INSTRUCTOR'S NOTES

The Everyday Writer

Fourth Edition

INSTRUCTOR'S NOTES

The Everyday Writer

Fourth Edition

Andrea A. Lunsford
Stanford University

Alyssa O'Brien
Stanford University

Lisa Dresdner
Norwalk Community College

Bedford/St. Martin's
Boston ♦ New York

Manufactured in the United States of America.

3 2 1 0 9 8
f e d c b a

For information, write: Bedford/St. Martin's, 75 Arlington Street, Boston, MA 02116 (617-399-4000)

ISBN-10: 0-312-48861-0
ISBN-13: 978-0-312-48861-1

Acknowledgments

"I Want a Wife" by Judy Brady. Originally published in *Ms.* Magazine, Vol. 1, No. 1, December 31, 1971. Reprinted with permission of the author.

"The War of 1812," excerpted from *The World Book Encyclopedia, 1988.* Copyright © 1988 World Book, Inc. Used with permission.

"Candidate for a Pullet Surprise," by Jerrold Zar. Used with permission of *The Journal of Irreproducible Results*, the science humor magazine, www.jir.com. This poem is reprinted in *This Book Warps Space and Time*, published by *The Journal of Irreproducible Results.*

Robert Francis, "The Pitcher" from *Collected Poems.* Copyright ©, 1960, 1985 by Robert Francis. Used with permission of Wesleyan University Press.

Emily Dickinson, "Much Madness is divinest Sense" from *The Poems of Emily Dickinson*, edited by Thomas H. Johnson. The Belknap Press of Harvard University Press, copyright © 1951, 1955, 1979 by the President and Fellows of Harvard College. Reprinted by permission of the publishers and the Trustees of Amherst College.

From *Beowulf*, translated by Michael Alexander. Revised edition copyright © 2003 by Michael Alexander. Used with permission of Penguin Group (UK), Ltd.

Preface

The *Instructor's Notes* for *The Everyday Writer* grew out of the notes published with the Sixth Edition of the *St. Martin's Handbook*. Developed over the past twenty years, they reflect the work of Cheryl Glenn, Roger Graves, R. Gerald Nelms, Dennis Quon, Melissa Goldthwaite, Jennifer Cognard-Black, Victor Mortimer, and Jeff Loew. The Fourth Edition of the *Notes* for *The Everyday Writer* builds on this strong foundation and works to extend and improve their usefulness for teachers of writing today.

The present edition signifies a major revision of the *Notes*, corresponding to the revised Fourth Edition of *The Everyday Writer*. Not only have we updated resources, added several new practical strategies, and responded to current trends in the field of writing, but we have also continued to develop new materials for teaching with technology—in addition to adding new chapters and restructuring the *Notes* to match the organization of *The Everyday Writer*.

Throughout, we have tested the materials for this new edition in our own classrooms, attempting in every case to make a connection between theory and practice. And as usual, we struggled to address both beginning and experienced instructors of writing. In approaching the question of audience, our first thoughts focused on everyday classroom needs: teaching suggestions, activities for student writers, answers to exercises, and so on. As we worked, we came upon materials and ideas for teaching that expanded our own horizons, providing not only the *what* to teach but also the *how* and the *why*.

In the past thirty years, the *what* has changed from a product-oriented approach to a process approach to a social process approach and most recently to a "postprocess" approach. Our teaching today focuses on the material conditions for student writing (and our teaching of it); on the social nature of writing and reading; on an enriched sense of rhetorical situations and the key writing occasions they entail; on dramatic changes in the nature, status, and scope of writing; on recently emerging genres of writing; and on the impact of technologies and visual culture on writing. Writing now includes forms of digital literacy, mediated writing for the screen, and the use of images and sound—not to mention color, innovative layout, and so on. And yet the need for traditional writing and writing abilities continues: students, perhaps more than ever, need deep experience in creating and sustaining clear, coherent, compelling arguments, in whatever genre and medium they choose to work. As a result, the stakes for teachers of writing have grown exponentially, and the shift in *what* we have described is necessarily paralleled by a shift to more effective pedagogy and research (the *how*) and greater understanding of our mission (the *why*). In our experience, the *what* of writing instruction can never be separated from the *how* and the *why*.

In this major revision, we have kept the best of the earlier notes, but with expanded notes on teaching multilingual writers, teaching with technologies, teaching with collaborative work, and teaching students with disabilities.

- **Background notes**, prefaced with "On," present useful historical, theoretical, and contextual information.
- **For Teaching notes** offer practical classroom strategies, exercises, and assignments.
- **For Collaborative Work notes** provide suggestions for group work.
- **For Multilingual Writers notes** offer suggestions for teaching writers whose home language is not English.
- **Teaching with Technology notes** offer classroom-tested strategies for using technologies effectively in the writing classroom.
- **Attending to Disabilities notes** provide advice for teaching students with disabilities as well as concrete strategies for including *all* students in classroom culture.
- **Useful readings** provide an annotated reference list of helpful books, articles, and Web sites.
- **Quotes about writing** suggest a starting point for class discussion.

We also offer a "Sample Syllabi" section, which provides useful syllabi that may be adapted for a variety of courses using *The Everyday Writer* in either a fifteen-week semester or a ten-week quarter.

We believe that the *Notes* make a particularly helpful supplement to *The Everyday Writer*: together they provide a wealth of practical pedagogical materials for teachers while keeping the textbook itself small, brief, and easy for students to carry in their book bags. And these *Notes* are themselves augmented by *The Everyday Writer*'s companion Web site, bedfordstmartins.com/everydaywriter, which offers a variety of supplementary resources including grammar exercises, diagnostic tests, documentation help, and useful Web links. You can also go to Bedford/St. Martin's Teaching Central Web site, bedfordstmartins.com/teaching central, and to the Just-in-Time Teaching site at bedfordstmartins.com/justintime, for a treasure trove of additional resources for teachers.

Our collaboration on this revision includes a number of friends and colleagues. At Bedford/St. Martin's we wish to thank our development editor, Stephanie Butler, as well as our managing editor, Shuli Traub, and our project editor, Harold Chester. The editorial team for *The Everyday Writer*, Fourth Edition, Carolyn Lengel and Nick Richardson, provided excellent assistance for our questions about these notes. For her research and contributions on visual exercises, we thank Dànielle DeVoss of Michigan State University. We are especially grateful to our colleagues at Stanford University, including Marvin Diogenes, Christine Alfano, Stacey Stanfield Anderson, and Jenn Fishman, whose timely advice helped provide material for these expanded *Notes*. In an important sense, however, this group extends to our students, from whom we continue to learn about writing and teaching, and all the instructors to whom this book is addressed.

Andrea A. Lunsford
Alyssa O'Brien
Lisa Dresdner

Ordering Information

To order any of the ancillaries for *The Everyday Writer*, please contact your Bedford/St. Martin's sales representative, e-mail sales support at sales_support@bfwpub.com, or visit our Web site at **bedfordstmartins.com**. Additionally, many of the resources listed below are available in various formats, packages, and bundles—please visit our Web site for more information.

Print and New Media Resources for *The Everyday Writer*

***The Everyday Writer* Student Center**
(bedfordstmartins.com/everydaywriter)

CompClass* for *The Everyday Writer
(yourcompclass.com)

Just in Time Teaching
(bedfordstmartins.com/teachingcentral)

CourseSmart e-book for *The Everyday Writer*, Fourth Edition
ISBN-10: 0-312-59016-4, ISBN-13: 978-0-312-59016-1

Exercises for The Everyday Writer, Fourth Edition
ISBN-10: 0-312-38653-2, ISBN-13: 978-0-312-38653-5

Answer Key to Exercises for The Everyday Writer, Fourth Edition
ISBN-10: 0-312-48858-0, ISBN-13: 978-0-312-48858-1

***Exercise Central to Go for Handbooks by Andrea A. Lunsford* CD-ROM**
ISBN-10: 0-312-43114-7, ISBN-13: 978-0-312-43114-3

***The Everyday Writer* Electronic Diagnostic Tests**
(bedfordstmartins.com/lunsforddiagnostics)

The St. Martin's Pocket Guide to Research and Documentation, Fourth Edition
Andrea A. Lunsford and Marcia Muth
ISBN-10: 0-312-44225-4, ISBN-13: 978-0-312-44225-5

From Theory to Practice: A Selection of Essays, Third Edition
ISBN-10: 0-312-46862-8, ISBN-13: 978-0-312-46862-0

Game Plans for Writers
ISBN-10: 0-312-56736-7, ISBN-13: 978-0-312-56736-1

Bedford/St. Martin's Research Pack
ISBN-10: 0-312-45950-7, ISBN-13: 978-0-312-45950-5

Writing Across the Curriculum (WAC) Pack
ISBN-10: 0-312-48275-2, ISBN-13: 978-0-312-48275-6

Bedford/St. Martin's Professional Resources

The St. Martin's Guide to Teaching Writing, Sixth Edition
ISBN-10: 0-312-45133-4, ISBN-13: 978-0-312-45133-2

The St. Martin's Sourcebook for Writing Tutors, Third Edition
ISBN-10: 0-312-44226-4, ISBN-13: 978-0-312-44226-2

Assigning, Responding, Evaluating, Fourth Edition
ISBN-10: 0-312-43930-X, ISBN-13: 978-0-312-43930-9

Second-Language Writing in the Composition Classroom, Fourth Edition
ISBN-10: 0-312-44473-7, ISBN-13: 978-0-312-44473-0

Disability and the Teaching of Writing, First Edition
ISBN-10: 0-312-44725-6, ISBN-13: 978-0-312-44725-0

Contents

Preface *v*

Sample Syllabi *1*

About College Writing

1 The Top Twenty: A Quick Guide to Troubleshooting Your Writing *10*
2 Expectations for College Writing *21*
3 Online and Multimedia Presentations *28*
4 Design for College Writing *37*

The Writing Process

5 Writing Situations *46*
6 Exploring Ideas *56*
7 Planning and Drafting *62*
8 Developing Paragraphs *71*
9 Reviewing and Revising *82*
10 Editing and Reflecting *98*

Critical Thinking and Argument

11 Critical Reading *110*
12 Analyzing Arguments *118*
13 Constructing Arguments *126*

Research

14 Preparing for a Research Project *136*
15 Doing Research *144*
16 Evaluating Sources and Taking Notes *152*
17 Integrating Sources and Avoiding Plagiarism *166*
18 Writing a Research Project *177*

Language

19 Writing to the World *186*
20 Language That Builds Common Ground *192*
21 Language Variety *201*
22 Word Choice and Spelling *209*
23 Glossary of Usage *224*

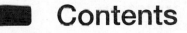

Sentence Style

24 Coordination, Subordination, and Emphasis *226*
25 Consistency and Completeness *234*
26 Parallelism *238*
27 Shifts *242*
28 Conciseness *248*
29 Sentence Variety *251*

Sentence Grammar

30 Basic Grammar *258*
31 Verbs *270*
32 Subject-Verb Agreement *280*
33 Pronouns *285*
34 Adjectives and Adverbs *294*
35 Modifier Placement *299*
36 Comma Splices and Fused Sentences *305*
37 Sentence Fragments *310*

Punctuation and Mechanics

38 Commas *316*
39 Semicolons *322*
40 End Punctuation *327*
41 Apostrophes *331*
42 Quotation Marks *334*
43 Other Punctuation Marks *339*
44 Capital Letters *344*
45 Abbreviations and Numbers *348*
46 Italics *352*
47 Hyphens *355*

MLA Documentation

48–51 MLA Documentation *360*

APA, *Chicago*, and CSE Documentation

52 APA Style *368*
53 *Chicago* Style *370*
54 CSE Style *372*

For Multilingual Writers

55 Writing in U.S. Academic Genres *376*
56 Clauses and Sentences *383*

57 Nouns and Noun Phrases *386*
58 Verbs and Verb Phrases *388*
59 Prepositions and Prepositional Phrases *390*

Writing in the Disciplines
60 Academic Work in Any Discipline *394*
61 Writing for the Humanities *399*
62 Writing for the Social Sciences *403*
63 Writing for the Natural and Applied Sciences *408*
64 Writing for Business *411*

Answers to Exercises in *The Everyday Writer with Exercises* *415*

INSTRUCTOR'S NOTES

The Everyday Writer

Fourth Edition

Sample Syllabi

Sample Syllabus for Fifteen-Week Semester

Structure of the Course

One of the best ways to learn to write is by writing, and for that reason students in this course will be asked to do a lot of inventing, drafting, and revising—that's what writing is. Sharing work with others, either in peer-response sessions, writing groups, or collaborative efforts, promotes learning about writing by widening the response writers get to their work. Finally, texts can help in learning to write by answering questions students may have or suggesting ways of going about the business of writing. Because each of these three principles operates powerfully in the classroom, they form the basis of the course schedule outlined below. To provide practice writing and sharing those writings, often the class will be devoted to writing workshops. These writing workshops give students the chance to see how other students have handled writing assignments, to practice editing skills by helping other students edit their own work, and to draft essays. Many class days will involve a class discussion of a student essay that demonstrates how the writing being done might best be handled. In addition, many classes will open with a short writing assignment, freewrite, or writing-log entry. Each week the class will read sections from *The Everyday Writer* that address issues about writing, guide students in their understanding of those issues, and suggest ways for them to broaden their knowledge and apply that knowledge to their writing.

Written Assignments

Students write five essays during the term. An acceptable draft of each essay must be turned in by the final due date for each essay. At any time during the term, a final grade may be assigned to the draft that each student judges to be his or her final effort on each essay. At least one week before the end of the term, students turn in four of five final drafts for final evaluation. Before the last day of classes, students turn in the fifth essay for a final grade. All final drafts must be typed or computer-generated.

Since students can suspend final evaluation of their progress until the end of the semester, this grading system provides students with the opportunity to have their best work evaluated.

Attendance

Because much of each student's most important work will take place in class, attendance in class should be mandatory. (Warn chronically late students once; after that, count each late appearance as an absence.)

Final Course Grades

Final course grades will be arrived at by combining grades for the five graded papers, class attendance, participation, and conferences with the teacher in the following manner:

portfolio of final, graded essays (4 × 15%)	60%
research essay (fourth essay)	20%
attendance	10%
conferences, writing logs, class discussion lists	10%

Course Schedule

Week Topics/Focus

1 Introduction: briefly outline the course; identify learning objectives from your perspective and ask the students to add some of their own; present guidelines for grading, plagiarism, late essays, attendance.

Diagnostic writing sample.

Considering rhetorical situations (Chapter 5); thinking about visuals (Chapter 4); rewrite diagnostic test to demonstrate drafting, learning through writing.

Assign the first essay: identify the task clearly, provide models of successful attempts, link the assignment to learning objectives, suggest ways for students to use the assignment to learn about something that interests them.

2 Invention techniques: mapping, brainstorming (Chapters 6 and 7); research as invention (Chapter 16). Apply invention methods to first assignment.

Draft of first essay due; peer response in class; teacher response: read for overall direction, scope, and suitability for your course and first assignment.

Revising and editing the draft (Chapters 9 and 10). Compare writing-log entries.

3 Second draft of first essay due; peer response in class; constructing strong paragraphs (Chapter 8).

Confer with students individually either during office hours or in classroom writing workshops. Identify specific error patterns you have noticed; conduct mini-lectures for students who share error patterns (the specific chapters you will need to refer to will emerge from the class's needs: see Chapters 24–51).

4 First essay due.

Assign the second essay: identify the task clearly, provide models of successful attempts, link the assignment to learning objectives, suggest ways for students to use the assignment to learn about something that interests them. Repeat invention techniques used for the first essay; repeat freewriting sessions and exchange freewrites to share ideas, approaches to the assignment.

5 Draft of the second essay due; peer response in class, teacher response to focus and questions to promote further research or development. Conciseness (Chapter 28); creating coordinate and subordinate structures (Chapter 24).

Writing workshop and/or individual conferences. Second draft of second essay due.

6 Understanding diction; enriching vocabulary; building common ground; considering language diversity (Chapters 19–21). Confer with students individually either during office hours or in classroom writing workshops. Identify specific error patterns you have noticed; conduct mini-lectures for students who share error patterns (the specific chapters you will need to refer to will emerge from the class's needs: see Chapters 24–51).

7 Second essay due.

Assign the third essay: identify the task clearly, provide models of successful attempts, link the assignment to learning objectives, suggest ways for students to use the assignment to learn about something that interests them. Repeat invention techniques used for the second essay; add tagmemic heuristic or clustering.

Thinking critically: constructing and analyzing arguments (Chapters 12 and 13).

8 Draft of the third essay due; peer response in class, teacher response to focus and questions to spur research or development. Creating and maintaining parallel sentence structures (Chapter 26); varying sentence structures (Chapter 29). Confer with students either individually in class or during office hours.

9 Identify specific error patterns you have noticed; conduct mini-lectures for students who share error patterns (the specific chapters

you will need to refer to will emerge from the class's needs: see Chapters 24–51).

10 Third essay due.

Assign the fourth essay (a research essay: identify the task clearly, provide models of successful attempts, link the assignment to learning objectives, suggest ways for students to use the assignment to learn about something that interests them).

Preparing for a research project (Chapter 14); conducting research (Chapter 15).

11 Research file due: a list of all sources consulted so far; notes; photocopies of relevant readings; summaries; quotations.

Evaluating and using sources (Chapters 16 and 17); writing a research essay (Chapter 18).

12 Draft of research essay due; confer individually with students; devote class time to writing workshops.

Emphasis (Chapter 24).

13 Second draft of research essay due; peer response in class.

Documenting sources (Chapters 48–54).

14 Final draft of research essay due.

Fifth assignment: rewrite or revise an essay from: (a) a course in the student's major, (b) a discipline that interests him or her, or (c) this course.

Writing about literature (Chapter 61); writing for social sciences and natural sciences (Chapters 62 and 63); writing for business (Chapter 64).

Due: a description of the conventions of the student's discipline; a description of the style of his or her field.

Due: typed, final drafts of first four papers for final grading.

15 Draft of the fifth assignment due; peer response in class, teacher response through individual conferences in class or during office hours; writing workshops in class.

Final draft of fifth essay due.

Course evaluations.

Sample Syllabus for Ten-Week Quarter

Structure of the Course

One of the best ways to learn to write is by writing, and for that reason students in this course will be asked to do a lot of inventing, drafting, and revising—that's what writing is. Sharing work with others, either in peer-response sessions, writing groups, or collaborative efforts, promotes learning about writing by widening the response writers get to their work. Finally, texts can help in learning to write by answering questions students may have or suggesting ways of going about the business of writing. Because each of these three principles operates powerfully in the classroom, they form the basis of the course schedule outlined below. To provide practice writing and sharing those writings, often the class will be devoted to writing workshops. These writing workshops give students the chance to see how other students have handled writing assignments, to practice editing skills by helping other students edit their own work, and to draft essays. Many class days will involve a class discussion of a student essay that demonstrates how the writing being done might best be handled. In addition, many classes will open with a short writing assignment, freewrite, or writing-log entry. Each week we will read sections from *The Everyday Writer* that address issues about writing, guide us in our understanding of those issues, and suggest ways for us to broaden our knowledge and apply that knowledge to our writing.

Written Assignments

Students write four essays during the term. An acceptable draft of each essay must be turned in by the final due date for each essay. At any time during the term, a final grade may be assigned to the draft that each student judges to be his or her final effort on each essay. At least one week before the end of the term, students turn in three of four final drafts for final evaluation. Before the last day of classes, students turn in the fourth essay for a final grade. All final drafts must be typed or computer-generated.

Since students can suspend final evaluation of their progress until the end of the semester, this grading system provides them with the opportunity to have their best work evaluated.

Attendance

Because much of each student's most important work will take place in class, attendance in class should be mandatory. (Warn chronically late students once; after that, count each late appearance as an absence.)

Final Course Grades

Final course grades will be arrived at by combining grades for the four graded papers, class attendance, participation, and conferences with the teacher in the following manner:

final, graded essays (4 × 20%)	80%
attendance	10%
conferences, writing logs, class discussion lists	10%

Course Schedule

Week Topics/Focus

1 Introduction: briefly outline the course; identify learning objectives from your perspective and ask the students to add some of their own; present guidelines for grading, plagiarism, late essays, attendance.

Diagnostic writing sample.

Considering rhetorical situations (Chapter 5); thinking about visuals (Chapter 4); rewrite diagnostic test to demonstrate drafting, learning through writing.

Assign the first essay: identify the task clearly, provide models of successful attempts, link the assignment to learning objectives, suggest ways for students to use the assignment to learn about something that interests them.

2 Invention techniques: mapping, brainstorming (Chapters 6 and 7); research as invention (Chapter 16). Apply invention methods to first assignment.

Draft of first essay due; peer response in class; teacher response: read for overall direction, scope, and suitability for your course and first assignment.

Revising and editing the draft (Chapters 9 and 10).

Compare writing-log entries.

3 Second draft of first essay due; peer response in class; constructing strong paragraphs (Chapter 8).

Confer with students individually either during office hours or in classroom writing workshops. Identify specific error patterns you have noticed; conduct mini-lectures for students who share error patterns (the specific chapters you will need to refer to will emerge from the class's needs: see Chapters 24–51).

4 First essay due.

Assign the second essay: identify the task clearly, provide models of successful attempts, link the assignment to learning objectives, suggest ways for students to use the assignment to learn about something that interests them. Repeat invention techniques used for the first essay; repeat freewriting sessions and exchange freewrites to share ideas, approaches to the assignment.

5 Draft of the second essay due; peer response in class, teacher response to focus and questions to promote further research or development. Conciseness (Chapter 28); creating coordinate and subordinate structures (Chapter 24).

Writing workshop and/or individual conferences. Second draft of second essay due.

6 Understanding diction; enriching vocabulary; building common ground; considering language diversity (Chapters 19–21). Confer with students individually either during office hours or in classroom writing workshops.

Identify specific error patterns you have noticed; conduct mini-lectures for students who share error patterns (the specific chapters you will need to refer to will emerge from the class's needs: see Chapters 24–51).

7 Second essay due.

Assign the third essay: identify the task clearly, provide models of successful attempts, link the assignment to learning objectives, suggest ways for students to use the assignment to learn about something that interests them. Repeat invention techniques used for the second essay; add tagmemic heuristic or clustering.

Thinking critically: constructing and analyzing arguments (Chapters 12 and 13).

8 Draft of the third essay due; peer response in class, teacher response to focus and questions to spur research or development.

Creating parallel sentence structures (Chapter 26); varying sentence structures (Chapter 29). Confer with students either individually in class or during office hours.

Identify specific error patterns you have noticed; conduct mini-lectures for students who share error patterns (the specific chapters you will need to refer to will emerge from the class's needs: see Chapters 24–51).

9 Third essay due.

Assign the fourth essay: rewrite or revise an essay from: (a) a course in the student's major, (b) a discipline that interests him or her, or (c) this course.

Writing about literature (Chapter 61); writing for social and natural sciences (Chapters 62 and 63); writing for business (Chapter 64).

Due: a description of the conventions of the student's discipline; a description of the style of his or her field.

Due: typed, final drafts of first three papers for final grading.

10 Draft of the fourth assignment due; peer response in class, teacher response through individual conferences in class or during office hours; writing workshops in class.

Final draft of fourth essay due.

Course evaluations.

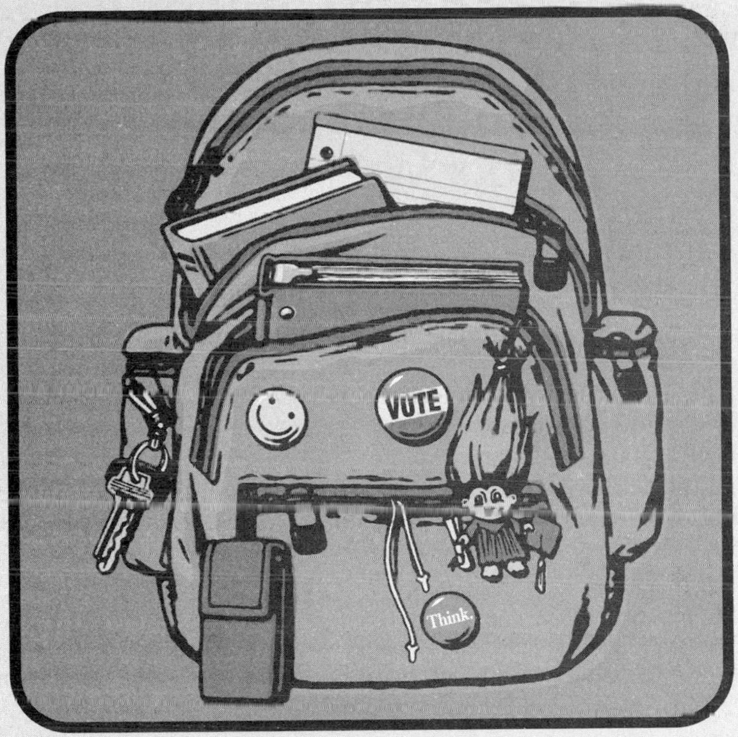

About College Writing

A mind that is stretched by a new experience can never go back to its old dimensions.

—OLIVER WENDELL HOLMES

1 The Top Twenty: A Quick Guide to Troubleshooting Your Writing

Recent research on students' approaches to college-level writing indicates that students are deeply invested in improving their rhetorical and argumentative skills in a way that confirms our scholarly insistence on "process" methodologies. As Richard Light discovered through his interviews with Harvard undergraduates, students are open to working through the acts of invention, organization, revision, and editing, and in fact desire the opportunity to do so. In his study *Making the Most of College: Students Speak Their Minds*, Light reflects:

> The findings from our survey dramatize the extraordinary importance that students put on good writing. . . . I was surprised by students' strong attitude toward writing. I would have guessed that they value good writing, but I didn't realize how deeply many of them care about it, or how strongly they hunger for specific suggestions about how to improve it.

Similarly, students at Stanford University told a group of writing teachers that they desired the freedom to make mistakes in their writing and rhetoric classes. They also voiced a hunger to take risks, receive suggestions, and analyze texts that they might use as models.

Our challenge as teachers is to provide the space for such risk-taking to occur. We might reconceptualize writing as an inevitable process of working through errors. In the words of Malcolm Gladwell, journalist for the *New Yorker* and author of *The Tipping Point*, the writer's inclination is to err. "Journalists write a lot," Gladwell told an audience at Stanford University in January 2002, "so sometimes you are just wrong."

Allowing—even encouraging—our students to embrace experimentation and error as integral parts of the writing process empowers them as practitioners and rhetoricians; it also provides us as teachers the opportunity to take risks in our facilitation of writing exercises and assignments. Above all, our task is to foster *critical thinking* about the errors—and the exceptional rhetorical strategies—in all writing. In this way, we can invite students to develop the ability to analyze the rhetorical situations in the textual, visual, and multimedia world around them and to transform their engagement into effective writing that contributes to the public sphere.

The Top Twenty encourages students to begin taking risks—not to fear failure, but to seize the opportunity to shape language into elegant, persuasive texts of rhetorical power and significance. The second chapter of *The Everyday Writer*, "Expectations for College Writing," and the Top Twenty together work as a mini-handbook, introducing students to the many facets of writing in an academic setting.

Additional information on the Top Twenty is available on *The Everyday Writer*'s companion Web site, **bedfordstmartins.com/everydaywriter**. Click on **The Top Twenty** or **Exercises** for practice identifying and correcting these writing problems.

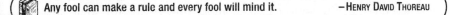

Any fool can make a rule and every fool will mind it. —HENRY DAVID THOREAU

FOR TEACHING: Taking a Writing Inventory

One way to encourage students to begin actively learning from their errors is through the use of writing inventories. Writing inventories help students take stock of their writing and think critically and analytically about how to improve their writing skills. After students have completed their first few assignments and have had time to review your comments, ask them to take a writing inventory using these ten steps:

1. Assemble copies of your first two or three pieces of writing, making sure to select those to which either your instructor or other students have responded.
2. Read through this writing, adding your own comments about its strengths and weaknesses.
3. Examine the instructor and peer comments carefully, and compare them with your own comments.
4. Group all the comments into the categories discussed in the Top Twenty.
5. Make an inventory of your own strengths in each category.
6. Study your errors, marking every instructor and peer comment that suggests or calls for an improvement and putting them all in a list.
7. Consult the appropriate sections of *The Everyday Writer* for more detailed help in those areas where you need it.
8. Make up a priority list of three or four particular writing problems you have identified, and write out a plan for improvement.

9. Note at least two strengths you want to build on in your writing.
10. Record your findings in a writing log, which you can add to as the class proceeds.

Students can access an electronic version of this inventory on *The Everyday Writer*'s companion Web site, **bedfordstmartins.com/everydaywriter**. Go to **Writing Resources** and click on **Taking a Writing Inventory**.

Before you ask students to take a full inventory of their writing, you might consider working through the beginning of a hypothetical inventory with them. To do so, distribute copies of a student essay (from your files or from another class), and ask the students to work with you to identify broad content issues, strengths or weaknesses in organization and language, and surface or citation errors.

To give students practice in taking a writing inventory on a more detailed level, ask them to examine a piece of writing for some specific feature—looking for every organizational "cue," for instance, or every transitional word or phrase. They can do this part of the assignment particularly well in groups. Then ask them to reflect on their findings and to draw one or more conclusions. Such an exercise asks students to move from observation to generalization, to "metadiscourse" about their own writing, or to what Shirley Brice Heath calls building theories about their own language use. The more students are able to make such mental moves, the better they will be at monitoring their own learning and at learning from their own errors.

On Looking for Strengths in Student Writing

Peter Elbow reminds us that it is characteristic of good teachers to *like* student writing, even though they see its weaknesses or failures. Elbow urges teachers to cultivate their enjoyment of student writing by (1) looking for "strengths, both real and potential"; (2) practicing "conscious, disciplined, positive reinforcement"; and (3) getting to know students through conferences, journals, and free topic choices. Elbow concludes:

> It's not improving our writing that leads us to like it, but rather our liking it that leads us to improving it. Liking writing makes it easier to criticize it—and makes criticism easier to take and to learn from. (Lecture delivered at Bread Loaf School of English, July 17, 1991)

On Learning from Your Errors

The greater the writer's fixation on error, the greater the difficulty that writer will have writing. The more the instructor focuses on error, the more the student will worry about error. In *The Concept of the Mind*, British philosopher Gilbert Ryle wrote that "errors are exercises in competence." And this new concept of error as "portals to discovery" became the mainstay of Mina Shaughnessy's study of basic writing. By 1981, Isabella Halsted was writing that errors are "*not* Sin, not Crime punishable by F." Errors are simply mistakes that we are all capable of, given the wrong circumstances: lack of sleep, deadline pressure, unfamiliarity with formal English. Halsted describes her own attitude toward error:

> Like soot on the pane, Error is something that gets in the way of the clear vision. . . . Error on all levels is distracting, annoying, obstructive. Error is inexcusable ultimately, yes, [but] not because it is Wrong per se. . . . In plain pragmatic terms, the absence of Error is useful; but when our students take pains to avoid it—by writing short sentences, by sticking to one tense, by writing as little as possible—I doubt very much that they do so in order to better communicate with a reader, but rather to play safe, to avoid the red marks.

At the same time, however, research by Larry Beason, in "Ethos and Error," suggests that errors impede more than communication; they also endanger a writer's credibility and character. Through quantitative research on fourteen businesspeople, Beason offers a rhetorical analysis of errors in terms of how textual transgressions lead readers to produce judgments of character and consequently construct "a negative ethos of the writer."

Beason's study provides compelling reasons for teachers to spend time helping students identify common errors in their writing: "Whether we believe it to be the optimum situation or not, errors have an impact on the writer's image and communicability. Error avoidance, I submit, should have a presence in the composition curriculum—but without overpowering it" (60). Focusing students' attention on the Top Twenty, covered in Chapter 1 of *The Everyday Writer*, can go a long way toward remedying such ethos-damaging errors.

> **Give me a fruitful error any time, full of seeds, bursting with its own corrections.**
>
> —VILFREDO PARETO

ATTENDING TO DISABILITIES: Learning from Errors

"[M]any of our students would gladly avoid composition classes because they fear any difficulties they have with writing will (once again) be interpreted as intellectual or moral flaws," write Brenda Jo Brueggemann, Linda Feldmeier White, Patricia Dunn, Barbara Heifferon, and Johnson Cheu in "Becoming Visible." This is especially true for students with disabilities who may already be at a disadvantage if the institution does not have the resources to facilitate their learning. Be sure to identify and meet with students at the beginning of the course in order to assess their writing fears and capabilities. A student information sheet can provide a quick way to ascertain students' perspectives, but be sure to follow up with individual conferences as soon as the course is under way. The reason for such early dialogue is clear. As Brueggemann and her colleagues assert:

> For decades we have spoken about "writing" as learning. We know that writing is about complex intellectual processes. We know that writing is intimately connected with issues of authority, identity, power, and confidence, and that if students are to become more sophisticated thinkers and writers, they should be both challenged and taken seriously. The rhetoric of the learning disability backlash interferes with this critical dynamic between writer and reader, between student and teacher, by introducing stereotype into the equation. (379)

FOR TEACHING: The Top Twenty

Here are twenty passages taken from the group of student essays on which Lunsford and Lunsford's research is based. Each passage contains one of the twenty most common student writing errors, and these passages are numbered to correspond with the Top Twenty in *The Everyday Writer*. These passages may be used in at least three different ways: (1) as a diagnostic test early in the semester to see how practiced your students are at recognizing these errors; (2) as a review test at the end of the semester or after concluding your class's study of this introduction; (3) as examples of the Top Twenty errors, supplementing those given in the text.

1. These essays were very contrasting.
2. The Beast which is one of the biggest roller coasters, has a thunderous ride of steep hills and turns. As you race down the first and biggest hill your coaster is engulfed by a tunnel at the end of the hill.
3. The author insists that the fur trade "is a game for wise old wolves, not new tenderfeet and fly-by-night gamblers."
4. Once you find where other surfers are, you can set up your camp. This entails claiming your own territory. You do this by laying out your oversized beach towel and by turning your radio on loud enough to mark your domain without disturbing anyone else. This should help you blend in with the locals.
5. Can we not say that statistics bare witness?
6. In "The Last Drop", he tries to explain why so many parts of the world do not have a regular supply of clean water.

7. There is also a stand up roller coaster called, the King Kobra, which goes upside down in the first loop, with plenty of tossing and turning. Like I said previously, King's Island also keeps the people with weaker stomachs in mind; there are rides all throughout the park which are a little slower paced.
8. The choices for English Language Learners are limited; Either assimilate quickly or be segregated.
9. After deciding to begin their college careers, many students are faced with the predicament of where to live. This is not such a problem for students from out of town, but it is for those who live in the same area which they attend school.
10. To give a recent example, Ellen Barry reported on a judge in Lebanon, Tennessee, who was presiding over a hearing of a child abuse case in which the person being charged was an eighteen-year-old immigrant mother, ordered to not only learn English but to learn it at the fourth grade proficiency by the next hearing.
11. The knights with armor and horses beautifully decorated participate in battles of jousting, target shooting with spears, archery, and duels of strategy and strength using swords and shields. During the evening, there is a break from the fighting, and a beautiful ceremony of marriage is acted out.
12. The good thing about its location is that it is right off the main highway, very easy to spot. There are also plenty of road signs pointing you in the direction of the park. And if you got extremely lost, pulling off and asking would be the easiest way to get on track.
13. I was gaining speed and feeling really good but when I looked back he wasn't there. I panicked. I saw him and my parents down at the other end of the street and forgot to look forward. When I finally did turn forward, I saw that I was rapidly closing in on my neighbor's car. How ironic; I was about to hit the car of the man who was trying to teach me how to ride a bike.
14. What I'm trying to get at is that because of this persons immaturity, many people have suffered. This persons lack of responsibility has turned peoples lives upside down.
15. I felt someone's hand shaking my shoulder. I lifted my head up to see my best friend Stephanie looking down at me. "That must have been some dream. Come on the bell rang class is over."
16. Chips and sauces are not the only thing that you get free refills on, you also get free refills on all non-alcoholic beverages, such as soda and tea.

The servers are very good about getting you more of both things when you need refills, usually you do not even have to ask.

17. On the other hand, what if you don't care for your partner—or even worse—they don't care for you? You know now that it is still okay to separate without the problem of obtaining a divorce. Many divorces that take place within the first years of marriage might have been avoided if the couple had lived together before marrying.
18. According to the *New York Times*, an open government site published "The documents, the experts say, constitute a basic guide to building an atom bomb" (Broad A1).
19. Her free-spirit was obvious in her artwork.
20. When I got to half court, the guy that was playing center on my team stood between the defensive player and me. As I dribbled around the center, he stopped the defensive player. Not by using his hands but by his big body. This is a strategy used to get a player open for a shot.

> **You can be a little ungrammatical if you come from the right part of the country.**
> **—Robert Frost**

FOR COLLABORATION: The Top Twenty

After students work through the previous twenty passages, ask them to work in groups of three to compare their findings. Then have them evaluate their own writing and develop a plan to recognize these errors in their work. Their plan should include categorizing the errors they make according to the catalog of errors in this chapter. They may want to determine the frequency of errors they make in each category. This simple exercise will establish their ability to evaluate their own work, an important skill each writer needs to develop.

> **But enough of these errors. The good writer masters grammar in order to control his words, and meaning is his target.**
> **—Ken Macrorie**

USEFUL READINGS

Bartholomae, David. "The Study of Error." *CCC* 31 (Oct. 1980): 253–69.

Beason, Larry. "Ethos and Error: How Business People React to Errors." *CCC* 53.1 (Sept. 2001): 33–64.

Bérubé, Michael. *Life as We Know It: A Father, a Family, and an Exceptional Child*. New York: Vintage-Random, 1998. In this important text about breaking stereotypes and not viewing your students through the lens of disabilities, Bérubé describes his own child with Down syndrome.

Booth, Wayne C. "The Rhetorical Stance." *Now Don't Try to Reason with Me: Essays and Ironies for a Credulous Age*. Chicago: U of Chicago P, 1970. Booth posits a carefully balanced tripartite division of rhetorical appeals, including "the available arguments about the subject itself, the interests and peculiarities of the audience, and the voice, the implied character, of the speaker" (27).

Brueggemann, Brenda Jo. *Enabling the Humanities: A Sourcebook for Disability Studies in Language and Literature*. New York: MLA, 2002.

———. *Lend Me Your Ear: Rhetorical Constructions of Deafness*. Washington, DC: Gallaudet UP, 1999. Writing out of both professional and personal experience with deafness, Brueggemann provides an astute analysis of rhetorical constructions and institutional traditions that limit deaf people; interviews and poetry make this a compelling text for the classroom.

Brueggemann, Brenda Jo, Linda Feldmeier White, Patricia A. Dunn, Barbara A. Heifferon, and Johnson Cheu. "Becoming Visible: Lessons in Disability." *CCC* 52.3 (Feb. 2001): 368–98. The authors scrutinize constructions of normalcy, writing, and composition in this groundbreaking article in disability studies.

Connors, Robert J., and Andrea Lunsford. "Teachers' Rhetorical Comments on Student Papers." *CCC* 44 (May 1993): 200–24.

Corbett, Edward P. J., Nancy Myers, and Gary Tate. *The Writing Teacher's Sourcebook*. 4th ed. New York: Oxford UP, 1999.

Daiker, Donald A. "Learning to Praise." *Writing Response: Theory, Practice, and Research*. Ed. Chris Anson. Urbana: NCTE, 1989. 103–13.

Epes, Mary. "Tracing Errors to Their Sources: A Study of the Encoding Processes of Adult Basic Writers." *Journal of Basic Writing* 4 (Spring 1985): 4–33. Epes makes a cogent argument for grammatical instruction that reflects standard academic English.

Halasek, Kay, Tara Pauliny, Edgar Singleton, Rebecca Greenberg Taylor, Kathleen R. Wallace, and Matt Wanat. *The Writer's Companion: A Guide to First-Year Writing*. Needham Heights: Pearson, 1999.

Halsted, Isabella. "Putting Error in Its Place." *Journal of Basic Writing* 1 (Spring 1975): 72–86.

Hartwell, Patrick. "Grammar, Grammars, and the Teaching of Grammar." *CE* 47 (1985): 105–27. Hartwell defines and explains the purposes of the various grammars.

Holberg, Jennifer, and Mary Tyler, eds. *Pedagogy: Critical Approaches to Teaching Literature, Language, Composition, and Culture*. Durham: Duke UP, 2000.

Jarratt, Susan C., and Lynn Worsham, eds. *Feminism and Composition Studies: In Other Words*. New York: MLA, 1998. This is an excellent collection of scholarship on feminist approaches to teaching.

Kolln, Martha. "Closing the Books on Alchemy." *CCC* 32 (May 1981): 139–51. While no direct relationship exists between grammar instruction and writing improvement, there are other important reasons for studying grammar—to analyze and to build shared vocabulary and conceptual frameworks.

Krishna, Valerie. "The Syntax of Error." *Journal of Basic Writing* 1 (Spring 1975): 43–49. Unlike the "classical" errors—verb agreement, punctuation, pronoun case—that are easily categorized, students' structural errors are unique. Krishna directs us in understanding that students' structural errors are the direct outgrowth of "a weak structural core" that is disjoined from the idea that a writer is trying to express.

Lanham, Richard A. *Analyzing Prose*. 2nd ed. New York: Continuum, 2002. Lanham applies Aristotelian classifications of style (such as noun and verb styles, parataxis and hypotaxis, and periodic and running styles) in order to provide both a descriptive and an evaluative approach to analyzing modern prose style.

Light, Richard J. *Making the Most of College: Students Speak Their Minds*. Cambridge: Harvard UP, 2001.

Lindemann, Erika. *A Rhetoric for Writing Teachers*. 4th ed. New York: Oxford UP, 2001. Lindemann provides background material for the teaching of writing, including a history of rhetoric, a survey of linguistics, and a useful bibliography.

Lunsford, Andrea A., and Lisa S. Ede. "Audience Addressed/Audience Invoked: The Role of Audience in Composition Theory and Pedagogy." *The Writing Teacher's Sourcebook*. 4th ed. Ed. Edward P. J. Corbett, Nancy Myers, and Gary Tate. New York: Oxford UP, 1999. Lunsford and Ede point out the limitations of two prominent concepts of audience, that of "audience addressed," which emphasizes the concrete reality of the writer's audience, and that of "audience invoked," which focuses on the writer's construction of an audience. They argue that a writer's audience may be both addressed and invoked.

Miller, Susan. "How Writers Evaluate Their Own Writing." *CCC* 33 (May 1982): 176–83. Miller argues that all writers should always end their writing process by evaluating the written product by answering two questions: How well did the audience respond to the piece of writing? How well did the writer meet his or her original intentions? But in the end, writers should measure their growth as writers, what Miller calls "author growth."

Paraskevas, Cornelia. "The Craft of Writing: Breaking Conventions." *The English Journal* 93.4 (Mar. 2004): 41–46. Paraskevas, a composition theorist and linguist, explains that grammar and punctuation rules are arbitrary in that they do not logically follow the way native English speakers use the language. Pointing out that conventions are often ignored in a variety of genres (such as newspapers, fliers, and magazines), she encourages writers not to think of conventions as strict rules and to recognize the value of occasionally violating the rules.

Pemberton, Michael A. *The Ethics of Writing Instruction: Issues in Theory and Practice*. Stamford: Ablex, 2000.

Pytlik, Betty P., and Sarah Liggett. *Preparing College Teachers of Writing: Histories, Theories, Programs, Practices*. New York: Oxford UP, 2002.

Ryle, Gilbert. *The Concept of the Mind*. New York: Barnes and Noble, 1949.

Schwegler, Robert. "The Politics of Reading Student Papers." *The Politics of Writing Instruction*. Ed. Richard Bullock, Charles Schuster, and John Trimbur. Portsmouth: Boynton, 1991. 203–26.

Shaughnessy, Mina. *Errors & Expectations: A Guide for the Teacher of Basic Writing*. New York: Oxford UP, 1977. Since the publication of this book, every scholarly work on error has referred to it.

Tate, Gary, Amy Rupiper, and Kurt Schick. *A Guide to Composition Pedagogies*. New York: Oxford UP, 2001.

Williams, Joseph M. "The Phenomenology of Error." *CCC* 32 (1981): 152–68. Williams argues that we need to view errors as simply socially inappropriate, easily remedied behavior.

———. *Style: Ten Lessons in Clarity and Grace*. 7th ed. New York: Longman, 2003. Intended as a how to manual for writers, this book outlines four principles of effective style: clarity, cohesion, emphasis, and concision. Williams also discusses punctuation and usage as matters of style.

Wolfram, Walt. "Teaching the Grammar of Vernacular English." *Language Variation in North American English: Research and Teaching*. Ed. A. Wayne Glowka and Donald M. Lance. New York: MLA, 1993. 16–27. This is a good basic guide (with bibliography) for working with speakers and writers of other Englishes.

USEFUL WEB SITES

The Bedford Bibliography for Teachers of Writing

http://bedfordstmartins.com/bb/

This is the electronic version of The Bedford Bibliography for Teachers of Writing *by Nedra Reynolds, Bruce Herzberg, and Patricia Bizzell.*

Centre for Disability Studies: University of Leeds, England

http://www.leeds.ac.uk/disability-studies/publish.htm

This site hosts an extensive list of recent publications in disability studies in England.

Kairos Special Issue: "Disability—Demonstrated by and Mediated through Technology"

http://english.ttu.edu/kairos/7.1

The Spring 2002 issue offers a range of articles and assignment ideas for composition.

Learning Disabilities Resources

http://www.ldresources.com

Read online columns and essays concerning learning disabilities, subscribe to the LD newsletter, read archived issues, keep informed on current happenings and conferences, contact people, find out about educational developments, access both high- and low-tech tools, and link to electronic books and videos.

Program in Writing and Rhetoric: Stanford University

http://pwr.stanford.edu

Stanford University's Program in Writing and Rhetoric site hosts a wealth of resources for students and teachers of writing.

Tools for Teaching

http://teaching.berkeley.edu/bgd/teaching.html

This is a compendium of resources from Barbara Gross Davis's Tools for Teaching *(San Francisco: Jossey-Bass, 1993).*

Expectations for College Writing

2

We must learn to reawaken and keep ourselves awake, not by mechanical aid, but by an infinite expectation of the dawn.

–HENRY DAVID THOREAU

Today, the job of teaching writing is a complex blending of at least two purposes: first, to help students see that they have a voice and to help them become comfortable with developing a writing process that can express it; second, to introduce them to the expectations and conventions of academic discourse, with its genres, levels of expertise, different tones, and sense of audience.

In your class are many students who know exactly what you expect of them: flawlessly executed, fully developed essays. Other students might feel lost in a college environment. They may not know what exactly is expected of them as writers, readers, and researchers at the university level. Others may be uncertain about what skills they can hope to learn in a college writing class. You might spend the first day of class discussing these expectations—of students, of writing, of applicability—in order to ease fears and build community.

Most of all, it is helpful to reassure students that their college writing classes are a means to awaken the mind, to begin to explore new ideas among a community of scholars at the college level, and to learn skills that will serve them well for years to come.

FOR COLLABORATION: Meeting Expectations (2a)

To help students develop a concrete understanding of the specific expectations they face as college writers, ask them to bring in the syllabi and assignment sheets for all of their classes. With students working in groups of three or four, ask each group to read and compare the syllabi and assignment guidelines from all the classes. Then have each group compose a list of key common features based on these questions:

- How are students addressed at the college level?
- What is asked of them in the guidelines in terms of work, commitment, performance, effort, originality, and contributions?
- What do different classes have in common in terms of what is expected of college writers?
- What are the technological or computer expectations?

Have the groups present their lists to the class. Conclude the activity with a discussion about how students might best begin to meet these particular college-level expectations.

TEACHING WITH TECHNOLOGY: Meeting Expectations (2a)

Using your class's electronic discussion board, blog, or chat room, initiate a conversation about how students have prepared for the work they need to do in college. Did they read admissions materials cover to cover? Did they talk with friends or family members who are currently or were recently college students? Did they read any books in preparation for the work they will need to do?

In the dynamic writing environment of the electronic discussion board, blog, or chat room, students can respond quickly to one another and post their fears and worries. Make sure to ask them to give their best advice to their peers about how to prepare to meet college expectations. In this way, they can begin to feel more comfortable about the challenges and opportunities ahead.

FOR TEACHING: Academic Writing (2b)

A good way to develop students' understanding of the expectations of college writers is to ask them to find a contemporary article on a subject of their choice from a recent periodical or academic journal. Conduct a rhetorical analysis of the article, examining the genre for its specific writing conventions.

- Is it a scientific piece divided into formal sections, such as "Observations," "Method," and "Significance"?
- Is it an opinion piece in a college newspaper using *I* and referring to current events?
- Is it an article in a literary journal containing a summary of a text and then a thesis offering an interpretation of the work?

Ask students to model their writing after the article's discipline-specific attributes.

FOR COLLABORATION: Academic Writing (2b)

To give students practice in learning the conventions of college writers, have them practice establishing authority and being direct in their everyday communication strategies.

- Ask students to phone a friend from another university or college and explain the assignment and their idea in the simplest possible terms. How does the idea sound? Does it tap into any current issue at the listener's college? Have the listener answer the following: Is the student speaking with authority? Is the idea being communicated clearly and directly? Once these goals are achieved, apply the successful spoken communication to the writing.
- Have students email a colloquial version of their assignment and potential topic to a friend or family member. Ask the person to answer the following: Does the student sound authoritative about his or her idea? Is the idea presented in a direct and compelling manner?

Often, communicating with a close friend or family member can help students develop skills in being authoritative and direct—that is, in meeting the expectations for college writers.

ATTENDING TO DISABILITIES: Academic Reading (2c)

In order to make sure that your teaching can accommodate the needs of all students, you might wish to distribute an information sheet for students to complete on the first day of class. You can ask students to voluntarily disclose any particular needs as writers and readers—an accommodation for a visually impaired student, a reliance on note-takers, an understanding about an emotional or social condition that might influence the student's ability to contribute to class discussions, or mobility requirements for sitting in class or taking field trips to the library.

Consult your campus office of accessible education for students with disabilities to learn what resources are available and how you can create a safe, welcoming learning environment for all students.

ATTENDING TO DISABILITIES: Electronic Communication in Academic Life (2d)

When working with technology in writing classes, be sure to comply with the Americans with Disabilities Act (ADA). A screen reader for visually impaired students can help facilitate complete participation in online analysis and writing activities. Software that translates spoken words into computer text is readily available and can ensure that all students contribute to in-class writing exercises. When posting material on a course Web site, ask your academic technology staff about design considerations that help meet ADA requirements and provide alternative pages for specially adapted Web browsers that might not be able to read fancy graphics or frames. Look to your institution's disability resource center for training sessions and a plethora of information to help you make writing projects accessible to all members of your class community. For more information, see the Learning Disabilities Resources Web page at www.ldresources.com.

To introduce the issue of accessibility to your students, John Slatin suggests the following exercises that you can conduct with the entire class:

> The Virtual Keyboard activity gives you a very slight hint of what using the Web and other software is like for people who cannot use their hands or voices to control the computer. It works like this: Download and install a virtual keyboard (for example, the Click-N-Type from Lake Software available at http://cnt.lakefolks.com). A virtual keyboard is an on-screen keyboard designed for people with limited or no use of their hands. People in that situation might use a puff-stick to aim a stream of breath at the screen, or a headmounted pointer to select each key. For this exercise, you can use your mouse to select the keys you need. Use the virtual keyboard for a week; again, you'll want to keep your journal handy to record your experiences and observations and to keep track of the problems you encounter—including the ones you solve and those you don't. (par. 21)

Slatin also recommends experimenting with the talking computer by installing a screen reader and putting away the mouse. This exercise enables students to "gain an understanding of what the Web and other applications are like as *auditory* experiences for people who are blind" (par. 22). Screen-reader demonstrations are available at no charge from www.freedomscientific.com.

FOR TEACHING: Email (2d)

In order to establish the ground rules for online communication, review the guidelines in Chapter 2 of *The Everyday Writer* as a class. You might also include a list of specific policies in your syllabus. Patrick Sullivan provides an excellent example of such a list of email etiquette in "Reimagining Class Discussion in the Age of the Internet" and urges teachers to "establish a strong online netiquette policy":

> Establishing such a policy is essential for creating a learning environment where students feel safe and comfortable enough to share their ideas and feelings. . . . It is important to establish ground rules about class discussion to ensure that conversations will not be confrontational, competitive, or unnec-

> essarily argumentative. Some level of conflict is, of course, usually desirable in a class discussion, but teachers who hope to create a positive class environment online need to make it very clear that class discussions will also be collaborative in nature and collegial in tone. (401–2)

In addition, you can model appropriate email style, tone, content, and use in your own correspondence with students. Be sure to discuss with your students the importance of having appropriate email addresses for an audience beyond their circle of friends. After discussing email etiquette, consider asking your students to send you an email explaining their writing strengths and weaknesses.

FOR COLLABORATION: Email, Lists, and Discussion Forums (2d)

Ask students to work in small groups to draw up a description of the ways in which email and listserv postings seem to differ from postal letters and from the academic writing they do for most of their classes. You can use their small group reports to generate a discussion about netiquette and about issues of style in different genres of writing.

> **I have keyboarded in so many emails, so many forum messages, so many arguments and replies, that I instinctively think of this activity as a conversation. —Roger Ebert**

FOR COLLABORATION: Web Logs and Social Networking Spaces (2d)

Ask students to brainstorm for a few minutes about all the blogs they know about or participate in. Then ask them to work in pairs to write a definition of *blog* and to try to categorize the major types of blogs. Finally, consider asking students to follow a blog for several days and then write a brief (one-page) review of it for class.

FOR COLLABORATION: Social Networking Spaces (2d)

Have students browse through their own and their friends' Facebook and/or MySpace pages, focusing primarily on three things: (1) the About Me information, (2) the public posts by friends, and (3) the photos and any related comments. Students should take notes and in groups compare what they find. First have them discuss the funniest and the most outrageous comments they find. Then, as a group, have them write a brief character analysis of one of the individuals, using the information posted as supporting documentation. The activities to this point will help develop students' analytical and interpretive skills using a social-networking element with which students are already familiar. Finally, to develop their awareness to the power of audience, ask students to write about how a potential employer or professor would think about the items posted. Have students write a character analysis from the employer's or professor's point of view.

FOR MULTILINGUAL WRITERS: Electronic Communication (2d)

The new digital dialogue and forms of writing found in Internet chat rooms, blogs, and social networking spaces may be hard for multilingual writers to follow. As *Telegraph Herald* writer Erik Hogstrom puts it, "To save time typing, chat room visitors and instant messaging users scrimp on the keystrokes to produce abbreviations for a variety of phrases and actions." This shorthand manifests itself in acronyms such as *IDG* ("I don't get it"), *BRB* ("be right back"), *LOL* ("laughing out loud"), and *TTYL* ("talk to you later"). Multilingual writers might find this condensing of the language to be a new challenge for communication; alternatively, they might offer ways of chatting electronically in shorthand that will be informative for the entire class.

> **Semicolons also have come to figure prominently in the newest of writing genres, email correspondence. A semicolon is an essential component in the wink or smirk: ;-).**
>
> **–JULIA KELLER**

USEFUL READINGS

Farr, Marcia. "Essayist Literacy and Other Verbal Performances." *Written Communication* 10 (Jan. 1993): 4–38. Farr argues that the essayist style of discourse used in most academic writing differs from the natural discourse of students from nonmainstream groups and that "many such students face difficulties in writing instruction that mainstream students do not face" (4). It is therefore important to teach essayist discourse explicitly and to learn about other discourse styles used by students.

Fulkerson, Richard. "Summary and Critique: Composition at the Turn of the Twenty-First Century." *CCC* 56.4 (June 2005): 654–87. Fulkerson provides an overview of composition studies through the past twenty years, suggesting that as a discipline it is less unified now than ever before. He claims that there are now three major ways to approach composition pedagogy: critical/cultural, expressivism, and rhetorical (which is further divided into argumentation, genre, and academic discourse).

Hampton, Sally. "The Education of At-Risk Students." *Practice in the Teaching of Writing: Rethinking the Discipline*. Ed. Lee Odell. Carbondale: Southern Illinois UP, 1993. 186–212. Hampton writes that "we are not likely to improve the chances of at-risk students to succeed academically until we examine the assumptions we currently hold about their needs and abilities, consider how those assumptions led to flawed educational practices, and enact new practices and assessment procedures based on what we know about what works and what does not work" (187).

Kinneavy, James. "The Basic Aims of Discourse." *CCC* 20 (1969): 297–304. This is a distilled version of Kinneavy's *Theory of Discourse*, in which he divides discourse into referential, persuasive, literary, and expressive, each emphasizing a particular element in the exchange between writer and audience about the subject of the discourse.

Moss, Beverly J., and Keith Walters. "Rethinking Diversity: Axes of Difference in the Writing Classroom." *The St. Martin's Guide to Teaching Writing*. 6th ed. Ed. Cheryl Glenn and Melissa A. Goldthwaite. Boston: Bedford, 2008. The authors make clear how "our" language informs the norms of the institution and how our students use language as their medium of resistance. They write that "acknowledging difference, examining it, and finding creative ways to build upon it—to make it the cornerstone of individual and corporate philosophies of educational theory and classroom practice—require that we see ourselves, our beliefs, and even our actions, from a new perspective, one that forces us, as Clifford Geertz has put it, to see ourselves among others."

3 Online and Multimedia Presentations

Talking and eloquence are not the same: to speak, and to speak well, are two things. –BEN JONSON

At the same time that oral discourse has been growing in importance in our culture, attention to orality has waned in college courses and in the college curriculum. This situation is, however, now being reversed, as many colleges and universities move to include attention to speaking and to oral presentations in their general education curriculum requirements. Students are being asked to give oral presentations in increasing numbers of classes, and they want and need help in responding to these demands.

New trends across the nation to incorporate multimedia presentations in the writing classroom also challenge us as teachers to reconsider our criteria for mastery and assessment in the first-year composition classroom. Alice Trupe raises this very issue in a *Kairos* article:

> The freshman essay and the research paper are vehicles through which students are expected to demonstrate their literacy. . . . Whereas these specialized genres for students have served as the measure of freshman writing ability for a hundred years, transformation of writing courses by computer technology is a recent phenomenon. Composition instructors first welcomed word processing because it facilitated production of the standard freshman essay. However, the move into electronic environments rapidly began to revolutionize classroom practices and genres. Today, the expanding possibilities for writing engendered through desktop publishing, email, Web-based bulletin boards, MOOs, Web page and other hypertext authoring, and presentation software show up the limitations the freshman essay imposes on thought and writing. (par. 2)

Trupe goes on to argue that despite our reliance on new technologies in the writing classroom, we still look to the essay as the "limiting genre that most of us expect first-year writers to master." Consequently, while "we may encourage them to explore the possibilities of interactive computer environments . . . in the final analysis, the test of what students have learned through classroom activities often remains the plain vanilla, five-paragraph essay, since that is what is assessed for a grade" (par. 1–6).

As you design your course syllabus to include a multimedia component and a final presentation, consider how valuable these forms of "writing" will be to students in their future academic and professional careers. It often helps to motivate students by sharing your insight into the applicability of presentation skills. But also consider granting value to their work by readjusting your assessment criteria.

> Moving from silence into speech is for the oppressed, the colonized, the exploited, and those who stand and struggle side by side, a gesture of defiance that heals, that makes new life and new growth possible. It is that act of speech, of "talking back," that is no mere gesture of empty words, that is the expression of our movement from object to subject—the liberated voice. —BELL HOOKS

FOR MULTILINGUAL WRITERS: Class Discussions (3a)

Most classes impose some form of class participation requirement on all students. But ESL students in particular may not yet be comfortable speaking in class or sharing their ideas—which may be still evolving—with a group of their peers. As Jim Fredal writes in "Beyond the Fifth Canon," our culture tends to ascribe certain qualities, values, and skills to people on the basis of their speaking. Usually these are seen to reflect "quality of mind" or "critical thinking" and moral values, sympathy, egotism, engagement, and so on. But these assumptions are not necessarily valid: great minds are not necessarily always highly articulate or eloquent. Poor speaking can mean lots of things besides poor thinking.

In addition, because speech—especially articulate, measured, orderly, progressive speech—is so highly valued, silence is devalued as a sign of boredom, laziness, confusion, stupidity, or aloofness. It may or may not reflect any of these things. How much one speaks and how often are heavily scripted by cultural expectations, with significant variations for gender, sexual, racial, ethnic, ability, and other differences. These expectations influence our estimations of students' abilities, but we don't think as much about, nor can we review carefully, what our students say in the same way as we can review what they write. Nor can we simply expect them to change in the space of ten (or sixteen) weeks, to match academic expectations (to talk more or in a certain way).

> Where's your spirit of innovation, of forging on, of damn-the-manual-full-speed-ahead? —LOU FOURNIER

FOR TEACHING: Effective Presentations (3b)

In "Town Meetings," Gerry Brookes recommends asking students to prepare to speak very briefly (three minutes) on a topic of concern to them. In "town meeting" sessions that occur once a week, two or three students make their presentations. After each one, Brookes says, the class always applauds. Then the teacher poses a series of questions designed to "allow people to suggest alternative points of view, to offer supporting evidence, or to point out misjudgments of audience, without breaking into open disagreement." This kind of controlled response to the presentations, Brookes argues, allows students and instructor to help the speaker even when they disagree passionately about what she or he has said. Brookes recommends writing response notes to each speaker instead of giving formal grades, using the notes as the basis for conferences, and "giving a bit of extra credit if the spoken text is especially good." This class activity can help students learn the elements of an effective oral presentation within a collaborative and safe space.

FOR COLLABORATION: Practicing the Oral Presentation (3b)

Students will benefit greatly from working with one another to prepare and practice oral presentations. To help them get started on this work, group them in twos or threes and allow them some class time to talk about their topics, to discuss their deadlines and time constraints, and to set up a schedule. Then ask them to hold group practice sessions outside of class. During these sessions, the listener(s) should take notes on three things: what they remember most vividly, what they don't understand, and what they need or want to hear more of. To encourage students to work seriously at these sessions, consider awarding some credit for this group work; ask them to write individual summaries of what they did during practice sessions, how the practices helped them, and what might be done to improve future practice sessions.

As an alternative activity, ask students to prepare two-minute introductions of themselves near the beginning of the term (ideally on the second day of class). In groups of three, they can practice and present with their peers. After the introductions of each group, use the remaining class time to talk about what was most effective in the presentations. Ask students to think about what was most memorable about these introductions, about what techniques seemed particularly successful, and about what was most threatening about this situation. As a follow-up exercise, ask students to write a journal entry about what conclusions and lessons they could draw from the oral introductions about their own strengths and weaknesses as presenters.

FOR TEACHING: Considering Task, Purpose, and Audience (3b)

Before students get started on developing an oral or multimedia presentation, ask them to brainstorm about the assignment. Have them answer the following questions to get their ideas flowing:

- Who is the main audience? What would work best for this audience?
- What, above all, do you want your audience members to take away from the presentation?
- What are your strengths as a writer and a creative individual? public speaking? creative design? humor? clear explication?
- What do you want to learn from the process of creating a presentation? new skills in oral communication? effective ways of using PowerPoint? practice for poster sessions?
- What should be most memorable in your presentation?
- What risks can you take?

On Incorporating Multimedia into Oral Presentations (3b)

Remind students that *multimedia* does not mean PowerPoint alone. Posters, handouts, props, and dramatic enactments can all be part of a multimedia presentation. Often students translate *multimedia* as *technology* and don't realize that a powerful presentation can be produced simply using a poster, a carefully constructed handout, or voice and gesture alone. Encouraging students to work on oral and multimedia presentations will also help foster their development as writers in multiple media, and hence to begin to see connections between genres. As James Inman, Rachel Hallberg, and Courtney Thayer argue, we need to ask our students to "imagine new and important connections between technology-rich and non-technological genres of writing" (par. 6).

Indeed, the advent of the Internet and World Wide Web and the increasing affordability of programs such as PowerPoint and Dreamweaver have highlighted the degree to which today's writing often combines media. But even before the Web, of course, what often appeared to be in one medium—a speech, let's say—was more accurately *multi*media: a televised speech and even a talk show host's monologue are delivered orally, but they have been previously written. And even the most traditional spoken lectures have long relied on illustrations that may include music, art, and other forms of media.

These possibilities of multimedia create special challenges for writing instructors who must learn how to discover, and then pass on, the best advice about how to create multimedia presentations that are rhetorically effective. Chapter 3 of *The Everyday Writer* is designed to help you and your students get started on working in and with these new discourses.

ATTENDING TO DISABILITIES: Visuals (3b)

Emphasize to students that their visuals should augment the power of persuasion in their oral presentations, not just serve as decoration or distraction. At the same time, raise the issue of attending to disabilities when using visuals. For students who may have vision impairments, visuals may be difficult to see from across the room. If such visuals are produced through technological means, such as on a Web site or through a PowerPoint presentation, there are many alternative methods of communicating that information. Here are two examples:

- Images on posters and handouts can be converted through alternative format production technology and printed as raised images on special paper, allowing a visually impaired person to feel the visual.
- Handouts or poster replicas can be translated into Braille or put on an audiotape through text-to-speech technology.

> **A man's work is nothing but this slow trek to rediscover, through the detours of art, those two or three great and simple images in whose presence his heart first opened.**
>
> —Albert Camus

FOR COLLABORATION: Evaluating Multimedia Presentations (3b)

Ask students to work in small groups to evaluate the examples of multimedia presentations in 3b of *The Everyday Writer* using the guidelines given there. You might ask some groups to concentrate on the PowerPoint presentation in 3b and other groups to evaluate the multimedia student samples on *The Everyday Writer*'s companion Web site, **bedfordstmartins.com/everydaywriter**, under **Student Writing Models**. Then ask each group to report the results of their evaluation to the entire class. As a follow-up exercise, the class might work together to draw up a set of their own tips for creating successful multimedia presentations.

FOR COLLABORATION: Evaluating Presentations (3b)

Ask students to join two or more classmates and attend a presentation of interest to them, either on campus or in the larger community. All members of the group should take notes during the presentation on what they find effective and ineffective. Then the team should meet to compare notes and, using the principles outlined in this chapter, write up a brief collaborative review of the presentation and bring it to class for discussion.

TEACHING WITH TECHNOLOGY: Peer Response (3b)

You may wish to ask students to evaluate one another's oral or multimedia presentations using an electronic peer response form. Consider giving them a set of categories or a rubric to guide their responses. For example, you could ask that they make comments on strategy (adaptation to audience, opening and closing, visual aids); content (supporting materials and language, clarity, line of argument, anticipating and answering objections); organization (overview of main points, signposting, main points); and delivery (eye contact, conversational style, voice quality, gestures).

After each presentation, allow for five minutes of questions and answers. Then ask students to write a short electronic commentary on the presentation and post it to your class's listserv, Web bulletin-board space, or shared electronic list. The benefits of asking students to provide their evaluative comments online are that the speaker can download and print all the comments at once, you avoid having to photocopy and assemble slips of feedback, and all class members can see what others have written and can learn from those peer responses how to rethink their own presentation strategies.

USEFUL READINGS

Brookes, Gerry H. "Town Meetings: A Strategy for Including Speaking in a Writing Classroom." *CCC* 44 (Feb. 1993): 88–92. This piece contains an especially interesting discussion of how norms and conventions of public speaking reflect cultural values.

Brueggemann, Brenda J.. *Lend Me Your Ear: Rhetorical Constructions of Deafness.* Washington, DC: Gallaudet UP, 1999. Brueggemann's important text redefines *speech* and *orality*, critiques what she terms "the will to speech," and presents compelling descriptions and analyses of powerful sign language presentations.

Dragga, Sam. "The Ethics of Delivery." *Rhetorical Memory and Delivery: Classical Concepts for Contemporary Composition and Communication.* Ed. John Frederick Reynolds. Mahwah: Erlbaum, 1993. 79–95. Although this essay doesn't deal with oral presentations per se, it offers a particularly cogent discussion of how delivery can be manipulated and perceived. Dragga's discussion of charts and other visuals is also useful for information on the successful and ethical use of visual aids.

Ehninger, Douglas, Bruce E. Gronbeck, Ray E. McKerrow, and Alan H. Monroe. *Principles and Types of Speech Communication.* 14th ed. Boston: Allyn & Bacon, 2003. This widely used textbook offers good advice on all aspects of public speaking. Particularly valuable is the "Speaker's Resource Book," a "collection of generally short presentations of materials especially relevant to some speaking situations or to particular speakers facing special problems."

Fredal, Jim. "Beyond the Fifth Canon: Rhetorical Constructions of Speech from Homer to Herder." Dissertation. Ohio State University, 1998. In this important study, Fredal uncovers the network of assumptions and ideologies inscribed in the Western world's "will to speech," focusing on ancient Greece and early Enlightenment Europe to illustrate his argument. This work will make all instructors of writing reconsider the definition of *speech* and its relationships to writing and to systems of value.

Garland, James C. "Advice to Beginning Physics Speakers." *Physics Today* (July 1991): 42–45. This is a witty and highly instructive address to science students on how to prepare for and deliver oral presentations.

Haas, Christina. *Writing Technology: Studies on the Materiality of Literacy.* Mahwah: Erlbaum, 1995. Haas's work examines the relationship between writing and technology. It also challenges the notions of technological transparency, demonstrating the ways in which writing is transformed by means of its inextricable link with technology.

Hindle, Tim. *Making Presentations.* New York: DK Publishing, 1998. This small guide to communicating effectively offers practical strategies with clear visuals.

Inman, James A., Rachel Fields Hallberg, and Courtney Thayer. "Disney Promotion Poster Analysis: A Post-Technology Assignment." *Kairos* 7.2 (Summer 2002) <http://english.ttu.edu/kairos/7.2/sectiontwo/inman>. The authors present a discussion of multimedia projects that help students to imagine new ways of writing in various technological and nontechnological environments.

Killingsworth, M. Jimmie. "Product and Process, Literacy and Orality: An Essay on Composition and Culture." *CCC* 44.1 (Feb. 1993): 26–39. Killingsworth explores the thesis that "just as the formulators of current traditionalism met the needs of their times—the nineteenth century with its burgeoning culture of literacy—so the advocates of process pedagogy face up to the demands of teaching writing in an age dominated by the nonprint media of mass culture."

Locker, Kitty. "Making Oral Presentations." *Business and Administrative Communication.* 4th ed. Homewood: Irwin, 1997. Although aimed primarily at those interested in business or technical communication, Locker's discussion of how to prepare for and deliver oral presentations provides valuable concrete advice for any student assigned to make an oral presentation.

Marzluf, Phillip P. "Diversity Writing: Natural Languages, Authentic Voices." *CCC* 57.3 (Feb. 2006): 503–22. Marzluf rethinks eighteenth-century natural language theory in light of contemporary diversity and identities and explains its usefulness in determining how marginalized individuals use language to relate to others and to the world.

Moss, Beverly J. "Creating a Community: Literacy Events in African-American Churches." *Literacy across Communities.* Ed. Beverly J. Moss. Creskill: Hampton, 1994. Chap. 5. Moss demonstrates how oral discourse functions in African American churches and relates this use of orality to students' home literacies, which are all too often undervalued in the academy.

Slatin, John. "The Imagination Gap: Making Web-Based Instructional Resources Accessible to Students and Colleagues with Disabilities." *Currents in Electronic Literacy* 6 (Spring 2002) <http://www.cwrl.utexas.edu/currents/spring02/slatin.html>.

Trupe, Alice L. "Academic Literacy in a Wired World: Redefining Genres for College Writing Courses." *Kairos* 7.2 (Summer 2002) <http://english.ttu.edu/kairos/7.2/binder.html?sectionone/trupe/WiredWorld.htm>. Trupe explores what it means to write in a computer-mediated environment, examining the rhetorical features of emerging genres and what academic literacy means in a "wired world."

Welch, Kathleen. "Classical Rhetoric and Contemporary Rhetoric and Composition Studies: Electrifying Classical Rhetoric." *The Contemporary Reception of Classical Rhetoric: Appropriations of Ancient Discourse.* Mahwah: Erlbaum, 1990. Chap. 6. Welch reviews the "orality/literacy debate" and relates issues of secondary orality to the contemporary technological revolution.

USEFUL WEB SITES

College Composition and Communication

http://www.ncte.org/ccc

The Web site for College Composition and Communication *offers an online version of the journal.*

Kairos: A Journal of Rhetoric, Technology, and Pedagogy

http://kairos.technorhetoric.net

The Summer 2002 issue's special focus on technology, popular culture, and the art of teaching is particularly enlightening to teachers interested in designing syllabi and assignments for collaborating online and off.

Ohio State University's Fast Facts for Faculty

http://www.osu.edu/grants/dpg/fastfact

This Web site offers excellent advice for designing classes with attention to students with disabilities. Read about the latest technologies, pedagogical approaches, and universal design resources. Sharing this information with all your students will greatly improve the class climate and the quality of students' oral and multimedia presentations.

Design for College Writing

4

Good visual design complements good writing; it does not replace it. Together writing and design are part of finding the best available means to communicate with readers.

–SUSAN HILLIGOSS

When addressing an audience, a speaker is judged visually and aurally. The speaker's appearance, tone of voice, and the degree to which he or she meets the audience's eyes all create an impression. Our rhetorical sense tells us that we ought to dress appropriately when we go before a committee to be interviewed for a scholarship. Classical rhetoricians called this aspect of our behavior *actio* or *pronunciatio*—delivery—and identified it as one of rhetoric's five arts or canons.

In classical rhetoric, *actio* referred exclusively to the delivery of a speech to an audience. In our literate culture, however, rhetoric must also include written communication, where the audience is removed from the writer's immediate proximity. The writer has a different set of cues than does the speaker on which to rely to get his or her image across to the reader. Some primary cues, of course, must come from the writing itself: what it says, how it presents the writer's ideas and feelings, how it reflects him or her. But increasingly in this digital age, the visual rhetoric of documents is taking center stage. Thus, today students *and* instructors need to pay special attention to the elements of design that add so much to the effectiveness of print documents.

For many instructors of writing, it has been all too easy to neglect *delivery*, which has long been cut out of the rhetorical tradition. Yet *action* is of great importance to students' writing and may well become more so in the future. You should consider the importance of such issues to your own writing and share your thoughts with students. Also, you need to make very clear your requirements concerning visual rhetoric—perhaps even spelling them out in your syllabus.

Additional information on effective design is available on the *The Everyday Writer*'s companion Web site, **bedfordstmartins.com/everydaywriter**. Click on **Student Writing Models** for examples of student writing in various formats, or go to **Writing Resources** and click on **Design Tutorials** for tutorials on document design for both print and Web projects.

On Document Design

In "*Actio*: A Rhetoric of Manuscripts," Robert Connors covers such document design concerns as "Type and Typefaces," "Paper," "Typography and Layout," and some "Minor Considerations." His overview ends with the following reminder regarding the powers—and limits—of any document design:

> The rhetoric of manuscripts is a very small part of the entire rhetorical presentation of a writer. At its best, *actio* effaces itself and allows readers to concentrate on comprehension, aware only that the texts they hold are pleasant to the eye and to the touch. The most wonderful manuscript, however, cannot turn a poor piece of writing into a good one or make a vacuous essay meaningful. The best that the suggestions here can do is prevent a good piece of writing from being sabotaged by silly or careless physical presentation. Like speakers, who are scrutinized as soon as they walk out onto the platform, writers are being sized up as soon as their manuscripts fall from a manila envelope or are pulled from a pile. Attention to the tenets of *actio* can make certain that both writer and speaker are able to present their messages in the most effective way. (76)

Paragraph breaks are also an element of *actio*. H. W. Fowler writes in *A Dictionary of Modern English Usage*, "Paragraphing is also a matter of the eye. A reader will address himself more readily to his task if he sees from the start that he will have breathing-spaces from time to time than if what is before him looks like a marathon course" (434–35). These principles are even more important in online documents, where space is at a premium.

TEACHING WITH TECHNOLOGY: Visual Structure (4a)

Most students today do their document design work on computers, and increasingly, they're distributing their work—to teachers, to other students, and to employers—electronically. Ask students to consider the advantages and disadvantages of this shift. What factors do the students take into account when considering print or electronic delivery methods? What word-processing system do the students use? Do they know of any problems between their version of their software and other versions? Will the recipient of an electronic document be able to access it? Will formatting be affected by electronic submission? Do students approach document design differently, depending on how they will ultimately distribute the product? Which method do they prefer and why? The students will be a rich source of information and advice for one another—as well as for the instructor.

ATTENDING TO DISABILITIES: Visual Structure (4a)

When considering document design—especially with the use of technology—it is important to keep all members of an audience in mind. Invite students to break from their standardized way of conceptualizing particular audience or class members. Often this means reconsidering peers with disabilities as group members with individual strengths, not weaknesses. John Slatin describes this paradigm shift in terms of an act of imagination:

> I become more convinced each day that practicing accessibility means closing the imagination gap that separates most people from people with disabilities. It means *imagining disability*, and working at it long enough to get over the first shock of being *un*able to do what you're accustomed to doing in the way you're accustomed to doing it—long enough so that you begin to find solutions and workarounds, long enough so that you can begin to tell the difference between good design and bad design, between things that you can't do because you haven't learned how to do them yet and things that you can't do because there's no way for a person in your (imagined) circumstances to do them. (par. 16)

When teaching students to create a visual structure, encourage them to use their imaginations and find solutions to include all audience members, no matter what their functional limitations (sight, hearing, or movement). Slatin's article offers a host of resources to help you do so.

FOR COLLABORATION: Appropriate Formats (4b)

Ask students to work in small groups to share information about their approaches to formatting layout and design for specific assignments or types of documents, taking into account the options available from their word-processing programs. Ask them to bring in samples of a variety of documents or provide examples of student or professional work. Working in groups of three or four, students should prepare a brief report for the class on the top ten best layout and design features available. After the groups report, you can use the information they provide to discuss the aesthetics of document design, formatting, and visual rhetoric of the page. Get them thinking along with you about which design features are most appropriate—and which ones are inappropriate—for most of their college writing assignments. What exceptions to these guidelines can they think of?

FOR MULTILINGUAL WRITERS: Effective Headings (4c)

Research in cognitive psychology has shown that breaking a document into sections through the use of headings helps readers follow and assimilate the text's meaning more easily. This is especially true for multilingual writers, who may have difficulty wading through a long, unbroken essay. Encourage your students to incorporate visual design elements such as headings to signal turns in the argument or new sections in the essay.

On Effective Visuals (4d)

In a 2000 issue of *College English*, Craig Stroupe argues that English studies "needs to decide not only whether to embrace the teaching of visual and information design in addition to verbal production, which some of the more marginalized elements of English Studies have already done, but, more fundamentally, whether to confront its customary cultural attitudes toward visual discourses and their insinuation into verbal texts" (608). Similarly, teachers in writing classes need to confront the idea that visual images are subordinate to the verbal, and that they serve as decoration to the true heart of the text that lies in its prose.

You can alert students to these preconceptions by asking them to take short articles from magazines and campus newspapers and analyze how the texts function when paired with visual images. How do placement, color, size, and relationality affect the power of persuasion inherent in visual–verbal combinations? Have students draw up a brief list of "visual rhetoric" criteria on which to evaluate the design of texts containing images. Then ask them to experiment with manipulating the images: What happens when a different image is used in conjunction with a text? How does changing the visual structure produce a change in rhetorical meaning?

TEACHING WITH TECHNOLOGY: Effective Visuals (4d)

According to Brian Krebs, the Ninth Circuit Court of Appeals ruled in February 2002 that "while Web sites may legally reproduce and post 'thumbnail' versions of copyrighted photographs, displaying full-sized copies of the images violates artists' exclusive right to display their own works" (par. 1). At stake was a technological technique called "framing" or "inlinking" that imports images and displays them in full size in the new browser window. Such an appropriation of images is not considered "fair use" and thus violates copyright law. Let your students know about this new consequence of using technology to incorporate images in their writing, particularly if they cut and paste images from the Web.

ATTENDING TO DISABILITIES: Effective Visuals (4d)

John Slatin's suggestion for collaborative work provides a way for you to attend to disabilities in your classroom at the same time that you develop all students' writing and production proficiencies. Ask students to assess a Web page for its visual elements and provide an alternative that would help disabled students access the content. Slatin writes:

> Divide the class into three groups: Art, Charts and Graphs, and News. Assign each group an appropriate image (a work of art, a recent news photo, a chart or graph presenting statistical information, etc.). Then further divide each group into pairs or trios. Each pair or trio should write ALT [alternative] text and a LONGDESC [long description] for the assigned image, and create a Web page that presents the image plus associated text. Students can evaluate each other's descriptions and alternatives, discussing how or whether different kinds of images call for different kinds of textual alternatives. In a subsequent activity, students would incorporate the image and its associated text into a more complex page design that includes navigation links, on-screen text, etc. Students can then discuss how the changing contexts created by these different designs affect their judgment about how to write text alternatives. (par. 28)

FOR COLLABORATION: Effective Visuals (4d)

As part of their next writing assignment, ask students to include a visual of some kind, labeled appropriately, according to the guidelines in 4d of the *The Everyday Writer*. Before allowing your students to hand in the final drafts of their papers, have them exchange these drafts for one final peer response, focusing purely on *actio*. To ensure that your students bring in a final typed draft, don't tell them ahead of time that these drafts will be reviewed. Provide each student with a pencil and eraser. Proofreading marks should be lightly made in pencil so that the author of the paper can erase them, if he or she chooses. It is important for students to realize that making or not making the suggested corrections is their choice. If a student finds substantial changes need to be made, then permit him or her to turn the paper in the next day.

FOR TEACHING: Sample Documents (4e)

Ask students to bring in various documents that they've received in other classes or through groups they belong to. They may want to form into small groups to analyze the design of each document, deciding what features make for successful or unsuccessful "delivery" of information. They also may want to consider if the document design enhances a mediocre or an already strong piece of information.

FOR COLLABORATION: Evaluating Sample Documents (4e)

Professor Kitty Locker reminds instructors that "a design that looks pretty may or may not work for the audience." To see how designs work with actual audiences, Locker suggests advising students to work with a reader to test their document's design, whether it be a home page, a set of PowerPoint slides, a poster, or some other multimedia document.

As the reader uses and reads the document, Locker suggests that the student writer should

- ask the reader to "think aloud" while completing the task, saying what he or she is thinking and doing.
- interrupt the reader at important points in the document, asking what he or she is thinking or feeling.
- ask the reader to describe what he or she thinks of the document in retrospect.

After completing this exercise, students can bring in their results and work in groups to improve their use of multimedia in their sample documents.

USEFUL READINGS

Berger, Arthur A. *Seeing Is Believing: An Introduction to Visual Communication.* 2nd ed. Mountain View: Mayfield P, 1998. Berger demonstrates the central role that visual phenomena play in our lives, arguing that our visual experiences are tied to our intellectual and emotional ones.

Connors, Robert J. "*Actio*: A Rhetoric of Manuscripts." *Rhetoric Review* 2 (1983): 64–73. Connors equates manuscript preparation with the last of the five canons of rhetoric. He discusses the rhetorical effects of typefaces, paper, and format.

Connors, Robert J., and Andrea A. Lunsford. "Frequency of Formal Errors in Current College Writing, or Ma and Pa Kettle Do Research." *CCC* 39.4 (December 1988): 395–409. The original research upon which Andrea A. Lunsford's handbooks are based.

Fowler, H. W. *A Dictionary of Modern English Usage.* 2nd ed. Rev. and ed. Sir Ernest Gowers. New York: Oxford UP, 1965.

Fox, Roy F., ed. *Images in Language, Media, and Mind.* Urbana: NCTE, 1994. The essays in this book demonstrate and examine the ways in which we create social meaning by interacting with images in areas ranging from teaching and politics to advertising and sexuality. Classroom implications and specific teaching strategies are introduced throughout, with the underlying thesis that "we can no longer separate visual literacy from verbal literacy, that we must treat word and image equally and simultaneously."

Garrett-Petts, Will F., and Donald Lawrence, eds. *Integrating Visual and Verbal Literacies.* Winnipeg, Manitoba: Inkshed, 1996. The essays in this collection offer various approaches to using multimedia literacies in the classroom; the editors contend that as technology makes the combination of image, text, and other media more accessible, the gap between authors and readers of these visual texts will diminish, and the roles of instructor and student will similarly change as classroom and other texts become interactive ones.

Hilligoss, Susan. *Visual Communication: A Writer's Guide.* 2nd ed. New York: Longman, 2002. This is a short, instructional guide on the mechanics of visual design.

Krebs, Brian. "Court Rules 'Thumbnail' Images OK, Full-Sized Copies Not." *Newsbytes* 7 (Feb. 2002) <http://www.computeruser.com/news/02/02/09/news3.html>. This is a brief on the court decision concerning copyright law on the Internet.

Lunsford, Andrea A., and Karen J. Lunsford. "'Mistakes Are a Fact of Life': A National Comparative Study." *CCC* 59.4 (June 2008): 781–806. An update of "Ma and Pa Kettle Do Research," the original Connors and Lunsford research upon which Andrea A. Lunsford's handbooks are based.

Reynolds, John Frederick, ed. *Rhetorical Memory and Delivery: Classical Concepts for Contemporary Composition and Communication.* Hillsdale: Erlbaum, 1993. Especially useful for this chapter is the updated version of Robert Connors's "*Actio*," listed above, which is included in this collection.

Shriver, Karen. "What Is Document Design?" *Dynamics in Document Design: Creating Texts for Readers.* New York: Wiley, 1997. 1–11. Shriver provides a discussion of terminology for document design.

Slatin, John. "The Imagination Gap: Making Web-Based Instructional Resources Accessible to Students and Colleagues with Disabilities." *Currents in Electronic Literacy* 6 (Spring 2002) <http://www.cwrl.utexas.edu/currents/spring02/slatin.html>. Slatin reminds teachers of their legal and ethical obligations to make their Web materials accessible to students with disabilities; he also suggests excellent group activities for raising student awareness of universal design.

Stafford, Barbara Maria, ed. *Good Looking: Essays on the Virtue of Images.* Cambridge: MIT P, 1998. Stafford argues for an "overarching and innovative imaging discipline," one that crosses disciplinary boundaries and continually questions the relations between words and images in all areas of society and all facets of perception. She urges a pragmatic, case-based approach to understanding our cognitive response to imagery, one that recognizes the complexity that emerges along with new and newly converging media technologies.

Stroupe, Craig. "Visualizing English: Recognizing the Hybrid Literacy of Visual and Verbal Authorship on the Web." *CE* 62.5 (May 2000): 607–32. Stroupe questions our ideological preference for the verbal text.

USEFUL WEB SITES

Graphion's Online Type Museum

http://www.typographia.org/1999/graphion-collection.html

This site provides information about the history and practice of typesetting, including good advice about indenting, using capitals, and spacing. The site's glossary of typographic terms offers a good starting point for anyone interested in design and layout both in print and online.

How Users Read on the Web

http://www.useit.com/alertbox/9710a.html

Claiming that most people visually scan a Web page rather than read it carefully, Jakob Nielson gives a brief overview of the importance of design on Web pages while simultaneously employing those specific design ideas on the Web site.

Yahoo! Computers and Internet: Graphics

http://dir.yahoo.com/computers_and_internet/graphics

This is a good source for links to design sites and journals.

The Writing Process

There may be people who like various aspects of the writing process. For some, it may be the excitement of facing a blank page. (Hate them!) For others, it could be a sense of getting a sentence just right. (Jerks!) There may be those who like the revision process, who can go over what they've produced with a cold eye and a keen ear and feel a satisfaction in making it better. (Liars!)

—RACHEL TOOR

5 Writing Situations

No writing takes place in isolation. As Wayne C. Booth wrote in his classic essay, "The Rhetorical Stance," all good writing establishes a relationship among content, reader, and writer. In texts from emails to research papers, there is a dynamic interplay among audience, persona, and message that signifies the "rhetorical situation." As they embark on a writing endeavor, your students will engage with this dynamic.

This interplay is made increasingly complex, in large part because technology has become such a mainstay of our lives that we must rethink our approaches to teaching and learning writing. Mary Hocks and Michelle Kendrick note the tensions related to the "encroachment of the visual into territory formerly held almost exclusively by text and print" (1) and encourage a shift from thinking about text versus image to imagining the *interplay* of text and image—and the historical significance and current technologies that facilitate such interplay. Hocks and Kendrick ask us to move beyond static binaries that separate visual/textual and image/word and to instead create spaces to focus on the "complex, interpenetrating relationships between words and images" (5).

On Writing to Connect (5a)

Within the discipline of rhetoric, the rhetorical situation has long been of paramount concern. The idea of the rhetorical stance was first put forward by Wayne Booth in a *CCC* article of the same name. A good rhetorical stance, said Booth, was the result of an effective balance between the three Aristotelian forms of proof: ethos, pathos, and logos. Too much emphasis on ethos, the wonderfulness of the writer, would result in an imbalance that Booth called the entertainer's stance. Too much emphasis on pathos, playing to the desires of the audience, would result in the advertiser's stance. And too much emphasis on logos, the message in itself, would result in the imbalance that Booth called the pedant's stance. Keeping these three elements at work but not allowing any one of them to predominate is the work of the successful writer.

Rhetoric calls for a careful investigation of the context in which any discourse appears, whatever the point of view. Aristotle offers categories of appeals (ethos, logos, pathos) that a writer should consider when addressing any audience. Kenneth Burke's scheme of dramatism is a pentadic method of analysis based on the categories of act, agent, agency, scene, and purpose. James Kinneavy explores what he calls "the rhetorical triangle" (writer or speaker, audience or reader, and text). Sandra Harding examines content from the perspective of feminist standpoint theory. New historicist and recent feminist theorists have also stressed the need to situate any act of writing within the fullest possible context or situation. In *A Pedagogy of Possibility: Bakhtinian Perspectives on Composition Studies*, Kay Halasek rereads the discipline of composition with special attention to rethinking the concept of rhetorical situation. Especially important are her applications of dialogism, heteroglossia, and other Bakhtinian concepts to composition in ways that reimagine familiar terms of the rhetorical situation—the student writer, audience, genre, and authority—and her description of a "pedagogy of possibility" that is based on dialogue, collaboration, and answerability.

> **A rhetorician, I take it, is like one voice in a dialogue. Put several such voices together, with each voicing its own special assertion, let them act upon one another in cooperative competition, and you get a dialectic that, properly developed, can lead to the views transcending the limitations of each.** —Kenneth Burke

On Understanding Rhetorical Situations (5b)

Whether the stimulus for writing comes from outside the writer (as in a class assignment) or grows from the writer's own desire to put thoughts into words, the decision to write is a deliberate act of commitment. When we commit ourselves to writing, we *prewrite* by assessing our writing (that is, rhetorical) situation, asking ourselves questions such as the following: Who is my audience? What does the audience expect of me? What do I already know about this subject? What must I find out? How can I best arrange my information and ideas? How much time do I have? How long should the composition be?

As soon as you make a writing assignment, encourage your students to respond to these questions by "thinking with a pencil in hand," jotting down ideas in their writing logs. Unlike experienced writers, students tend to spend little time prewriting. You might want to remind your students that almost all writers, even experienced ones, dread the blank page. Many authors say that the quickest way to face that challenge is to cover the blank page with writing, allowing anything to find its way onto the page. You might remind your students that they should *write* to think rather than *wait* to think.

FOR TEACHING: Understand Rhetorical Situations (5b)

You can provide students with experience writing in a variety of academic genres by offering them freedom to choose the rhetorical stance for a particular assignment. Have them select the disciplinary parameters for their essays by modeling their work on published academic writing in the fields of literary analysis, film review, scientific writing, social science research, or computer science. A good way to develop students' critical reading and writing skills in terms of genre and academic discourse is to ask them to find a contemporary article on a subject of their choice from a recent periodical or academic journal. Conduct a rhetorical analysis of the article, examining the genre for its specific writing conventions. Then have students model their own writing after the article's discipline specific attributes.

FOR TEACHING: Assignments (5b)

Some instructors—and writing programs—believe that three to five pages is an appropriate page length for most composition-course essays. Three- to five-page papers demand development of a topic beyond simple description of a problem or narration of an event, yet they are short enough to require significant narrowing of the topic. In contrast, other instructors require progressively longer and more challenging assignments, culminating in a fifteen- to twenty-page research paper. Whatever the length of the assignment, take the time to create *detailed* and *directive* assignment sheets that explain the purpose, goals, length, format, content, and grading criteria for the assignment. Clarifying the evaluation criteria makes your expectations transparent and eliminates the guessing game students often play in trying to figure out what you want.

Consider assigning due dates for drafts. A day or two after introducing invention strategies, assign an exploratory draft. A couple of days later, schedule conferences with your students to discuss their work. Within the next few days, have them bring their revisions—along with all their planning notes and earlier drafts—to class. Setting deadlines for drafts reinforces the importance of starting early.

After designing and distributing your assignment, make time in class to read through the detailed handout and answer any questions. Too often we leave this step up to the students and, consequently, problems arise concerning expectations, which could have been avoided with a general class discussion. Stress the importance of comprehending and addressing the rhetorical situation before beginning to write.

FOR COLLABORATION: Brainstorming the Topic (5c)

Use small groups to generate ten to twenty possible topics or questions for several subject areas, such as interesting people, current controversies, cultural trends, problems on campus, intriguing scientific discoveries, possibilities for progress or decay, and so on. Students can use these topics or questions as starters for prewriting activities (see 6a), which may lead directly to an essay draft.

FOR TEACHING: The Topic and Writing Logs (5c)

Ask your students to keep a section in their writing logs dedicated to compiling essay topics on subjects that interest them. The log can also be a place to store ideas, facts, observations, and provocative quotations from public figures or from students' reading (academic or otherwise). Organizing these entries under general subject headings (of the teacher's suggestion or the writer's invention) can provide some initial development of the topics.

GAME PLAN: Analyze the Writing Situation (5c–d)

The Game Plan to Analyze the Writing Situation provides a dynamic way for students to navigate the rhetorical triad in the beginning stages of their writing process. This game plan works effectively as an individual exercise, in small groups, or as a whole class. For example, you might have the students come up with a specific topic and define an audience for an assignment you've presented them with. Then put the students in pairs so that half the class works on the questions for the topic and half works on the questions for the audience. After a limited amount of time, the students should report back orally while you or a recorder writes down results. The range and variety of results become the basis for a discussion on the effect of and importance of defining topic and audience to give shape to the writing. At this point, you might put the students in different pairs or create slightly larger groups: have those students who brainstormed the audience shift their discussion to the question "What topic will appeal to this audience?" and the other half of the students discuss the question "How will an audience react to this topic?" After discussing topic and audience, ask the students to consider the questions about purpose. While some of these questions will be dictated by the requirements of the assignment, some will require deeper thinking. If your students seem to stall at this point, use it as an opportunity to brainstorm the many kinds of purposes writing has.

FOR TEACHING: Analyze Your Audience (5c)

In *A Pedagogy of Possibility*, Kay Halasek discusses audience in ways that are helpful to teachers and students alike. Halasek briefly describes the uses of six kinds of audience that writers have available to them: projected audience (those imagined or invoked by the writer), previous audience (those the writer is responding to or is in conversation with), immediate audience (such as peer group members), textual audience (what some call the "implied" reader or the audience in the text), public audience (those to whom the text will be sent), and evaluative audience (the teacher, employer, or group that will assess the text).

FOR TEACHING: Analyze Your Audience (5c)

Dealing with questions of audience is one of the most complex problems facing any writer, and face-to-face oral communication doesn't completely prepare students for the intricacies of attending to audience in written texts. Discuss the six types of audience presented in the preceding discussion with your students and ask them to brainstorm examples of each type from their daily lives. Try the exercises that follow to continue educating students about the crucial importance of audience in the writing process. You can use the questions listed in 5d of *The Everyday Writer* for oral or written practice in getting students more comfortable with writing for a wider or more diverse audience than they may be used to.

Ask students to prepare to write an essay describing the college health service's policies on distribution of birth control information. They should answer the bulleted list of questions in 5d with two audiences in mind: a women's student group at another college and a faith-based scholarship committee. This exercise can be done either individually or in groups, and in either case the writing is followed by class discussion on the kinds of problems each audience presents to a writer.

A student's first response to the question of audience is usually to assume that the instructor is the audience as well as the evaluator of the essay. Help your students distinguish between the two by asking them to write a *general audience profile*. If, for example, their general topic is *part-time worker, full-time student*, their audience profile might read something like this: *My audience is seventeen- and eighteen-year-olds who are either attending or planning to attend college and who have experienced the dual obligations of work and school.*

By writing an audience profile for each paper, your students will begin to see that they are constructing an audience that goes beyond you. As they begin to visualize their audience, they can write directly to it instead of directly for you. It will also be easier for you to evaluate their work when they have defined their audience.

You might also ask each student to bring in an article, editorial, or column from a newspaper and to circle elements in the writing that deliberately include or exclude certain kinds of audiences. Ask students to read the circled excerpts and talk about whether the writer seemed to be aware of or in control of his or her effects, and how and why the writer made the choices he or she made concerning the inclusion or exclusion of audiences. Ask students to bring in local newspapers and magazines that target speakers of languages other than English. Discuss the audiences for each periodical.

> **Only presidents, editors, and people with tapeworm have the right to use the editorial "we."**
> —MARK TWAIN

FOR COLLABORATION: Analyze Your Audience and Peer Response (5d)

If your students are working on an essay, have them exchange their drafts and write audience profiles based on one another's topics. After they have returned the profiles and drafts, the students may need to rethink their original audience. This type of collaborative work often helps students grasp the significance of addressing an audience and the way in which they need to revise their stance, strategic use of appeals, and language to match readers' expectations.

FOR TEACHING: Analyze Your Position as a Writer or Speaker (5e)

Students may have trouble coming up with a succinct statement of purpose for a piece of writing they are currently working on. Often their purpose will be little more than a simple statement like *My purpose is to tell the story of how I felt after I wrecked my dad's Buick* or *My purpose is to describe how stupid it is to shoplift.* Try pushing students beyond these simple statements into purpose statements that include some effect on the audience, since audience and purpose are always linked. The intended audience for most first drafts is usually *either people in the class*, or *you, the instructor*. Again, asking students to go beyond audiences that are immediately available will increase their repertoire of abilities. In talking with or writing to the student, keep asking how the writing would change if written for some other audience.

FOR COLLABORATION: Analyze Your Position as a Writer or Speaker (5e)

Ask students to join with two other members of the class. Each team should choose one of the following assignments and brainstorm how these topics might be approached depending on the writer's purpose. To guide students' work, ask them to refer to the questions in 5e. Have students take notes during their collaborative work and bring their notes to class for discussion.

1. Compare two book-length studies of Malcolm X.
2. Discuss the controversies surrounding the use of genetic engineering to change characteristics of unborn children.
3. Analyze the use of headlines in a group of twenty advertisements, and then analyze what relationship those headlines have with the visual image in the advertisement.
4. Describe a favorite spot in your hometown.
5. Explain the concept of virtual reality.

On Language and Clarity (5f)

In an interview in the *Council Chronicle* (Feb. 1994), Maya Angelou was asked if city schools should teach the languages of their neighborhoods, or if they should teach the English language. Her strong response follows:

> I think they should teach the English language primarily. Fundamental Standard English language in every environment—because the language is so flexible, there are particularities and peculiarities which will be absorbed into the language. [The neighborhood language] becomes what the West Africans call the *sweet language*. That then makes a person bilingual. He or she speaks Standard English, which he needs in the marketplace. He or she also speaks the *sweet language*, which is used to make contact with a beloved, a family member, a lover. I think what should be taught is the Standard English language. The other languages of the neighborhood are so in flux that you can't really teach them. You can learn them, but you can't really teach them. (8 ff.)

We may not be able to teach our students the "*sweet languages*," but we can use examples such as the one Maya Angelou discusses to teach students about the importance of *discourse communities*. Have students develop an awareness of how different language conventions are used for different audiences across the country—whether by region, race, profession, or class. What kind of discourse communities exist in the students' hometown, on campus, in the dorms, or between different majors? When students begin writing, they should consider such differences and select the most appropriate language to match the expectations of their audience.

FOR COLLABORATION: Tone and Style (5f)

To help students consider how words and images work together to create tone, ask them to gather a collection of magazine advertisements. As a class, analyze a few ads, closely reading and assessing how the text works—or doesn't work—with the visuals in the ads. Engage in a large-group discussion about the arguments that advertisements make to us, as potential consumers, through text and through images. Then explore possible examples of resistance or appropriation—for instance, the "spoof ads" hosted at adbusters.org (adbusters.org/spoofads). Finally, ask students to choose a particular ad and to revise or rewrite the text. For instance, the text for an ad for couture jeans that features a thin model might read "Skip lunch, buy our jeans." An ad for beer that features a fit man with exposed and muscled abdominals might read "Beer gut?" An ad for deodorant that promises a "radical breakthrough in dryness protection" might be revised to read "Once upon a time in America, revolution meant the overthrow of a government and radical meant never-before-known ideas and discoveries."

FOR COLLABORATION: Tone and Style (5f)

In addition or as an alternative to the preceding exercise, ask students working in pairs or small groups to visit the Web sites of different types of organizations or businesses (e.g., museums, nonprofits, hospitals). Have each group identify the type of site they are exploring and present to the class how visuals are used within the site to create a feel, a voice, an identity, and a tone. Then ask students to find and carefully read the mission statement or About Us sections of the sites and analyze how effectively the tone of the writing matches the tone of the imagery.

On Writing Web Texts (5f)

In his essay "Escaping from Flatland," Lawrence M. Hinman says that the new dynamic, interactive, multimedia-filled Web page has led him to realize that "I no longer write as well as I used to. The medium has changed, and now I realize there are areas of writing in which I am less skilled." Like Hinman, most teachers of writing learned to write a text that was composed solely of words. The past decade, however, has brought the changed medium Hinman talks about, and students are making projector-based presentations, Web pages, podcasts, videos, and all sorts of multimedia "writing." While conventions to guide writers in these new forms are evolving, teachers need to become keen observers, taking note of features we find most effective in Web texts and beginning the hard work of creating a pedagogy to encompass them.

At the same time, the development of Web texts should not be limited to student writers. As Sheila Offman Gersh reminds us, we can dramatically revitalize and improve our pedagogy through rhetorically sound Web texts that engage and educate our student audience:

> Teachers . . . can use the Internet to link their students to other classes to work collaboratively to further enrich any topic they are learning. This creates the "shared learning" environment around classroom instruction. (par. 8)

USEFUL READINGS

Booth, Wayne C. "The Rhetorical Stance." *CCC* 14 (Oct. 1963): 139–45.

Britton, James. *The Development of Writing Abilities*. London: Macmillan, 1975.

Doheny-Farina, Stephen. *The Wired Neighborhood*. New Haven: Yale UP, 1996. This book examines how writing allows for engagement with the global village and considers the ethical implications involved in online rhetorical contexts.

Ede, Lisa, and Andrea Lunsford. "Audience Addressed/Audience Invoked: The Role of Audience in Composition Theory and Pedagogy." *CCC* 35 (1984): 155–71. Rpt. in *The Writing Teacher's Sourcebook*. Ed. Gary Tate and Edward P. J. Corbett. New York: Oxford UP, 4th ed., 2000. Ede and Lunsford point out the limitations of two prominent concepts of audience, that of "audience addressed," which emphasizes the concrete reality of the writer's audience, and that of "audience invoked," which focuses on the writer's construction of an audience.

Faigley, Lester. "Literacy after the Revolution." *CCC* 48 (1997): 30–44. In his 4Cs Chair's Address, Faigley puts the electronic "revolution" in global perspective and reminds instructors of the economic and political concerns raised by the increasing importance of online rhetorical situations.

Glenn, Cheryl, and Melissa A. Goldthwaite. *The St. Martin's Guide to Teaching Writing*. 6th ed. Boston: Bedford, 2008. Chapter 4 provides more on "Successful Writing Assignments."

Halasek, Kay. *A Pedagogy of Possibility: Bakhtinian Perspectives on Composition Studies*. Carbondale: Southern Illinois UP, 1999.

Hinman, Lawrence M. "Escaping from Flatland: Multimedia Authoring." *Syllabus Magazine* <http://ethics.sandiego.edu/lmh/Papers/Escaping%20 from %20Flatland.html>.

Hocks, Mary E. "Understanding Visual Rhetoric in Digital Writing Environments." *CCC* 54.4 (2003): 629–56. Hocks provides an excellent framework for academic hypertext and student work.

Kroll, Barry M. "Writing for Readers: Three Perspectives on Audience." *CCC* 35 (1984): 172–85. Kroll examines three prominent views of audience—the "rhetorical," the "informational," and the "social." For each view he offers an analysis of its theoretical assumptions, its pedagogical implications, and its limitations.

Spack, Ruth. "Initiating ESL Students into the Academic Discourse Community: How Far Should We Go?" *TESOL Quarterly* 22 (1988): 29–47. Spack argues that teachers must help students enter the academic discourse community by setting up a process-centered writing course that clearly articulates academic expectations, demands, and standards.

White, Edward. *Assigning, Responding, Evaluating: A Writing Guide.* 4th ed. New York: Bedford, 2007. Practical advice on approaching writing assessment, using evaluations, and creating assignments and tests.

6 Exploring Ideas

In any work that is truly creative, the writer cannot be omniscient in advance about the effects that he or she proposes to produce. The suspense . . . is not just in the reader, but in the writer, who is intensely curious about what will happen.
—MARY MCCARTHY

Classical rhetoric consisted of five canons: *inventio* (invention), *dispositio* (arrangement), *elocutio* (style), *memoria* (memory), and *pronunciatio* (delivery). The process of discovery implied by the Latin *inventio* and the Greek *heuresis* parallels our modern concept of prewriting. Since *prewriting* is often used to refer both to "invention" and to "planning," your students might want to think of invention as a process of exploring what to say about a topic; of planning as the choices of what, when, and how to say it; and of prewriting as the first stage in the writing process, when invention and planning most often occur. While drafting can and should occur throughout the process of exploring and planning, at some point you will want to help students compile all their drafting into an official first draft. Encourage your students to be creative in their approach to a topic, the prewriting process, and the planning of organizational strategies.

ATTENDING TO DISABILITIES: Exploring Ideas

Barbara A. Heifferon teaches Nancy Mairs's intimate account of writing and disability in *Carnal Acts: Essays* to enable students to explore the links among writing, identity, emotion, and meaning making in the world. For one of her male students, "the disability text opened up an opportunity for him to express his own grief and loss. The introduction of her honest text and the chance to write in response to that honesty reinforce our notions that writing is closely linked to how we form our identities" (Brueggemann et al., 386–87). Heifferon's reflection on her pedagogy offers writing teachers an important lesson:

> Texts on disability, honest, real, open texts such as Mairs's essay, have a valuable place in the writing classroom, particularly in a culture that continually blasts the able-bodied, idealized, and commodified body into our eyes and ears, and in a culture that often denies men the right to express their innermost feelings. I doubt a tamer text or a text that did not confront such stereotypes could have moved students so far from the previously unquestioned assumptions they carried with them, invisible and silent assumptions that render those with disabilities invisible and silent. Thus we moved from dismay to discussion past dissonance to the discovery of a place where disability texts in the classroom help students confront issues of authority and power. Students' ability to grapple with such texts that challenge the views they take for granted increases their confidence and enables identification with persons different from themselves. (Brueggemann et al., 386–87)

Have your students respond to a powerful textual account of living with disabilities as a way to break through conventional categories of meaning making.

FOR TEACHING: Exploring Ideas and Writing Logs

Peter Elbow suggests in *Writing without Teachers* that students who sincerely want to improve their writing keep a freewriting diary:

> Just ten minutes a day. Not a complete account of your day; just a brief mind sample for each day. You don't have to think hard or prepare or be in the mood: without stopping, just write whatever words come out—whether or not you are thinking or in the mood. (9)

You might suggest that students keep a section of their logs dedicated to a freewriting diary.

On Brainstorming (6a)

Exploring a topic through brainstorming works particularly well with groups of three to five students, but it generates even more energy when conducted with the entire class. Whether you or your students suggest the topic is not as important as getting started. Appoint two students to record ideas suggested by the rest of the class. After about ten minutes, break up the class into groups of four, and ask each group to choose an idea and develop a thesis from it. Share with your students the following ways to facilitate brainstorming:

- Write down as many ideas you can think of *without stopping*. Go back and edit your list later, selecting the most promising topics.
- Speak into a tape recorder as you walk through campus, commenting on what you notice as interesting.

- Keep a reaction journal in which you jot down your responses to course lectures, reading materials, news items, and public conversations in dorms or dining halls.
- Find the most provocative article you can on a topic that matters to you, and forge a constructive response to it.
- Interview five people in your community on a matter of historical, intellectual, or personal interest. Transcribe their responses into a dialogue, and insert your own voice in an attempt to discover your own stance.

FOR COLLABORATION: Brainstorming (6a)

Distribute 5 × 7 index cards to each student. Each student will write a topic at the top of a card and pass it on to the student to the right. The next student poses a question about that topic. Have the students continue passing the cards and responding with more questions until the cards are filled. The questions may lead in a direction previously not considered and give ideas to the writers about what their audience may want to know.

On Freewriting (6b)

James Moffett, in *Teaching the Universe of Discourse*, and Janet Emig, in *The Composing Processes of Twelfth Graders*, posit that freewriting not only increases verbal fluency but also provides a means for discovering ideas. In *Writing without Teachers*, Peter Elbow writes:

> The habit of compulsive, premature editing doesn't just make writing hard. It makes writing dead. Your voice is damped out by all the interruptions, changes, and hesitations between the consciousness and the page. (6)

Freewriting eliminates the beginning writer's most frustrating habit: focusing on correctness rather than content. During final drafting, your students will need to focus on correctness—but not until then.

TEACHING WITH TECHNOLOGY: Looping (6b)

Looping is a way to activate students' critical thinking. If you are teaching with a course email distribution list or an electronic bulletin board, have each student post an initial one- to two-sentence description of an idea that might provide the beginning of a paper. Then ask students to respond to one or two posts and identify what is most interesting about the topics. Have the first student, in turn, respond to the reactions of the class by developing and amplifying the focus of the topic. Encourage students to pose questions in their responses to generate even more ideas. This form of collaborative looping, facilitated by technology, can offer a fast and meaningful way to encourage your students' exploration of writing topics.

TEACHING WITH TECHNOLOGY: Clustering (6d)

Recent versions of Word enable students to follow the flow of their ideas through diagrams that resemble clouds, circles, or squares. Arrows can begin to show relations between items and, in the software program Inspiration, students can click a drop-down menu and convert their clusters of ideas into an outline.

On Asking Questions (6e)

The questions in 6e of *The Everyday Writer* are meant to stimulate the writer's thinking and are based on various heuristics (prompts for thinking that involve questioning and other guides for investigation). Ultimately, all such heuristics derive from the *topoi*, the "topics" or "commonplaces" of classical rhetoric.

In *Classical Rhetoric for the Modern Student*, Edward P. J. Corbett explains that the topics helped writers find appropriate ways to develop any subject. Special topics are those classes of argument appropriate to particular kinds of discourse: judicial, ceremonial, or political. Aristotle names the common topics, those that could be used for any occasion, as definition, comparison, relationship, testimony, and circumstance.

Like the questioning strategies in this section, the *topoi* provide a way to find something to say about a subject.

FOR MULTILINGUAL WRITERS: Questioning (6e)

Another questioning technique that works well with students comes from the yoga technique of empathetic listening. This strategy can be particularly successful with multilingual students who may be shy about voicing questions during class.

Have students sit in pairs and ask each other the questions that follow. Tell them not to respond to the answers, but to facilitate continued talk through asking a subsequent question. These prompts are particularly effective in helping students develop argumentative research papers or position papers.

What really matters to you, and why?

Go on, can you tell me more about it?

What do you want me to do about it?

At the end of ten minutes, have students write down what focused thoughts emerged as a consequence of this questioning/empathetic listening technique. You can modify the questions to match the purpose of your own class's particular writing assignment.

> **Just get it down on paper, then we'll see what to do with it.** —Maxwell Perkins

ATTENDING TO DISABILITIES: Questioning (6e)

For students with hearing impairments, you can conduct the preceding questioning exercise through an email discussion group, an instant-message chat, or a networked bulletin board exchange. The advantage of using a word processor is that students will have a textual copy of their work in progress, including brainstorming questions, answers, and reflections. For students with visual impairments, provide a tape recorder at the time of the questioning session so that the conversation can be recorded for later reference.

On Working Collaboratively (6g)

To ensure that students take ownership of their individual contributions to group work, have the students identify the characteristics they value and come up with their own rubric for assessment that they can fill out anonymously.

> **Here it is, My Theory about Writing: It's hard. No good writing is easy.** —Dave Barry

USEFUL READINGS

Brueggemann, Brenda Jo, Linda Feldmeier White, Patricia A. Dunn, Barbara A. Heifferon, and Johnson Cheu. "Becoming Visible: Lessons in Disability." *CCC* 52.3 (Feb. 2001): 381.

Corbett, Edward P. J., with Robert Connors. *Classical Rhetoric for the Modern Student*. 4th ed. New York: Oxford UP, 1999. This text provides a thorough, cogent, and readable exposition of Aristotelian rhetoric and a brief history of the Western rhetorical tradition.

Elbow, Peter. "The Loop Writing Process." *Writing with Power*. New York: Oxford UP, 1981. 59–77. Elbow provides a refinement of freewriting that he calls loop writing—"a way to get the best of both worlds: both control and creativity" (59).

———. *Writing without Teachers*. 2nd ed. New York: Oxford UP, 1998.

Emig, Janet. *The Composing Processes of Twelfth Graders*. Urbana: NCTE, 1971.

Flower, Linda. "Writer-Based Prose: A Cognitive Basis for Problems in Writing." *CE* 41 (1979): 19.

Lauer, Janice M. "Issues in Rhetorical Invention." *Essays on Classical Rhetoric and Modern Discourse*. Ed. Robert J. Connors, Lisa S. Ede, and Andrea A. Lunsford. Carbondale: Southern Illinois UP, 1984. 127–30. Various prewriting techniques imply various assumptions about the composing process. Lauer distinguishes prewriting methods according to such factors as "the genesis of writing, exploratory acts and their relationship to judgment, and the province of invention."

Moffett, James. *Teaching the Universe of Discourse*. Portsmouth: Boynton, 1987.

Reid, Joy. "The Radical Outliner and the Radical Brainstormer: A Perspective on Composing Processes." *TESOL Quarterly* 18 (1984). 529–33.

Smitherman, Geneva. "'The Blacker the Berry, the Sweeter the Juice': African American Student Writers." *The Need for Story*. Ed. Anne Haas Dyson and Celia Genishi. Urbana: NCTE, 1994. 80–101. Smitherman suggests four general ways of drawing on African American rhetorical traditions. First, capitalize on the strengths of African American cultural discourse; it is a rich reservoir that students can and should tap. Second, encourage students toward the field dependency style, which enables them to produce more powerful, meaningful, and highly rated essays. Third, design strategies for incorporating the African American imaginative storytelling style into student production of other essay modalities. Further, deemphasize your and your students' concerns about African American English vernacular grammar; overconcentration on these forms frequently suppresses the production of African American discourse and its rich, expressive style.

USEFUL WEB SITE

Step by Step Guide to Brainstorming

http://www.jpb.com/creative/brainstorming.html

This site provides tips for brainstorming and a method for choosing the best ideas from the brainstorming process.

7 Planning and Drafting

Some writers begin drafting as soon as they start to think about a topic or problem; others like to plan extensively before beginning even a rough draft. Your students need to think about how drafting works best for them, and they would also do well to consider the consequences of a particular method of drafting. The writer who begins drafting right away, for example, can expect to go through several drafts and to revise extensively.

FOR COLLABORATION: Craft a Working Thesis (7b)

Ask your students to exchange their preliminary working theses and evaluate them, using questions such as the following:

1. Does the thesis arouse your interest? How can it be made more engaging?
2. Is the thesis clear and specific? How can you make it more so?
3. What is the "so what?" of the thesis? How might the writer push the argument further?
4. Does the thesis seem manageable within the limits of time and length? Does the writer promise to do too much? How can the writer narrow the thesis?

The value of this peer-review exercise is greater perspective. What is patently obvious to the writer may not be so discernible to a reader whose information is limited to the text.

On Gathering Information (7c)

There are many ways to orient students to the wealth of materials available to them in the form of verbal and visual information for writing projects. Your own field research into the ever-increasing information available to students will help make their research projects more exciting.

- Explore the online resources of your institution's library and research facilities in order to point students to helpful resources.
- Look into archives and special collections that host specialized information in terms of documents, visual material, digitized collections, sound collections, and more.
- Investigate your institution's office of undergraduate research to find out if there are Web sites listing faculty mentors (for possible interviews), scholarships and research grant opportunities for students (for continuation of their e-projects), and workshops in research skills on campus.

GAME PLAN: Develop a Working Thesis (7b)

The Game Plan to Develop a Working Thesis offers students two different ways to approach a working thesis, depending on where they are in the drafting process. Consider using the game plan as a collaborative exercise with the whole class, choosing a general topic and beginning with the arrow and column on the left before moving to the right side. Once you have created a working thesis as a class, have the students individually go through the directives to test the sentence and then compare results. Once students are familiar with the process, you can assign the directive questions as out-of-class work to prepare for a lesson, or set aside time during class for students to use the questions as a brainstorming exercise. After each student has written a tentative working thesis, put them in groups of three or four to test the theses. Individual members of a group can be responsible for addressing one of the four "test" statements for each thesis as it is circulated, thus providing students with a range of feedback.

FOR TEACHING: Gathering Information (7c)

Many students—including juniors and seniors—have little experience with research projects or familiarity with a campus library. You might consider holding a class in the library and asking a reference librarian to describe the general resources of the library (including electronic resources) and to explain their location and usefulness.

For more about teaching library, online, and field research, see Chapter 15.

FOR COLLABORATION: Organizing Verbal and Visual Information (7d)

Ask your students to read and comment on one another's drafts, looking first at organizational patterns in individual paragraphs and then throughout the entire paper. Ask them to write in the margin what type of organization the paragraphs exhibit. Toward the end of class, call on several students to read paragraphs that illustrate different forms of organization. Some paragraphs may defy classification because of the ingenuity of the writer or the rough condition of the draft.

Another effective teaching strategy entails asking students to produce an outline *after* completing their draft essays. Use these outlines to double-check the organization and flow of the essay as well as the strategic use of both visual and verbal information.

On Organizing Visuals (7d)

In their book, *Web Style Guide: Basic Design Principles for Creating Web Sites*, Patrick J. Lynch and Sarah Horton talk extensively about "visual logic," showing how spatial organization of text and graphics on Web pages can "engage readers with graphic impact, direct their attention, prioritize the information they see, and make their interactions with your Web site more enjoyable and efficient." Students can profit from Lynch and Horton's advice by aiming to create a consistent and memorable visual hierarchy that emphasizes important elements and organizes the content in ways that are predictable to most readers. Getting real readers to respond to their site design is thus of great importance, since this kind of user feedback will help in revision of the design.

ATTENDING TO DISABILITIES: Visuals and Web Texts (7d)

In "The Imagination Gap," John Slatin reminds us that we need to teach universal design when instructing students in the step-by-step process of creating Web texts:

> None of us would knowingly build a course Web site that students of color, or students who are women, or students who are men, would be unable to use simply by virtue of their racial or ethnic status or their gender. It should be equally unthinkable for us to design Web resources for our classes that are inaccessible to students or colleagues with disabilities simply because of those disabilities. (par. 1)

Slatin suggests the following techniques that you can use in your classroom as you work to create Web texts:

- The Mouseless Week (shifting from mouse to keyboard)
- Week of No Images (Web pages from a blind person's perspective)
- The Great Blow Up (loss of context for those with limited vision)
- The Virtual Keyboard (for those who can't use voice or hands)
- Talking Computer (the Web as an auditory experience)

Slatin concludes that these exercises can help students understand the importance of universal design and accessibility when working with computers. But it can also bring students together to brainstorm the best possible approach—and medium—for their word-processing projects in mediated environments.

FOR TEACHING: Visuals and Multimedia (7d)

In the October 1999 special issue of *Syllabus Web: Useful Information on Technology Used to Enhance Education*, the editors discuss the benefits of multimedia and digital content on the Web:

> Today's classrooms have come alive with dynamic animations, simulations, and visualizations that help illustrate complex concepts. Through multimedia, instructors can present material that might be difficult or impractical to bring to the lab or lecture hall. And with more advanced Web technologies, such as Java applications, back-end databases, and streaming media, multimedia content resources can be leveraged online to support campus-based courses or to reach distant learners.

Model the best rhetorical practices of using visuals and multimedia in your teaching. This will inspire students to incorporate dynamic technological visualizations in their own Web texts.

Miriam Schacht, for example, nervous about teaching in a computer-assisted classroom for the first time, asked her students to create multimedia autobiographical Web texts as part of their final writing projects. She used the assignment to model possibilities to the students and turned her "lack of expertise" to pedagogical advantage by modeling the learning process as well. The success of this experiment manifests itself on many levels, as seen in the student projects available through her online article's hypertext.

FOR MULTILINGUAL WRITERS: Using Visuals and Multimedia (7d)

Loretta F. Kasper argues in "Print, Film, and Hypertexts" that incorporating multimedia in your pedagogy increases learning for ESL students in three ways: it develops content-area knowledge, enhances linguistic proficiency, and increases overall motivation to learn and work in class.

> At the click of a mouse, hypertext resources present students with a diverse collection of authentic English language texts dealing with a wide array of interdisciplinary topics, and at each Web page link, students have the advantage of reading print texts with the benefit of immediate visual reinforcement provided by pictures and/or slide shows, facilitating the collaborative effects of print and visual information processing. (408)

FOR TEACHING: Make a Plan (7e)

Even the most proficient pre-draft outliners need to know that outlines are not unalterable or absolute; they are merely guides. The outline must conform to the paper—not the paper to the outline. Outlines, like the papers they help organize, must be revisable.

If you require an unchangeable, formal outline, your students may not be able to adhere to it. Instead, ask them to prepare a "writing plan," a backbone for the body of the paper. Then allow them to develop their papers as much by their drafting processes, which reveal form, as by their plan. Another possibility is to suggest that they write each idea on a note card. They can then easily rearrange their ideas and experiment with various orders. They will also learn that some ideas are expendable.

FOR TEACHING: Storyboarding Web Texts (7e)

As students plan their Web texts, ask them to fill out a brief form that can help them carry out an ongoing evaluation of their plan:

- title of my Web text or site
- purpose of my Web text or site
- the personality I want my Web text to have
- audiences for my Web site
- necessary links for my Web text (and why they are necessary)

Ask students to work in pairs or groups of three to lay out or storyboard plans for a Web text. Suggest that they use index cards, one to represent the home page and another for each major page of the text that readers can gain access to from the home page. For this early planning exercise, ask them to organize the Web site hierarchically—putting the home page at the top and then arranging the additional pages below. One goal of this exercise is to ask students to show the relationship of each page to the other pages. Finally, ask them to bring their storyboard plan to class for discussion and criticism.

TEACHING WITH TECHNOLOGY: Essays and Web Texts (7e)

The Summer 2002 issue of *Kairos* offers an entire host of assignments concerning hypertext and Web texts. Patricia Ventura, for example, in her essay for *Kairos*, asks students to translate a written essay into what she calls a "Websay." Her purpose is to have students "examine the ways in which Web writing both differs from and resembles traditional writing so that [they] will be able to produce Web projects that take full advantage of this medium." To do so successfully, students need to consider carefully the elements of visual design. Ventura emphasizes that they need to "transform," not "transfer," their documents for the Web. Experiment with a similar exercise in your class before assigning a more complex Web text project.

On Writing Out a Draft (7f)

Remind your students that first drafts are never perfect. Among many other scholars and researchers who believe that first drafts are rarely directed toward an audience, Linda Flower has listed the features of what she calls "writer-based prose." According to Flower, this stage of writing is

1. typically narrative or chronological in structure.
2. usually filled with private terms that may not be meaningful to another reader.
3. sometimes elliptical.
4. filled with unclear referents and causal relations.
5. frequently loaded with self-referents, such as "I believe," "I feel," "in my opinion."

Flower views writer-based prose as a natural stage in the composing process, one that allows for discovery and growth and that should not be criticized because it is not yet "reader-based."

Often, proficient writers can skip the stage of writer-based prose and move directly to reader-based prose. These writers seem to internalize their writer-based drafts, unlike many beginning writers.

FOR TEACHING: Write Out a Draft (7f)

Anne Lamott's famous advice to writers in "Shitty First Drafts" in *Bird by Bird: Some Instructions on Writing and Life* merits repeating to students embarking on producing a draft: "Now, practically even better news than that of short assignments is the idea of shitty first drafts. All good writers write them. This is how they end up with good second drafts and terrific third drafts" (21).

Help students overcome their own fears about first drafts by giving them permission to make errors, to explore intellectual content, to try strategies of argument, and to play with variations in their writing style and persona. Allow them to experiment with voice in a first draft, to be comfortable with not having all the answers, and to write for the sake of discovering meaning. The open, encouraging attitude of a teacher can go a long way toward getting that first draft down on paper.

FOR MULTILINGUAL WRITERS: Write Out a Draft (7f)

Diane Belcher, director of Ohio State University's English as a second language (ESL) program, advises multilingual writers to "slow down the writing process as much as possible—to allow as much time as possible to concentrate on content and form first, grammar and style later."

While using the first or most comfortable language can be very useful during invention, Belcher warns that "thinking in a first language" at later stages of the writing process is far less likely to be beneficial and can lead to negative transfer as a result of translating rather than composing in English.

Mary Shapiro also warns that many ESL students have had little or no experience writing in English for *any* purpose, have never written a research paper, and have had no access to sources—let alone the opportunity to make proper use of them. She goes on to say that many ESL students come from backgrounds in which linear argumentation is not the norm. Many have never written an outline, do not know how to write introductions and conclusions (or even seem aware that this is necessary), and have no experience writing footnotes or bibliographies.

Therefore, each ESL student must be made aware that every essay, regardless of purpose, method of organization, or intended audience, requires a title, an introduction of topic and thesis, adequate development of ideas with appropriate transitions, an appropriate style, a conclusion, proper documentation, and most often linear progression.

USEFUL READINGS

Ballenger, Bruce. "Methods of Memory: On Native American Storytelling." *CE* 59 (1997): 789–800. This fine example of an essay uses association as a mode of organization.

Bolter, Jay David. "Hypertext and the Rhetorical Canon." *Essays on Rhetorical Memory and Delivery*. Ed. Fred Reynolds. Mahwah: Erlbaum, 1993. 97–111.

Carbone, Nick. *English Online: A Student's Guide to the Internet and the World Wide Web*. 3rd ed. Boston: Houghton, 2000. This extremely clear and helpful volume is intended as a student's companion to working online. It is also of great help to instructors, especially for its careful explanation of how to enter the Internet and how to create a basic Web page.

Crowe, Chris, and Keith Peterson. "Classroom Research: Helping Asian Students Succeed in Writing Courses." *TETYC* (Feb. 1995): 30–37. The authors offer concrete suggestions for helping with organization, transitions, and use of sources.

Flower, Linda. "Writer-based Prose: A Cognitive Basis for Problems in Writing." *CE* 41 (1979): 19.

Kaplan, Robert B. "Cultural Thought Patterns in Intercultural Education." *Composing in a Second Language*. Ed. Sandra McKay. Cambridge: Newbury, 1984. 43–62. Different cultures produce different rhetorical patterns of discourse that ESL teachers should be aware of. Kaplan discusses Semitic, Oriental, Romance, and Russian writing and rhetorical patterns. He recommends that ESL instructors teach "contrastive rhetoric" and provides pedagogic exercises for doing just that. Though Kaplan's work is very controversial, the patterns he describes offer a starting point for thinking about rhetorical and cultural differences.

Kasper, Loretta F. "Print, Film, and Hypertexts: A Multimedia Model for Discipline-based ESL Instruction." *TETYC* 26.4 (1999): 406–14. Kasper argues that using multimedia to present discipline-based content improves ESL instruction.

Schacht, Miriam. "Converting to the Computer Classroom: Technology, Anxiety, and Web-Based Autobiography Assignments." *Currents in Electronic Literacy* 6 (Spring 2002) <http://www.cwrl.utexas.edu/currents/spring02/schacht.html>. One teacher eases her anxieties concerning teaching with technology by creating an autobiographical Web assignment.

Slatin, John, M. "Reading Hypertext: Order and Coherence in a New Medium." *CE* 52.8 (1990): 870–83. This article provides a foundational overview of how written text must necessarily transform itself when moving to the Web and how writers must accommodate different reading strategies on the Web as well.

Ventura, Patricia. "The Essay and the Websay." *Kairos* 7.2 (Summer 2002) <http://english.ttu.edu/kairos/7.2/binder.html?sectiontwo/ventura/websay_assignment.htm>. Ventura's assignment details the purpose and necessary steps for transforming a traditionally written essay into a Web text. The sample assignment topics provide excellent models for using visual images.

USEFUL WEB SITES

American History Exhibit

http://americanhistory.si.edu/disabilityrights/exhibit_technology.html

This Smithsonian Institution Web site explores the significant role of technology in bringing together people with disabilities, particularly in conjunction with the Internet starting in the early 1990s.

Kairos: A Journal of Rhetoric, Technology, and Pedagogy

http://kairos.technorhetoric.net/

For an exploration of writing for the computer screen, see Veronica Austen's Flash-based text "Writing Spaces: Performances of the Word" (1:8) and the Spring 2003 issue devoted to new media.

Purdue University's Online Writing Lab: Guides to Planning (Invention)
http://owl.english.purdue.edu/owl/resource/673/01
Different methods of invention are described.

Web Developer's Virtual Library
http://www.wdvl.com
This site includes tutorials for HTML and javascript, articles on Web authoring and design, and thousands of images and icons.

Developing Paragraphs

8

Learning is fundamentally about relationships.

–RICHARD RODRIGUEZ

Earlymanuscriptsranwordstogetherlikethis

Words were not considered individual entities; rather, they formed the continuum of oral language. Later manuscripts, however, began to sacrifice precious paper by leaving space between the words and putting special marks in the margin as an aid to the reader. In fact, the paragraph as we know it today—with its qualities of consecutiveness and loose order of propositions—did not begin to emerge until the late seventeenth century and did not attain full codification until the eighteenth. Not until the mid-nineteenth century did the first systematic formulation of paragraph theory appear, in Alexander Bain's *English Composition and Rhetoric* (1866).

Bain's theories on essay structure generated categories we still use today, including narration, description, exposition, and argumentation. Suddenly the text—and the units of paragraphs within it—were characterized as fundamentally relational and affective. A text attempts to influence its readers, but readers also come to a text with particular expectations based on their social and cultural contexts, their purpose in reading the material, and their knowledge of the field.

On Developing Paragraphs

In his essay "Structure and Form in Non-Narrative Prose," Richard Larson explains what he sees as the three categories of paragraph theory: paragraphs (1) as expanded sentences, governed by comparable syntactical forces; (2) as self-contained units of writing with their own unique principles; and (3) as parts of the overall discourse, informed by the strategies a writer chooses for the overall piece.

Today, partially as a result of the poststructuralist and feminist critique, scholars are challenging conventional paragraph norms. In *Marxism and the Philosophy of Language*, V. N. Volosinov notes that "to say that a paragraph is supposed to consist of a complete thought amounts to absolutely nothing." Beginning with this provocative insight, Kay Halasek's book *A Pedagogy of Possibility* shows the ways in which composition textbooks have traditionally taught the paragraph in strictly traditional ways, as unified, coherent, and tightly linear. But Halasek works to redefine the paragraph as dialogic, as a negotiation among writer, audience, subject, and other textual elements that surround it. Most important, Halasek insists, is for instructors of writing to understand that the process of producing "unified," "cohesive" paragraphs calls for ignoring, erasing, or otherwise smoothing out a diversity of discourses and voices. Thus teaching students to be aware of this process not only illuminates a great deal about how "good" paragraphs get constructed but also introduces them to a philosophy of language that is not based on current traditional positivism or objectivism.

FOR TEACHING: Developing Paragraphs

For many of the reasons Halasek identifies, students often have problems with conventional academic paragraphing—with development and cohesion. And their problems are often diagnosed in various ways. For instance, George Goodin and Kyle Perkins argue that because students fail to subordinate effectively, their writing is replete with digressions and afterthoughts. Betty Bamberg argues that cohesion comes with the successful movement from "writer-based" to "reader-based" prose. Writer-based prose often consists of elliptical expressions, sentences that have meaning for the writer but that omit information necessary for the reader's understanding.

Successful prewriting—and the kind of analysis Halasek calls on both students and instructors to do—may be the best cure for both of these paragraphing "problems." By planning ahead what to say and how to say it, writers can better stay on course. Therefore, reaffirm the need for prewriting as you introduce paragraphing. Adequate prewriting will result in the more orderly text characteristic of academic paragraphs.

FOR COLLABORATION: Developing Paragraphs

Encourage your students to browse through their favorite nonacademic reading materials—newspapers, magazines, novels, nonfiction—looking for effective long and short paragraphs. They should bring their samples to class, either copies to be distributed or one copy to read aloud. Have students work in groups of three or four to explain the paragraphing conventions of their chosen publications and authors. In small groups, they'll need to answer the following questions:

1. What idea or topic does each paragraph develop?
2. What special effects do the paragraphs create, if any?
3. How do these effects move forward the main idea?

This exercise will serve to heighten students' awareness of paragraphing techniques—their own as well as those of their favorite authors. Remind students that all writers tend to imitate the styles of their favorite authors, consciously and unconsciously.

On Focusing on a Main Idea (8a)

The notion that one sentence in every paragraph should announce the main idea of that paragraph was derived from the fourth law of Alexander Bain's "seven laws" for creating paragraphs: "Indication of theme: The opening sentence, unless obviously preparatory, is expected to indicate the scope of the paragraph."

Although most compositionists agree with Bain that every paragraph should have a unifying theme or purpose, not all agree that it should be announced by a topic sentence. On one hand, in his study of professional writers, Richard Braddock found that topic sentences are used far less than we have traditionally believed; his research calls into question the teaching of topic sentences. On the other hand, Frank D'Angelo argues that despite Braddock's findings, the use of topic sentences improves the readability of a paragraph.

FOR TEACHING: Topic Sentences (8a)

If your class uses a reader, have students turn to *any* essay in it and see whether they can find a topic sentence in each paragraph. Have them answer the following questions: What is the placement of the topic sentence? What are the key terms in that topic sentence? How does the information in that paragraph relate to those key words?

TEACHING WITH TECHNOLOGY: Topic Sentences (8a)

Ask students to repeat the preceding analytical exercise using their own drafts. With students working in small groups of two or three, project each student's essay on a shared plasma screen. Change the font color of the topic sentence of each paragraph. At the end of the allotted time, ask students to select three paragraphs from their papers that show different strategies for positioning a topic sentence. Display the models for the entire class, and discuss the pros and cons of each approach. Allow students to speak about their selections and to describe how the placement functions as a persuasive act.

FOR COLLABORATION: Relating Each Sentence to the Main Idea (8a)

One practical way to have students check whether each sentence relates to the main idea of the paragraph is through a collaborative highlighting exercise. Ask students to exchange papers in writing groups. Have each student go through one essay, highlighting the main idea of each paragraph and noting the relevance of each sentence in a given paragraph to the highlighted one. Then ask the groups to discuss their reviews together. Provide them with the following questions to help their analysis:

- Does each paragraph stand on its own as a unified whole?
- Are there too many new ideas in a given paragraph?
- Do the details of each paragraph fit together to support the topic sentence?

Encourage the peer-review groups to revise one paragraph from each essay collaboratively by relying on the strengths of each group member.

FOR COLLABORATION: Provide Details (8b)

Have students work in pairs to rewrite the following undeveloped paragraphs by adding concrete supporting details, examples, and reasons. The groups should bring their collaboratively revised paragraphs to class for discussion.

1. *The introduction to an essay tentatively titled "A Week on $12.80"*
Nothing is more frustrating to a college student than being dead broke. Not having money for enough food or for the rent, much less for entertainment, is not much fun. And of course debts for tuition and books keep piling up. No, being broke is not to be recommended.

2. *The introduction to a humorous essay contrasting cats and dogs*
Have you threatened your cat lately? If not, why not? Why not get a real pet—a dog? Dogs, after all, are better pets. Cats, on the other hand, are a menace to the environment.

On Effective Methods of Development (8c)

No such thing as a pure definition or division/classification or comparison/contrast essay exists outside of the classroom, and to teach or assign these techniques as discourse structures is to confuse means with ends.

Discourses are, perhaps without exception, motivated by multiple aims. However, we can identify primary aims and primary organizing principles in order to construct essays using dynamic and reciprocal notions of function and form.

FOR TEACHING: Methods of Development (8c)

To give students practice using *narrative* (or *chronological order*), suggest that they write a paragraph about their morning routines. Then ask them to mark the controlling idea. Do they have a topic sentence? Or did they come to one after they wrote the paragraph?

To give students practice using *description* (or *spatial order*), suggest that they write about their view of their bedrooms or dorm rooms upon waking. After they record the information, ask them to read their essays to see if they started out or ended up with a controlling idea. Remind them to identify the topic sentence.

Ask students to brainstorm a series of *examples* in order to experiment with this type of paragraph development. Have them study an advertisement from a popular magazine and freewrite a series of sentence fragments in response. Then have them revise their freewriting into a short opinion essay to be submitted to the magazine using their responses as evidence for their argument. When they are done, encourage them to reflect on the process: Did they begin with a strong response and move toward a conclusion? How did they turn their freewriting into support?

Have students practice using *division and classification* (or *logical order*) by writing a paragraph describing their possessions—academic/personal; from home/from school; old/new; personal/public. They may want to look around their rooms as they write. Did they start out or end up with a controlling idea? What is it? Do they have a topic sentence?

TEACHING WITH TECHNOLOGY: Division and Classification (8c)

As a way of introducing the idea of classifying, consider asking the class to answer the following series of questions on their computers or through a threaded email discussion:

1. What are your strengths and weaknesses as a writer?
2. Is your writing process linear or recursive?
3. How do you learn in this class: from writing? from taking notes? from reading and responding to your friends' work?
4. What are your reasons for taking this course?

Then, with students working in groups of three, have them use their answers to these questions to classify each other into different groups. Ask students to draft a chart presenting the results of their classifications and to discuss different strategies for dividing and classifying. Project the results on a shared overhead screen to enable further class discussion.

FOR TEACHING: Consider Paragraph Length (8d)

Modern stylist William Zinsser advises nonfiction writers to keep their paragraphs short. Visually, such paragraphs are more inviting because they have more white space around them. But he does not mean that all paragraphs should be the same length. Paragraph length should vary with purpose: long paragraphs often introduce a character, a setting, or a situation, whereas short paragraphs add emphasis or move the reader through the text.

Ask your students to find a magazine article and a newspaper article that cover the same story. Which medium has more consistent paragraph length? Is one story more comprehensive? Does one have longer, more developed paragraphs that continue to introduce new information? Can students account for the different styles and lengths of paragraphs?

FOR TEACHING: Repeating Key Words and Phrases (8e)

Repetition of key words and phrases is an age-old technique for pulling together thematically related units; moreover, the rhythm of such verbal/visual echoing effectively holds the audience's attention. We are all familiar with various repetitive devices.

Single word

> Vanity of vanities, saith the preacher, vanity of vanities; all is vanity.
> —ECCLESIASTICUS 1:1

Syntactic structure

> The thoughts are but overflowings of the mind, and the tongue is but a servant of the thought.
> —PHILIP SYDNEY

Anaphora (initial repetition)

> Say that I was a drum major for justice. Say that I was a drum major for peace. That I was a drum major for righteousness. And all of the other shallow things will not matter.
> —MARTIN LUTHER KING JR.

> Why am I compelled to write? Because the writing saves me from this complacency I fear. Because I have no choice. Because I must keep the spirit of my revolt and myself alive. Because the world I create in the writing compensates for what the real world does not give me. By writing I put order in the world, give it a handle so I can grasp it.
> —GLORIA ANZALDÚA

FOR MULTILINGUAL WRITERS: Repeating Key Words and Phrases (8e)

Students from non-English-speaking cultures will often mention the rich variations in language that exist in their home countries, particularly with regard to patterns of repetition and common phrases. You can encourage all students to develop an awareness of culturally based patterns of repetition by sharing with them translated texts from other languages. Alternatively, ask students to bring in materials from language and literature courses for collective study, or assign readings of your own. Gloria Anzaldúa, for instance, uses a unique blend of eight languages—two variations of English and six of Spanish—in *Borderlands/La Frontera: The New Mestiza*.

FOR TEACHING: Repetition and Parallelism (8e)

As students read the following paragraph from the famous 1971 essay "Why I Want a Wife" by Judy Syfers Brady, have them identify every use of repetition and parallel structure. In addition, ask them to explain, in a brief paragraph, how the writer uses these structures to build coherence in the paragraph.

> I would like to go back to school so that I can become economically independent, support myself, and, if need be, support those dependent upon me. I want a wife who will work and send me to school. And while I am going to school I want a wife to take care of my children. I want a wife to keep track of the children's doctor and dentist appointments. And to keep track of mine, too. I want a wife to make sure my children eat properly and are kept clean. I want a wife who will wash the children's clothes and keep them mended. I want a wife who is a good nurturant attendant to my children, who arranges for their schooling, makes sure that they have an adequate social life with their peers, takes them to the park, the zoo, etc. I want a wife who takes care of the children when they are sick, a wife who arranges to be around when the children need special care, because, of course, I cannot miss classes at school. My wife must arrange to lose time at work and not lose the job. It may mean a small cut in my wife's income from time to time, but I guess I can tolerate that. Needless to say, my wife will arrange and pay for the care of the children while my wife is working.

FOR TEACHING: Commonly Used Transitions (8e)

Read aloud to the class the following selection from Chapter 34 of Charlotte Brontë's *Jane Eyre*. As you read, your students should jot down the transitional devices they hear.

> My first aim will be to *clean down* . . . Moor House from chamber to cellar; my next to rub it up with beeswax, oil, and an indefinite number of cloths, till it glitters again; my third, to arrange every chair, table, bed, carpet, with

> mathematical precision; afterwards I shall go near to ruin you in coals and peat to keep up good fires in every room; and lastly, the two days preceding that on which your sisters are expected will be devoted by Hannah and me to such a beating of eggs, sorting of currants, grating of spices, compounding of Christmas cakes, chopping up of materials for mince-pies, and solemnising of other culinary rites, as words can convey but an inadequate notion of to the uninitiated like you. My purpose, in short, is to have all things in an absolutely perfect state of readiness for Diana and Mary before next Thursday; and my ambition is to give them a beau-ideal of a welcome when they come.

Diane Belcher, director of the English as a Second Language program at Ohio State University, notes that overuse of taxonomies of transitions are of very limited help to multilingual writers, pointing out that such lists may lead students to conclude an essay with "at last" rather than "in conclusion"—*without* humorous or ironic intent (personal correspondence).

You might also ask students to think of linking paragraphs in terms of the game of dominoes. Each paragraph needs to share a similarity with the previous one: just as in dominoes, you can only connect two game pieces that have the same number of points on them. Drawing a spatial model of the dominoes game on the board for students often helps open their eyes to the way in which writing also works as a series of relationships within and between paragraphs. Translate this visual exercise to the students' writing by having them begin with the first paragraph and write out the last sentence followed by the first sentence of the next paragraph. Repeat this with each paragraph and look for repetition of key words, ideas, and phrases as effective links between the paragraphs. The visual impact of seeing the first and last sentence of each paragraph also helps students to determine if the paragraph is unified (8a).

FOR COLLABORATION: Using Transitions (8e)

After students review the list of commonly used transitions in 8e of *The Everyday Writer*, have them break into groups and trade drafts of current essays. As they read one another's papers, they should draw arrows between or circles around key terms and ideas; mark transitional phrases with heavy underlining; and label parallel structures with *//sm*. By stopping to analyze patterns in their writing, students can better understand the elements of unity and coherence necessary for constructing effective paragraphs.

FOR TEACHING: Opening and Closing Paragraphs (8f)

Ask students to bring in magazine articles in which you will highlight the various purposes served by particular paragraphs, especially the introductory and concluding paragraphs. Alert students to the presence and function of transitional paragraphs in especially long prose texts. It is important to stress that of all the paragraphs in a piece of writing, none is more important than the first. In fact, outside of classroom assignments—in job applications, newspaper articles, and fund raising appeals, for example—the quality of the opening paragraph often determines whether readers bother to read further.

One high school student, Ted Frantz, found himself concentrating hard on his opening paragraph as he worked on a college application essay describing his "major academic interest." Following is the paragraph he came up with to get his readers' attention and introduce his subject.

> Picture a five-year-old boy with a stack of cards in his hands, not baseball cards but presidential flash cards. He would run around asking anybody to question him about presidents; this kid knew incredible facts and could name every president in the correct order from Washington to Bush. I was this little boy, and ever since I was five, I have had a passion for studying history.

Consider asking students to take some time to look at the opening paragraphs in the reading they normally do: newspapers or magazines, textbooks, junk mail. How well do such paragraphs get and hold their attention? Ask students to bring the paragraphs to class for discussion.

FOR COLLABORATION: Closing Paragraphs (8f)

Ask students to draft three different attempts at concluding their essays. Have them share these samples in writing groups and talk about what works and what doesn't work in each draft. If the essay is only two or three pages in length, you can ask students to read through to the penultimate paragraph and then jot down their thoughts on how best to conclude the essay *before* turning to the three conclusion attempts.

USEFUL READINGS

Bain, Alexander. *English Composition and Rhetoric*. London: Longman, Green, and Co., 1866.

Ball, Arnetha F. "Cultural Preference and the Expository Writing of African-American Adolescents." *Written Communication* (Oct. 1992): 501–32. Researcher Arnetha Ball identifies embedded narrative and two other patterns of development that are characteristic of spoken discourse.

Bamberg, Betty. "What Makes a Text Coherent?" *CCC* 34 (1983): 417–29.

Braddock, Richard. "The Frequency and Placement of Topic Sentences in Expository Prose." *Research in the Teaching of English* 8 (Winter 1974): 287–302. After analyzing the use of topic sentences by professional writers,

Braddock concludes that topic sentences are used far less than textbooks claim. We should not deceive our students on the subject.

Christensen, Francis. "A Generative Rhetoric of the Paragraph." *CCC* 16 (1965): 144–56. Christensen exemplifies the view that paragraphs are determined by forces similar to those that determine sentences and explains the three principal kinds of paragraphs: coordinate, subordinate, and a mixture.

D'Angelo, Frank. "The Topic Sentence Revisited." *CE* 37 (1986): 431–41. Citing work in psycholinguistics, D'Angelo argues that the use of topic sentences improves readability, which justifies teaching them.

Fleckenstein, Kristie. "An Appetite for Coherence: Arousing and Fulfilling Desires." *CCC* 43 (1992): 81–87. The author urges instructors to help students practice looking at parts of their texts from the reader's point of view, as a means of understanding what devices can be used to make the text "cohere" for the reader.

Goodin, George, and Kyle Perkins. "Discourse Analysis and the Art of Coherence." *CE* 44 (1982): 57–63.

Halasek, Kay. *A Pedagogy of Possibility: Bakhtinian Perspectives on Composition.* Carbondale: Southern Illinois UP, 1999. Halasek devotes a significant part of one chapter to a rereading of paragraph pedagogy from a Bakhtinian perspective, suggesting that we have lost quite a bit in a narrow drive for "unity" and "coherence" at all costs.

Halliday, M. A. K., and Rugaiya Hasan. *Cohesion in English.* London: Longman, 1976. The authors provide a classification of cohesive ties in paragraphs and essays: reference, substitution, ellipsis, conjunction, and lexical ties.

Larson, Richard. "Structure and Form in Non-Narrative Prose." Rpt. in *Ten Bibliographic Essays.* Ed. Gary Tate. Fort Worth: Texas Christian UP, 1987. 39–82. Larson provides an exposition of his own paragraph theory as well as an overview of contemporary theory.

Markels, Robin Bell. *A New Perspective on Cohesion in Expository Paragraphs.* Carbondale: Southern Illinois UP, 1984. Investigating paragraph cohesion from a perspective that focuses both on semantics and structural (syntactic) cohesiveness, Markels offers useful alternative backgrounding to the grammatical concept of unity.

National Council of Teachers of English. *The Sentence and the Paragraph.* Urbana: NCTE, 1963. This important collection includes essays by Francis Christensen on the generative rhetoric of the sentence and the paragraph, Alton L. Becker's "A Tagmemic Approach to Paragraph Analysis," and a symposium on the paragraph by Francis Christensen, A. L. Becker, Paul C. Rodgers Jr., Josephine Miles, and David H. Karrfalt.

Root, Robert L., Jr. "Beyond Linearity: Writing the Segmented Essay." *Writing on the Edge* 9.2 (Spring 1998): 27–34. Root argues that we should teach "segmented" essays, which are not traditional, beginning with a thesis and presenting a linearly linked set of supports. In contrast, the segmented essay organizes by juxtaposition, parallelism, accumulation, or patterning. He offers examples of a number of assignments.

Selfe, Cynthia, and Susan Hilligoss. *Literacy and Computers: The Complications of Teaching and Learning with Technology*. New York: MLA, 1994.

Witte, Stephen P., and Lester Faigley. "Coherence, Cohesion, and Writing Quality." *CCC* 32 (1981): 189–204. Using an adjusted version of Halliday and Hasan's classifications, the authors conclude that cohesion is connected to our perceptions of how well the text fits its context.

9 Reviewing and Revising

> *"I never have time to rewrite; I always wait until the night before."*
> *"How can I improve my first draft when I don't know whether it's good?"*
> *"I don't care about what I'm writing. I just want to get it over with."*
> *"I'm such a bad writer that I hate to read my own writing."*
> *"If I can't get it right the first time, I must be stupid."*

Such typical attitudes toward revision support Erika Lindemann's claim that "for most students, *rewriting* is a dirty word." Students tend to view rewriting as an indication of failure, as punishment, or as simply a "filler" for classroom time. Because students have often been trained to outline carefully or to follow the format of a five-paragraph essay, revising means nothing more than making their words "prettier" or moving from handwriting to type or fixing misspelled words and mispunctuated sentences. In fact, many student writers are under the misapprehension that "real" writing is perfectly formed and flows onto the page at the touch of the Muse's hand. It is important for them to realize that almost all experienced writers revise their work repeatedly.

Marcel Proust wrote that "the real voyage of discovery consists not in seeking new landscapes, but in having new eyes." Revision *is* a process of "*re*-vision" or looking at an essay with new eyes. You can help students grasp the benefits of rigorous review and in-depth revision by sharing with them Proust's insight and teaching them to look at rewriting as a journey of discovery.

For more student writing samples, go to *The Everyday Writer*'s companion Web site at **bedfordstmartins.com/everydaywriter** and click on **Student Writing Models**. For peer review information go to **Writing Resources** and click on **Working Online**. If you're using **Comment** in your course, your students can take part in peer-review activities online.

> I have made this [letter] longer, because I have not had the time to make it shorter.
> —BLAISE PASCAL

FOR TEACHING: Reread (9a)

When instructing students to reread their drafts, be sure to distinguish between revising and editing. Students often confuse revising (making changes in content) with editing (correcting mechanical errors). To reinforce this important distinction:

1. Try to observe the distinction yourself.
2. Discuss revising and editing on separate days, as separate class topics.
3. Plan separate practice exercises for revising and editing.

Finally, try to structure your assignment schedules with ample time for students to be able to look at a piece of writing with fresh eyes. In particular, check to see that there is sufficient space between the due dates for the rough draft, the peer review, and the final version.

TEACHING WITH TECHNOLOGY: Reread (9a)

Have students post their papers online through an electronic discussion board or a course Web site. Provide students with an online peer-review sheet, asking them questions based on the information in 9a of *The Everyday Writer*. Ask students to assess their own drafts through the lens of these topics and questions. You can then move into peer review, but it is crucial to develop in students the ability to reread their drafts from a more impartial and critical vantage point. Vary this exercise by having students read one another's drafts focusing on just one area: meaning, purpose, audience, stance, organization, or use of visuals.

On Getting Responses from Peers (9b)

Having students respond to one another's work is probably the most common type of collaboration in composition classes. Peer review helps students (1) move beyond an exclusive focus on the instructor as audience; (2) learn to accept and use constructive criticism; (3) practice analyzing written texts, including their own; and (4) acquire the vocabulary of composition.

Nevertheless, many students are reluctant to share their writing with other students. They may regard the instructor as the only one qualified to give advice or criticism; hence, time spent with peers is perceived as wasted. Moreover, some students are embarrassed to show what they fear is poor writing to peers who will judge them personally. They lack experience in offering constructive criticism. Your students may need help in learning how to respond to one another's work—how to temper excessive criticism with tact, how to balance *what* has been said with *how* it has been said, both in terms of the writer's text and the reader's comments. In this way they will learn how to respond to drafts and how to trust and help one another, both vital aspects of a productive composition course.

FOR COLLABORATION: Peer Response (9b)

Here are a few exercises you can use to help students gain comfort sharing their drafts and learning to give and receive critiques:

1. At the beginning of the term, have groups of students read and comment on one another's writing. You may wish to suggest a number of your own questions as well as those in the text to help them respond to what they read: What stands out most or is most memorable in what they are reading? What is the writer's main point—and what makes that point clear or not clear? How does the essay in question respond to the assignment?
2. Using an anonymous, imperfect model draft, provide at least one or two practice sessions before the class undertakes its first peer-review session. During these preliminary discussions, check their responses and help students who have trouble offering comments.
3. To encourage group discussion, you may wish to share one of your own preliminary drafts or an example of a work in progress and have students comment on it.
4. Ask your students to keep a record of peer responses to their work. Do certain problems recur? As they become increasingly aware of their writing profiles, your students will develop self-critical faculties that they can apply to their own writing. What they can do today in group discussions with peers, they will be able to do individually and by themselves in the future.
5. Group students into threes or fours and have each student read her or his paper aloud to the others. The students then vote on which of the papers they think is the strongest; make sure they can articulate why. Then pair the groups, so that the larger group has two strong papers. Again, have those students read their papers aloud to the group, and have

the group vote on the strongest of the two papers. Encourage discussion to articulate why one paper is stronger than the other. Finally, have the students with the resulting strong papers (likely three to four at this point, depending on the size of the class) read them aloud to the whole class, and have the students discuss which one is the strongest and why.

ATTENDING TO DISABILITIES: Peer Response (9b)

Some students may have particular learning disabilities (such as dyslexia) that merit careful and sensitive responses in peer-review situations. Identify such students at the beginning of your course, and make sure they have ample support from your institution's disability resource center and writing center. In addition, reiterate to all students that their job in peer review is not to edit corrections in a negative way but to make students aware of frequent patterns of errors in their writing.

FOR MULTILINGUAL WRITERS: Peer Response (9b)

Realize that students from diverse cultures have different comfort levels with giving and receiving peer feedback. Matsuda and Silva refer to a study conducted by George Brain, who found that multilingual students often commented on not feeling "comfortable" in their classes: "During peer review of papers in groups, these students felt that the [native English-speaking (NES) students] were impatient with them, and one student said that he overheard a[n] [NES] student complain to the teacher about her inability to correct the numerous grammatical errors. . . ."

Some students may feel shy about making comments, afraid of offending the writer or being rude; their reviews may be excessively formal in tone, exceedingly positive in nature, and polite to the point of being unhelpful. Gently encourage these students to develop the skill of providing *constructive criticism* and to see themselves as important readers of the texts under review. Often, these students doubt their own authority to suggest changes and they need to be coached into becoming confident, collaborative peer reviewers. A different sort of challenge is that students can make quick and often incorrect judgments about others. To solve this problem, spend some time at the beginning of the class modeling effective peer-review strategies. If possible, ask a group of former students (as culturally mixed as possible) to come into class and present a peer-response session for your current students.

Finally, multilingual students are often able to point out the excessive use of clichés, cultural shortcuts, and other common patterns of tired writing. From their vantage point of what Karl Manheim would call "intellectuals" on the cusp between cultures, multilingual writers are invaluable members of any writing class community.

FOR TEACHING: Peer Response (9b)

To make sure your students are offering more than yes/no comments when reviewing other writers' drafts, consider collecting and evaluating their responses. Reinforce specific responses that quote a word or phrase or that refer to a specific paragraph or line. Your interest will underscore the value of peer response.

To vary the peer response exercises, randomly distribute copies of each student's paper and have the recipient write a letter to the writer. This exercise (used as a homework assignment) encourages students to articulate their constructive criticism more clearly and with more elaboration than responding to questions. It also allows you to reinforce letter-writing skills and gives you an opportunity to grade the peer reviewer.

Rather than hand out your own list of questions you want addressed in a peer review group, have each student write three specific areas she or he wants the peer reviewer to address in the paper. Doing so compels a student to acknowledge that her writing is still in process and to recognize where her weaknesses might be.

Limit your peer-response groups to three or four students so as not to overwhelm students with too many suggestions and questions, and assure them that they need not heed all the advice, but to weigh all advice carefully. However, if several comments point in the same direction, the writer should take them seriously.

When students are faced with conflicting advice, they will naturally turn to you for the "right" answer. Because this is an impossible request, you will have to encourage them to reach their own decisions. Have them ask other students to respond to their particular problems. Ask about their original writing choices and about the potential effect of suggested changes. Using others' comments to make independent decisions should be a goal of every writer.

Ask students to write a brief summary of their peer reviewers' comments and clarify what they plan to do differently in their next revision of their paper. Ideally, peer-review sessions will be so effective, profitable, and stimulating that your students will initiate sessions outside the classroom. Realistically, however, they will probably hesitate to ask others who have no peer-review experience or training. Therefore, you may want to provide them with several questions or statements for introducing a session:

1. "Would you mind telling me what you think of this?"
2. "The point I want to make in this paper is ______."

3. "How well did I succeed?"
4. "What do you think of my support?"
5. "I had trouble with this part. Does it make sense to you? What can I do to improve it?"

At least once during the term, have students initiate a review session with someone other than a classmate. Ask them to report on their success.

TEACHING WITH TECHNOLOGY: Peer Response (9b)

Have students compose online entries or threaded email responses on their perceptions of the advantages and disadvantages of peer review. Have them respond to one another's entries or put together a class Web page on the possibilities and potential problems. Knowing their concerns will allow you to explain the nature of peer review more fully and thus alleviate many of their initial concerns. Having them communicate their concerns will help build class community and alleviate individual fears. Then you can more easily model and introduce collaborative writing activities (including the ones in this chapter).

On Learning from Instructor Comments (9c)

It is important for students to recognize the larger questions informing the writing process: What is the purpose of this writing project? Who is the audience? What is the main argument? Is there sufficient evidence?

When you present a writing assignment to your students, provide them with a detailed list of questions or criteria to follow in composing their work. Research shows that students need to continue to work on broad content issues, including the frequently commented-on categories in the chart in 9c of *The Everyday Writer*. Provide a rationale for understanding each of these broad content issues as part of your assignment sheet in order to facilitate students' own critical thinking about broad content issues in their writing. Have students refer to the instructor comment chart when they read over your comments on drafts.

Remember, though, that one of the most frustrating and troubling experiences for a college student can be when the student can neither decipher nor understand the comments provided on an essay. To avoid this, take time at the beginning of class to review your expectations for submitted work. Distribute a brief handout explaining the kinds of marginal and closing comments you are likely to provide on student writing. You might even create a chart, showing the shorthand words and symbols you use and what they mean.

Alternatively, you could give students a copy of a commented paper from a previous class (with the student writer's permission, of course) to illustrate and review your process of providing feedback. It is most important, however, that you should take time to explain your reasons for making the kinds of comments you anticipate making and illustrating to students how you hope your feedback will enable them to improve and develop as writers at the college level.

Feedback doesn't need to be monumental, but its influence often is. —NANCY SOMMERS

FOR TEACHING: Instructor Comments — Overall Impression (9c)

Surprisingly few studies have been done on the nature of teachers' written comments on student writing, and no studies have looked at large numbers of essays commented on by large numbers of teachers. In 2005, Andrea Lunsford and Karen Lunsford analyzed teachers' global comments on student essays gathered from teachers throughout the United States. The most common global comments—those that address issues of rhetoric, organizational structure, longitudinal writing development, mastery of content, and so on—are discussed in the chart in 9c of *The Everyday Writer*. Their study suggests that teachers care a great deal about such matters and that, contrary to popular opinion, they comment on them rather than only pouncing on surface errors. The chart in 9c of *The Everyday Writer* translates these global comments into actions that students can take to improve their writing.

On Instructor Comments and Organization and Presentation (9c)

Often students, in their focus on content and purpose, overlook the importance of organization and presentation. Ask them to consider the impression that one makes in going to a job interview with the appropriate clothes and demeanor. Would someone wear crumpled, dirty, or inappropriate clothing? It's just as crucial for writers to attend to formal qualities of their writing, including overall organization, sentence structure and style, paragraph structure, format, and documentation.

FOR COLLABORATION: Learning from Instructor Comments (9c)

Ask students to bring in copies of papers returned to them from instructors in other classes. Have them make a chart of the kinds of feedback they were given. The students can work in small groups, aiding one another in translating the comments into lessons about how to improve as writers and thinkers. If students are unsure of the meaning of some comments, they can refer to the chart in 9c of *The Everyday Writer* for some common comments and their meanings.

Each group should then compose a short "message pitch": What is the message that the writer is being given through the comments? What strategies for growing and developing as college writers can all students in class learn from these comments?

FOR TEACHING: Instructor Comments — Purpose (9c)

When designing your writing assignments, list "Purpose" as a separate category in order to develop students' critical thinking about the importance of purpose in the writing process. Ask students to compare the purposes of writing done for different classes and different audiences. Have students bring in the prompts for writing assignments distributed in other classes and participate in a group analysis of the language of these documents. A class dialogue on purpose, using concrete examples from students' courses and extracurricular activities, will help illuminate this concept.

FOR MULTILINGUAL WRITERS: Instructor Comments — Audience (9c)

An exercise on audience can help multilingual writers begin to distinguish between different kinds of writing in English. On the first day of class, ask students to write a brief paragraph addressed to you explaining what they hope to gain from your course. Then have students rewrite the paragraph with two different audiences in mind — their parents, their best friend from home, their summer employer, their coach, and so on. When the students finish writing, take some time to discuss the diction, tone, and appeals particular to each rhetorical situation.

FOR TEACHING: Instructor Comments — Organization (9c)

Ask students to find a recent essay or assignment with instructor comments on organizational issues and to bring the example to class for discussion. Have them refer to the common instructor comments in 9c of *The Everyday Writer* when necessary. Ask students to write a short letter to that instructor. Their letters should do three things:

1. Respond to the instructor's comments, telling that instructor what they think he or she is asking them to do.

2. Explain why the students organized their writing in the way they did in the first place.
3. Explain how they would reorganize the essay or assignment according to the instructor's comments and their own improved understanding.

FOR COLLABORATION: Instructor Comments — Sentence Structure and Style (9c)

Have students exchange papers in peer-review groups and use pens to circle repetitive phrases in their sentence patterns. Often a particular tendency will emerge in student writing, and each student can develop an awareness of his or her own individual preferences by having peers help identify these patterns. Students can use a highlighter to emphasize particularly compelling phrases in the work of their peers. Ask students to share their findings with one another and to discuss the benefits of different sentence lengths, sentence sequences, and ordering strategies.

FOR TEACHING: Instructor Comments — Paragraph Structure (9c)

You can use post-draft outlines to emphasize the importance of logical paragraph structure in the writing process. Ask students to make an outline of the points covered in their drafts, and then have them assess the effectiveness of their paragraph order and structure. You might give students a list of questions to answer, including the following:

- Do the paragraphs help readers follow the thread of thought?
- Is there a tendency to use underdeveloped paragraphs (one or two sentences in length)?
- Does each paragraph deal with one significant idea (or are there too many)?
- Is there a cumulative development of ideas from beginning to end?
- Does the argument build or do the paragraphs need to be rearranged/restructured to provide a more forceful progression?
- Are there strong transitions between paragraphs?

FOR TEACHING: Instructor Comments — Format (9c)

Sylvan Barnet and Hugo Bedau assert the necessity of assessing format and presentation in terms of visual persuasion. It may be helpful to share this rationale with your students: "Every paper uses some degree of visual persuasion, merely in its appearance: perhaps a title page, certainly margins (ample—but not so wide that they tell the reader that the writer is unable to write a paper of the assigned length), double spacing for the convenience of the reader, paragraphing (again for the convenience of the reader), and so on" (96). Ask students to complete a format checklist in peer-review groups or on their own before handing in their revised drafts.

TEACHING WITH TECHNOLOGY: Instructor Comments—Sources (9c)

Using a computer projector, display sample writing passages from student papers to demonstrate the effective use of sources. A large computer screen or shared plasma screen works particularly well, as all students can see the text on the screen.

Once you display a sample text, ask students to participate in analyzing the use of the source as evidence: Is there an effective lead-in to the citation? Does the passage identify the source of the citation? Is there an effective comment on the citation to propel the argument forward? Solicit suggestions for revision from the students, and make changes with the keyboard, demonstrating each correction to the class.

Try to offer different kinds of examples when teaching the proper use of sources. For instance, demonstrate a paraphrase, summary, and direct quotation. Show students how to integrate visual sources into their writing. Provide a Web source, an e-text of a published article, and a book entry. Use this opportunity to begin a conversation about the evaluation of sources and the importance of consulting a range of sources.

FOR COLLABORATION: Instructor Comments—Documentation (9c)

Students respond well to checklists that help them assess proper documentation. You can provide the following questions to help them work on their drafts in peer-review groups before turning in a final revision:

- Are there specific primary sources cited throughout the essay?
- Are there secondary sources integrated as frame and support for the argument?
- Is all the material in the quotes necessary and appropriate?
- Are quotes integrated well (with proper signal phrases), so that the context or source is understood?
- Is there sufficient analysis and explanation after each quotation to propel the argument forward?

For MLA citation:

- Is there a source reference for every quotation?
- Are page numbers or paragraph numbers cited parenthetically after each quotation?
- Does each citation list the author's last name (or, if no author, the title's key words)?
- Are quotes of four lines or more introduced with a colon and indented five spaces?
- Are quotes of less than four lines set off with quotation marks?
- Does the format follow MLA style with punctuation after the parenthesis?
- Is the works-cited list in correct MLA format?

In addition to distributing checklists to students, it is worth spending time in class discussing the importance of proper documentation. Analogies to scientific notation (for science majors), correct "code" (for computer science majors), or proper form and training (for athletes) often work to open students' minds to considering the value of proper format.

GAME PLAN: Work with Peer Reviewers and Revise with Reviewer Comments (9b and d)

The Game Plans to Work with Peer Reviewers and to Revise with Reviewer Comments work well together: each outlines the basic steps that writers and reviewers should take in the peer review process. Even if you provide a structured set of questions for the peer review process, these game plans are an effective review before the students begin. Students can also use these as a checklist upon the completion of a peer review session to ensure that all the steps have been followed. Additionally, the questions in both these game plans make good short writing prompts: Work with Peer Reviewers emphasizes the importance of being specific when acting as a peer reviewer; Revise with Reviewer Comments encourages writers to reflect on the process.

FOR TEACHING: Organization (9d)

Ask your students to locate a story, an article, or a book they especially enjoyed reading. Either in class or as homework, have them analyze the piece by outlining its organization. Then ask them to answer the following questions and cite examples from the text:

1. Why do you suppose the author started this way? Is there a flashback? a provocative question? a description?

2. Does the author "hook" you? If so, how?
3. At what point in the piece did you become interested and decide to go on?
4. How is the piece held together? Find appropriate transitional devices, repetition of key words, or repetitive sentence structures.
5. How does the author prepare you for the information in the middle and the end of the piece?
6. How does the author end the piece? Was it satisfying to you? predictable? surprising?

In class, discuss students' responses to the questions. How can they apply their responses to their own written drafts?

I have not failed. I've just found 10,000 ways that won't work. —Thomas Edison

FOR COLLABORATION: Organization (9d)

Assign each student a partner; ask students to read and outline each other's essays. This activity will give students an idea of how well their organization comes across. If possible, and if time allows, have students exchange essays with more than one reviewer so they can compare various outlines of their essays. This exchange will help all students pinpoint possible areas of confusion.

A useful kind of outlining exercise is the "Says/Does" outline: have students examine each paragraph in terms of what it "says" (the point of the paragraph) and what it "does" (how the paragraph functions in the essay as a whole and/or in relationship to preceding and subsequent paragraphs). Students can write their "says/does" responses in the margins.

FOR COLLABORATION: Titles (9d)

With students working in groups of three, have them review each other's drafts and answer the following questions:

- Look at the title. Does it seem appropriate to you now that you've finished the piece? Why, or why not?
- Did the title seem appropriate when you started reading?
- Can you improve on the title or provide an alternative?

A good title should be like a good metaphor: it should intrigue without being too baffling or too obvious. —E. B. White

TEACHING WITH TECHNOLOGY: Titles (9d)

A great way to get students to understand the importance of titles is through an assessment of their function. Begin by discussing the crucial aspects of titles—what function they serve and what makes them effective. Students might suggest the following attributes that you can write on the board or project from a computer screen (we call this list the "three *I*'s for effective titles"):

- *I*nformative (or clear and relevant to the topic)
- *I*nteresting (or captivating—perhaps through humor, shock, or emotion)
- *I*ndicates stance (or begins to suggest the writer's thesis or perspective on the topic)

Once you have discussed this working rubric, ask students to evaluate one another's titles. This activity works well in a computer-networked classroom, where you can cut and paste the titles of all students' drafts into a PowerPoint presentation while they are in peer-review groups. Then lead them through a slide show in which you show increasing levels of complexity, from simple one-word titles to more engaging, funny, and elaborate titles. Make the presentation interactive by asking students for on-the-spot revisions as you go. At the end of class, ask them to read out loud their revised titles and save them for future use. (Note: If you can't create a PowerPoint presentation during peer review in class, then simply ask students to post or email their papers to you so you can develop the presentation before your class meeting.)

FOR TEACHING: Introductions (9d)

"First impressions count," Emily Post wrote, speaking about one's manners and personal appearance. Similarly, the writer's introductory paragraph gives the reader a first impression of the writer. Have students work in small groups to answer the following questions about the effectiveness of their introductory paragraphs:

1. What tentative conclusions can you draw about the writer's style and tone from the introduction? Is the writer intelligent, well-informed, and confident? Is the writer ill at ease or uncommitted to the topic?
2. Can you determine the intended audience from the first paragraph? Or does the introduction seem to be directed at no one in particular? Describe the intended audience.

FOR TEACHING: Conclusions (9d)

Padded endings are common in student writing. Inexperienced writers may sense that the paper is finished, but lacking confidence in their own writing, may feel compelled to restate the thesis or summarize the entire essay. Have students find and copy into their logs the endings (the final paragraph or sentence) of three to five essays or articles they particularly like. Have them each select an ending to share in class and discuss the features that make it effective. Then have them read the endings of their own essays aloud in small groups to see if they can identify any possibilities for making them more effective (more concise, clear, powerful, and so on).

FOR TEACHING: Introductions and Conclusions (9d)

To emphasize the impact of revision, have students play with writing different introductions or conclusions for one another's papers: students can exchange three or four of their body paragraphs and, using this text as a base, other students can write new introductions and conclusions, using models and the information from 8f as reference.

FOR TEACHING: Design (9d)

If students are integrating visuals as support of evidence in their papers, ask them to review their use of visuals by considering the following questions:

- Are visual elements introduced properly (using the notation "Figure 1," for example)?
- Are the visuals explained adequately in the essay?
- Are they placed effectively, either next to the corresponding text or appended at the end of the essay?
- Is there a source notation for the visual—either beneath it in a caption or at the end of the essay in the works-cited list?

USEFUL READINGS

Bishop, Wendy. *Released into Language: Options for Teaching Creative Writing*. Urbana: NCTE, 1991. Bishop offers us two chapters on responding to student writing: "Responding and Revising" and "Evaluating and Responding" (131–76). Besides her fine explanations of the politics of responding to student writing, Bishop provides clearly articulated response questions that are accessible to students at any level. See also her "Helping Peer Writing Groups Succeed," in *Teaching English in the Two-Year College* 15 (1988): 120–25.

Brannon, Lil, Melinda Knight, and Vera Neverow-Turk. *Writers Writing*. Upper Montclair: Boynton, 1983. Arguing that writing and revising should not be considered two separate stages in the writing process, the authors provide examples of successive drafts by both student writers and professional writers.

Cook, Devan. "Revising Editing." *TETYC* 29.2 (Dec. 2001): 154–61. Cook challenges the common distinction between revising and editing by showing how an attention to the rhetorical effects of punctuation as purposeful and meaning making helps students discover new ideas as part of the revision process.

Faigley, Lester, and Stephen Witte. "Analyzing Revision." *CE* 32 (1981): 400–14. The authors distinguish between surface revision (usually at the phrase or word level) and text-based revision (at the structural level).

Flower, Linda. "Writer-Based Prose: A Cognitive Basis for Problems in Writing." *CE* 41 (1979): 19–37. Flower suggests that early drafts are frequently directed not to readers but to the writer. A significant part of revision is the movement from writer-based to reader-based prose.

Flower, Linda S., John R. Hayes, Linda Carey, Karen Schriver, and James Stratman. "Detection, Diagnosis, and the Strategies of Revision." *CCC* 37 (Feb. 1986): 16–55. This award-winning essay discusses three revision methods employed by successful writers in order to move from intention to goal: detecting problems in the text, diagnosing the problems, and selecting a strategy. A focus on purpose and audience shifts attention from proofreading to more elaborate revision.

Horvath, Brooke K. "The Components of Written Response: A Practical Synthesis of Current Views." *Rhetoric Review* 2 (1984): 136–56. Horvath identifies seven types of "formative" responses to student writing that treat the text as part of an ongoing process rather than as a finished product, including responses that correct, emote, suggest, question, remind, and assign. Horvath also provides an eighty-one-item annotated bibliography.

Lindemann, Erika. *A Rhetoric for Writing Teachers*. 4th ed. New York: Oxford UP, 2001.

Rubin, Lois. "'I Just Think Maybe You Could . . .': Peer Critiquing through Online Conversations." *TETYC* 29.4 (May 2002): 382–92. Rubin's study refutes the myth that politeness in peer review signifies low power status and instead analyzes it as a strategy of negotiation that in fact increases power and effectiveness in communication.

Rutz, Carol. "Recovering the Conversation: A Response to 'Responding to Student Writing' via 'Across the Drafts.'" *CCC* 58.2 (Dec. 2006): 257–62. As part of the Re-Visions series in *CCC*, Rutz references Nancy Sommers's evaluation of her 1982 essay and, in doing so, emphasizes the importance of establishing a dialogue between instructor and students to explain how instructor comments should be read.

Sommers, Nancy. "Across the Drafts." *CCC* 58.2 (Dec. 2006): 248–57. As part of the Re-Visions series in *CCC*, Sommers revisits her 1982 essay, "Responding to Student Writing." She argues that her original essay did not accurately reflect real-life situations with students, and she now recognizes that a partnership must exist between instructor and students to create an effective environment for honest, constructive criticism through comments on papers. She further notes that comments should focus on specific, targeted areas rather than everything at once.

———. "Revision Strategies of Student Writers and Experienced Adult Writers." *CCC* 31 (Dec. 1980): 378–88. Rpt. in *Landmark Essays on Writing Process*. Ed. Sondra Perl. Davis: Hermagoras, 1994. Sommers analyzes the differences between revision strategies of students and older writers, examining the range from choosing words to rearranging form in order to meet the needs of an audience. She argues that revision is a recursive process essential to developing ideas, rather than a surface cleaning of diction or the final step in a writing progression.

Tinberg, Howard. "From 'Self-Righteous Researcher' to 'Fellow Teacher.'" *CCC* 58.2 (Dec. 2006): 262–66. As part of the Re-Visions series in *CCC*, Tinberg's commentary on Nancy Sommers's revision of her 1982 essay, "Responding to Student Writing," highlights the recursive nature of the writing process and the necessity of revisiting "foundational scholarship."

Tomlinson, Barbara. "Tuning, Tying, and Training Texts: Metaphors for Revision." *Written Communication* 5 (1988): 58–81.

Welch, Nancy. *Getting Restless: Rethinking Revision in Writing Instruction.* Portsmouth: Boynton, 1997. Drawing from feminist and psychoanalytic theories and utilizing ethnographic, case-study, and autobiographical research, Welch seeks to demonstrate ways composition teachers can support "revision as restlessness," a process that leads to revisioning and making real-life changes.

10 Editing and Reflecting

The difference between the right word and the almost right word is the difference between lightning and the lightning bug.
—Mark Twain

Students often think that becoming a better writer means that one does not have to attend to the smaller units of composition—paragraphs, sentences, words, and tone. But even the most prolific and accomplished writers struggle with revision of these small parcels of meaning. The popular humor writer Dave Barry offers the following reflection on revision *How to Write Funny*, which you might want to share with your students:

> Writing humor takes discipline and hard work. I have this theory. Here it is, My Theory about Writing: It's hard. The humor doesn't just flow as easily as people think. A funny idea has to be tooled and shaped so that it's funny to others when it's read. People think that because humor is light and easy to read that it's just as simple to write. Nothing could be more untrue. You have to work at it. Writer's block, for example. Here's My Theory about Writer's Block: People simply give up and don't want to put forth the effort to work through the barriers. No good writing is easy. It has to do with overcoming the obstacles we find in the way of our creativity. You have to have the determination to do it.

FOR COLLABORATION: Edit (10a)

Assign a draft due at the start of class. Ask the students to identify the best three- to five-sentence paragraph from their drafts. After dividing the class into small groups, ask each student to read his or her paragraph to the rest of the group. The rest of the group then decides which passage is most effective and analyzes it for sentence length, sentence variety, word choice, and tone. Accentuate the positive and encourage possible revisions.

> But many writers who have earned their reputations through hard work agree that one writes at first just to have something to rewrite. —David Madden

FOR COLLABORATION: Edit (10a)

Have students work in groups of three or four to compare and contrast the paragraph structures in a popular newsmagazine (such as *Time* or *Newsweek*) and an academic journal (*Critical Inquiry* or the *Journal of Modern History*) of their choosing. Ask students to note that paragraph length, organization, layout, and use of visuals vary from news magazine to academic journal. Ask each group to write a short response essay on the following question: How do the paragraphs you looked at compare with those you and your classmates typically write?

FOR TEACHING: Sentence Openings (10a)

Have students underline the first four words of each sentence in several random paragraphs. If the basic syntax is the same in too many sentences, ask them to find ways to reword the sentence, by beginning with dependent clauses. See Chapter 29 in *The Everyday Writer* for more ideas.

FOR TEACHING: Sentence Length (10a)

Ask students to choose two random paragraphs from their paper and count the words in each sentence. If the number for each sentence is too similar, ask them to combine and condense their sentences for variety in length.

FOR COLLABORATION: Opening with *It* and *There* (10a)

Following are two sentences featuring *it is* or *there is* from the first draft of a student's paper. Ask students to work collaboratively with a classmate to make at least two revisions that eliminate these constructions. All pairs of students should bring their revisions to class and be prepared to explain their revision process.

1. In today's world of CNN, e-journals, and Newsweek.com, it is often easy to forget how pervasive a medium the magazine was prior to the advent of television.
2. There is no denying that this strategy worked brilliantly, as this inviting image of Santa Claus graduated from the pages of *Saturday Evening Post* to become the central figure of the most celebrated and beloved season of the year.

After your students have written two versions of each of the *there is* and *it is* sentences, ask them to see how many variations they can create as a class.

FOR TEACHING: Document Design (10a)

It's crucial that students become aware of the entire package and presentation of their work, from the opening words to the overall format of their essays. You can help facilitate such attention by providing students with a "final checklist" to use in assessing their last revisions. Give students a handout or post questions on your course Web site. Delineate your precise expectations for document design, the way a paper will be formatted. It is also helpful to have a class dialogue about the different formatting expectations across disciplines and classes.

On Tone (10a)

Word choice produces tone, and tone carries implications for a writer's voice. The work of theorist Mikhail Bakhtin has been particularly useful in helping to examine traditional notions of voice as something unique and authentic to any individual. This traditional view, much elaborated and advocated by Peter Elbow, Donald Murray, and many others in composition studies, fails to recognize the constructed nature of all voices. More important, it fails to recognize the multiplicity (what Bakhtin calls "heterogeneity") of voice. Like all writers, students have many voices they can deploy in various ways, and these voices are always, according to Bakhtin, in dialogue with others. Teachers can help students locate differing voices in their texts, some their "own" and others that belong to institutional discourse, such as the voice of big business or of higher education.

Instructors can teach students how to study and learn from the tensions among these voices. By emphasizing that students examine carefully their use of words or diction, teachers can begin to raise student awareness about the presence and importance of voice in writing.

FOR TEACHING: Word Choice (10a)

Joseph Williams, in *Style: Ten Lessons in Clarity and Grace*, points out that avoiding passive and agentless constructions will usually make one's choice of words more vigorous and direct. He gives these examples for comparison:

> The money was found by me.
> I found the money. (80)

However, as Williams points out, "often we don't say who is responsible for an action, because we don't know or don't care, or because we'd just rather not say." Consider the following examples:

The president *was rumored* to have considered resigning.
Those who *are* guilty of negligence *can be fined*.
Valuable records *should always be kept* in a fire proof safe. (82)

After giving students these examples, have them select one page of a current draft and highlight every passive construction they can locate. They can work individually, in pairs, or in groups to determine if each instance of the passive voice is justified or not.

FOR TEACHING: Proofreading the Final Draft (10a)

Many students cut out the final stage of editing because they are eager to finish, because they stay up too late, or because they lose interest in the writing. You may want to provide them a last-minute opportunity to proofread and make final edits. Before they hand in their papers, give them ten minutes of class time to read over their final drafts; or ask them to trade papers and proofread one another's final drafts. Encourage students to proofread from the end to the beginning: by reading the document backward, sentence by sentence, the students are more apt to catch mistakes because they are reading out of context.

> **I have rewritten—often several times—every word I have ever published. My pencils outlast their erasers.**
> **—Vladimir Nabokov**

FOR COLLABORATION: A Student's Revised Draft (10a)

Ask students to work in small groups and list all the different ways Emily Lesk's edited and proofread draft (in 10a) differs from her original draft (in 9b). Articulating the differences helps them to understand how significant revision can be.

FOR TEACHING: A Student's Revised Draft (10a)

Distribute an early and a late draft of a paper from a previous class and have students read both versions and discuss. Ask them to write a one-page summary of the specific ways the revised version differs from the original draft and explain why those differences strengthen or weaken the paper.

On Portfolios (10b)

One of the best ways to capture the kinds of changes that take place over time with the writing process is by assembling either a print or electronic writing portfolio. One salutary result of the "process" movement in composition studies has been the increased understanding of how and when particular student writers move back and forth among the acts of inventing, revising, drafting, editing, rethinking, drafting, and so on, most often in nonlinear and highly recursive ways, and portfolios are one way to document that process. In turn, these new understandings have highlighted the importance of critical thinking to writing, not only in terms of invention and expression of ideas but also in more global ways.

Often referred to as *metadiscourse*, this high-order kind of critical thinking calls on writers to step back and survey their own work, analyzing its strengths and weaknesses and articulating its inner workings—its diction, syntax, and rhetoric. Research in composition indicates that the ability to exercise this kind of critical thinking is an important part of what enables growth in writing.

At the same time, the benefits to the student of assembling a writing portfolio are immeasurable. By tracking, compiling, and reflecting on their work, the way their writing has changed, and how they have developed strategies of invention, composition, and delivery, students produce a metadiscourse about the recursive nature of their writing lives. Moreover, once introduced to the value of assembling and maintaining a writing portfolio, students often continue the practice throughout their academic and professional careers. In this way, they continue to learn about themselves as writers and as critical thinkers.

The overlapping terms *portfolio*, *journal*, *log*, *diary*, and *daybook* refer to a wide range of writing practices whose origins may be as old as writing itself. Thus, when leading students in the assembly and completion of portfolios, take time to explain how these various writing genres all serve a similar purpose: the portfolio is a crafted representation of the writer's work. However, as an instructor, you should be clear in your own mind what purpose you want the portfolio to serve: Do you want it to be a showcase portfolio—a collection of the best work from a specific course? Do you want it to be a process portfolio—a collection of work that documents progress through drafts, revisions, and final copies? Do you want it to function as a professional portfolio that students could use for job searches (common in art, teaching, and nursing disciplines)? Will the portfolio be used to evaluate or assess the student? the program? What portion of the course grade will it be? What criteria will you use to evaluate it?

> **It would do us all good to remember that the focus of portfolio assessment is the student, not the instructor.**
>
> —Marcia Dickson

FOR TEACHING: Portfolios (10b)

When giving students guidance on what elements to include in their portfolios, be sure to spend time discussing the importance of organization and format. Susan Hilligoss and Tharon Howard delineate some of the key concerns students should keep in mind when designing portfolios: A portfolio is a unique genre, with much opportunity for visual creativity, yet it calls for many of the navigational features of more conventional long documents. Because it projects your ethos and because readers may be rushed or unfamiliar with portfolio layouts, the portfolio should have a unified look, a visual impact that supports your ethos and the communicative purpose, and clear organization. (87)

As Richard Larson argues in "Portfolios in the Assessment of Writing," *portfolio* should designate "an ordered compilation of writings. A casual gathering up of papers one has written over a year or two probably does not deserve to be called a 'portfolio.' A portfolio ideally should be a deliberate compilation, gathered according to some plan, for use by an identified reader or readers for specific needs or purposes." Teachers who wish to use portfolios in their classrooms or programs might well begin by following Larson's lead here: determine the principles by which the portfolio will be compiled, decide how it will be organized, identify the intended audience(s) for the portfolio, and enumerate the purposes the portfolio will serve. You should emphasize to students the three key concepts of a portfolio: collect, select, and reflect.

Write about what makes you different. —SANDRA CISNEROS

FOR COLLABORATION: Portfolios (10b)

If your entire class is structured on a portfolio, then you will have determined the portfolio's purposes and the criteria by which it will be evaluated. However, if the portfolio is only a portion of your class or if it is an option, then, if possible, engage students in developing the criteria by which their portfolios will be evaluated. This way, the entire class participates in the portfolio planning process. Ask students to work in groups to come up with at least half a dozen (or more if possible) items they think are characteristic of first-rate portfolios. Use these lists as the basis for class discussion on how you can recognize these characteristics in the pieces of writing in the portfolio and how credit should be apportioned for them. Then if the portfolio is to be a major part of your course, you might wish to have students form groups of three to work together as an editorial board, reviewing and responding to one another's portfolios throughout the term.

Suggest that students work in groups of two or three to brainstorm what each of them would most like his or her portfolio to accomplish—and which pieces of writing will best meet these goals. Students should take notes during their conversations with team members and bring these notes to class for discussion. Each team member should be prepared to explain his or her choices for the portfolio.

FOR MULTILINGUAL WRITERS: Portfolios (10b)

Yu Ren Dong advocates asking multilingual students to write autobiographies about their native literacy experiences in order to facilitate more responsive and effective instruction. Such literacy autobiographies can work particularly well when students develop them into comprehensive writing portfolios. Do they have samples of their writing from earlier years and in multiple languages? Can they compose short, self-reflective introductions to each sample in order to lead the reader through the portfolio? Their narrative of literacy education will trace developmental turns in their writing process across years and languages. Ask them to conclude with a critical reflection on the goals they seek to achieve next in their writing process.

> **Exploratory writing can have a range of postures, from the personal to the objective.**
> —William J. McCleary

TEACHING WITH TECHNOLOGY: Portfolios (10b)

Leading the field forward, Carl Young and Margo Figgins use an electronic portfolio, called the Q-folio, in research and writing classrooms at the University of Virginia. They designed and implemented the tool in the classroom in an attempt to "reawaken the imagination to critical inquiry and reinvent traditional notions of research and composition portfolios" (par. 1).

More and more students keep track of all their writing on their computers. You can transform this careful habit into a productive and dynamic electronic portfolio. Electronic portfolios, or ePortfolios, are more than simply an electronic version of a paper portfolio, in part because of the many creative ways students can project their work on the Web. With an ePortfolio, students must consider how their audience will navigate their portfolio and what kinds of connections they want their readers to see. Additionally, an electronic portfolio fosters community, because students can invite others—even around the world—to view their work; it invites reiteration because it exists over time and can be added to; and it facilitates new ways of engaging with the learning process. Help students brainstorm ways of compiling both their work and their reflections through imaginative and informative electronic portfolios. Remember to attend to disabilities; review the guidelines provided throughout this manual to make sure that all interested readers can access the electronic materials.

FOR TEACHING: Reflective Statements (10b)

Reflective statements can be structured in a variety of ways, but it is imperative that you clarify your expectations about what the statement should cover: Should it be comprehensive, including quotes from the papers as supporting statements, or should it focus on specific items determined by you or the students? Or do you want shorter reflective statements for specific assignments? For example, a reflective statement might be written as a letter to a reader other than the instructor; it might focus specifically on error analysis—explaining what specific errors have been identified and strengthened throughout the course; and it might also be an argumentative essay showing that the student has met the required outcomes for the class. Metacognitive writing takes practice, though, and you will want to teach the process and show models of the kind of writing you expect.

FOR COLLABORATION: Edit and Reflect (10a–b)

Even writing that has reached final draft stage can be revised through one last editing pass, and often very effectively. Have students read the excerpt of Emily Lesk's final draft in 10a of *The Everyday Writer* and, working with two or three other students, plan and carry out a last editing pass. They should begin by reading the paragraphs aloud once or twice and jotting down items in three columns: a "plus" column for words, phrases, or ideas they especially like; a "minus" column for words, phrases, or ideas they *don't* like; and a "question" column for words, phrases, or ideas that seem unclear or questionable. Then they can compare notes and together draft a revision plan to change words or phrases that were not as strong as they could be. Finally, have them compare their edits with the original paragraphs and report to the class, explaining the changes and describing what they have done to improve the essay as a whole through this final editing. You might have students access Emily's full final draft on *The Everyday Writer*'s companion Web site and have each group review different sections of the paper. Go to **bedfordstmartins.com/everydaywriter** and click on **Student Writing Models**.

> **Sometimes the delete key is your best friend.** —STEVE MARTIN

USEFUL READINGS

Barrett, Helen C., and Judy Wilkerson. "Conflicting Paradigms in Electronic Portfolio Approaches: Choosing an Electronic Portfolio Strategy That Matches Your Conceptual Framework" <http://electronicportfolios.org/systems/paradigms.html>. This article addresses the philosophical foundation of electronic portfolios, presenting a variety of perspectives on the most effective strategies in using them.

Belanoff, Pat, and Marcia Dickson, eds. *Portfolios: Process and Product.* Portsmouth: Boynton, 1991. A classic in the field, this anthology is vital to any teacher or program using portfolios as classroom-based or programmatic assessment tools. The anthology provides case-study examples from liberal arts and land grant secondary institutions; advice for how to structure portfolios in the composition, basic writing, and biology classrooms; theoretical pieces on the connections between portfolios and learning; and the political questions and consequences of instituting portfolio-based assessment programs.

Berlin, James A. *Writing Instruction in Nineteenth-Century American Colleges*. Carbondale: Southern Illinois UP, 1984.

Bishop, Wendy. "Designing a Writing Portfolio Evaluation System." *English Record* 40.2 (1990): 21–25.

Dong, Yu Ren. "The Need to Understand ESL Students' Native Language Writing Experiences." *TETYC* 26.3 (Mar. 1999): 277–85.

Elbow, Peter, and Pat Belanoff. "Portfolios as a Substitute for Proficiency Examinations." *CCC* 37 (1986): 336–39.

———. "Using Portfolios to Increase Collaboration and Community in a Writing Program." *WPA: Journal of the Council of Writing Program Administrators* 9 (Spring 1986): 27–40.

Hilligoss, Susan, and Tharon Howard. *Visual Communication: A Writer's Guide*. 2nd ed. New York: Longman, 2002. This book provides brief but specific guidelines on the visual design of portfolios and other texts.

Jafari, Ali and Catherine Kaufman, eds. *Handbook of Research on ePortfolios.* Hershey: Idea, 2006. This thorough and comprehensive compilation of articles from ePortfolio specialists covers the most current scholarship in the field, ranging from chapters on using ePortfolios to foster critical thinking and learning to chapters on using them for goal setting and assessment. The sourcebook also includes case studies that address institutional as well as student concerns.

Larson, Richard L. "Portfolios in the Assessment of Writing: A Political Perspective." *Assessment of Writing: Politics, Policies, Practices*. Ed. Edward White. New York: MLA, 1996. 271–83. Larson examines the issues of power relations in portfolio assessment, particularly consent, as instructors may be forced to use this method, and privacy, as student writing may be assessed by outside parties. He advocates an approach in which administration works with instructors to gain their acceptance of the portfolio method, and that makes clear the uses to which such assessment will be put.

Murphy, Sandra, and Barbara Grant. "Portfolio Approaches to Assessment: Breakthrough or More of the Same?" *Assessment of Writing: Politics, Policies, Practices*. Ed. Edward White. New York: MLA, 1996. 284–300. The authors examine various theoretical models of how the portfolio method aids in the assessment of student writing, and further discuss the problems and practicalities of implementing such models, in particular decisions regarding standardization versus contextualization and top-down versus collaborative assessment.

Nelson, Alexis. "Views from the Underside: Proficiency Portfolios in First-Year Composition." *TETYC* 26.3 (Mar. 1999): 243–53. Students' stories about portfolio assessment shed light on how they work and why they sometimes don't.

"Portfolio Assessment: An Annotated Bibliography." *Quarterly of the National Writing Project and the Center for the Study of Writing* 10 (Oct. 1988): 23–24.

Riedinger, Bonnie. "Mining for Meaning: Teaching Students How to Reflect." *Handbook of Research on ePortfolios*. Ed. Ali Jafari and Catherine Kaufman. Hershey: Idea, 2006. 90–101. Riedinger provides a comprehensive overview of how reflection has been used in portfolios, both its challenges and its benefits, and offers a variety of strategies for teaching reflection.

Yancey, Kathleen Blake, and Irwin Weiser, eds. *Situating Portfolios: Four Perspectives*. Logan: Utah State UP, 1997. One of the most recent anthologies on portfolios in English, this collection explores four contexts for writing portfolios: the theory behind portfolios in the field and their power as assessment tools for secondary educational institutions; portfolio pedagogy, especially in terms of student literacy and the classroom community; portfolios as reflective and professional instruments for teachers themselves; and the interstices of technology and portfolios, particularly hypertext portfolios, email, and the electronic classroom. All four contexts address how portfolios transform student writing and the teaching of composition.

Young, Carl A., and Margo A. Figgins. "The Q-Folio in Action: Using a Web-Based Electronic Portfolio to Reinvent Traditional Notions of Inquiry, Research, and Portfolios." *Contemporary Issues in Technology and*

Teacher Education 2.2 (2002) <http://www.citejournal.org/vol2/iss2/english/article1.cfm>. This article discusses the design and implementation of the Q-folio at the University of Virginia as an electronic tool for transforming traditional composition and the imagination.

White, Edward M. "The Scoring of Writing Portfolios: Phase 2." *CCC* 56.4 (June 2005): 581–600. This article addresses the challenges of holistic scoring of portfolios and suggests a two-part, efficient method of scoring them: (1) a clear articulation of the goals for the portfolio and (2) a reflective letter written by the student that uses the documents in the portfolio for support.

Williams, Joseph M. *Style: Ten Lessons in Clarity and Grace*. 5th ed. New York: Addison, 1997. This practical guide for revising gives special attention to the sentence. Individual chapters deal with such problems as overuse of nominalization and passive voice, prose sprawl, and lack of coherence and emphasis.

USEFUL WEB SITE

ePortfolio at Laguardia Community College

http://www.eportfolio.lagcc.cuny.edu

A leader in ePortfolio use, LaGuardia Community College built this Web site that provides an overview of ePortfolio, extensive resources, and access to student ePortfolios.

Critical Thinking and Argument

To repeat what others have said requires education; to challenge it requires brains.

—MARY PETTIBONE POOLE

11 Critical Reading

The peace I am thinking of is the dance of an open mind when it engages another equally open one—an activity that occurs most naturally, most often in the reading/writing world we live in. –TONI MORRISON, "The Dancing Mind"

One of the primary benefits of teaching students the conventions of academic discourse is that it demonstrates to them the mutual reciprocity between the reading and writing processes. The interconnection between reading and writing has received a great deal of attention during the past decade. It has become clear that writing teachers are doing far more than teaching sentence structure—we are helping to introduce students to a discourse with which many of them are unfamiliar. Standard academic discourse is more than just correctness; it is a style of presentation that involves awareness of audience, grasp of subject, and confidence in the writer's own ethos and abilities. As David Bartholomae says in "Inventing the University,"

> Every time a student sits down to write for us, he has to invent the university for the occasion—invent the university, that is, or a branch of it, like history or anthropology or economics or English. The student has to learn to speak our language, to speak as we do, to try on the peculiar ways of knowing, selecting, evaluating, reporting, concluding and arguing that define the discourse of our community. . . . The student has to appropriate (or be appropriated by) a specialized discourse, and he has to do this as though he were easily and comfortably one with his audience, as though he were a member of the academy or an historian or an anthropologist or an economist; he has to invent the university by assembling and mimicking its language while finding some compromise between idiosyncrasy, a personal history, on the one hand, and the requirements of convention, the history of a discipline, on the other. He must learn to speak our language. (134–35)

In order to become part of the conversation of academic discourse, students must be exposed to it. Readings in a writing course assist this process in several ways: they provide models of good writing (as well as models of writing to be avoided); they provide content issues that can be discussed; they provide analyses of the decisions that writers have made; and they can illuminate the composing process. We use all of these elements in the reading exercises and the examples from works by various writers throughout *The Everyday Writer*.

Additional information on critical reading is available on *The Everyday Writer*'s companion Web site, **bedfordstmartins.com/everyday writer**. Go to **Writing Resources** and click on **Argument Resources**.

FOR TEACHING: Think Critically about Written Texts (11a)

Encourage students to follow the guidelines for critical reading that are listed here for any kind of text, whether written, visual, or a combination of the two. Emphasize that they should employ their critical reading skills when working with digital and new media texts as well.

Guidelines for critical reading

Preview for preliminary questions:

- What does the title tell you?
- What do you already know about the subject?
- What information can you find about the author and his or her expertise or biases?
- What does the time and place of publication tell you?
- What effects do the visuals and headings have?
- What do you expect the main point to be?

Read and annotate the text:

- What key terms and ideas do you identify?
- With which statements do you agree? disagree?
- What sources does the text cite?
- What do you find confusing or unclear?

Summarize what you have read; jot down questions.

Analyze the text:

- Do the main points match your expectations?
- What evidence does the text provide? What counterevidence occurs to you or is missing?
- Are the sources trustworthy?

- How do the words and visuals work together?
- What are the author's underlying assumptions?
- Is the author's purpose accomplished?
- What is intriguing or irritating about the text?
- What would you like to know more about?

Reread the text, and check your understanding.

FOR TEACHING: Think Critically about Written Texts (11a)

Use journal assignments to have students keep a reading log of their assigned reading. Require them to note unfamiliar words and define them, pose questions about the text, and record which arguments confuse them. Use these logs at the beginning of class to start discussion, or have students, in small groups, share and compare what they found.

On Thinking Critically about Visuals (11b)

The emphasis in composition classrooms on considering visual arguments is becoming more and more prominent in curricula across the country. From analyzing a photograph in the news to interrogating the function of a Web site, students are participating in the "pictorial turn" by moving from passive consumers to active readers and eventually writers of visual media. As Sylvan Barnet and Hugo Bedau remind us, "premises and assumptions tend to remain unstated in visual persuasion; deciphering them requires highly active reading" (93). Whether visual images are found online or in a photo gallery, in a mall or on a monument, in combination with words or on their own, visual culture offers a form of argument that we need to consider in our writing classes.

Much theoretical work in visual culture has been done since W. J. T. Mitchell identified the "pictorial turn" in composition studies. New journals such as *Enculturation* merge visual cultural studies and rhetoric, while the Summer 2002 issue of *Kairos* (an online journal of rhetoric, technology, and pedagogy) hosts a series of articles exploring the intersections of technology, popular culture, and the art of teaching.

> The omnipresence of cameras persuasively suggests that time consists of interesting events, events worth photographing. After the event has ended, the picture will still exist, conferring on the event a kind of immortality (and importance) it would never otherwise have enjoyed.
> —SUSAN SONTAG

ATTENDING TO DISABILITIES: Think Critically about Visuals (11b)

Teachers who "rely exclusively on word-based pedagogies," Patricia Dunn tells us, are guilty of "setting up a false dichotomy" that "position[s] students against each other rather than against banking-model teaching" and absolves teachers "from having to rethink their epistemological assumptions, philosophical goals, or classroom practices" (qtd. in Brueggemann, White, Dunn, Heifferon, and Cheu 377). When you construct materials for teaching arguments, think about how using visual arguments for presenting your lessons will expand students' understanding of how different media can provide modes of argumentation. As you teach visual literacy, consider how you might be reaching certain members of your class while excluding others. As Dunn explains:

> Granted, a writing class must be about writing. But composition professionals may, unwittingly, be privileging a way of knowing with which we ourselves are most comfortable, perhaps not realizing that our students have other talents we might use even as we teach writing. We may, unwittingly, play a part in disabling some of our best thinkers by overusing one pathway—writing—in the many intellectual tasks leading up to a finished piece: written journals, written peer responses, freewriting, written proposals or outlines, written email discussions, and so on. (qtd. in Brueggemann, White, Dunn, Heifferon, and Cheu 379)

Make sure you model more diverse ways of considering visual arguments by designing your pedagogy with all learners in mind.

> **Writing is a visual art. If I don't know where to begin, I describe.** —DONALD M. MURRAY

TEACHING WITH TECHNOLOGY: Questions about Design (11b)

A great way to get students to appreciate the significance of the design choices of visual arguments is to ask them to manipulate selected images with standard computer programs such as Adobe Photoshop or Paintbrush. What happens when a picture of the human genome is juxtaposed over a baby? a sick patient? a field of identical tomatoes? an industrial smokestack? How does the color scheme affect the power of persuasion in the image? Ask students to explore black and white versus color, sepia versus primary colors. What audiences are addressed by different color schemes, font sizes, and visual tropes?

You might also ask students to write three paragraphs analyzing the effect of each visual manipulation. What have they learned from manipulating images about size, color, placement, font, and composition? Project several examples from the class up on a large screen, and ask students to read their essays out loud to the class. Then spend some time getting feedback on both the images and essays from the class as a whole.

FOR TEACHING: Rhetorical Analysis and Visuals (11b)

Doreen Piano, in "Analyzing a Web Zine," asks students to "choose a zine of interest to write a rhetorical and cultural analysis." As part of the assignment, students examine "not only textual aspects such as purpose, audience, design and layout, and content but [also] extra-linguistic features such as reception and consumption of the zine" (par. 2). Her purpose is to show students that the visual images help make the Internet "an ethnographic site, a space where people convene and create different kinds of cultures, some that are in opposition to mainstream culture or that present points of view that may not be represented in the media" (par. 1).

By emphasizing the point that visual arguments speak to an audience, you can help students apply their analysis of argument skills to visual images. Moreover, they can assess both content and design aspects with an eye to the larger purposes such visual arguments serve.

> **A visual experience is vitalizing. Whereas to write great poetry, to draw continuously on one's inner life, is not merely exhausting, it is to keep alight a consuming fire.**
>
> —KENNETH MACKENZIE CLARK

GAME PLAN: Read Critically

The Game Plan to Read Critically functions on multi-levels, and, significantly, it underscores the strong relationship between reading and writing skills. Each section of this game plan can be used autonomously, as prereading, reading, or post-reading activities, or the sections can be used together for one activity.

Use the section asking students to preview the reading as a way to (1) emphasize the importance of a critical approach to reading from the outset, and (2) remind the students that their background knowledge and experience can be used to inform their reading.

The questions in the section about reading carefully are an opportunity to teach students the distinction between main and supporting ideas, particularly in the service of a summary. Often, students are embarrassed to admit that they are confused with a text, so consider having students share in small groups their responses to what they find confusing. Doing so will not only demonstrate to them that their peers are in similar situations, but it also encourages them to work through the confusing parts together. You can address the questions regarding sources, audience, and purpose as a group, or have students answer them individually; point out how these questions play a key role in analyzing the text. Call attention to the question about whether students are part of the intended audience, as their responses can generate discussion on the importance of audience awareness and on their role as students in an academic community.

One of the skills in critical reading is being able to summarize a text, and, as this game plan illustrates, being able to describe the text to someone else is a way to check one's own understanding. Additionally, the verbal summary demonstrates another pre-writing strategy that students can use before a written exercise.

Finally, the section on analyzing the text asks students to think about several parts of the critical reading process: the subjective question of what they like the most validates their opinions; the questions regarding whether the parts work together and the text's purpose help them to understand how various parts of a text function in relationship to one another; the question on whether the expectation was met provides an opportunity for reflection based on their initial expectations articulated in the preview section; and, finally, the important question of "What else do I need to know?" reinforces the notion that reading critically often engenders further questions and further reading.

This game plan is also effective when used in conjunction with the game plan on peer review, as it asks students to think about how their own writing might be read critically.

USEFUL READINGS

Ahern, Jennifer. "Reading/Writing the *X-Files*." *Kairos* 7.2 (Summer 2002) <http://english.ttu.edu/kairos/7.2/binder.html?sectiontwo/ahern>. Ahern's assignment develops students' skills as readers, writers, researchers, and editors of visual texts.

Barnet, Sylvan, and Hugo Bedau. *Current Issues and Enduring Questions*. Boston: Bedford, 2008. Chapter 4 provides an excellent discussion of "Visual Rhetoric: Images as Arguments."

Bartholomae, David. "Inventing the University." *When a Writer Can't Write: Studies in Writer's Block and Other Composing Process Problems*. Ed. Mike Rose. New York: Guilford, 1985: 134–65. Bartholomae argues that in order to succeed in college, students need to learn to speak the language of the university, "to try on the peculiar ways of knowing, selecting, evaluating, reporting, concluding, and arguing" that are valued by various academic discourse communities.

Berger, Arthur Asa. *Seeing Is Believing: An Introduction to Visual Communication*. 2nd ed. New York: McGraw, 1998. This primer of visual communication offers helpful chapters on photography, television, and film.

Brooks, Charles, ed. *The Best Editorial Cartoons of the Year*. Gretna: Pelican, 2002. A wonderful resource of political cartoons that students can use in constructing visual arguments.

Brueggemann, Brenda Jo, Linda Feldmeier White, Patricia A. Dunn, Barbara A. Heifferon, and Johnson Cheu. "Becoming Visible: Lessons in Disability." *CCC* 52.3 (Feb. 2001): 368–98. A compelling case for thinking beyond "word-based pedagogies."

Charlton, James I. *Nothing about Us without Us: Disability Oppression and Empowerment*. Berkeley: U of California P, 1998. Examining the emergence of disability rights activists in the United States and across the globe, Charlton traces the "the political-economic and cultural dimensions" of what he calls "the dominant culture's oppression of people with disabilities" and offers pedagogues crucial reading (interviews, international research, and local practices).

Corrigan, Dagmar Stuehrk, and Chidsey Dickson. "Ezines and Freshman Composition." *Kairos* 7.2 (Summer 2002) <http://english.ttu.edu/kairos/7.2/sectiontwo/corrigan/description.html>. The authors ask students to analyze and produce an ezine as a collaborative learning tool.

Glenn, Cheryl, and Melissa A. Goldthwaite. *The St. Martin's Guide to Teaching Writing*. 6th ed. Boston: Bedford, 2008. Part 2 provides more on "Teaching Composing Processes."

Hilligoss, Susan. *Visual Communication: A Writer's Guide*. 2nd ed. New York: Longman, 2002. A short guide to visual design, this text suggests ways that students can use computers to produce effective graphic communications.

Kelman, Mark, and Gillian Lester. *Jumping the Queue: An Inquiry into the Legal Treatment of Students with Learning Disabilities*. Cambridge: Harvard UP, 1998. While the controlling metaphor of this book suggests a "special treatment" epistemology, the authors constructively promote inclusive learning communities. This is a valuable source for reconsidering reading and writing processes in your classroom.

Kleege, Georgina. "Voices in My Head." *Yale Review* 85 (1997): 1–18. In this beautifully crafted essay, Kleege explores books on tape as another way to read, focusing on the ways that people with disabilities use this and other techniques of reading.

Lay, Nancy Duke. "Response Journals in the ESL Classroom: Windows to the World." *TETYC* (Feb. 1995): 38–44. Lay's article describes ways to use journals to help students with reading and with getting to know one another.

Messaris, Paul. *Visual Persuasion: The Role of Images in Advertising*. Thousand Oaks: Sage, 1997. This is an excellent resource book for teaching students how to consider visual arguments in the advertising world all around us.

Mitchell, W. J. T. *Picture Theory: Essays on Verbal and Visual Representation*. Chicago: U of Chicago P, 1994. A classic text by the guru of visual representation theory.

Murray, Donald M. "Teaching the Other Self: The Writer's First Reader." *CCC* 33 (1982): 140–47. According to Murray, all writers have an "other self" that is capable of reading a piece of writing in progress and giving advice to the writer about how the writing should proceed. Murray argues that the instructor should teach a student's "other self" by giving the writer's "other self" the chance to speak in teacher-student conferences and in small and large workshops with other writers.

Piano, Doreen. "Analyzing a Web Zine." *Kairos* 7.2 (Summer 2002) <http://english.ttu.edu/kairos/7.2/binder.html?sectiontwo/piano/webzinehome.htm>. Piano offers a practice assignment sequence for analyzing the content and design of Web sites.

Shiflet, E. Stone. "Shifting the Triangle: Critical Thinking through the Mediation of Forensic and Media Discourse." *Kairos* 7.2 (Summer 2002) <http://english.ttu.edu/kairos/7.2/sectiontwo/shiflet>. Shiflet uses the methodology of Paolo Freire to develop students' critical literacy with regard to visual mediations of news events.

Stroupe, Craig. "Visualizing English: Recognizing the Hybrid Literacy of Visual and Verbal Authorship on the Web." *CE* 62.5 (May 2000): 607–32. Stroupe examines the changing professional trends as more institutions question the teaching of both visual and verbal literacies.

Wilson, James C., and Cynthia Lewiecki-Wilson, eds. *Embodied Rhetorics: Disability in Language and Culture.* Carbondale: Southern Illinois UP, 2001. The editors unite rhetoric and disability studies to rethink educational practices.

USEFUL WEB SITES

Disability Studies Quarterly

http://www.dsq-sds.org

The online site for the Center on Disability Studies at the College of Education.

Kairos: A Journal of Rhetoric, Technology, and Pedagogy

http://kairos.technorhetoric.net

The focus of the Summer 2002 issue on technology, popular culture, and the art of teaching offers excellent articles suggesting strategies for teaching visual arguments.

Learning Disabilities Resource Center Online

http://www.ldresources.com

An important resource for developing pedagogical materials attending to disabilities: read online columns and essays, subscribe to the LD newsletter, keep informed on current happenings and conferences, contact people, find out about educational developments, access both high- and low-tech tools, and link to electronic books and videos.

12 Analyzing Arguments

Responding to culture—clarifying, explicating, valorizing, translating, transforming, criticizing—is what artists everywhere do, especially writers involved in the founding of a new nation.
–Toni Morrison

The classical period in Greece was long thought of as being characterized by stable values, social cohesion, and a unified cultural ideal, and thus for many years our conception of classical rhetoric held that it was primarily concerned with argument based on reasonable appeals made within a rational culture.

More recent scholarship has argued that the Western rhetorical tradition has been one of exclusion and agonism, that the classical period was not nearly as complacent and rational a world as earlier scholars thought, and that our view of classical rhetoric was incomplete. Following some of the ideas of that group of early Greek thinkers known as the sophists, many contemporary rhetoricians view humankind as "symbol-using animals" who live in a fragmented world mediated by and through language. In *A Rhetoric of Motives*, philosopher and critic Kenneth Burke refers to that society when he writes that "rhetoric is concerned with Babel after the Fall" (23) and goes on to substantiate the modern goal of rhetoric as "communication," differing from the traditional goal of combative or coercive "persuasion": "Wherever there is persuasion, there is rhetoric. And wherever there is 'meaning,' there is 'persuasion' " (127).

In *Modern Dogma and the Rhetoric of Assent*, Wayne Booth builds on the work of Burke, positing that good rhetoric is "the art of discovering good reasons, finding what really warrants assent because any reasonable person ought to be persuaded by what has been said" (xiv).

Although good reasons *ought* to guarantee assent, sometimes they do not, for each person finds a reason to believe or not. Sometimes, the reason is not a rational one. However, in *Classical Rhetoric for the Modern Student* Edward P. J. Corbett and Robert Connors echo Aristotle:

> Rationality is humanity's essential characteristic. It is what makes people human and differentiates them from other animals. Ideally, reason should dominate all of people's thinking and actions, but actually, they are often influenced by passions and prejudices and customs. To say that people often respond to irrational motives is not to say that they never listen to the voice of reason. We must have faith not only that people are capable of ordering their lives by the dictates of reason but that most of the time they are disposed to do so. (37)

Speech professors Sonja Foss and Cindy Griffin expand the scope of rhetoric still further—to include forms of discourse that do not involve the intent to change the behavior or beliefs of others and are not solely tied to reason. Their 1993 presentation to the Speech Communication Association offers a new taxonomy that includes rhetorics of conquest, conversion, advice, and invitation. The first three categories involve a conscious intent to persuade that is not present in the fourth.

Invitational rhetoric proposes to create an environment that enables a transformation, should individuals choose to change. The communicative options of invitational rhetoric are (1) modeling, (2) the creation of external conditions for change, and (3) a belief that audience and rhetoric are equal, both expert in their own lives.

Students need guidance in exploring the uses of argument, and in challenging the traditional view that the only object of argument is winning.

FOR COLLABORATION: Analyzing Arguments

The At a Glance box that precedes 12a provides pertinent questions that help writers explore and develop a topic. Break the class into groups, and have them answer these questions as they relate to "A Curse and a Blessing," the student essay in 12g. These are the kinds of questions that the group will want to use again and again as they write essays and review the essays of the other group members.

ATTENDING TO DISABILITIES: Think Critically about Argument (12a)

You might want to begin your class by asking students whether they are auditory, visual, or hands-on learners. Then, rather than relying on the label "learning disabled," emphasize the strengths in a student's learning style and help locate the resources available to maximize that particular approach to learning. Find out whether any students have particular needs that might be served by such aids as screen readers, lecture note takers, recording devices, video magnifiers, or ergonomic work stations. The on-campus disability resource center often has technology to help compensate for different learning styles, which can be particularly helpful when you are teaching students about recognizing and analyzing arguments.

TEACHING WITH TECHNOLOGY: Think Critically about Argument (12a)

Building on students' familiarity with the Internet, ask them to work in small groups to identify three favorite Web sites. Each group should select two Web sites from the batch to present to the class. Perhaps one Web site is quite obviously an argument. But the second one may be a much more subtle form of persuasion. What is the Web site's message, pitch, or purpose? How does it sell something, convince the audience to believe something, or make a claim? Display the selected Web sites on a projector screen for the entire class to analyze. Let students present the major features of argument in each Web text. You might consider asking them to analyze popular social networking sites for arguments, as well. Are these arguments easy to identify? Are students aware of these arguments in their daily use of these sites or networks?

> **So much of what we receive from others—from family and friends to thirty-second blurbs on TV—is intended to persuade. Recognizing how this is done gives greater power to choose.**
>
> —VICTOR VILLANUEVA JR.

FOR COLLABORATION: Recognize Cultural Contexts (12b)

To foster understanding of how any event or topic has multiple points of view, have the students choose a topic or event as a class. In small groups, students should research and discuss the perspective of a specific cultural group. For example, a discussion of Muslim women's dress code could take the points of view of Islamic scholars, Muslim women, American feminists, among others. After each group presents its perspective, the class will have a better understanding of the cultural biases and assumptions inherent in arguments.

FOR MULTILINGUAL WRITERS: Recognize Cultural Contexts (12b)

In *Decoding ESL*, Amy Tucker articulates the problems for our students who are "Trying to Handle Two Languages at Once," the title of her opening chapter. Throughout her book, Tucker tries to take the point of view of ESL students rather than the more familiar stance of the instructor.

And in the manner of Mina Shaughnessy, Tucker helps us see what our students are "trying" to do as well as what they are, indeed, doing. Thus we have both their method and their goal.

In Chapters 6 and 7, which are especially pertinent to argumentation, Tucker discusses the rhetorical preferences of Japanese and Americans, with Americans being more direct, opinionated, and aggressive. "Some 'Japanese' and 'American' Rhetorical Preferences" and "In Which the Emphasis of Chapter 6 Is Shifted: Some 'American' and 'Japanese' Rhetorical Preferences" demonstrate the specific ways that Japanese students, for instance, may initially have problems reconciling their native linguistic and behavioral patterns with some of the demands made on them by the syllabi in American college composition courses, which typically include personal narratives, journals, procedural essays, and persuasive or argumentative papers (171).

FOR COLLABORATION: Identify an Argument's Basic Appeals (12c)

To help students understand Aristotle's three appeals, assign one essay that contains instances of all three types of appeals and have students divide into three small groups to analyze the presence of each appeal. Jonathan Swift's famous essay "A Modest Proposal" works particularly well for this activity, and many students may have already encountered the essay earlier in their education. If so, they can then serve as content advisers for their small group, explaining the essay's purpose and meaning.

For collaborative work, ask each group to identify passages that make use of one of the appeals (pathos, ethos, or logos) and to comment on the function and efficacy of each appeal in the essay. Each group should provide a short presentation to the class. You might also ask each group to formulate a contemporary argument equivalent to Swift's essay and create a mock appeal for that topic.

Another, more contemporary, essay that students would have fun analyzing for appeals is Leon Kass's essay, "The End of Courtship." Readily available in three parts, allowing for analysis of shorter or longer pieces, the provocative essay generates much discussion for both traditional and nontraditional students. It can be found on the Web zine Boundless.org. You might also ask students to find recent political essays or speeches to analyze how they employ pathos, logos, or ethos. Suggested topics include world hunger, war, genocide, AIDS, poverty, and the energy crisis. Get students to come up with their own analogies and appeals, and then have them share these with the class.

FOR COLLABORATION: Identify an Argument's Basic Appeals (12c)

To help students identify how word choice can create bias, make two columns on the board labeled "We" and "They." As a class, identify the kinds of words that would be used in each column. For example, We plan/They plot; We are clever/They are sneaky; and so on. You might have them examine editorials, blogs, or other opinion writing to help them recognize such language.

FOR TEACHING: Analyze the Elements of an Argument (12d)

Ask students to analyze Teal Pfeifer's essay about the effect of images in the media on women's perceptions of themselves in 13k, reading it now for its implicit argument. Have them analyze the essay using the five Toulmin categories described in 12d, focusing especially on the assumptions that underlie the writer's claims. Does the essay succeed as an argument? Why, or why not?

FOR COLLABORATION: Analyze Visual Arguments (12e)

Ask students to bring in examples of their favorite advertisements from print sources (such as magazines and campus or national newspapers) and the Internet. In small groups, have students use the questions in the At a Glance box in 12e to examine the images. Also have students ask what difference the medium makes (print versus digital; national press versus campus paper; fashion magazine versus independent journal).

Have each group select two images that work particularly well as visual arguments and present their analysis collaboratively to the class. Then, as a means of reinforcing what was learned, assign students the task of finding another, more subtle visual argument to bring to the next class.

> In my mind's eye, I visualize how a particular . . . sight and feeling will appear on a print. If it excites me, there is a good chance it will make a good photograph. It is an intuitive sense, an ability that comes from a lot of practice. —ANSEL ADAMS

FOR MULTILINGUAL WRITERS: Analyze Visual Arguments (12e)

Realize that the argumentative claims and assumptions of a visual argument may not be readily accessible or obvious to all students. Depending on their country of origin, students come to visual texts with different perspectives. You can emphasize this difference in the classroom by discussing what happens at the "point of encounter." Find a political cartoon, and ask students to write a caption for it. Each student will offer a different visual/verbal combination, one that makes a unique argument. Multilingual writers, however, will offer increased complexity by adding an alternative national lens, one that straddles the border between cultures.

> **Visualization and belief in a pattern of reality,**
> **Activates the creative power of Realization.**
> —A. L. LINALL JR.

FOR TEACHING: Think Critically about Fallacies (12f)

Writers who rely on manufactured methods of persuasion—distorting evidence, misquoting, misrepresenting opposing views—do not trust their own position on an issue and may not be able to represent that position believably. Encourage students to rely on the strengths of their personal experience as well as the facts they have selected to support their position on an issue.

Ask students to bring in ads that *do not* fairly represent a product, or an editorial or a letter to the editor that presents distorted evidence. What are the contexts for the examples? What specifically is slanted or unfair? Then ask students (1) to write out their responses to the examples and (2) to rewrite the ad or example according to fair standards. By doing such analyses, your students will sharpen their critical thinking, reading, and writing skills.

After talking about logical appeals, ask students to look again at the misleading ads, editorials, or columns they brought to class, this time analyzing them for logical appeals. Often unfair text is based on emotional rather than logical or ethical appeals.

FOR COLLABORATION: Think Critically about Fallacies (12f)

Instruct the students that they should consider themselves masters of manipulation, and their job is to teach unscrupulous people how to gain influence over others. Then, have the class choose a controversial topic and split the class into two groups—pro and con. Each group of master manipulators should deliberately use as many fallacies as possible (they could think of them as "tricks") to show how to "win" the argument at all costs. Role-playing like this will help them to recognize fallacies more frequently.

FOR COLLABORATION: Analyzing Arguments

Assign each pair of students a brief argumentative text—a letter to the editor or editorial, a "My Turn" essay from *Newsweek* or an essay from *Time*, something from the school newspaper, or an advertisement or editorial cartoon. Then ask students to work together to analyze this text, playing both the believing and the doubting game, and identifying claim(s), reason(s), assumption(s), evidence, and qualifiers, as well as emotional, ethical, and logical appeals. Then, still working together, students should write a two-page, double-spaced critical response to the text. Finally, ask the pairs to bring their texts and critical responses to class, and to be prepared to present the results of their analysis.

USEFUL READINGS

Belcher, Diane. "An Argument for Nonadversarial Argumentation: On the Relevance of the Feminist Critique of Academic Discourse to L^2 Writing Pedagogy." *Journal of Second Language Writing* 6 (Jan. 1997): 1–21. In this extremely helpful essay for instructors of multilingual writers, Belcher demonstrates the ways in which traditional notions of agonistic argument are *un*helpful to L^2 learners.

Booth, Wayne. *Modern Dogma and the Rhetoric of Assent*. Chicago: U of Chicago P, 1974. This is a classic discussion of the art of "good rhetoric."

Burke, Kenneth. *A Rhetoric of Motives*. Berkeley: U of California P, 1969. Burke's emphasis on rhetoric as being communicative, not combative, is worth sharing with your students.

Corbett, Edward P. J., and Robert Connors. *Classical Rhetoric for the Modern Student*. 4th ed. New York: Oxford UP, 1999. This text provides a thorough, cogent, and readable exposition of Aristotelian rhetoric and a brief history of the Western rhetorical tradition.

Corbett, Edward P. J., and Rosa A. Eberly. *The Elements of Reasoning*. 2nd ed. New York: Longman, 2000. This short, practical summary of common strategies of argumentation—definition, cause and effect, evaluation, proposal—based on classical rhetoric includes chapters on the appropriate arena of argument, on forms of argument, and on logical fallacies.

Foss, Sonja, and Cindy Griffin. "Beyond Persuasion: A Proposal for an Invitational Rhetoric." *Communication Monographs* 62 (1995): 2–18. Describing the characteristics of what they term "invitational"—as opposed to agonistic or oppositional—rhetoric, Foss and Griffin urge scholars and instructors to adopt and practice this useful category.

Lamb, Catherine. "Beyond Argument in Feminist Composition." *CCC* 42 (1991): 11–24. Lamb describes teaching a feminist approach to argument, one that emphasizes the use of negotiation and/or mediation in order to resolve a disagreement in a mutually satisfying way.

Lynch, Dennis, Diana George, and Marilyn Cooper. "Agonistic Inquiry and Confrontational Cooperation." *CCC* 48 (1997): 61–85. The authors describe two courses on argument that move beyond traditional disputation and opposition to urge students to explore complexities rather than merely to take sides.

Toulmin, Stephen. *The Uses of Argument.* New York: Cambridge UP, 1958. According to Toulmin, the persuasiveness of our arguments ("claims") depends on both the general principles ("warrants" or assumptions) that underlie our interpretations of data and the reasons we provide for them.

Tucker, Amy. *Decoding ESL.* Portsmouth: Boynton, 1995. See Chapters 6 and 7 on argumentation.

13 Constructing Arguments

The art of writing has for backbone some fierce attachment to an idea.
—VIRGINIA WOOLF

Argumentation, persuasion, rhetoric—these terms may bring to mind images of hostility, manipulation, deception, overpowering, overmastering, and outmaneuvering. In *A Rhetoric of Motives,* Kenneth Burke postulates that the image of persuasion should not be bellicose, but rather that

> a speaker persuades an audience by the use of stylistic identifications; his act of persuasion may be for the purpose of causing the audience to identify itself with the speaker's interests; and the speaker draws on identification of interests to establish rapport between himself and his audience. (46)

Identification, Burke reminds us, occurs when people share some principle in common—that is, when they establish common ground. Persuasion should not begin with absolute confrontation and separation but with the establishment of common ground, from which differences can be worked out. Such common ground can help students establish their credibility and understand where their audiences are coming from.

When teaching students how to construct arguments, you may wish to reiterate Burke's emphasis on identification and common ground. At the same time, it is helpful to encourage students to advance their own ideas: as Virginia Woolf notes, "fierce attachment to an idea" makes for powerful writing. This balance of identification and originality might be best understood as contributing a new idea to an ongoing conversation. Teaching thesis statements as beginnings of conversations rather than as statements of finality, D. Diane Davis suggests, emphasizes "the encounter" present in all writing.

Additional help with argumentation is available on *The Everyday Writer*'s companion Web site, **bedfordstmartins.com/everydaywriter**. Go to **Writing Resources** and click on **Argument Resources**. To read other sample essays, click on **Student Writing Models**.

> There are only three things, after all, that a [piece of writing] must reach: the eye, the ear, and what we may call the heart or mind. It is most important of all to reach the heart of the reader.
> —ROBERT FROST

ATTENDING TO DISABILITIES: Understand What Counts as Argument (13a)

Ask students to review the purposes of argument mentioned in 13a of *The Everyday Writer*: to win, to convince, and to explore an issue. Then give students one of the following assignments adapted from a list by Beth Haller of Towson University. All four assignments (which have been modified into argument prompts) deal with awareness of disabilities on campus and in U.S. culture. They can be conducted either by students with disabilities to encourage them to develop their own stances on access or by all class members collectively using the environment around them as material for constructing arguments.

- Have students meet with someone from a local center for independent living to take an "audit" of the campus's compliance with the Americans with Disabilities Act; ask them to argue why noncompliance hurts all community members.
- Through individual or group analysis of ads, TV programs, and movies, ask students to explore the stigmatizing media images of people with disabilities and make an argument on how such images can be changed for the better.
- Through interviews with university disability resource centers and academic computing, have students investigate how improved technology for people with disabilities better integrates them into society; ask students to formulate an argument based on their findings.
- Have students evaluate their own attitudes about interactions with people with disabilities or their experiences as people with disabilities; collectively, this group can make an argument for disability etiquette.

FOR COLLABORATION: Purpose, Audience, and Support in Thesis Statements (13b–d)

Have students work in small groups to evaluate the purpose, audience, position, and support in each of these thesis statements:

1. My essay will deal with the issue of recruiting college athletes. My audience is made up of coaches and administrators, and I want to point out

that it is their insistence on winning seasons that often causes coaches to resort to unethical recruiting practices.

2. In this essay, I will argue that this university discriminates against people who live off campus and who must drive to school. I know this is true because I am a commuter and can never find a parking spot. If there's a blizzard, the university doesn't close because residence-hall students can walk to class. The university schedules two or three hours between classes for commuter students and then doesn't provide them with any place to go except the library, where you can't even get a soda.

How can these statements be improved? Should the proposed audience be reconsidered? Ask each group to provide a revision of one of the statements, working together to formulate a better thesis using the guidelines in 13b–d.

FOR COLLABORATION: Shape Your Appeal to Your Audience (13d)

Once students have determined their main argument, have them identify two different audiences. Ask them to brainstorm in pairs about the diverse approaches they might take to reach the different audiences. This exercise will help them to write an effective argument and will also generate more specific counterarguments.

FOR MULTILINGUAL WRITERS: Establish Credibility through Ethical Appeals (13e)

The multilingual writers in your classes may come from different cultures or nations where the deliberate establishment of ethos as a persuasive appeal is discouraged. Some students may consider it rude or arrogant to advance their own credibility as experts in an area or as originators of an idea. For these students, emphasize that writers can build respect and credibility not simply by demonstrating knowledge through claims of expertise, but also in more graceful ways, such as by building common ground, appealing to authority, citing evidence uncovered during the research process, and referring to others who have previously participated in the conversation on the topic at hand. When students focus on making connections with their audience and on building identification rather than animosity, they develop a more collegial, less blatantly aggressive voice that has more persuasive power in an argument.

FOR COLLABORATION: Establishing Common Ground (13e)

Your students will better understand the concept of common ground if you provide them with an opportunity to demonstrate how opposing parties can reach agreement. Divide the class into pairs of students who hold opposing views, and ask each pair to establish a first principle of agreement, their common ground. Use frustrating situations that the students experience as well as the following rhetorical situations:

1. Your roommate keeps an annoying schedule. (For example, if an early bird and a night owl are roommates, they may keep antagonistic schedules. Yet when they discuss their unhappiness, both agree that they each need quiet for sleeping and noise for relaxing. They have thus established common ground, a starting point for working out their differences.)
2. Your English instructor doesn't accept late papers.
3. You show your parents your 3.0 average.
4. You'd like permission (and money) to go to Florida during spring break.
5. Your roommate constantly borrows your belongings.
6. You need help with child care or household duties.

FOR TEACHING: Demonstrating Fairness (13e)

MOOR EEFFOC—that's "COFFEE ROOM" backwards when you look through the glass from the other side. Ask students to try to see the point of view of the "opposition" and honestly consider counterarguments. When they try to decipher MOOR EEFFOC, they show their willingness to go over to the other side to get a better view of the rhetorical situation. They also demonstrate their developing skills in constructing arguments.

FOR TEACHING: Use Effective Logical Appeals (13f)

Students in Western countries often look to logical appeals as *the* most effective way to persuade an audience. Students from math and science backgrounds, steeped in logical positivism, frequently declare that "hard evidence" such as statistics and "concrete logic" such as rational arguments and syllogisms are the only certain modes for convincing an audience. These students may benefit from reading Darrell Huff 's *How to Lie with Statistics* and other texts that analyze how scientific information and statistics are manipulated, selected, and presented to an audience using loaded language and claims to authority. In short, teach students that the most persuasive argument does not merely employ logos, but rather interweaves Aristotle's three appeals in a strategic crafting of knowledge.

> **Writing is different from speaking. Organize your written thoughts so that you don't have to stud your sentences with asides, sudden additions, curses or last minute entries.**
>
> —William Safire

FOR TEACHING: Examples, Precedents, and Narratives (13f)

Judith Gardner of the University of Texas at San Antonio warns that college writers can get into trouble through overdependence on stories and cautions that writing from sources is not telling a story; narrative should be used to support the point, not *be* the point.

> **I will tell you something about stories. . . . They aren't just entertainment.**
>
> —Leslie Marmon Silko

FOR TEACHING: Authority and Testimony (13f)

Student writers sometimes rely too heavily on authority figures because they doubt the power of their own strongly held opinions—opinions that might well influence their readers. Encourage your students to cite authorities to support—not substitute for—their own positions on an issue.

While you help students consider the appropriateness and proportion of their use of authority, ask them to consider the authority of celebrities when they tell students to stay in school or appear in other public service announcements. Do students pay any attention to or respect these campaigns? Do they buy hamburgers, athletic shoes, soft drinks, or other products on the advice of the celebrities who endorse them? You might bring in several examples of such celebrity advertisements—from television, print ads, or a document printed from the Internet—for discussion.

Often students overlook the testimony of ordinary people as a means of identifying with their readers; they don't realize that the testimony of someone with firsthand experience lends powerful credibility to an argument. Although Nancy Reagan conducted a very visible "Just say no to drugs" campaign, her credibility was perhaps not as strong as that of an inner-city resident who had witnessed the effects of the drug trade at close range.

Ask students to identify current celebrities and public figures who are campaigning for a cause, and discuss how their status works for or against their appeal. How do these compare with campaigns that utilize ordinary people? Which type do students find more persuasive and why?

FOR TEACHING: Causes and Effects (13f)

Cause-effect relationships are often complex: what appears at first glance to be the obvious cause of an event turns out to be only a secondary influence, which obscures the primary cause-effect relationship. For example, one student felt sure that her migraine headaches were brought on by stress, air pressure, and certain food allergies. Only after several seizures was she convinced otherwise: she had a small brain tumor. Encourage your students to persevere in finding the real connections between events and their causes.

For practice, ask students to identify the obvious and not-so-obvious connections in the following statements of cause and effect:

1. A large increase in church membership in recent years shows that people are becoming more religious.
2. Older women sometimes fall and break their hips because they don't consume enough calcium.
3. Because of its elderly population, Florida is the best place to buy a gently used car.
4. Republican victories in nearly every presidential election since 1968 show that the country has repudiated social welfare programs.

On Inductive and Deductive Reasoning (13f)

Most of us live our lives according to inductive generalizations: we are aware of the probability that we will miss the heavy traffic if we take a particular route to school each day; that we can stay in the hot sun only so long without getting burned; that we must eat and exercise a specific amount if we are to stay in shape; or that certain foods, animals, and plants provoke an allergic reaction in us. Many such generalizations stem from inductive reasoning: morning traffic is heavy; sun can burn the skin; too many calories make one fat; poison ivy causes a rash.

One of Aristotle's greatest contributions to rhetorical theory was the use of deductive as well as inductive logic: he used the enthymeme, whose essential difference from the syllogism in logic is not so much that one of the premises is left unstated as that the argument is based on premises that are probably true rather than absolutely true and that the opening premise is agreed on by speaker and audience. In his analysis of inductive reasoning, Aristotle put great emphasis on the importance of examples.

FOR TEACHING: Use Appropriate Emotional Appeals (13g)

Although emotional appeals have traditionally been ignored or devalued as inappropriate to "good" arguments, they are widely used—and frequently effective. Indeed, some emotional appeals, including bandwagon and various kinds of flattery as well as boasting and exaggeration, are well-known and highly effective appeals characteristic of African American rhetorical strategy. For suggestions on ways of drawing on this rhetorical tradition, see Geneva Smitherman's article "'The Blacker the Berry, the Sweeter the Juice': African American Student Writers."

FOR COLLABORATION: Visuals That Make Emotional Appeals (13g)

Divide the class into small groups, and ask students to find visuals to support an argument for one of the following topics. Have them speculate on what subtopics might be created to support these arguments, write out the working thesis, and then work to construct a set of rough notes for each argument. They should also locate two to three visuals to use as ethical, logical, and emotional appeals for one of the topics:

1. banning smoking in all public places
2. two-career marriages
3. "returning" students
4. a topic of current import on campus

TEACHING WITH TECHNOLOGY: Consult Sources (13h)

You can help students get started on their own arguments by walking them through a "model" example in the computer classroom. Have students choose one of the following statements and make notes regarding any personal experience they have that supports or refutes the statement:

1. Vegetarians have a lower incidence of heart attacks than do meat-eaters.
2. College degrees mean higher incomes.
3. To succeed, college students must resort to various forms of dishonesty.
4. Students should graduate from college if only to be four years older and wiser when they join the job market.
5. Exercise relieves stress.
6. We are returning to the moral standards of the fifties.
7. AIDS is the worst disease the United States has ever known.
8. Student loans, grants, and scholarships are becoming scarce.

Then have them use library and online sources to gather as much additional evidence as possible. (You might have students work together in small groups to do this research.) Finally, ask them to use this information and their notes on personal experience to outline a short essay arguing for or against the statement. Project one or two outlines on a large screen for collective class analysis and revision.

FOR TEACHING: Organize Your Argument (13i)

Help clarify the five-part classical argument by providing the class with an essay that follows this format. The "My Turn" column in *Newsweek* is a good choice, as are the editorials in city and campus newspapers. Ask students to analyze the essay, identifying the introduction, background, lines of argument, refutation, and conclusion. As you proceed through this exercise, use the board to outline the thesis statement as well as the five major headings.

You can extend this exercise by asking students to find an essay on their own that uses this form of argument and to write a short commentary on the claim.

USEFUL READINGS

Belcher, Diane. "An Argument for Nonadversarial Argumentation: On the Relevance of the Feminist Critique of Academic Discourse to L^2 Writing Pedagogy." *Journal of Second Language Writing* 6 (Jan. 1997): 1–21. In this extremely helpful essay for instructors of multilingual writers, Belcher demonstrates the ways in which traditional notions of agonistic argument are *un*helpful to L^2 learners.

Bridwell-Bowles, Lillian. "Discourse and Diversity: Experimental Writing within the Academy." *CCC* 43 (1992): 349–68. The author explores the ways in which experimental forms, including narrative, can function well in academic writing.

Bruner, Michael, and Max Oelschlaeger. "Rhetoric, Environmentalism, and Environmental Ethics." *Landmark Essays on Rhetoric and the Environment*. Ed. Craig Waddell. Mahwah: Erlbaum, 1998. 209–25. Bruner and Oelschlaeger emphasize the importance of pathos, claiming that an argument can produce social change only if it "evoke[s] sentiment." Relying on Richard McKeon's description of transformative rhetoric as "architectonic," they urge artistic rhetoric with the purpose of social change.

Burke, Kenneth. *A Rhetoric of Motives*. Berkeley: U of California P, 1969. Burke's emphasis on rhetoric as communicative, not combative, is worth sharing with students.

Davis, D. Diane. "Finitude's Clamor; or, Notes toward a Communitarian Literacy." *CCC* 53.1 (Sept. 2001): 119–45. A compelling alternative to the "adversarial academy" as it manifests itself in the classroom, Davis's article offers a theoretical and scholarly assessment of "communitarian literacy" in contrast to mastery goals in writing instruction, or what Davis calls the "rhetoric of assertion."

Haller, Beth. "Integrating Disability Issues into Skills Classes," NCA presentation, Nov. 1998. <http://www.towson.edu/~bhalle/ideas.html>. An excellent list of collaborative ideas for getting students to attend to disabilities and for students with disabilities to argue their own perspectives on issues of access.

Hindman, Jane E. "Special Focus: Personal Writing." *CE* 64.1 (Sept. 2001): 34–108. This collection of short essays on the role and function of personal writing in academic and professional situations opens with an instructive literature review and overview before moving into articles debating the place of the personal in professional research methodologies, in pedagogical settings, and in rhetorical structures within academic writing.

Huff, Darrell. *How to Lie with Statistics*. New York: Norton, 1993. This book is a delightful look at the deceitful presentation strategies and scientific flaws in the media's use of statistics.

Lynch, Dennis, Diana George, and Marilyn Cooper. "Agonistic Inquiry and Confrontational Cooperation." *CCC* 48 (1997): 61–85. The authors describe two courses on argument that move beyond traditional disputation and opposition to urge students to explore complexities rather than merely to take sides.

Smitherman, Geneva. "'The Blacker the Berry, the Sweeter the Juice': African American Student Writers." *The Need for Story: Cultural Diversity in Classroom and Community*, Ed. Anne Haas Dyson and Celia Genishi. Urbana: NCTE, 1994. Smitherman suggests ways of drawing on the rhetorical tradition that characterizes African American discourse as reliance on emotional appeals.

Spigelman, Candace. "Argument and Evidence in the Case of the Personal." *CE* 64.1 (Sept. 2001): 63–87. Spigelman analyzes arguments for and against the personal in scholarly and student writing, tracing the debates in composition studies, feminist scholarship, and rhetoric. She builds on Aristotelean rhetorical theory to argue that "narrative too offers claims, reasons and evidence for serious analysis and critique" (83).

Research

Research is formalized curiosity. It is poking and prying with a purpose.

—ZORA NEALE HURSTON

14 Preparing for a Research Project

Wisdom begins in wonder. – SOCRATES

The fifteenth edition of the *New Encyclopaedia Britannica* (*NEB*) (1987) attributes the dominance of human beings on earth to the "innate ability to communicate and to store, retrieve, and use knowledge so that each generation does not have to relearn the lessons of the past in order to act effectively in the present." Research is the activity that enables us to process, create, and communicate knowledge. But research goes beyond simply gathering data and passing it on. In its most beneficial sense, research is the process of investigating information or data for a purpose: to make decisions about our lives, to understand our world, or to create or advance understanding. Far from being restricted to work on a college "research essay," research informs much of what we do throughout our lives, especially in the age of electronic media. Research carried out for *The Everyday Writer*, in fact, revealed just how much research students today are doing online for *non*school-related uses, from tracking the performance of stocks or sports teams to comparison shopping for an MP3 player.

Regardless of the field of study, researching, writing, and learning are interconnected. James Britton's distinction between expressive and transactional writing helps explain this interconnection. We write in order to learn; that is, we think on paper, using writing to process information and to probe ideas. This function of writing, a form of self-expression and exploration, Britton calls *expressive*. It serves the writer; it enables him or her to learn and understand information. We also write to communicate learning. We use language to inform, to persuade, or to help someone else understand. This function Britton calls *transactional* to emphasize the exchange or transmission of information for an audience's learning purposes. Similarly, Janet Emig views writing as a means of discovery in which research, writing, and learning are intrinsically connected. She argues that the notes, outlines, and drafts that make up the research and writing process provide a record of the growth of learning.

> **We don't receive wisdom; we must discover it for ourselves after a journey that no one can take for us or spare us.** —MARCEL PROUST

FOR TEACHING: Analyze the Research Assignment (14a)

As preparation for a discussion of the nature and process of college-level research, have students write in their logs about their previous experiences with research (including online research) and research papers.

> **Before ideas come to fruition, they must germinate. The most important direct consequence of an idea is that it gives rise to more ideas.** —ANATOL RAPOPORT

FOR COLLABORATION: Analyze the Research Assignment (14a)

Working with one or two members of the class, students should come up with a list of everyday research tasks they have done lately—on what bike or DVD player to buy, on where to take a vacation, on where to go to college, and so on. Next, the groups should choose two of these everyday research projects and detail their information-gathering processes. All groups should bring the results of their work to share with the class. In your closing discussion of this activity, ask students to identify the steps each group took to find the information they needed. What patterns can the students find among these processes?

> **The test of a first-rate intelligence is the ability to hold two opposed ideas in mind at the same time and still retain the ability to function.** —F. SCOTT FITZGERALD

FOR COLLABORATION: Analyze the Topic (14a)

Have students work in groups of three. Ask them to create some possible research questions on topics and then exchange these with two other groups. If students have difficulties with this, ask them to focus on what they'd like to find out about the topic that they don't already know. Ask the other groups to analyze the topic for the purpose of the research, the audience, the scope, and length limits. This will help each student narrow the topic into a more feasible and focused project.

FOR TEACHING: Analyze the Audience (14a)

Have students bring to class three research assignments from other classes. Use these as the basis for group discussions of the purpose, scope, and audience implied in the assignments. Identifying the audience will likely pose problems for your students. Answering the questions in 14a of *The Everyday Writer* for each of the research assignments brought in by the groups will help students understand that they must consider the audience when deciding on word choice, tone, strategy, and presentation.

Point out to your students that one of their responsibilities as researchers and writers is to make information available and understandable to a variety of audiences. To do so involves making choices about language and development that depend on their analysis of the purpose of the research, the scope of the project or topic, the specific audience, and so on. For example, the physiologist presenting material on limb regeneration should judge how much he or she needs to explain the significance of *blastema* and the relevant aspects of it on the basis of purpose, audience, and scope. Clearly, colleagues in the writer's field, unlike a general audience, will not require a preliminary basic working definition of the term *blastema*. On the other hand, this physiologist would need to define the term and others particular to the field if the essay were written for an audience made up of readers outside the field.

FOR COLLABORATION: Formulate a Research Question and Hypothesis (14b)

One way of moving students from research questions toward a working hypothesis is to have them brainstorm ways to refine the topic. After students have explored and narrowed their topics using some of the techniques presented in 7a, ask them to explain their topics to the class individually. They should briefly explain their interest in the topic, give some background or contextual information, and identify their research question.

Next, open up the discussion to the class. Encourage students to ask questions and to respond to the topic. By fielding the class's questions and responses, students will develop a sense of the possible directions their topics can take. This informal class brainstorming session can help them identify perspectives that interest others in the topic. By the end of the session, in response to the student questions, the speakers can have generated a working hypothesis—their stance on the issue.

Limit each student's individual session to fifteen minutes—five minutes for the student to present his or her topic, and ten minutes for the class to respond and ask questions. At the end of the fifteen minutes, have each student freewrite for ten to fifteen minutes, noting (1) suggestions for focusing, narrowing, or phrasing the research question; (2) a statement or working hypothesis on his or her own interest in or possible approach to the topic; or (3) remarks on matters of purpose, audience, scope, or length.

To make the most of the activity, have at least four individual sessions, with no more than two topics presented in any one class. Then break up the class into groups of four or five to work through this activity. The small group activity gives the entire class practice at working out possible topics.

FOR COLLABORATION: Plan Your Research (14c)

Have students work in peer-review groups, and ask each student to take a turn serving as a "designated respondent" who will ask a crucial question about another group member's topic. This process of interactive questioning can help students begin to identify what they do know and what they will need to investigate in their research process.

TEACHING WITH TECHNOLOGY: Plan Your Research (14c)

You can provide students with a sample schedule on your course Web site and ask them to download it to their own research files. Alternatively, keep a class time line on your Web site and update it weekly to show your collective progress in meeting the class research deadlines. Since one of the main challenges students have with research projects is managing their time, requiring students to check in electronically on a regular basis helps them to keep up with the process. It also gives you an opportunity to regularly post time-saving tips on the research process and links to time-management workshops on campus, and to use email and discussion forums as a means of submission for works in progress.

FOR TEACHING: Plan Your Research (14c)

Scientist and writer Lewis Thomas recommends taking alternate routes to exploring a question or research topic, including going in the opposite direction from what seems most natural or just "fiddling around." "Fiddle around," he says, ". . . but never with ways to keep things the same, no matter who, not even yourself." As students begin to formulate a preliminary research plan, encourage them to "fiddle around" as part of the process.

FOR TEACHING: Set Up a Research Log (14d)

A research log (or a section of the writing log set off for such a purpose) is a good place to keep track of reading, note-taking, and writing progress;

to ask questions; and to formulate tentative syntheses or conclusions. But no less important, it is a good place to write about the blocks, obstacles, or challenges any researcher inevitably faces. Point out these uses to your students, and ask them to make several log entries on their research processes. You can use these as the basis for class discussions on how to make research most efficient and productive.

ATTENDING TO DISABILITIES: Set Up a Research Log (14d)

When providing research log models on a course Web site, remember to take students with disabilities into consideration. This means conforming to standards of universal design. As Patricia Dunn and Kathleen Dunn De Mers explain, "The philosophy of universal design and its principles can help generate multi-modal intellectual pathways to writing pedagogies. As teachers and students put elements of their writing classrooms and studies online, everyone benefits from the site owner's understanding and application of the principles of universal design" (par. 1). Restructuring your pedagogy to make the research process more inclusive and flexible means using the technological tools at your disposal to benefit *all* of your students. Invite students to explore note-taking strategies that signify alternatives to word-focused methods, such as sketching, voice recording, and oral record keeping. Allow students to transfer texts from a database onto a CD-ROM for future reference or to transfer written texts into audio files using your institution's disability resource center or technology support staff. Moreover, when you take your students to the library, note if there are any hard-to-reach stacks or library resource areas that may present obstacles to the successful completion of a research project for certain writers.

FOR MULTILINGUAL WRITERS: Set Up a Research Log (14d)

Multilingual writers have an expanded range of research materials available to them because of their proficiency in two or more languages. Encourage students to read widely in other languages but to keep careful notes on their research and reading process. You might suggest that if they find a passage they wish to cite, they should record both the original text and their own translation of it in their research logs. Then, on the final paper, they can provide the translated text in the body of their paper and insert a footnote or endnote with the original text and full source information. The words *translation mine* should be placed after the translated passage.

TEACHING WITH TECHNOLOGY: Set Up a Research Log (14d)

Students are often hungry to learn practical and successful methods for completing the research process. Suggest to them that they work directly with technology as they begin the research process and construct their research logs. When they are exploring library databases online, they can cut and paste citation information right into a working bibliography. If they find potentially useful quotations or images, they should attach the source information below the copied text. Some students are able to download articles from large databases such as First-Search, Academic Universe, LexisNexis, and Medline, and then burn a CD-ROM of cited materials. If you require students to hand in photocopies of all works cited and consulted, the use of a CD-ROM or flash drive can save both time and trees. Students should be encouraged to take advantage of the bibliography tool in their word-processing programs, such as the one included in Office 2007.

FOR TEACHING: Move from Hypothesis to Working Thesis (14e)

As students work on their research projects, remind them that their focus and working hypotheses will naturally shift. Share with them stories about famous researchers who might serve as role models.

In the following passage from *Boca's Brain*, for example, astronomer Carl Sagan describes the excitement of the kind of research in which he is engaged, research that makes you "really think" and consequently "experience a kind of exhilaration." Ask students to read Sagan's description carefully. Have they done any research that fits his description? What kind of research would allow them to experience "exhilaration"? How might their own research process develop in this way?

> . . . the main trick of [doing research in] science is to *really* think of something: the shape of clouds and their occasional sharp bottom edges at the same altitude everywhere in the sky; the formation of a dewdrop on a leaf; the origin of a name or a word—Shakespeare, say, or "philanthropic"; the reason for human social customs—the incest taboo, for example; how it is that a lens in sunlight can make paper burn; how a "walking stick" got to look so much like a twig; why the Moon seems to follow us as we walk; what prevents us from digging a hole down to the center of the Earth; what the definition is of "down" on a spherical Earth; how it is possible for the body to convert yesterday's lunch into today's muscle and sinew; or how far is up—does the universe go on forever, or if it does not, is there any meaning to the question of what lies on the other side? Some of these questions are pretty easy. Others, especially the last, are mysteries to which no one even today knows the answer. They are natural questions to ask. Every culture has posed such questions in one way or another. Almost always the proposed answers are in the nature of "Just So Stories," attempted explanations divorced from experiment, or even from careful comparative observations.
>
> But the scientific cast of mind examines the world critically as if many alternative worlds might exist, as if other things might be here which are not. Then we are forced to ask why what we see is present and not something else.

Why are the Sun and the Moon and the planets spheres? Why not pyramids, or cubes, or dodecahedra? Why not irregular, jumbly shapes? Why so symmetrical, worlds? If you spend any time spinning hypotheses, checking to see whether they make sense, whether they conform to what else we know, thinking of tests you can pose to substantiate or deflate your hypotheses, you will find yourself doing science. And as you come to practice this habit of thought more and more you will get better and better at it. To penetrate into the heart of the thing—even a little thing, a blade of grass, as Walt Whitman said—is to experience a kind of exhilaration that, it may be, only human beings of all the beings on this planet can feel. We are an intelligent species and the use of our intelligence quite properly gives us pleasure. In this respect the brain is like a muscle. When we think well, we feel good. Understanding is a kind of ecstasy.

USEFUL READINGS

Belcher, Diane, and George Braine, eds. *Academic Writing in a Second Language: Essays on Research and Pedagogy*. Norwood: Ablex, 1994.

Brent, Douglas. *Reading as Rhetorical Invention: Knowledge, Persuasion, and the Teaching of Research-Based Writing*. Urbana: NCTE, 1992. The author provides an excellent overall discussion of research-based college writing.

Britton, James, et al. *The Development of Writing Abilities*. London: Macmillan, 1975.

Clark, J. Milton, and Carol Peterson Haviland. "Language and Authority: Shifting the Privilege." *Journal of Basic Writing* 14.1 (1995): 57–66. Clark and Haviland describe an assignment that shifts linguistic privilege in the classroom in order to facilitate the acceptance of greater linguistic inclusiveness. They describe how, working with magazines written in French, Spanish, and Chinese, students expand their scope and research focus and participate in "genuine collaboration."

Dunn, Patricia, and Kathleen Dunn De Mers. "Reversing Notions of Disability and Accommodation: Embracing Universal Design in Writing Pedagogy and Web Space." *Kairos* 7.1 (Spring 2002) <http://english.ttu.edu/kairos/7.1/binder2.html?coverweb/dunn_demers/index.html>. Dunn and De Mers argue that as writing teachers and students put their pedagogical work online, they need to incorporate universal design in order to make their work accessible to all learners. Calling Web accessibility a "civil rights issue," the authors offer concrete guidance, Web links, and suggestions for alternative teaching methods to challenge narrow reliance on writing as a mode of learning.

Emig, Janet. "Writing as a Mode of Learning." *CCC* 28 (1977): 122–28. Emig's view of writing as a means of learning informs the interconnection among researching, writing, and learning.

Glenn, Cheryl, and Melissa Goldthwaite. *The St. Martin's Guide to Teaching Writing*. 6th ed. Boston: Bedford, 2008. Chapter 4, "Successful Writing Assignments," offers more information on creating research-based assignments.

Langer, Judith A. "Learning through Writing: Study Skills in the Content Areas." *Journal of Reading* 29 (1986): 400–406. Langer reports that writing essays encourages content learning more effectively than do taking notes and answering questions.

Rodrigues, Dawn. *The Research Paper: A Guide to Library and Internet Research*. 3rd ed. Upper Saddle River: Prentice, 2003. Rodrigues offers students and teachers a walk-through of library and Web search strategies in the context of the research process.

15 Doing Research

Knowledge is of two kinds. We know a subject ourselves, or we know where we can find information upon it.

–SAMUEL JOHNSON

According to Charles Bazerman, "gathering convincing data is not easy." The method that a researcher uses greatly determines the evidence that supports the research, the conclusions that the researcher is able to draw, and ultimately the effectiveness with which the research will influence others to accept its claims. In other words, the way that a researcher explores and produces data will affect how an audience responds to the research.

Will it be believable? Is it accurate? reasonable and reliable? thorough? careful? appropriate? significant? Bazerman advises researchers that "method is so central to the understanding and evaluation of the final written product that in many disciplines a writer is obliged to describe as part of the statement the method used to produce and analyze the data. In this way, many articles contain stories of how they were made" (331).

To appreciate the importance of choosing the methods appropriate to different research projects, researchers need to know that methods vary across disciplines and within them, and that they often change with time. For example, on the one hand, in linguistics many sociolinguists believe that understanding the way words change in meaning is most accurately explained by observing the way words are used in different social contexts. Historical linguists, on the other hand, prefer to explain meaning changes in terms of the historical origins of words and language groups.

The issue of method is especially important today, as many students are conducting research online. They need to understand the disadvantages as well as the advantages of such research methods. Researchers, for instance, are in some ways at the mercy of whatever search engine they are using: What are its principles of exclusion and inclusion? Discussing these difficult issues in class will pay off—for you as well as your students.

Additional coverage on conducting online research is available on *The Everyday Writer*'s companion Web site, **bedfordstmartins.com/everydaywriter**. Go to **Research Resources**.

> **All great masters are chiefly distinguished by the power of adding a second, a third, and perhaps a fourth step in a continuous line. Many a man had taken the first step. With every additional step you enhance immensely the value of your first.**
>
> **—Ralph Waldo Emerson**

FOR TEACHING: Understand Different Kinds of Sources (15a)

Have your students list the sources of information they would use to help you decide on which portable MP3 player to buy. They will probably mention their own experiences or their family's experience with a reliable or unreliable player. They will probably mention consumer guides. They'll also likely mention newspaper and television advertisements as well as pertinent Web sites. Have them classify these sources as either primary or secondary and explain their classifications.

For example, students' own experiences can be classified as a primary source. The fact that they have owned a particular system for many years and that they have recommended it to relatives and friends who have had trouble-free experiences is a form of raw data. If they mention an article that praises their MP3 player, the magazine is a secondary source.

FOR COLLABORATION: Understand Different Kinds of Sources (15a)

Ask students to work in groups of three to draw up a list of reference sources that would be relevant for the following topics. Then ask them to choose one topic, go to the library, and, using both online and print sources, find the necessary facts. Have them write a brief summary, noting where they found the facts and what strategy they used to do so.

- the top ten scorers in the WNBA in 2008
- the articles published on Epstein-Barr syndrome in 2003
- a description of the elements of deconstructive architecture
- information on the 2008 Summer Olympics
- reviews of *A Million Little Pieces* by James Frey
- all the critical articles published on Gabriel Garcia Márquez's *One Hundred Years of Solitude* between 1991 and 2001

- information on the life of Barack Obama
- a description of the progress of research on global warming
- information on Cynthia McKinney, the Green Party presidential candidate in the 2008 election
- the ten most often-cited articles on superconductivity in 2007

FOR TEACHING: Reference Librarians (15b)

Set up a meeting for your class with a reference librarian, or ask a librarian to attend your class, to discuss the resources in your particular library and how best for students to get access to them. At many schools, reference librarians are prepared to do a demonstration of online searches for your students as well as to provide an overview of the library. Planning a special class session devoted to using the library early on will benefit students throughout the term, and if you provide the librarian with your students' assignment, the librarian may be able to tailor the demonstration to your class needs.

FOR TEACHING: Catalogs and Databases (15b)

Encourage students to explore the range of resources available in the library. Spend some time discussing the differences between online library resources that an institution pays for by subscription—such as JSTOR, FirstSearch, Project Muse, Academic Universe, and LexisNexis—and other, less academic and unregulated search engines such as Google.

TEACHING WITH TECHNOLOGY: Find Library Resources (15c)

If you are teaching in a technology-enhanced classroom, you can take advantage of the computers available to you by walking students through interactive exercises in finding library resources. Specifically, ask students to conduct research with different kinds of searches. Put students into groups of three, and have them brainstorm together on the best keywords to use in a database search on the following topics: computer viruses, white-collar crime, contemporary rap, sexual harassment in the military, upcoming NASA missions, and the cost of a college education.

Ask each group to go online and collaboratively find the three most promising sources for their topic. Have each group repeat this exercise with the library's catalog, a subscription database, a book index, a review index, and an e-journal catalog or periodical index. At the end of class, have each group give a five-minute oral presentation on the advantages and disadvantages of each method. Have students write up a short reflection on their investigations into library resources and add this reflection to their research files.

FOR COLLABORATION: Find Library Resources (15c)

To help students understand library resources, ask them to join one or two classmates and pay a visit to the main library on your campus. The team should bring back answers to the following questions: How are the library's materials organized? What resources can you use to find out what your library owns and where these materials are located? What electronic encyclopedias, indexes, and databases are available? What electronic journal collections does your library subscribe to? Each team should write up a brief report that answers these questions, and comment on those aspects of the library that the group found most interesting or helpful, most confusing or difficult to use. Review the reports in a larger class discussion.

To help students understand the different ways to research periodicals, pair up students to and enter the keywords for each of their research projects in at least three different periodical indexes. They can then compare results: How many references did each search yield? What kinds of journals turned up in each different search? What other differences between searches can they note?

FOR TEACHING: Search the Internet (15d)

While most students are now producing their college assignments on computers, and most students are comfortable using the Internet—even creating their own blogs, MySpace accounts, or Facebook personas—most still need solid instruction in how to harness the Internet for academic research purposes. Your students need to know how to determine which information is reliable and how to conduct effective searches for their topics. For these reasons, you may want to work through 15d of the *The Everyday Writer* with your students, explaining how to track searches and bookmark useful sites, and exploring the various search engines with the same set of keywords.

TEACHING WITH TECHNOLOGY: Search the Internet (15d)

Arrange for a workshop to take place in a computer lab, where students can work online together to conduct some preliminary research. Alternatively, ask if someone in the library or at a public computing site could help you set up such a workshop. Then lead students through a simple search, showing them how to apply the "rules" of various search engines and how to evaluate what they find on the Web. Realize that some students in your class can probably serve as facilitators. This will create a strong community and enable students to learn from one another. Emphasize that popular texts found on the Web may not necessarily be bad, depending on the purpose of the search and the nature of the assignment. To analyze the marketing strategies of rap artists, for instance, Google might produce better results than would LexisNexis.

> **The Web site you seek / cannot be located but / endless others exist.**
>
> —FOUND ON THE WEB

FOR TEACHING: Conduct Field Research (15e)

Students may believe that they will simply "get the facts" when they observe and that they will not or do not bring their own interpretive frames to their observations. Students in one class, for instance, decided to spread out across campus and observe instances of graffiti, taking notes on their observations. This task seemed very straightforward to them. They soon realized, however, that recording the graffiti out of context changed it in significant ways. The examples of graffiti—for example, scrawled in giant letters sideways on a door—just didn't mean the same thing printed neatly in a notebook. Nor did the students record their observations in the same ways, or even with the same consistency. In this case, the very act of writing down the data changed their context. The students decided to try to capture something of the spatial orientation and surrounding context of the graffiti by copying the form as well as the content and noting other contextual details. As a result, their data were much richer and more multidimensional than before. You might wish to share this example with students, and ask them to talk in class about how they themselves affect the data they gather.

ATTENDING TO DISABILITIES: Conduct Field Research (15e)

Students with mobility, hearing, or viewing limitations may wish to turn to technological aids to enhance their field research experiences. Vast collections of library resources are now available through university and library Web sites or digitized collections. Interviews with famous scholars or area specialists can now be conducted on the telephone (with special transcribing devices) or through email, forgoing the need for an in-person meeting. Full-text versions of academic and popular articles can be accessed through library databases, making stack searching and photocopying a thing of the past. Spend time in class discussing the options available to your students. Consult with your local disability resource center or librarian as well.

FOR MULTILINGUAL WRITERS: Conduct Field Research (15e)

Writers from various backgrounds and with expertise in multiple languages may find the research process similar to ethnographic work. The process of defamiliarization, which accompanies what Beverly Moss calls "ethnography in composition," can be transformed into a fruitful learning experience for your students if you communicate with them about the unique challenges and opportunities presented by field research.

FOR COLLABORATION: Interviews (15e)

Ask students to work in pairs, first preparing tentative interview questions and then practicing these questions on their partners. Each partner, in turn, provides a critique of the questions. As an alternative, set up one mock interview for your class. Then lead a class discussion on the strengths and weaknesses of the interview.

For additional practice, ask students to choose a professor in a field of study that interests them and interview that person about the research that the professor tends to do. Encourage them to draw up a list of questions they would like answered about the kind of research questions asked in that field, the most typical methods of answering them, and the kinds of sources most often used. After the interview, have students summarize in two or three paragraphs what they have learned.

Use their findings for a class discussion on how to conduct an effective interview, on the etiquette of interviewing, and on the ethics of interviewing (whether to change a subject's words to correct a "mistake," for example).

FOR TEACHING: Observation (15e)

Suggest that most students assume the role of reporter, using the *who*, *what*, *when*, *where*, *why*, and *how* questions to note down what they see and hear at home, in their dorms, and in other classes that arouses their curiosity (see 6e). At least in the trial run, these questions can help guide students' observation.

FOR COLLABORATION: Opinion Surveys (15e)

Though you will often assign research to be carried out individually, you might ask students to work in teams on a project in order to conduct field research in the form of a survey of their peers or of members of their community.

As one possibility, have students work in research teams to gather information for a report on the condition, the level of use, and any needed changes of the bike paths (or commuter parking lots) on campus. Allow a week or so for them to organize their efforts and to decide what kind of survey they will need to do. Have them identify the target audience, generate a list of survey questions, and decide on a method of recording the data (paper survey, Web-based questionnaire, microphone, video recorder). Then ask them to write together a brief summary of how they have proceeded, noting problems they have encountered and projecting ways to solve them.

USEFUL READINGS

Bazerman, Charles. *The Informed Writer: Using Sources in the Disciplines*. 5th ed. Boston: Houghton, 1995. See Chapters 11–15 for an in-depth discussion of the ways different disciplines gather data for research. Bazerman describes the various methods of data gathering in the social and natural sciences and in the humanities and theoretical disciplines.

Bishop, Wendy. "I-Witnessing in Composing: Turning Ethnographic Data into Narratives." *Rhetoric Review* 11 (Fall 1992): 147–58.

Carbone, Nick. *Writing Online: A Student's Guide to the Internet and World Wide Web*. 3rd ed. Boston: Houghton, 2000.

Grobman, Laurie. "'I Found It on the Web, So Why Can't I Use It in My Paper?': Authorizing Basic Writers." *Journal of Basic Writing* 18.1 (1999): 76–90. Grobman argues for the use of Internet sources in writing classrooms as a tool to help basic writers join the "conversation of ideas" and authorize them as members of an academic community.

McCartney, Robert. "The Cumulative Research Paper." *Teaching English in the Two-Year College* 12 (1985): 198–202. This article provides a model for allowing students to conduct in-depth research on one topic through several assignments.

Moss, Beverly J. "Ethnography in Composition: Studying Language at Home." *Methods and Methodology: A Sourcebook for Composition Researchers*. Ed. Gesa Kirsch and Patricia Sullivan. Carbondale: Southern Illinois UP, 1992. 153–71.

Schmersahl, Carmen. "Teaching Literary Research: Process, Not Product." *Journal of Teaching Writing* 6 (1987): 231–38. The author provides a sequence of assignments designed to lead students through the stages of a research-based essay.

Spitzer, Michael. "Local and Global Networking: Implications for the Future." *Computers and Writing: Theory, Research, Practice*. Ed. Deborah H. Holdstein and Cynthia L. Selfe. New York: MLA, 1990. 58–70. Spitzer discusses local area networks, mainframe networking, computer conferencing, and electronic libraries. He also suggests activities to introduce students to these resources.

USEFUL WEB SITES

The Bedford Research Room

http://bedfordstmartins.com/researchroom

This site collects helpful instruction, tutorials, and links to give students resources and hands-on practice doing research and source-based writing.

Craig Branham, "A Student's Guide to Research with the WWW"

http://www.slu.edu/departments/english/research

This tutorial walks students through the steps of online research.

Stanford University, Student Research Resources: Program in Writing and Rhetoric

http://www.stanford.edu/group/pwr/students/wr_resources/research.html

You can direct your students to Stanford University's online resources for conducting research.

UCLA College Library: Thinking Critically about World Wide Web Resources

http://www.library.ucla.edu/libraries/college/help/critical

Overseen by Esther Grassian of UCLA College Library, this site lists many questions intended to help instructors and students think critically about Web resources.

Widener University, Wolfgram Memorial Library: Evaluate Web Pages

http://www3.widener.edu/Academics/Libraries/Wolfgram_Memorial_Library/Evaluate_Web_Pages/659/

This part of the Wolfgram Memorial Library site is devoted to evaluating Web resources and includes a number of useful teaching materials.

16 Evaluating Sources and Taking Notes

Every mind must make its choice between truth and repose.
It cannot have both. –Ralph Waldo Emerson

In ordinary language, we say we have received information when *what we know* has changed. The bigger the change that occurs to our knowledge base, the more information we have received. Information, like energy, does work. But whereas energy does physical work, information does logical work. While this view that increased information changes what we know is largely true, it's intellectually disastrous to accept blindly and unquestioningly our information sources. A judicious, practiced researcher learns that not everything she or he reads in journals, magazines, or scholarly books, whether online or off, is true simply because it appears in a text. The truly inquisitive researcher understands that no source is totally beyond dispute.

Additional resources on evaluating sources are available on the *The Everyday Writer*'s companion Web site, **bedfordstmartins.com/everydaywriter**. Click on **Student Writing Models** for examples of annotated bibliographies and student research papers.

FOR TEACHING: Understand Why You Should Use Sources (16a)

To help students understand what factors determine their decisions for using one source rather than another, ask them to look for biases in the sources they consult in their research areas. Is there such a thing as an unbiased source? If not, why use sources? What purpose do they serve? Challenge students to consider the merits of evaluating and selecting several authoritative sources on their topic to widen the scope of their research. By using a range of carefully chosen perspectives, students can broaden and extend the research questions and offer a new contribution to the ongoing conversation.

Books, like friends, should be few and well-chosen. —SAMUEL JOHNSON

FOR COLLABORATION: Understand Why You Should Use Sources (16a)

Ask students to work with one or two members of the class for this collaborative activity. Each group should read the following passage, in which MIT psychologist Sherry Turkle, in *Life on the Screen*, questions whether the state of flux in which we now live may be not a transitional stage but a permanent feature of our existence. Then discuss why the writer may have used each one of the sources cited. What purpose does each source serve? Bring the results of the group analysis to class for discussion.

> As we stand on the boundary between the real and the virtual, our experience recalls what anthropologist Victor Turner termed a liminal moment, a moment of passage when new cultural symbols and meanings can emerge (108). Liminal moments are times of tension, extreme reactions, and great opportunity. In our time, we are simultaneously flooded with predictions of doom and predictions of imminent utopia. We live in a crucible of contradictory experience. When Turner talked about liminality, he understood it as a transitional state—but living with flux may no longer be temporary. Donna Haraway's characterization of irony illuminates our situation: "Irony is about contradictions that do not resolve into larger wholes [. . .] about the tension of holding incompatible things together because both or all are necessary and true" (148).

FOR TEACHING: Create a Working Bibliography (16b)

Students can begin to evaluate sources even as they initially construct a list of sources that seem promising for use in their project. Ask students to record all the source information and a brief description of the writer's bias toward the topic. Many students, especially those in the sciences, will deny that the author's or researcher's perspective influences research. In science, they may claim, researchers look at phenomena objectively, without interpretive bias. However, while the bias may not be apparent in the analysis of the data, the conclusions cannot avoid some degree of bias. Conclusions result from the interpretive analysis of data.

For a striking example, see Anne Fausto-Sterling's *Myths of Gender: Biological Theories about Women and Men*. Fausto-Sterling, a biologist, demonstrates that many of the questionable distinctions between males and females that scientists have "proved" derive from their research methods and the kinds of questions they have asked. For instance, male superiority in athletic performance can be "proved" when it is measured by muscle strength rather than other criteria such as resiliency or endurance. Have students reflect on this example and attempt to notice the bias—or types of questions most interesting to the writer—for each source they consult in their research project.

Students often do not understand the amount of research they will need to do just to find sources relevant to their topic or argument and will, then, try to "fit" whatever research they do into their paper. To help them understand the value of broad research, have them create both an annotated and a "detonated" bibliography. The "detonated" bibliography notes should explain why the student will not use that source; the traditional annotated one will describe their reasons for choosing to include sources.

TEACHING WITH TECHNOLOGY: Evaluate a Source's Usefulness and Credibility (16c)

In "The Web Demands Critical Thinking by Students," Kari Boyd McBride and Ruth Dickstein remind instructors that students no longer get most materials for research writing from traditionally reputable print sources available in the library. Because the Web is awash in all kinds of undifferentiated material—some junk, some masterful—we have a special obligation to focus on critical reading, writing, and thinking. To carry out this goal, McBride and Dickstein use an exercise asking students to research a topic using several different sources—a book, an article, a reference work, a work identified through use of a CD-ROM index, and a Web site. Students then report on one of these resources, "summarizing the information it contains and evaluating the reliability of the author and the plausibility of the argument." While the authors created the exercise to help students think critically about electronic sources, they found that it had a much wider payoff: it has shown students that even encyclopedia articles can be biased and led them to look closely at a writer's sources and to ask what makes an argument authoritative and persuasive, whether in print or online. Why not develop and use a similar exercise with your students?

FOR TEACHING: Evaluate a Source's Usefulness and Credibility (16c)

Reading through sources with one's research question in mind is the ideal way of reading with focused efficiency. However, students do not always have a research question in mind when they start. If students haven't formulated one, encourage them to look through the table of contents of several sources on a general topic for a perspective or subheading for potential research subjects. Before they begin to skim through, they might ask themselves a question about the topic based on the subheadings in the table of contents.

Remind students not to underestimate the value of an index. Skimming the index can give the student a sense of the depth of information the book includes about a topic and also give students ideas for different approaches.

FOR MULTILINGUAL WRITERS: Evaluate a Source's Usefulness and Credibility (16c)

Multilingual writers unfamiliar with publishing houses or incorporated institutions in the United States can turn to their peers for help in evaluating the usefulness and credibility of sources. Specifically, students may want to exchange research logs with a writing partner in order to evaluate the publisher or sponsor of the sources in their collection. This collaboration can provide a fruitful learning experience for both parties, as hierarchies of authority vary from context to context. You can share these differences with the class to broaden the scope for research possibilities: include international and translated research materials.

FOR TEACHING: Read Critically and Interpret Sources (16d)

Ask students to read the following two passages about the War of 1812, the first from an American encyclopedia and the second from a Canadian history book. Have students read each one carefully, with a critical eye, and then answer the following interpretative questions, noting any differences in the two accounts:

1. What motivated the War Hawks?
2. Who attacked whom at the beginning of the Battle of Tippecanoe?
3. What did the War of 1812 mean in British, American, and Canadian history?
4. Why did the Treaty of Ghent end up restoring the prewar boundaries?

Then ask students to answer these questions about both passages:

1. What is the perspective, tone, and argument of each passage?
2. How does each passage make clear its point of view?
3. Can you find at least one example in each passage that seems to show how the author's point of view accounts for or affects the interpretation of events?
4. Why do you think each passage takes the view it does?
5. How would you, as a researcher, evaluate and use these sources?

Have students compare their own critical reading and interpretation with those of other students in your class, and remind them to be prepared for a full class discussion.

From the *World Book Encyclopedia*

The War of 1812

The War of 1812 was in many ways the strangest war in United States history. It could well be named the War of Faulty Communication. Two days before war was declared, the British Government had stated that it would repeal the laws which were the chief excuse for fighting. If there had been telegraphic communication with Europe, the war might well have been avoided. Speedy communication would also have prevented the greatest battle of the war, which was fought at New Orleans fifteen days after a treaty of peace had been signed.

It is strange also that the war for freedom of the seas began with the invasion of Canada, and that the treaty of peace which ended the war settled none of the issues over which it had supposedly been fought.

The chief United States complaint against the British was interference with shipping. But New England, the great shipping section of the United States, bitterly opposed the idea of going to war. The demand for war came chiefly from the West and South, although these sections were not really hurt by British naval policy.

When we add that both sides claimed victory in the War of 1812, it becomes clear that the whole struggle was a confused mass of contradictions. These must be explained and cleared up before we can understand why the democratic United States sided with Napoleon I, the French dictator, in a struggle for world power. . . .

The War Hawks. A group of young men known as "War Hawks" dominated Congress during this period. Henry Clay of Kentucky and John C. Calhoun of South Carolina were the outstanding leaders of the group. Clay was then Speaker of the House of Representatives. Like Clay and Calhoun, most of the War Hawks came from western and southern states, where many of the people were in favor of going to war with Great Britain.

The people of New England generally opposed going to war, because war with Great Britain would wipe out entirely the New England shipping trade which had already been heavily damaged. Another reason New England opposed war was because many New Englanders sympathized with Great Britain in its struggle against the dictator Napoleon.

Many historians believe that a leading motive of the War Hawks was a desire for expansion. The people of the Northwest were meeting armed resistance in their attempt to take more land from the Indians, and they believed that the Indians had considerable British support. An American army was attacked by Indians at the Battle of Tippecanoe in the Wabash Valley in November, 1811, and British guns were found on the battlefield. The Westerners, therefore, were anxious to drive the British out of Canada. Southerners looked longingly at Florida, which belonged to Great Britain's ally, Spain. The South had also suffered a serious loss of markets. But the deciding motive for war seems to have been a strong desire for more territory.

Progress of the War

Declaration of War. On June 1, 1812, President Madison asked Congress to declare war against Great Britain. He gave as his reasons the impressment of United States seamen and the interference with United States trade. He charged also that the British had stirred up Indian warfare in the Northwest. Congress declared war on June 18, 1812. Two days earlier, the British Foreign Minister had announced that the Orders in Council would be repealed, but word of this announcement did not reach America until after the war had begun.

Because President Madison asked for the declaration of war, many Federalists blamed him for the conflict, calling it "Mr. Madison's war." But it was more the War Hawks' war than it was Madison's. . . .

Treaty of Ghent. The British public was tired of war and especially of war taxes. The British Government therefore proposed discussing terms. Commissioners of the two countries met at Ghent, Belgium, in August, 1814.

The British at first insisted that the United States should give up certain territory on the northern frontier, and set up a large permanent Indian reservation in the Northwest. But American victories in the summer and fall of 1814 led the British to drop these demands. A treaty was finally signed on December 24, 1814, in Ghent, Belgium. By its terms, all land which had been captured by either party was to be given up. Everything was to be exactly as it was before the war, and commissions from both of the countries were to settle any disputed points about boundaries. Nothing whatever was said in the treaty about impressments, blockades, or the British Orders in Council, which supposedly had caused the war. The treaty was formally ratified on February 17, 1815.

Results of the War

One important result of the War of 1812 was the rapid rise of manufacturing in the United States. During the war, United States citizens were unable to import goods from Great Britain, and had to begin making many articles for themselves. The war also increased national patriotism, and helped to unite the United States into one nation.

The war settled none of the issues over which the United States had fought. But most of these issues faded out during the following years. In the long period of peace after 1815, the British had no occasion to make use of impressments or blockades. Indian troubles in the Northwest were practically ended by the death of the chief Tecumseh and by the British surrender of Detroit and other posts. The United States occupied part of Florida during the war, and was soon able to buy the rest of it from Spain.

One indirect result of the War of 1812 was the later election to the Presidency of Andrew Jackson and of William Henry Harrison. Both of these men won military fame which had much to do with their elections. Another indirect result was the decline of Federalist power. New England leaders, most of them Federalists, met secretly in Hartford, Conn., to study amendments to the Constitution. Their opponents charged that they had plotted treason, and the Federalists never recovered. . . .

Chief Battles of the War

The War of 1812 was not an all-out struggle on either side. For the British, the war was just an annoying part of their struggle with Napoleon. For many

Americans, it was an unjustified attempt to gratify the expansionist ambitions of the South and West.

From *Canada: A Story of Challenge*

Danger on the Western Border

From the Treaty of Versailles in 1783 until the outbreak of a second war with the United States in 1812, the western border of young Canada was never secure. Trouble arose in the lands south of the Great Lakes; in the Ohio country which had been officially granted to the United States in 1783, but which had remained tied to the St Lawrence fur trade. The final consequence was open war. The trouble began almost with the signing of peace in 1783, when Britain quickly came to regret the ready surrender of so much of the West, and sought at least to delay its transfer to the United States.

The chief reasons for delay arose from the fur traders and the Indians who were still the masters of the unsettled Ohio West. The Canadian fur merchants of the St Lawrence drew most of their trade from that country, and they asked that the transfer be postponed for two years until they could adjust their business to this heavy loss. The Indians supplied the major reason, however. They declared that they had been ignored in the Treaty of Versailles and that Britain had handed over their lands, which they had never ceded, to the United States. There was danger that if the West was transferred and opened to American settlement the Indians would, in revenge, attack the thinly held and almost unprotected British settlements in Upper Canada.

Taking advantage of vague wording in the peace treaty, therefore, the British held on to the military and trading posts in the West below the Lakes, giving as their reason the failure of the Americans to carry out the term of the treaty that called for the restoration of Loyalist property. It was a sound reason, but not the chief one for failing to transfer the West.

This situation dragged on into the 1790's, while the Americans feared that the British were arousing the Indians against them, and the British feared that the Indians would become aroused. Dorchester, as governor, darkly expected a new war with the United States, and had some hope of building an Indian state in the Ohio country that would stand between the Americans and the Upper Canadian frontier and help to protect the latter. The Americans, meanwhile, were pressing forward from the region south of the Ohio, and sending forces against the Indians in order to break their hold on the western country. In 1794 one of these expeditions completely defeated the tribes at the battle of Fallen Timbers, and hope of an Indian "buffer state" collapsed. The tribes ceded their lands to the United States. . . .

The rapidly advancing western states of the American union made good use of the growing warlike spirit in the republic. They held that the place to punish Britain was in Canada. Filled with the forceful confidence and expansive drive of the frontier they wanted to add Canada to the American union: a Canada which American frontier settlement had already invaded. Was not Upper Canada by now practically an American state? The "war hawks" of the American West clamoured for an easy conquest. Their chance seemed to arrive in 1811.

In that year the western Indians, being steadily pushed back by advancing American settlement, attempted a last stand. Led by the chief Tecumseh, they formed a league to resist further inroads. The Americans saw this as the threat of a new Pontiac uprising, of savage Indian raids on the frontier. They attacked the Indians, and by their victory at the battle of Tippecanoe, destroyed Tecumseh's league. Yet the American West was not satisfied. It was fully convinced that the British had been behind the Indians, although the Canadian government had actually sought to keep the Indian league at peace. It seemed that the West would only be safe when the British had been driven out of Canada. The war hawks cried for blood, the American frontier wanted new lands to conquer, and the American East was newly aroused by fresh skirmishes over the right of search. The United States declared war in June, 1812, and set out to capture Canada.

The Second Struggle with the Americans

The War of 1812 in British history is only a side-show, not altogether successful, during the huge and victorious contest with Napoleon. In United States history it is a second war of independence, chiefly against the weight of British sea-power. In Canadian history it is above all a land war, a second struggle against American invasion. All these pictures are partly true; and in studying the Canadian version one must bear in mind that it portrays only the War of 1812 as it affected Canada. Yet for Canada the war was vitally important; far more important than it was for Britain, and much more dangerous than it was for the United States. . . .

Thus the war ended late in 1814 in a stalemate, which was probably a good thing for future peace.

It was not completely a stalemate. Britain still held the West and some of the Maine coast, and the British naval blockade was strangling American commerce. But in the peace negotiations the Americans made clear their readiness to go on fighting rather than yield territory. Faced with a revival of Napoleon's power in Europe at that very moment, Britain did not press the point. As a result the Treaty of Ghent of 1814 simply stopped the fighting, restored the pre-war boundaries, and said little about the problems that had caused the conflict.

Nevertheless in the next few years many of these problems disappeared. The question of the right of search ended with the Napoleonic Wars, and vanished in the long years of peace after 1815. The Indian problem declined as American settlement filled in the old West; the tribes had been too weakened by the war to offer any further resistance. The American war-hawks had found Canada no willing mouthful, and the United States was turning away to expand in a new direction, towards the south. . . .

The War of 1812 thus tended to bring British North America together and strengthened the bond with Britain. Any common feelings among the colonists, however, were largely directed against the United States. This anti-American spirit was still a narrow basis on which to build a Canadian nationalism. Anti-Americanism was particularly evident in Upper Canada. Further American settlement was largely prevented there, and American settlers already in the province were in danger of persecution—the Loyalists' case in reverse—if their declarations of British sentiments were not loud enough. Nevertheless, on the whole these reactions to the strain of the War of 1812 were understandable; and not an extreme price to pay for the survival of British North America.

–J. M. S. Careless

FOR COLLABORATION: Synthesize Sources (16e)

Ask students to work in small groups and share their responses to the preceding passages about the War of 1812. Then have students synthesize the data and arguments presented by the readings. When students are satisfied that they have captured the main point of each passage, ask them to reflect on their syntheses, drawing out implications and points for discussion. Finally, ask them to work together to develop an interpretation of these sources that all members of the group can agree on. Have them present this synthesis to the class.

FOR TEACHING: Synthesize Sources (16e)

To teach students how to begin synthesizing their material, ask them to keep a record of the main points that emerge from their research about their topic. Under each point, have them make two columns: "similar/ agree" and "contrast/disagree." A brief note with the similar or contrasting perspectives and the respective source for each one will allow them to start seeing the bigger picture of how their sources engage one another.

ATTENDING TO DISABILITIES: Synthesize Sources (16e)

As your students move from finding and critically reading sources to the important work of synthesizing sources, make sure that you as an instructor are facilitating the best possible research experience for all students. To do so, keep in mind the following guidelines from Brenda Jo Brueggemann, associate professor of English and coordinator of Ohio State University's American Sign Language Program and Interdisciplinary Disability Studies Minor:

- Provide opportunities to review students' research in individual conferences.
- Encourage multimodal approaches to the research process in topic development, organization, source collection, and the like. (These should be approaches that involve alternatives to reading- and writing-intensive activities, such as spatial, kinesthetic, and tactile approaches to the subject.)
- Engage students in class discussions about time on task and knowing the extent of the subject to be covered.
- Offer in-class opportunities for, and discussions about, prewriting, arrangement, and organization techniques in writing.

Ohio State University's Fast Facts for Faculty Web site, http://ada.osu .edu/resources/fastfacts/index.htm, gives more examples of multiple types of writing, outlines common problems students have with them, and suggests the best writing practices to help students of varying abilities.

> **An educated person is one who has learned that information almost always turns out to be at best incomplete and very often false, misleading, fictitious, mendacious—just dead wrong.**
> —RUSSELL BAKER

GAME PLAN: Synthesize Sources (16e)

The Game Plan to Synthesize Sources delineates the many steps involved in one of the most difficult, but important, skills students must learn. By asking students to begin with identifying good sources, you immediately demonstrate the necessity of research and how to evaluate sources, from the relevance of the source to its validity. Use the questions in this part of the game plan to review how to evaluate sources.

This game plan asks students to move beyond a simple summary and engage in a dialogue with the source as well as put the sources in dialogue with each other. Remind students that this stage of synthesis is often the messiest and they can approach it in several ways. They can write down several points from each source in separate columns and draw lines to see where and how the points relate to one another; they can summarize the main points from each source and write a brief, personal response as a way to clarify their own perspectives; or they can write down their topic and the points of the sources and, through clustering or webbing, make connections. Encourage students to use the patterns that begin to emerge as a foundation for another way of thinking through the topic. The patterns also might provide a structure for organizing their thoughts and their papers.

Finally, when students are organizing their research, ask them to consider carefully the questions about the uses of the sources in relationship to their thesis. Remind them that the right balance of source material to their own writing is crucial in establishing their credibility. This step is also an opportunity to evaluate sources even more critically as students articulate the necessity of each source, thus emphasizing the recursive nature of writing.

FOR TEACHING: Take Notes and Annotate Sources (16f)

Suggest to students that they use the following process when photocopying or downloading research materials:

1. Photocopy or download only the most important material, after reading and selecting it.

2. Highlight essential passages.
3. Quote, paraphrase, or summarize those passages on note cards.
4. Write a brief comment or response to the material to help you remember how you might want to use it.
5. Remember to ask permission to use material found on the Internet.

TEACHING WITH TECHNOLOGY: Take Notes and Annotate Sources (16f)

Students can save precious time during the research process by taking notes and composing annotations right on a computer. Remind students to list the complete information for each source and to provide quotations in full. Have them follow the guidelines in 16f of *The Everyday Writer*.

Moreover, some students now download full-text files to their computers and burn a CD-ROM of works cited to turn in with their final research papers. Suggest to students that they apply a critical eye to sources before downloading to avoid having to delete unnecessary files later on. Evaluating sources while engaging them with technology will allow for students' research agendas to evolve as they read and assimilate source materials.

TEACHING WITH TECHNOLOGY: Quoting (16f)

The cut-and-paste operation of any word-processing program can be extremely helpful in taking down quotations from a source. However, with this ease comes great danger of plagiarism. Make sure that you remind students to follow the example of David Craig, whose research is shown in Chapters 14, 16, and 18, in attributing the full source and page number for any quotation. Students might also take a moment to describe the context for the quotation and indicate how—and where—they hope to use the quotation in their final paper.

FOR TEACHING: Paraphrasing (16f)

Paraphrasing is a skill that has twofold value. It helps us communicate, but it also helps us do something else that isn't always readily apparent to students: it helps us in our learning. Because a paraphrase requires us to put someone else's meaning into our own words, we have to understand the meaning of the original. If we have trouble with the paraphrase, our difficulty likely indicates that we don't have an adequate grasp of the original passage. The measure of how well we understand what we've read is the paraphrase (or the summary). In expressing our understanding we are involved in a process of learning.

For this reason, the importance of paraphrasing cannot be overestimated. As students take paraphrase notes in their research logs, make sure to point out the following to students:

1. Often a paraphrase may seem to make sense to the writer, but it may not to a reader because of the writer's familiarity with the original passage and because the paraphrase is in his or her choice of language.
2. There are at least two purposes of paraphrasing, one to help the writer understand, and another to present the information to another person to understand.
3. Much research involves paraphrasing or explaining ideas in the researcher's own words.
4. Having others respond to their writing helps writers learn how to judge and use language for audiences that are different in their levels of understanding and expertise with a subject.
5. The paraphraser is in some ways always in danger of misrepresenting another, or of satirizing or even parodying another, by taking meanings out of context. Thus, like summaries and quotations, paraphrases should be used with care.

FOR COLLABORATION: Paraphrasing (16f)

Whenever students paraphrase, have them compare versions and explain similarities and differences. Collaborating on a second version will help them appreciate not simply where their troubles lie but also the learning effectiveness of collaboratively talking out, working out, and writing out material they are studying.

For additional practice with paraphrasing, divide the class into groups of six, and present them with these instructions: choose for paraphrasing a short passage of about one hundred words from a text, an essay, or an article. Each member of the group should first individually restate the original passage in his or her own words. Keep in mind that the paraphrase requires a writer to include all major and supporting details. Once they have produced their paraphrases, have them break into three groups of two, and, working together, cowrite a paraphrase of the original excerpt. Then they should discuss the similarities or differences among the three versions. Ask students to try to explain them, especially the differences, focusing on the following guiding questions:

1. Working in pairs, did you disagree over terms and their meaning in the original passage?
2. Was it easy to agree on synonyms or on paraphrases of ideas and concepts?
3. Did you agree on the information to include? to leave out?
4. How similar are the three coauthored versions? Why, or why not?
5. What does trying to agree on a paraphrase tell you about how different people read and interpret a passage? about how they choose to rephrase it?

FOR COLLABORATION: Summarizing (16f)

Have students read a short article and come to class with the main points they would include in a summary. Appoint a student to record everyone's points on the board, marking when a point is noted more than once. Then have students comment on whether they agree with what emerges as the main points and whether some of the points aren't as important to a summary as they may have initially thought.

USEFUL READINGS

Brown, M. Neil, and Stuart M. Keeley. *English on the Internet: Evaluating Online Resources*. Upper Saddle River: Prentice, 2001. A detailed and comprehensive guide to finding and evaluating online resources for writing projects.

Carbone, Nick. *Writing Online: A Student's Guide to the Internet and World Wide Web*. 3rd ed. Boston: Houghton, 2000. This useful and clearly written guide can help students get started writing and conducting research online.

Fausto-Sterling, Anne. *Myths of Gender: Biological Theories about Women and Men*. New York: Basic, 1987.

Goodwin, Doris Kearns. "How I Caused That Story." *Time* 4 Feb. 2002: 69 <http://www.time.com/time/nation/article/0,8599,197614,00.html>. Goodwin explains how her citations from Lynne McTaggart's book ended up in her publication, *The Fitzgeralds and the Kennedys*, despite her meticulous note-taking techniques: "Though my footnotes repeatedly cited Ms. McTaggart's work, I failed to provide quotation marks for phrases that I had taken verbatim, having assumed that these phrases, drawn from my notes, were my words, not hers." Once her son showed her the footnote function in her word-processing program, she began indicating sources as she inserted notes in her draft—which is an excellent strategy to share with your students.

Harris, Robert A. *Using Sources Effectively: Strengthening Your Writing and Avoiding Plagiarism*. Los Angeles: Pyrczak, 2002. A slim guide of ninety-eight pages, this text helps students confront two key writing issues: unintentional plagiarism and ineffective use of source material.

McBride, Kari Boyd, and Ruth Dickstein. "The Web Demands Critical Thinking by Students." *Chronicle of Higher Education* 20 Mar. 1996: B6.

USEFUL WEB SITES

Cornell University Library: Critically Analyzing Information Sources

http://www.library.cornell.edu/okuref/research/skill26.htm

Among the critical reading guides available online, this Web page published by Cornell University Library provides a useful set of guidelines to follow in evaluating sources. The page's primary focus concerns assessment of a source's credentials and validity.

Dartmouth College: Sources—Their Use and Acknowledgment

http://www.dartmouth.edu/~sources

This comprehensive online guide to using sources walks students through every step of the process, from a discussion of reasons to acknowledge sources to five ways to cite sources to an extensive list of FAQs.

UCLA College Library: Thinking Critically about World Wide Web Resources

http://www.library.ucla.edu/libraries/college/help/critical

Overseen by Esther Grassian of UCLA College Library, this site lists several questions intended to help instructors and students think critically about Web resources.

Widener University, Wolfgram Memorial Library: Evaluate Web Pages

http://www3.widener.edu/Academics/Libraries/Wolfgram_Memorial_Library/Evaluate_Web_Pages/659

This part of the Wolfgram Memorial Library site is devoted to evaluating Web resources and includes several useful teaching materials.

17 Integrating Sources and Avoiding Plagiarism

By necessity, by proclivity, and by delight, we all quote.
—Ralph Waldo Emerson

The process of integrating sources into your writing can be similar to hosting a conversation at a stimulating dinner party. As the dialogue unfolds, various participants have the chance to contribute. But the writer remains the moderator, orchestrating the ebb and flow of conversation. Deciding how and when a source should enter this dialogue is a skill developed best through practice, observation of successful models, and attention to rhetorical purpose. Invite your students to begin the conversation, and look to this chapter for advice on how best to guide them through this process.

While teaching integration of sources, do not discount the importance of helpful examples. Stuart Swirsky, in a review of Candace Spigelman's *Across Property Lines: Textual Ownership in Writing Groups*, stresses the way in which models can lead students toward mastery of complex writing processes such as integrating sources:

> As any writing instructor well knows, a co-requisite to becoming a competent writer is to engage in a tremendous amount of careful and critical reading. Perhaps more than anything else, what students really need is more models for writing, models that are readily available in texts. Getting students to do more reading may be as important as getting them to open up to more collaboration in the classroom.

ATTENDING TO DISABILITIES: Integrating Sources

Remember that your college or university disability resource center has a wealth of technological aids to help students work on integrating sources. Consider some of the following techniques:

- *Scanners*: Entire books can be scanned into a computer using a high-speed scanner, converted to computer-readable text with OCR software, then printed out in Braille or read aloud via a text-to-speech screen reader.

- *Integrating visuals*: Diagrams and line drawings can be printed as raised images on special paper, allowing a visually impaired person to "feel" the drawing.
- *Viewing sources*: Video magnifiers can enlarge text and pictures for those with visual impairments.
- *Auditory services*: Specialized tape recorders read books on tape and FM listening devices offer help for students with hearing impairments or attention difficulties.

FOR COLLABORATION: Decide Whether to Quote, Paraphrase, or Summarize (17a)

Ask students working in pairs to select an article from a major journal in a field of interest to them. Have them identify each occurrence of paraphrase, summary, or quotation and the function that each serves. These functions may be to:

- provide background information.
- define terms.
- provide a position for rebuttal.
- explain quoted material.
- illustrate a point.
- show disagreements among sources.
- cite authorities and, hence, to reinforce claims, statements, or credibility.
- state a point more precisely, powerfully, or accurately than with a paraphrased version.
- challenge, resist, or even parody the source.

Once two students have identified the functions, have them exchange their article with another pair. Have them repeat the exercise and then compare versions and findings.

FOR COLLABORATION: Incorporate Quotations, Paraphrases, and Summaries (17b)

Ask students to bring in five pages of the rough draft of a research essay in progress, making sure to choose pages that include quotations, paraphrases, and summaries, and having underlined or highlighted all signal verbs and phrases. Then ask them to work in pairs to examine their use of these verbs and phrases. Can they explain why each signal verb or phrase was chosen and what rhetorical effect it has?

FOR TEACHING: Incorporating Quotations (17b)

Quoting is ordinarily taught as a way to let the quoted person "speak for herself." But to what degree is that actually possible? Consider sharing with your students the perspective of Kay Halasek who, in *A Pedagogy of Possibility*, builds on the work of Bakhtin and Volosinov to question traditional ways of teaching quoting as if this practice were ideologically or politically neutral. When we quote, after all, we take another's words out of context, putting them into contiguous relationship with our own words.

In addition, when we teach use of quotations as a way to build authority, we implicitly teach students to defer to the authority's quoted words. Halasek wisely suggests that we alert our students to these often invisible aspects of quoting and to show them at least some of the ways in which quotations can be used not to defer to an authority but to resist or even parody that supposed authority.

To check that students understand why they are using specific quotes, have them follow each excerpt in their text with an explanation of its significance.

FOR TEACHING: Incorporating Paraphrases and Summaries (17b)

Like the paraphrase, the summary is a useful learning and communicating skill. Writing summaries gives students practice identifying and coordinating the main points of a passage. Students don't have to write summaries using their own words, but if they do, if they rephrase the main points of an original passage, they will better understand what they are reading. This practice of rephrasing summarized (and paraphrased) information will also help them work source material into their research projects more easily. For this reason, discourage your students from simply pulling out phrases, sentences, or chunks of the original, and then merely stringing them together.

TEACHING WITH TECHNOLOGY: Integrate Visuals Effectively (17c)

When teaching students to select and integrate visuals into their writing, be sure to discuss issues of copyright and permissions. Students should carefully note the source of the image. The use of visuals in students' papers is generally considered fair use, but like any source, visuals must be cited in the text. If students intend to post to an unprotected Web site any work that includes visuals from another source, they must seek permission from the rights holder.

FOR TEACHING: Check for Excessive Use of Source Material (17d)

Recall the conversation analogy introduced at the beginning of this chapter. Have students review their drafts and ask themselves: "Am I still the moderator of this conversation? Is my voice clear, compelling, and original? Do I allow my own argument to emerge as foremost in this piece?" Note that this last question may be difficult for multilingual writers familiar with different kinds of writing conventions. They may feel that emphasizing their own voice is rude or arrogant, or they may feel that they do not have the authority to advance their views. Challenge them to see the emphasis of their own argument as a strategy of ethos, one of the most effective ways for persuading an audience. Indeed, writing instruction aims to build confidence and thereby to develop a compelling and informed voice that can contribute in important ways to the public sphere. As Bill Beattie observes:

> The aim of education should be to teach us rather how to think, than what to think—rather to improve our minds, so as to enable us to think for ourselves, than to load the memory with thoughts of other men.

Have students use three different colored highlighters: one for the signal phrase or verb, one for the quote itself, and one for the explanation of the quote. Students should be able to scan their paper to determine if they have an abundance of quotes in relationship their own writing.

> Enough! Or too much? —William Blake

FOR TEACHING: Understand Why You Should Acknowledge Your Sources (17e)

You might explain the way in which the demand for originality in writing impelled an ideology of ownership. Peter W. Morgan and Glenn M. Reynolds tell us that it was not until the romantic era that the creation of new material became culturally paramount. In classical times, imitation was not a crime:

> The term "plagiarism" came from the word *plagiarius*, which literally meant "kidnapper." It was first used by the poet Martial regarding someone who had "kidnapped" some of his poems by copying them whole and circulating them under the copier's name. But while copying so as to take credit for another's work was wrong, use of another's work to create something of one's own was not. The goal was to take an idea that someone else might have had first, but to improve on it, or its execution. (par. 13)

Help your students see the proper acknowledgment of sources as a professional, economic, and scholarly responsibility—one that respects the livelihoods of other writers—so that they can begin to understand why they need to be vigilant and extremely careful in their note-taking and writing processes.

FOR TEACHING: Know Which Sources to Acknowledge (17f)

Have students work in peer-review groups to read one another's drafts for any passages that stand out as unfamiliar and mark them with a highlighter. Often students can help point out to their peers what knowledge is most probably not readily available to them without the help of sources. Peer reviewers can also point out material that is common knowledge and doesn't need to be cited.

> Immature poets imitate; mature poets steal. —T. S. Eliot

On Avoiding Plagiarism (17g)

Rebecca Moore Howard, director of the writing program at Syracuse University, challenges us as teachers to rethink our pedagogical approach to teaching proper use of sources:

> In our stampede to fight what *The New York Times* calls a "plague" of plagiarism, we risk becoming the enemies rather than the mentors of our students; we are replacing the student-teacher relationship with the criminal-police relationship. Further, by thinking of plagiarism as a unitary act rather than a collection of disparate activities, we risk categorizing all of our students as criminals. Worst of all, we risk not recognizing that our own pedagogy needs reform. ("Forget" par. 7)

Her insights are valuable ones; students often don't understand the nuances and complexities of proper citation. As Howard explains, "Encouraged by digital dualisms, we forget that plagiarism means many different things: downloading a term paper, failing to give proper credit to the source of an idea, copying extensive passages without attribution, inserting someone else's phrases or sentences—perhaps with small changes—into your own prose, and forgetting to supply a set of quotation marks" ("Forget" par. 11). Howard suggests that instead of relying on Web sites such as Turnitin.com or Plagiarism.org, we should develop more interesting and challenging assignments, foster increased dialogue on student drafts, and offer ourselves as an authentically engaged audience for student writing.

Nick Carbone provides a lengthy and insightful discussion of pedagogical approaches to possible plagiarism in his online column, "Technology and Teaching," on the Bedford/St. Martin's TechNotes Web site:

> Turnitin.com was originally founded by John Barrie—a neurobiology graduate student—as Plagiarism.org, which still exists as a marketing arm of Turnitin.com.
>
> . . . It assumes the worst about students and the worst about teachers. It assumes students have no honor and need always to be watched and followed electronically, a big brother welcome to academic traditions. It assumes teachers are too beleaguered and inept to design classroom assignments and practices that teach students how to write responsibly. Much of what Turnitin.com proposes to detect can be avoided by careful assignment planning and teaching. . . , by paying better attention early on to students and the work they do. (pars. 5 and 15)

Your manuscript is both good and original. But the part that is good is not original, and the part that is original is not good. —Samuel Johnson

FOR TEACHING: Uphold Your Academic Integrity, and Avoid Plagiarism (17g)

As you prepare to discuss with students the important topic of academic integrity and plagiarism, consider for a moment how you will approach the subject and present it to your students.

In a lecture called "Why Is Plagiarism Wrong?" given at DePauw University on November 11, 1987, Barry M. Kroll outlined the five different approaches instructors take to discourage plagiarism. The most traditional—and apparently least effective—approach involves *prohibitions*. The instructor simply tells students, typically in moralistic terms, that plagiarism is wrong. Kroll warns us, "Virtually all college students already 'know' that plagiarism is a prohibited act. But despite that knowledge, a significant number of students do not appear to take the prohibition seriously enough to be dissuaded from plagiarizing in their college papers."

The second approach involves *prevention*, an attempt to make it difficult to plagiarize. Some strategies of this approach include assigning different textbooks and paper topics from term to term and not using books for which *Cliffs Notes* exist. Unfortunately, this approach does little to teach students not to plagiarize.

Some instructors and institutions try to deter students from plagiarizing by establishing *penalties* for those caught plagiarizing. This approach gains effectiveness when supported by the institution. However, it turns instructors into police, and most instructors dislike such a role, because it tends to undermine instructor–student rapport. More recent software, such as that available at Turnitin.com, similarly constructs a policing role for the writing instructor and breaks down the trust necessary for learning. It's much more effective to discuss the rationale for acknowledging sources, give students the benefit of the doubt, and provide excellent models for them to examine.

However, some instructors and institutions reject the notion that without penalties cheating would increase. Their remedy for plagiarism is to provide students with *practice* in using source material. This perspective assumes that most plagiarism is caused by unfamiliarity with the conventions of citation, sloppiness and neglect, and insufficient practice in citing sources. Unfortunately, we have ample evidence that students often do plagiarize intentionally.

The fifth approach to plagiarism—and the one that Kroll recommends—consists of teaching the *principles* behind society's attitudes toward plagiarism. In a separate study of how first-year students actually view plagiarism, Kroll discovered that they understood what it was and took it seriously, and that they could explain the wrongness of plagiarism with reference to three principles: fairness to authors; responsibility to one's education; and ownership of ideas. The latter two principles, Kroll argues, are inadequate, and the first incomplete. Kroll found no reference by students to the idea that plagiarism is wrong because it is deception. Yet, Kroll recommends that principle as being the best argument against plagiarism. Such deception is morally unacceptable and is detrimental to the institution, to the community, and to the character of the individual. Moreover, this principle is the basis for the other approaches: "For unless our students understand the reasons that plagiarism is wrong and destructive, they are likely to see our prohibitions as outmoded, to see the practices of careful documentation as merely tedious exercises, and to see the penalties for plagiarism as irrationally punitive." In the final analysis, plagiarism can be both personally and rhetorically devastating. Whatever the personal consequences, plagiarism inevitably undermines the writer's ethos. The writer who plagiarizes loses all authority, and thus persuasion becomes impossible.

In "Plagiarisms, Authorships, and the Academic Death Penalty," Rebecca Moore Howard raises a number of additional issues that, as instructors of writing, we should consider, such as examining our own assumptions and preconceptions about the ownership of texts and ideas as preparation for discussing these issues with students.

Education's purpose is to replace an empty mind with an open one. –Malcolm S. Forbes

USEFUL READINGS

Barks, Debbie, and Patricia Watts. "Textual Borrowing Strategies for Graduate Level ESL Writers." *Linking Literacies: Perspectives on L2 Reading/Writing Connections*. Ed. Diane Belcher and Alan Hirvela. Ann Arbor: U of Michigan P, 2001. The authors present three ideas for teaching "textual borrowing strategies to ESL students at the graduate level": classroom discussion, modeling of practices, and ethnographic approaches.

Bloch, Joel. "Plagiarism and the ESL Student: From Printed to Electronic Texts." *Linking Literacies: Perspectives on L2 Reading/Writing Connections*. Ed. Diane Belcher and Alan Hirvela. Ann Arbor: U of Michigan P, 2001. Bloch's article examines different cultural norms concerning citation and explores the significance that new technologies have on writing processes in what he calls "less-developed" countries.

Carbone, Nick. "Turnitin.com, a Pedagogic Placebo for Plagiarism." *Bedford/St. Martin's TechNotes: Technology & Teaching*. 5 June 2001 <http://bedfordstmartins.com/technotes/techtiparchive/ttip060501.htm>. Carbone criticizes the methodology of new software technologies as "the wrong way to teach students about plagiarism, copyright, and intellectual property."

DeSena, Laura Hennessey. *Preventing Plagiarism: Tips and Techniques*. Urbana: NCTE, 2007. This brief, practical guide emphasizes the importance of creating assignments that foster original thinking and helps to prevent the opportunities and students' perceived needs to plagiarize. DeSena offers a variety of tips drawn from her own classroom experience.

Goodwin, Doris Kearns. "How I Caused That Story." *Time* 4 Feb. 2002: 69 <http://www.time.com/time/nation/article/0,8599,197614,00.html>. Goodwin explains how she unintentionally plagiarized one of her sources; her new technological approach to note taking offers a concrete strategy you can share with your students.

Hafner, Katie. "Lessons in the School of Cut and Paste." *New York Times* 28 June 2001: E1. Hafner describes the usual signs that a student has lifted a paper off the Web and explains how teachers are now instructing students in the consequences of using the Web to unethical ends.

Halasek, Kay. *A Pedagogy of Possibility*. Carbondale: Southern Illinois UP, 1999.

Harris, Robert. *The Plagiarism Handbook: Strategies for Preventing, Detecting, and Dealing with Plagiarism*. Los Angeles: Pyrczak, 2001. With a positive approach to teaching students about academic honesty and appropriate use of sources, Harris emphasizes empathy with students' perspectives and gives concrete strategies for holding productive conversations about this difficult issue.

Howard, Rebecca Moore. "Forget about Policing Plagiarism. Just *Teach*." *Chronicle of Higher Education* 16 Nov. 2001: B24 <http://chronicle.com/weekly

/v48/i12/12b02401.htm>. Howard asserts that new policing technologies such as Turnitin.com are indicative of our "mass hysteria" regarding plagiarism. She advocates instead pedagogical reform in terms of better assignments, an authentic audience, and real dialogue about the writing process.

———. "Plagiarisms, Authorships, and the Academic Death Penalty." *CE* 57 (1995): 788–806. Howard argues that plagiarism is widely misunderstood and, as a result, mistaught. Teachers of writing need to acknowledge the extent to which all writers rely on the work of others, and to teach what Howard calls "patchwriting" as a practice students can use as they learn to weave sources (fully credited) into their own texts. It is a thought-provoking review of an issue of ongoing concern to writing instructors.

Kennedy, Mary Lynch. "The Composing Process of College Students Writing from Sources." *Written Communication* 2 (1985): 434–56. Based on a protocol analysis of six students writing from sources, Kennedy argues that fluent readers read the sources "with pencil-in-hand," doing more planning, rereading, and note taking prior to writing than the less-able readers.

Kroll, Barry M. "How College Freshmen View Plagiarism." *Written Communication* 5 (1988): 203–21. Kroll describes the results of a study in which 150 first-year college students wrote their explanations of why plagiarism is wrong, rated five standard explanations, and responded to statements about the seriousness and possible consequences of plagiarism.

Levinson, Arlene. "Paper Chase." *Portland Press Herald* 3 Sept. 2001: 2A. Levinson looks at the seedy underbelly of term-paper supply companies on the Internet.

Martin, Brian. "Plagiarism: A Misplaced Emphasis." *Journal of Information Ethics* 3.2 (Fall 1994): 36–47. Martin examines what he calls "the vast amount of institutionalized plagiarism," such as ghostwriting and non-attribution of authorship, and argues for reducing the stigma of plagiarism in academic contexts.

Masur, Kate. "Papers, Profits, and Pedagogy: Plagiarism in the Age of the Internet." *Perspectives Online* 39.5 (May 2001) <http://www.historians.org/perspectives/issues/2001/0105/0105news3.cfm>. Masur offers an overview of how students access online Web databases to plagiarize papers.

McNenny, Geraldine, and Duane H. Roen. "Collaboration or Plagiarism—Cheating Is in the Eye of the Beholder." *Dialogue: A Journal for Writing Specialists* 1 (Fall 1993): 6–27.

Morgan, Peter W., and Glenn H. Reynolds. "A Plague of Originality." *Idler* 23 (Jan. 2002) <http://www.the-idler.com/IDLER- 02/1-23.html>. This electronic version of Chapter 5 of *The Appearance of Impropriety* begins with the ironic observation that the University of Oregon's teaching assistant handbook plagiarized Stanford University's section on plagiarism.

The article then provides an eye-opening history of plagiarism and offers a compelling case for considering the ethics of the practice.

Scanlon, Patrick M., and David R. Neumann. "Internet Plagiarism among College Students." *Journal of College Student Development* 43.3 (May–June 2002): 374–85. Professors from the Rochester Institute of Technology have found that students do not plagiarize from the Internet as much as we might think: out of 698 students, only a minority reported cutting and pasting material without citations. More interesting is their finding that, statistically speaking, the numbers remain the same for print-based theft as for Web site theft.

Sherrard, Carol. "Summary Writing: A Topographical Study." *Written Communication* 3 (1986): 324– 43. In studying paragraph-length summaries written by university students, Sherrard found that most of the summaries were "remarkably mechanical." Summary strategies most favored included omitting text sentences, mapping existing sentences into summary sentences, and combining only those sentences that were next to each other.

Swirsky, Stuart. Rev. of *Across Property Lines: Textual Ownership in Writing Groups*, by Candace Spigelman. *CCC Online* 52.4 (June 2001): 662–66.

USEFUL WEB SITES

Antiplagiarism Strategies for Research Papers

http://www.virtualsalt.com/antiplag.htm

Drawn from his book The Plagiarism Handbook, *this site by Robert Harris delineates strategies of awareness, detection, and prevention.*

Online Writing Lab: Starting Points for Internet Research

http://owl.english.purdue.edu/internet/tools/research.html

This online writing lab page provides an excellent list of Web-based primary source documents organized by discipline and is prefaced with a brief guide to Internet research strategies.

Plagiarism and the Web

http://www.wiu.edu/users/mfbhl/wiu/plagiarism.htm

Bruce Leland lists several commercial Web sites from which students can procure papers and offers concrete strategies for teachers to use in order to confront would-be "borrowers" and so avoid plagiarism.

Plagiarism.org

http://plagiarism.org

This subscription-based service allows you to submit student papers for scrutiny and to get reports on whether the work was plagiarized. Feedback can include directions to the site on the Web from which the paper was obtained and charts analyzing how much of a paper was plagiarized.

TechNotes: Thinking and Talking about Plagiarism

http://bedfordstmartins.com/technotes/techtiparchive/ttip102401.htm

An excellent discussion of alternative approaches to teaching students about plagiarism (rather than policing them), Nick Carbone's page offers excerpts from his own syllabi as well as an invaluable list of links.

Tools for Teaching: Preventing Academic Dishonesty

http://teaching.berkeley.edu/bgd/prevent.html

From her book Tools for Teaching, *Barbara Gross Davis provides concrete steps and general strategies that teachers can use to help prevent academic dishonesty.*

UC Berkeley Library: Primary Sources on the Web

http://www.lib.berkeley.edu/instruct/guides/primarysourcesontheweb.html

This annotated list of research collections on the Web is a terrific place for students to start the process of integrating sources. Maintained by the University of California at Berkeley Library, the page provides descriptions and Web links to digital collections of primary sources in a wide range of disciplines.

Writing a Research Project

18

Nothing will work unless you do. —MAYA ANGELOU

The contemporary idea of research for an essay seems not to have gained much currency in college classrooms until the older idea of *all* reading (and especially the keeping of commonplace books) as research began to fade during the nineteenth century. Robert Connors notes that as students could be "counted on less and less for the sorts of commonplace knowledge that the older classical curriculum specialized in, teachers found general assignments worked less and less well. One solution was to ask students to go to the library (a place not easily accessible for most people, even college students, until about 1869 and after) and look up information in books." But this solution only led to more difficulties, notably copying verbatim or "plagiarizing." As a result, according to Connors, "teachers came to turn more and more to assignments that had at least some element of first-person experience." Research could then be used to support this experience, and such assignments grew increasingly common during the 1890s. The first handbook to include a full chapter on the research paper appears to have been Hodges's 1941 *Harbrace Handbook*, and by the 1950s this assignment was firmly entrenched in the college curriculum.

The idea of writing a research-based essay may seem daunting to many students, especially first-year composition students or students who have never written more than a brief response paper. Your job will be as much to motivate, inspire, and lead them through this process as it will be to supervise their research and writing. Most of all, students need encouragement and assurance that they can indeed join the community of scholars.

Every noble work is at first impossible. —THOMAS CARLYLE

ATTENDING TO DISABILITIES: Refine Your Writing Plans (18a)

Realize that students with disabilities may need extra time and support to complete research-based writing projects. For students with attention-deficit disorders or other learning impairments, you can offer invaluable assistance with the structure and schedule by providing a syllabus with clearly delineated due dates. However, be flexible if these students have a hard time meeting course deadlines. Meet with them and collaborate to create a makeup schedule, or allow them extra time to incorporate materials and write the paper.

Students with visual impairments may need extra time to access textbooks, library materials, and films. Make sure that your institution has a range of adaptive technologies, such as Braille readers, printer-to-voice conversion software, and voice-to-text production technology. For students with severe hearing impairments, remember that English is a second language; these students may need extra tutoring in grammar and mechanics. Provide them with guided notes on your Web site for any lectures on research-based essays, and make sure your Web site is ADA compliant and works with adaptive technology.

FOR TEACHING: Refine Your Writing Plans (18a)

To help your students appreciate the value of the questions at the beginning of 18a of *The Everyday Writer*, point out that they help students to

- identify the intended audience.
- judge whether to define basic terms or to take for granted that the audience is already familiar with the research topic. For example, students wouldn't need to define *regeneration* for an audience of senior-level students working in molecular genetics or *apartheid* for senior-level political science students. But they might want to define and explain that term fully in a paper examining *economic disparity* in South Africa that they are writing for a composition class.
- evaluate their sources and determine how to use them. For a general audience, students cannot assume that a simple mention of a researcher's claims will give the audience sufficient understanding. If the source material requires an advanced level of understanding, careful explanations will be necessary.
- consider how to present themselves to the audience, how to define their relationship with the audience, and how to establish common ground with audience members.

- consider further how they view their subject. What are they trying to prove or explain? What is their purpose in relation to the audience?
- reconsider the thesis with a specific audience in mind. Is the thesis unfamiliar to the audience? Or is it a reexamination of something that the audience already assumes or accepts?

FOR COLLABORATION: Developing an Explicit Thesis (18a)

To make full use of the thesis statement activity in 18a of *The Everyday Writer*, call on one student to present his or her thesis to the class. Ask the writer to clarify or define any unfamiliar terms or vague points. Also ask the student to explain his or her topic choice. Then open up the class to a brainstorming session in which the student writer elaborates on the thesis and purpose by answering the questions posed by members of the class. In fielding the class's questions, the writer will clarify the project in his or her own mind, noting where difficulties lie, where command of the subject is lacking, and where elaboration is warranted. The writer may also discover that the topic is too broad and that the thesis needs refining.

Once you have demonstrated this activity for the whole class, have students work in groups of two or three to develop one another's thesis statements.

FOR TEACHING: Organize and Draft (18b)

Just as we all have different preferred modalities for learning, we also have different approaches to organizing information. Engage your students in discussion about how they shape their research notes into a draft. Do they begin with an outline? Do they freewrite several pages to discover their direction? Do they group information by subject headings?

The point cannot be overemphasized: a full formal outline is devilishly hard to write before one has actually produced at least a revised draft. A working outline that guides or reflects planning is all that students should expect to produce. Assure your students that an outline is flexible and is subject to revision once they've started writing. This advice rests on the thinking that not until writers put something down on paper can they really judge and plan the appropriateness of the content and format to purpose and audience.

FOR COLLABORATION: Organize and Draft (18b)

A new program at Stanford University called "How I Write: Conversations with Faculty" allows students to hear firsthand about the research strategies of senior faculty members across the disciplines. By learning about different strategies for approaching research and producing texts, students become critically aware of their own writing processes. One student, Angela, reflected, "I was glad to find that I wasn't the only one who gets stuck when I write . . . other students and even other professors do, too! I guess it is always a challenge to write something that really expresses what you want to say, and that's why it always takes a longer time to revise and revise, until you are satisfied with the writing."

Set up a similar conversation in your own classroom by asking students to interview each other about the writing process. How do they approach the organization of information? Do they need music or food in order to write? How do they work through writer's block? Do they rely on an outline or note cards grouped by subject headings?

Ask students to exchange drafts of their research projects with another student and outline their partner's draft using the text alone—that is, without asking for clarification from the writer. Next, have each pair examine these outlines together. How well does the outline reflect what the student writer intended in the draft? What points, if any, are left out? What does the outline suggest about the organization of the draft and the coverage of the topic? In what ways can this retrospective outline help the student revise the draft?

TEACHING WITH TECHNOLOGY: Organize and Draft (18b)

Almost all students now compose on computers. With their cut-and-paste function, quick saving capability, and ability to interface with online databases and image banks, computers are effective for drafting research-based essays. However, there are several practical tips for working with technology that you should bring to the attention of your students:

- *Save often*—and not just on the hard drive. You might ask students to use an external hard drive or CD-ROM to back up their work. Students can send their files to their home directories via FTP over the Internet, send backup copies to their email accounts, or save files to a flash drive.
- *Print out draft versions.* Encourage students to print out their drafts at each stage in order to keep a record of their writing process. A printed copy can also be a lifesaver if the document file is lost.
- *Revise on paper as well as on-screen.* Remind students that revising and editing an entire paper document versus blocks of text on a screen can differ in significant ways. Ask them to reflect on the kinds of revisions they tend to make on paper versus on a computer screen.

FOR COLLABORATION: Introduotions and Conclusions (18b)

Have students work in groups of five to brainstorm lists of specific purposes for the introduction and the conclusion. Once they've compiled these lists, ask them to find articles in major journals in various fields and to note the writers' purposes in several introductions and conclusions. Here are some possibilities they may come up with:

1. *Introductions*

   State the problem or topic to be explored.

   Briefly give the background or context for the question or topic.

   Get readers interested.

   Briefly give the reason for discussing or researching a topic.

2. *Conclusions*

   Answer the question initially raised in the introduction.

   Confirm the hypothesis.

   Repeat the main idea or point that the article has worked to explain.

   Confirm the importance of the question or subject.

   Suggest areas for further research.

Have students read aloud to one another their introductions followed by their conclusions. Doing so will help them to hear whether they are merely repeating or summarizing what they have already said or whether their conclusion pushes their readers' thinking further.

FOR TEACHING: Review and Get Responses to Your Draft (18d)

Have students read out loud the questions for reviewing drafts in 18d of *The Everyday Writer*. Next, ask students to copy these questions into their logs to use them as a handy reference during the drafting process. The writing log is a good place to reflect on the current state of any draft students may be working on.

FOR MULTILINGUAL WRITERS: Review and Get Responses to Your Draft (18d)

For students whose first language is not English, collaborative readings of a draft can greatly enhance their understanding of how a text accomplishes its purpose. Pair up students and ask them to read their drafts out loud to each other. Not only will the auditory expression of the text reveal errors in usage, logic, and organization, but it will also provide multilingual writers with an immediate audience response to their draft.

FOR TEACHING: Revise and Edit Your Draft (18e)

You might suggest that students use pens or highlighters of different colors to work through the various responses they receive on their drafts. In addition, have them respond to the steps in 9d of *The Everyday Writer* by writing a brief reflection on their revision process.

> **I am strongly in favor of intelligent, even fastidious revision, which is, or certainly should be, an art in itself. . . .** —Joyce Carol Oates

TEACHING WITH TECHNOLOGY: Prepare and Proofread Your Final Copy (18g)

Remind students that the word processor's spell-check and grammar-check functions will not catch every mistake. In fact, these editing tools often *create* mistakes, such as with homonyms and wrong-word errors. Advise students to proofread their final copy by reading it aloud, by showing it to a friend, and by scanning the text backwards.

> **I rewrite so much that the first chapter of a book sometimes may be rewritten forty or fifty times. . . . It's this way, see—when a writer first starts out, he gets a big kick from the stuff he does, and the reader doesn't get any; then, after a while, the writer gets a little kick and the reader gets a little kick; and finally, if the writer's any good, he doesn't get any kick at all and the reader gets everything.** —Ernest Hemingway

USEFUL READINGS

Bazerman, Charles. *The Informed Writer: Using Sources in the Disciplines*. 5th ed. Boston: Houghton, 1995. See especially Bazerman's discussion and examples of literature reviews.

Brent, Doug. *Reading and Rhetorical Invention: Knowledge, Persuasion, and the Teaching of Research-Based Writing*. Urbana: NCTE, 1992.

Dickson, Marcia. *It's Not Like That Here: Teaching Academic Writing and Reading to Novices*. Portsmouth: Boynton, 1995. See especially Dickson's cogent discussion of research and writing in Chapter 4, "Putting It All Together: Reading, Writing, and Research" (pp. 75–122).

Dinitz, Susan, and Jean Kiedaisch. "The Research Paper: Teaching Students to Be Members of the Academic Community." *Exercise Exchange* 31 (1986): 8–10. The authors suggest that rhetorical concerns—purpose and voice—should be primary concerns for research papers.

Gay, Pamela. "Dialogizing Response in the Writing Classroom: Students Answer Back." *Journal of Basic Writing* 17.1 (Spring 1998): 3–17. Gay proposes a dialogic approach to teacher commentary on student-written texts wherein students respond to a teacher's comments immediately after receiving them. She also proposes that students write letters to teachers, identifying their goals, strengths, and weaknesses.

Jeske, Jeff. "Borrowing from the Sciences: A Model for the Freshman Research Paper." *Writing Instructor* 6 (Winter 1987): 62–67. This helpful four-part model for writing the research essay encourages students to reflect on the research process itself while they are producing the research project.

McCormick, Kathleen. *The Culture of Reading and Teaching of English*. Manchester: Manchester UP, 1994. See especially Chapters 4 and 5 on research-based writing.

Moran, Mary Hurley. "Connections between Reading and Successful Revision." *Journal of Basic Writing* 16.2 (Fall 1997): 76–89. Moran examines the view that reading drafts aloud produces successful writing by attending to the correlation between reading ability and the efficacy of this activity. Her findings—that reading drafts aloud is beneficial to students with adequate or good reading skills but does not make any significant difference in the case of poor readers—have consequences for classroom practices and should encourage teachers to consider the reading-proficiency levels of their students.

USEFUL WEB SITES

DO-IT Program: Disabilities, Opportunities, Internetworking, and Technology

http://www.washington.edu/doit

This site is a series of Web pages for students, teachers, administrators, and nonacademic professionals, with instructional pages, links, and resource information.

Ohio State University: Fast Facts for Faculty

http://www.osu.edu/grants/dpg/fastfact/writing.html

This site offers concrete advice and resources for teachers to design their pedagogy with students with disabilities in mind.

Language

There is nothing wrong, really, with any word—all are good, but some are better than others.

—WILLIAM STRUNK JR. AND E. B. WHITE

19 Writing to the World

As we see more diversity both in our classrooms and in our professional circles, we need to reevaluate what it means to "write to the world." How can we teach students to communicate across cultures and with various audiences, using appropriate evidence and structures, and with an eye toward what it means to "write well" in a particular context or community? Perhaps the best lesson we can teach our students is that all language use is embedded in multiple contexts and gains meaning in and through those contexts. Thus what is utterly persuasive in one context fails miserably in another; what is elegant in one is tacky in another; what is clear and well organized in one may be anything but in yet another.

Scholars of contrastive rhetoric have been trying to teach us these lessons for a long time. The Sapir-Whorf hypothesis, for instance, proposes a kind of linguistic relativism that recognizes the intricate relationship between language and culture — but we have yet to apply this hypothesis to teaching American students how to write well. The early work of Robert Kaplan, arguing that language and writing are culturally embedded and that varying languages are characterized by different patterns of organization, logic, and so on, gained widespread attention, including charges of essentialism. Today Kaplan's early work is still relevant, and it has been expanded by several others who are helping teachers understand writing as a cultural activity. Ideally, our students would all learn to engage in contrastive rhetorical analysis in order to understand their own preferences for particular writing patterns and styles as well as those of others. Chapter 19, "Writing to the World," asks students to begin this important work.

On Writing to the World

The concept of world writing draws on the powerful work of Maria Lugones. In "Playfulness, World Traveling, and Loving Perception," Lugones uses the term "world traveling" and says, "The reason I think that traveling to someone's 'world' is a way of identifying with them is because by traveling to their 'world' we can understand *what it is to be them and what it is to be ourselves in their eyes*" (17).

On What You Consider "Normal" (19a)

Disability scholar Lennard J. Davis has shown that the terms *normal* and *normality* didn't enter English usage until 1857. These terms, Davis tells us, were mobilized in Western Europe and the United States by pioneers in the fields of statistics and eugenics to signify "constituting, conforming to, not deviating or differing from, the common type or standard, regular, usual" (24). As educators in composition, we can make our students aware of the historical baggage associated with the term *normal* and work instead for a more global, open acceptance of difference in both the writing we require and the standards we teach.

ATTENDING TO DISABILITIES: What You Consider "Normal" (19a)

Realizing that appropriate behavior, discourse, and conventions are culturally and community bound, you might encourage a discussion of "normalcy" on the first day. Try engaging your students in a critical analysis of the social norms perpetuated by the media, advertising, popular movies, and magazines. Design your lesson plan with the following questions from Johnson Cheu in mind:

> What are students' preconceptions about disability, and how should their literacies regarding disability influence pedagogy and curriculum?
>
> How does a teacher validate students' "uneasy" feelings and experiences surrounding disability yet assist them in finding their own way of engaging with the subject matter? (qtd. Brueggemann, White, Dunn, Heifferon, and Cheu, 387)

Teach students that being a world writer means expanding one's conception of the world to include all participants. Let your students with disabilities share their perspectives on encountering obstacles to learning with other students so that together, we can begin to change the social norms that constrict our understanding of what seems normal.

FOR COLLABORATION: What You Consider "Normal" (19a)

Ask students to work in groups of three to answer the following questions. Ask each group to draw up a report of their findings and present it to the class.

1. What do you think are the "good manners" of writing? That is, how do you show politeness in writing?
2. In general, what kind of evidence is most persuasive to you, and why?
3. What styles and tones in writing appeal to you most? Which carry the most authority? Which work best in college?

FOR COLLABORATION: Defining Your Terms (19b)

Paul Kei Matsuda and Tony Silva offer a classroom exercise focused on raising awareness and understanding of cultural differences. In this "cultural profile" exercise, students form into groups of three, with each student representing a different cultural group. Students interview one another, trying to learn all they can about cultural practices that differ from their own. In Matsuda's and Silva's own classes, students have discussed such issues as arranged marriage in Japan and India, the status of women in Indonesia, and the use of physical punishment by teachers in Korea. Students identified "dissonances" between their own and others' cultural practices and then interviewed each other again, trying to gain a better understanding of the particular practice in its local culture.

FOR TEACHING: Defining Your Terms (19b)

Brainstorm with students about the kinds of things they listen for and their purposes in listening. Then ask them to do an "intentional listening" exercise: have them choose one specific strategy to listen for throughout a specific time frame. They might listen for how people—in conversations, films, or activities—persuade, encourage, motivate, inform, critique, pacify, and so on. What culturally based differences did they notice in these conversations? How did speakers overcome (or fail to overcome) those differences? The point is to focus their listening on a specific strategy and take notes in their writing logs about how communication is accomplished. Have them bring the logs to class and explain those discoveries to others in the class. This activity should make for lively discussion—and perhaps for more effective listening and communicating.

On Your Own Authority as a Writer (19c)

Helen Fox, author of *Listening to the World: Cultural Issues in Academic Writing*, reminds us that language and power are closely related. Noting that North American business style dominates the world, Fox says "the ethnocentrism of the powerful is more significant, in a global environment, than the ethnocentrism of weaker countries. According to the 1999 United

Nations Human Development Report, global communication occurs mainly in English and mainly in the richer countries. The same report reveals that while English is used in roughly 80 percent of Web sites, fewer than one in ten people in the world speaks this language." Such statistics point out the importance of teaching students to examine their own inevitable ethnocentrism—without somehow feeling guilty about it—and to understand their own linguistic values and preferences in light of that knowledge.

TEACHING WITH TECHNOLOGY: Your Responsibility to Your Audience (19d)

A way to study and learn the differences in audience expectations across the globe is to use the Internet. Ask students to locate three Web pages on the same topic posted in different countries. Then have them conduct a rhetorical analysis of each Web page's formal properties, strategies of address, use of argumentative diction, and placement of images. Ask them to post their reflections on the differences among national audiences to your class discussion list. Alternatively, have students work collaboratively and create their own Web page analyzing the differences in audience expectations.

This exercise works particularly well for multilingual writers. Loretta Kasper argues that "as ESL students become more comfortable surfing the Internet, they discover that it is a vast resource that can be used to develop not only content area knowledge, but also linguistic proficiency" (408).

TEACHING WITH TECHNOLOGY: What Counts as Evidence (19e)

Ask students to keep an electronic journal on their computers concerning their awareness of differences in film and visual texts. Have them watch a movie that will help them learn about what counts as evidence in a culture other than their own. For example, *Smoke Signals*—a film adaptation of Sherman Alexie's collection of stories *The Lone Ranger and Tonto Fistfight in Heaven*—was written, directed, and acted by Native Americans. It offers cultural representations based on their own, rather than another culture's, points of view. Other possibilities include Julie Dash's *Daughters of the Dust*, which uses film strategies and figures drawn from African culture; or *Rabbit-Proof Fence*, a film adaptation of Doris Pilkington Garimara's book, *Follow the Rabbit-Proof Fence*, which tells the story of "the stolen generation" of mixed-race aboriginal children in Australia and also reveals how others might see their colonizers (in this case, the British). After you and the class draw up a list of films, ask students to view one of their choosing and to make an entry in their electronic journals about what they learned from the film in terms of "evidence" or proof, organization, style, and so on. They can also post their responses to the class discussion list and begin a dialogue online about evidence across cultures.

> **Writing...keeps me from believing everything I read.** —GLORIA STEINEM

FOR COLLABORATION: What Counts as Evidence (19e)

Divide students into small groups, and ask them to brainstorm answers to the following questions. Each group should be ready to report its answers to the class.

1. What should you rely on as evidence? How might your views differ from those from other cultures or with different beliefs?
2. In general, what kind of evidence is most persuasive to you?

On Organization and Style (19f–g)

We can identify several historical reasons that led to preferences for verbally elaborate style and structure in some European countries (such as Spain) and for "plain talk" and explicit structures in England and the United States. Some scholars trace this development of preferences to the utilitarian movement, whereas others argue that it is related to the growing power of democracy. In any case, it is clear that such linguistic preferences are culture specific.

USEFUL READINGS

Davis, Lennard J. *Enforcing Normalcy: Disability, Deafness, and the Body*. London: Verson, 1995. This pioneer in disability studies examines the historical uses and social implications of the terms *normal* and *normality*.

Fox, Helen. *Listening to the World: Cultural Issues in Academic Writing*. Urbana: NCTE, 1994. Using personal stories and experiences of students to inform her thinking, Fox discusses the difficulty that "minority" students have in learning to write according to American academic conventions.

Kaplan, Robert B. "Cultural Thought Patterns in Intercultural Education." *Language Learning* 16: 1–20.

Li, Xiao-Ming. *"Good Writing" in Cross-Cultural Context*. Albany: SUNY P, 1996. In an ethnographic account of teachers' perceptions of good writing in China and America, Li builds a dialogue between expert teachers in the two countries in order to show that "good writing" is a complex interaction between student texts and the teachers who read and judge that writing.

Lugones, Maria. "Playfulness, World Traveling, and Loving Perception." *Hypatia* 2 (1987): 17.

Matsuda, Paul Kei, and Tony Silva. "Cross-Cultural Composition: Mediated Integration of U.S. and International Students." *Composition Studies* 27 (1999): 15–30.

Severino, Carol, Juan C. Guerra, and Johnella E. Butler, eds. *Writing in Multicultural Settings*. New York: MLA, 1997. This collection addresses the challenges presented by the racial, ethnic, gender, class, religious, age, and physical-ability differences among college writing students. See, especially, the essays by Juan Guerra and Ulla Connor.

20 Language That Builds Common Ground

The thought of Kenneth Burke in *A Rhetoric of Motives* informs much contemporary work in rhetoric and composition, and it certainly informs *The Everyday Writer* in general and this chapter in particular. Burke's key term is *identification*:

> A is not identical with his colleague B. But insofar as their interests are joined, A is *identified* with B. Or he may *identify himself* with B even when their interests are not joined, if he assumes that they are, or is persuaded to do so. . . . To identify A with B is to make A "consubstantial" with B.
>
> . . . Here is perhaps the simplest case of persuasion. You persuade a man only insofar as you can talk his language by speech, gesture, tonality, order, image, attitude, idea, *identifying* your ways with his. (20, 55)

Burke's concept of identification underlies the advice in this chapter, which is meant to remind student writers of the many ways that language can promote—or destroy—identification. Ironically, given the extensive attention Burke devotes to identification, his own texts exclude half of humankind with their consistent use of the generic *he* and *man*.

Of course, you don't have to look far to see *dis*-identification at work. We overheard a fourteen-year-old exclaim to his aunt: "I am *not* a 'kid' anymore, so please stop calling me that!" The nephew objected to a label he found both inaccurate and disrespectful, one that clearly built no common ground, no source of identification, between him and his aunt. Ask students to think of situations when they've struggled to find just the right words to avoid offending someone: what salutation to use instead of "Dear Sir" when they are not sure who will read the letter, for instance, or how to describe an eighty-year-old without calling him or her "old," or what besides "mailman" to call someone who delivers the mail—especially when that person is *not* a man. These are choices student writers must make every day in trying to build common ground and communicate with others.

FOR TEACHING: Diversity in the Classroom

One good way to get the class to start thinking about differences and common ground is to ask students to look around the classroom and try to describe the class in writing. After all, generations of college students have found themselves in classes filled with people both like them and different from them. Here is Eudora Welty, describing her first year (1926) at Mississippi State College for Women in *One Writer's Beginnings*:

> There I landed in a world to itself, and indeed it was all new to me. It was surging with twelve hundred girls. They came from every nook and corner of the state, from the Delta, the piney woods, the Gulf Coast, the black prairie, the red clay hills, and Jackson—as the capital city and the only sizeable town, a region to itself. All were clearly differentiated sections, at that time, and though we were all put into uniforms of navy blue so as to unify us, it could have been told by the girls' accents, by their bearings, the way they came into the classroom and the way they ate, where they'd grown up. This was my first chance to learn what the body of us were like and what differences in background, persuasion of mind, and resources of character there were among Mississippians—at that, among only half of us, for we were all white. I missed the significance of both what was in, and what was out of, our well-enclosed but vibrantly alive society.

Take time to have students read this passage and then talk about where they've come from—their ages, ethnicities, hometowns, religions, and so on. Use the discussion to help them focus on their own diversity.

On Common Ground and Educational Opportunity

Mike Rose, in his extraordinary book *Lives on the Boundary*, talks about the sorts of sensitivity that will be necessary to build the common ground that will enable many people to be well served by our schools:

> We are in the middle of an extraordinary social experiment: the attempt to provide education for all members of a vast pluralistic democracy. To have any prayer of success, we'll need many conceptual blessings: A philosophy of language and literacy that affirms the diverse sources of linguistic competence and deepens our understanding of the ways class and culture blind us to the richness of those sources. A perspective on failure that lays open the logic of error. An orientation toward the interaction of poverty and ability that undercuts simple polarities, that enables us to see simultaneously the constraints poverty places on the play of mind and the actual mind at play within those constraints. We'll need a pedagogy that encourages us to step back and consider the threat of the standard classroom and that shows us, having stepped back, how to step forward to invite a student across the boundaries of that powerful room. Finally, we'll need a revised store of images of educational excellence, ones closer to egalitarian ideas—ones that embody the reward and turmoil of education in a democracy, that celebrate the plural, messy human reality of it. At heart, we'll need a guiding set of principles that do not encourage us to retreat from, but move us closer to, an understanding of the rich mix of speech and ritual and story that is America. (238)

> A writer lives in awe of words, for they can be cruel or kind, and they can change their meanings right in front of you. They pick up flavors and odors like butter in a refrigerator.
>
> –JOHN STEINBECK

FOR TEACHING: Unstated Assumptions and Stereotypes (20a)

To help students see that writing has powerful effects, ask them to write about a time when someone—a friend, parent, teacher, employer—wrote or said something about them that affected the way they thought or felt about themselves, that labeled them in some way that led to disidentification and misunderstanding. Then ask them to write about a time when their words had an important effect on someone else. Use these entries as a starting point for class discussion about the power of language.

FOR MULTILINGUAL WRITERS: Unstated Assumptions and Stereotypes (20a)

Students whose first language is not English are often familiar with the power of language as both a tool of respect and as a tool that inflicts harm. Ask your students to relay their experiences with the class in order to forge identifications across differences. Do multilingual speakers have to combat damaging assumptions about their countries of origin or intellectual abilities?

FOR COLLABORATION: Unstated Assumptions and Stereotypes (20a)

Have students work in groups of three, and give each group a few paragraphs from Jonathan Swift's *A Modest Proposal*; distribute the pages evenly among the groups. Ask each group to identify language that stereotypes certain groups—the Irish, women, or Americans, for example. Then ask the groups to consider such stereotyping in relation to Swift's *satiric purpose*. Particularly in the case of satire, such labeling may serve to argue for exactly the opposite of what it seems to be saying. In such cases, do the students find such stereotypes offensive or useful? Ask them to look at contemporary political satire and to address the same questions about it.

TEACHING WITH TECHNOLOGY: Assumptions about Gender (20b)

Ask students to read the opening of the Declaration of Independence and to consider what groups of citizens are made invisible by the document's language.

> When in the Course of human events, it becomes necessary for one people to dissolve the political bands which have connected them with another, and to assume among the powers of the earth, the separate and equal station to which the Laws of Nature and of Nature's God entitle them, a decent respect to the opinions of mankind requires that they should declare the causes which impel them to the separation.—We hold these truths to be self-evident, that all men are created equal, that they are endowed by their Creator with certain unalienable Rights, that among these are Life, Liberty and the pursuit of Happiness.—That to secure these rights, Governments are instituted among Men, deriving their just powers from the consent of the governed.

Following class discussion, ask students to post an entry on your electronic discussion board on the term *sexist language*. Ask them to try to define the term and to offer examples of terms that are or may seem to be sexist or that make certain assumptions about language. These computer entries should then be used to initiate a class dialogue.

On Assumptions about Race and Ethnicity (20c)

In a 1991 *New York Times* article Daniel Goleman reported on an experiment done by Smith College psychologist Dr. Fletcher Blanchard that led him to conclude that "a few outspoken people who are vigorously antiracist can establish the kind of social climate that discourages racist acts." After asking 144 Smith College students for their reactions to a racist incident on campus, Dr. Blanchard found that students who heard others making racist remarks were more willing to make racist remarks themselves. These findings suggest that the peer group in the writing classroom could serve as an effective mechanism for encouraging students to consider the influence their language could have on others.

FOR TEACHING: Assumptions about Race and Ethnicity (20c)

Ask students to write a paragraph or two about their own ethnic heritage. Some may want to talk with parents or grandparents about their own ethnicity. Such research would form the basis for class discussion and for a writing assignment about "where I come from." In addition, you may want to ask students to spend a few minutes asking "what's in a name?" and discussing the terms used to refer to their own ethnic group and, perhaps, their own names. Some students may not know, for instance, that Booker T. Washington long ago wrote that former slaves must change their slave names and that this impetus is related to the practice of taking names that reflect African or Islamic influence: Malcolm Little to Malcolm X and then to Malik Al-Shabazz; Cassius Clay to Muhammad Ali; Lew Alcindor to Kareem Abdul-Jabbar. What names might students choose to reflect their own ethnicity? What terms do they prefer to use when referring to their own ethnic group, and why?

FOR TEACHING: Assumptions about Race and Ethnicity (20c)

Ask students to read the following excerpt from Carol Lee Sanchez's description of the language that white culture has used to characterize Native Americans. Have students contrast these stereotypes with Native Americans' perspective of themselves, their way of life, and the white culture that threatens them. Who is Sanchez's audience in this article? How does she build common ground with readers? Are students persuaded by her arguments?

> On the negative side, to be Indian is to be thought of as primitive, alcoholic, ignorant (as in "Dumb Indian"), better off dead (as in "the only good Indian is a dead Indian" or "I didn't know there was any of you folks still left"), unskilled, non-competitive, immoral, pagan or heathen, untrustworthy (as in "Indian-giver") and frightening. To be Indian is to be the primary model that is used to promote racism in this country.
>
> How can that happen, you ask? Bad press. One hundred and fifty years of the most consistently vicious press imaginable. Newspapers, dime novels, textbooks and fifty years of visual media have portrayed and continue to portray Indians as savage, blood-thirsty, immoral, inhuman people. When there's a touch of social consciousness attached, you will find the once "blood-thirsty," "white-killer savage" portrayed as a pitiful drunk, a loser, an outcast or a mix-blood not welcomed by, or trusted by, either race. For fifty years, children in this country have been raised to kill Indians mentally, subconsciously through the visual media, until it is an automatic reflex. That shocks you? Then I have made my point. . . .
>
> The Indian Way is a different way. It is a respectful way. The basic teachings in every Tribe that exists today as a Tribe in the western hemisphere are based on respect for all the things our Mother gave us. If we neglect her or anger her, she will make our lives very difficult and we always know that we have a hardship on ourselves and on our children. We are raised to be cautious and concerned for the *future* of our people, and that is how we raise our children—because *they* are *our* future. Your "civilization" has made all of us very sick and has made our mother earth sick and out of balance. Your kind of thinking and education has brought the whole world to the brink of total disaster, whereas the thinking and education among my people forbids the practice of almost everything Euro-Americans, in particular, value.

If you want to talk with somebody you have to arrive at the same language somehow. And/but talking the same language cannot and must not mean "my language and not yours" or "your language and not mine." It means finding a way to understand, not to change or to eclipse or to obliterate but to understand each other. —JUNE JORDAN

ATTENDING TO DISABILITIES: Other Kinds of Difference (20d)

As a culture, how reliant are we on metaphors of mobility, visibility, and ability? You can discuss ways of building common ground that attend to disabilities by asking students to examine common patterns of speech or colloquial expressions. Johnson Cheu, for instance, normalizes wheelchair mobility by using the following expression:

> Some time after the class was over, one of the students stopped me as I was rolling on campus. (qtd. in Brueggemann, White, Dunn, Heifferon, and Cheu 390)

Brenda Jo Brueggemann and her colleagues point out some of these common expressions, reminding us that we need to be aware of varieties of language that inclusively transform the way our culture demarcates people as able-bodied or "dis-abled":

> Another concern lies in the metaphor of visibility . . . in the very ways that the language we and our students use is laden with metaphors of ability. Not that we would want to police the propriety of sight equaling insight; the political power gained with "visibility" in our culture; the importance of "hearing others' voices"; the meaning of "throwing our own voices," "turning deaf ears," or coming up with "lame ideas." To do so would pretty much have emptied out the 1999 CCCC's program book, which was overladen with these very metaphors. (369)

Ask students to create innovative linguistic expressions for their own experiences of mobility, ability, vision, and hearing.

> **Disability studies . . . invite us all to at least consider the able-bodied agenda lurking in the way we make meaning through so many crippling metaphors, in the way we compose and communicate that disables even as it might be attempting to "enable."**
>
> —Brenda Jo Brueggemann

On Other Kinds of Difference: Sexual Orientation (20d)

Students should be aware that people whose sexual orientation is not strictly heterosexual constitute a significant minority of our world and inhabit all walks of life. They should also be aware that, as with many other labels, the terms used to describe sexual orientation are in flux. *Sexual orientation* itself is the term preferred by many who view sexuality as genetically determined or as the result of very early socialization (or as some combination of the two). *Sexual preference*, on the other hand, is preferred by many who see sexuality as primarily a matter of personal or political choice.

It is also worth noting that style sheets for most organizations recommend using the term gay only as an adjective; *homosexual* and *lesbian* are used as both adjectives and nouns.

FOR COLLABORATION: Language That Builds Common Ground

Because campus speech codes often ban slurs and epithets, they are most usually referred to as "Hate Speech Codes." And when these speech codes are enforced, they usually fire up controversies about what exactly constitutes "hate speech" as well as what kinds of speech violate First Amendment rights.

Form students into groups to investigate the campus speech codes at your college, reporting to the rest of the class on their content as well as instances of when—if ever—they have been enforced. How have the codes been applied in the past? What were the results? How were violations of the codes addressed? Are there situations on your campus now that merit application of the campus speech codes?

FOR COLLABORATION: Language That Builds Common Ground

To reinforce the learning in this chapter, share the following message with your students:

> Like you, generations of college students have found themselves in classes filled with people both like them and different from them. Take time now to examine where you've come from—your age, ethnicity, hometown, religion, and so on.

Ask students to write a short response to the message. Then ask them to examine one or more of their classmates. Have them write a paragraph about the differences and the common ground they see, and then study their paragraph for any assumptions their language reveals. Finally, ask students to meet with two other classmates to read their paragraphs and share what they have learned about finding common ground.

USEFUL READINGS

Ball, Arnetha, and Ted Lardner. "Dispositions toward Language: Teacher Construction of Knowledge and the Ann Arbor Black English Case." *CCC* 48 (1997): 469–99. Ball and Lardner explore the effects of language-based stereotypes and offer important ways to teach beyond these stereotypes for all instructors interested in inclusive writing instruction.

Brueggemann, Brenda Jo. "On (Almost) Passing." *CE* 59 (1997): 647–60. The author explores her "coming out as a deaf person" and traces the effect of this rite of passage on herself, her teaching, and her writing.

Brueggemann, Brenda Jo, Linda Feldmeier White, Patricia A. Dunn, Barbara A. Heifferon, and Johnson Cheu. "Becoming Visible: Lessons in Disability." *CCC* 52.3 (Feb. 2001): 368–98. Calling for increased awareness of disability in composition studies, the authors argue that such an awareness can productively disrupt notions of "writing" and "composing" at the same time it challenges "normal"/"not normal" binarics in the field.

Burke, Kenneth. *A Rhetoric of Motives*. Berkeley: U of California P, 1969.

Carpenter, Carol. "Exercises to Combat Sexist Reading and Writing." *CE* 43 (1981): 293–300. Carpenter describes three activities designed to explore the implications of sexism while building reading and writing skills.

Davis, Lennard. "Deafness and Insight: The Deafened Moment as a Critical Modality." *CE* 57 (1995): 881–900. In this wonderfully provocative essay for teachers of writing, Davis examines the notion of "disability" in order to uncover the "epistemological bases and dialectical relations inherent in any notion of aesthetics."

Frank, Francine Wattman, and Paula A. Treichler. *Language, Gender, and Professional Writing: Theoretical Approaches and Guidelines for Nonsexist Usage*. New York: MLA, 1989. This book addresses the issue of linguistic sexism in scholarly and professional writing, presenting relevant ideas and research and a set of guidelines for nondiscriminatory usage.

Goleman, Daniel. "New Ways to Battle Bias: Fight Acts, Not Feelings." *New York Times* 16 July 1991: B1+.

Keating, Ann Louise. "Interrogating 'Whiteness': (De)Constructing 'Race.'" *CE* 57 (1995): 901–18. Keating argues that teachers must complicate existing concepts of race — both by "exploring the many changes that have occurred in all apparently fixed racial categories and by informing students of the political, economic, and historical factors shaping the continual reinvention of 'race.'"

Mairs, Nancy. "Body in Trouble." *Waist-High in the World: Life among the Nondisabled*. New York: Beacon, 1997. The author of the now-classic "On Being a Cripple" and *Carnal Acts* writes with particular insight and passion about living with and beyond disabilities.

Matthews, Anne. "Brave, New 'Cruelty Free' World." *New York Times* 7 July 1991. A teacher of nonfiction writing at Princeton University, Matthews satirizes current expressions that, in attempting to be "cruelty-free," actually deny or trivialize difficult human conditions.

A Media Guide to Disability. East Hartford: CDD Council, 1985 <http://www.state.ct.us/ctcdd/mediaguide.html>. This is a discussion of language most often used in professional literature and most preferred by people with various disabilities.

Moss, Beverly J., and Keith Walters. "Rethinking Diversity: Axes of Difference in the Writing Classroom." *Theory and Practice in the Teaching of Writing: Re-thinking the Discipline.* Ed. Lee Odell. Carbondale: Southern Illinois UP, 1993. 132–85.

Nilsen, Aileen Pace. "Winning the Great 'He'/'She' Battle." *CE* 46 (1984): 151–57. Nilsen uses examples from manuscripts submitted for publication to illustrate the complexities involved in using "inconspicuous sexfair language." Based on an analysis of these examples, she offers four principles for instructors and students who lack the sometimes considerable skill necessary for writing in a gender-neutral manner.

Okawa, Gail Y. "Diving for Pearls: Mentoring as Cultural and Activist Practice among Academics of Color." *CCC* 53.3 (Feb. 2002): 507–32. This discussion of Geneva Smitherman and Victor Villanueva, two senior scholars of color, shows that mentoring is far more than an academic exercise and helps build a multiethnic/multiracial professoriate in our discipline.

Rose, Mike. *Lives on the Boundary.* New York: Penguin, 1989.

Stockton, Kathryn Bond. "Reading Details, Teaching Politics: Political Mantras and the Politics of Luxury." *CE* 64.1 (Sept. 2001): 109. Stockton examines the repetition of received cultural norms in teaching and scholarship.

Wise, Tim. *On White Privilege.* "The Pathology of Privilege: Racism, White Denial, and the Costs of Inequality." DVD. This 57-minute disk provides an eye-opening account of race and racism from the "inside out." Wise, author of *White Like Me*, disarms the often defensive mode individuals take in discussions of race by presenting a frank and unapologetic perspective of the privileges of being white and its dire consequences to people of all races.

Language Variety

21

[I]f you want to really hurt me, talk badly about my language. Ethnic identity is twin skin to linguistic identity—I am my language. Until I can take pride in my language, I cannot take pride in myself.

–Gloria Anzaldúa

Linguist Walt Wolfram has done a great deal to explicate and map varieties of English and to demonstrate that such variations are not only extensive but also strongly influenced by a number of factors, including region or geographical location, social status, ethnicity, age, and gender. "Cutting across and intersecting with these variables," Wolfram says, "are the dimensions of formality of style and occasion of use of the language." In spite of the work of such scholars, and because the language is constantly changing, we still have only a limited picture of the current diversity within English. Instructors of writing will benefit from learning what we can about *all* the varieties of English that inform our students' literate practices.

In "English in Our Language Heritage," Shirley Brice Heath explains that several languages played important roles in the early life of this country, and that the use of different languages was encouraged. Only in the late nineteenth century, according to Heath, did political and ideological forces move to champion monolingualism. Today, as this chapter demonstrates, the United States is once again using—and appreciating—multiple languages and varieties of English.

Keith Walters, in an essay on "Dialects," provides an excellent discussion of "the nature of language and dialect and the role they are likely to play in the construction of individual and group identity in a multicultural society that prides itself on a democratic way of life." He goes on to explain:

> Teaching students about . . . the many dialects of American English will surely not rid the country of prejudice, but it might be a first step in helping those whose native dialect differs from that of the academy appreciate the tasks they are engaged in as they strive to acquire Standard English. It would likewise

help those from mainstream backgrounds appreciate the challenge some of their classmates face. Surely, it would help prepare future citizens to live in a society characterized by increasing linguistic diversity.

> **Is it that we think the brain too small a place to hold more than one language at a time?**
>
> —DELL HYMES

On Standard Varieties of English (21a)

In *The Language Instinct*, Steven Pinker demystifies any questions speakers of so-called standard English might have about varieties of the English language, particularly about African American English vernacular, one of the most widely used languages in the United States. Responding to the labeling of such English as a "non-logical mode of expressive behavior," Pinker writes:

> If the psychologists had listened to spontaneous conversations, they would have rediscovered the commonplace fact that American black culture is everywhere highly verbal; the subculture of street youths in particular is famous in the annals of anthropology for the value placed on linguistic virtuosity. Indeed, . . . a number of ethnic varieties of English display linguistic virtuosity and power. In addition to African American vernacular English, Walt Wolfram lists Italian, Jewish, Irish, German, Puerto Rican, Chicano, American Indian, and Vietnamese Englishes as of interest to scholars and teachers. Students in your class may be familiar with still other ethnic varieties of English.

In *Speak Standard, Too—Add Mainstream English to Your Talking Style*, Mary I. Berger encourages her students to speak standard English whenever they are "out there" and to speak their home dialect at home. Her advice is controversial, especially given what many linguists feel is the political nature of such switching and shifting. Geneva Smitherman tells us in *Talkin' and Testifyin': The Language of Black America* that we expect only the "colonized" person to make linguistic shifts, and she writes:

> An individual's language is intricately bound up with his or her sense of identity and group consciousness. In the history of man's inhumanity to man, it is clearly understandable why the conqueror forces his victim to learn his language, for as black psychiatrist Frantz Fanon said, "every dialect is a way of thinking." Certainly this principle has been operative in the history of colonized people where the colonizer's language and culture occupy a position superior to that of the colonized, even among the oppressed persons themselves. (The fact that America was once a colony of England goes a long way toward explaining why British English still commands such great prestige in this country—despite the real communication barrier it poses for most Americans. Fanon would label this the "colonized mentality" of White America. . . .)

> In the American context, the negative attitude toward black speech is but a variation on this same theme. Historically, Black English has been the usage pattern associated with plantation figures like Uncle Remus and Uncle Tom. Contemporaneously, it is the dialect associated with black urban "ghetto" types. . . . Since the Civil War, and in the twentieth century especially, upward mobility for Black Americans has come to mean the eradication of black language (and black culture) and the adoption of the linguistic norms of the white middle class. . . . Moreover, some blacks contend that being bidialectal not only causes a schism in the black personality, but it is also like saying black talk is "good enough" for blacks but not for whites. (171–73)

> **A standard language is a dialect with an army and a navy.**
>
> —OLD ONE-LINER AMONG SOCIOLINGUISTS

On Ethnic Varieties of English (21b)

In recent years, the debate over standard English—as well as over "English only"—has become increasingly virulent, as we saw in the uproar over Ebonics, a term that combines the words *ebony* and *phonics* and that was coined well over twenty years ago. Instructors of writing need to be aware of these debates and to help their students think and talk through the issues involved. The Useful Readings and Useful Web Site listed at the end of this chapter provide many resources.

FOR TEACHING: Regional Varieties of English (21c)

John Algeo recommends using a quiz like the following one to introduce students to the subject of regional variation in English:

Match each lettered term with its numbered meaning:

a. Coney Island butter	1. sandstorm
b. Boston dollar	2. burro
c. Adam's ale	3. razorback hog
d. Albany beef	4. downpour
e. Arizona cloudburst	5. mustard
f. Arkansas dew	6. penny
g. Carolina racehorse	7. sturgeon
h. Colorado mockingbird	8. water

(key: a – 5, b – 6, c – 8, d – 7, e –1, f – 4, g – 3, h – 2)

Algeo says that students in any level class can make up similar quizzes, exercises that could lead to a survey of oral language use among their families and friends—and provide rich material for class discussion of regional variation in English.

Following this exercise, you might ask students to bring to class some examples of a regional variety of language they know well, to demonstrate the use of these words or phrases in context and to explain the nuances of their meanings.

> **Impassable and impossible distances were measured by the distance from "Hog to Kick 'em Jenny." Hog? Kick 'em Jenny? Who knew until I was . . . grown that these were two little reefs in the Grenadines, between Grenada and Carriacou. –Audre Lorde**

FOR MULTILINGUAL WRITERS: Other Languages (21d)

Gloria Anzaldúa was known for weaving English and Spanish together in her texts. Following her lead, students may wish to integrate other languages in their papers. Such interweaving can be an extremely successful rhetorical strategy. Share with your students examples of imbricated texts that work well by bringing in many varieties of language.

FOR COLLABORATION: Other Languages (21d)

We all shift regularly among varieties of English, often automatically and especially in speech, in response to changing situations and audiences. Ask students to try listening to themselves talk—at work, with parents or other authority figures, with close friends, and so on. Each student should take notes on his or her own use of language by jotting down any words and patterns that are from languages other than English or that are characteristic of a specific region, job, or cultural group. Then, working with a partner, students should spend half an hour or so comparing notes, asking which of these words they might use in writing as well as in speaking. Why would they use them, and for what effect? They should also compile a list of differences between their speech patterns and decide which differences are due to regional, occupational, ethnic, or other varieties of English. Students should bring the results of this collaborative exploration to class for discussion.

FOR TEACHING: Language Variety

In his "Mr. Language Person" columns, Dave Barry often mixes the language of a hypothetical English instructor with his own brand of outrageous examples:

Q. What are the rules regarding capital letters?

A. Capital letters are used in three grammatical situations:

1. At the beginning of proper or formal nouns. *Examples*: Capitalize "Queen," "Tea Party" and "Rental Tuxedo." Do *not* capitalize "dude," "cha-cha" or "boogerhead."

2. To indicate a situation of great military importance. *Example*: "Get on the TELSAT and tell STAFCOM that CONWIMP wants some BBQ ASAP."

3. To indicate that the subject of the sentence has been bitten by a badger. *Example*: "I'll just stick my hand in here and OUCH!"

USEFUL READINGS

Algeo, John. "DARE in the Classroom." *Language Variation in North American English*. Ed. A. Wayne Glowka and Donald M. Lance. New York: MLA, 1993. 140–43. One essay in a collation that covers theories of vernacular, regional, ethnic/social, gender, and historical variations of English.

Berger, Mary I. *Speak Standard, Too —Add Mainstream English to Your Talking Style*. Chicago: Orchard, 1994.

Brueggemann, Brenda Jo, Linda Feldmeier White, Patricia A. Dunn, Barbara A. Heifferon, and Johnson Cheu. "Becoming Visible: Lessons in Disability." *CCC* 52.3 (Feb. 2001): 368–98. Calling for increased awareness of disability in composition studies, the authors argue that such an awareness can productively disrupt notions of "writing" and "composing" at the same time it challenges "normal"/"not normal" binaries in the field.

Campbell, Kermit E. "The Signifying Monkey Revisited: Vernacular Discourse in African American Personal Narratives." *Journal of Advanced Composition* 14.4 (Fall 1994): 463–73. Campbell argues that signifying is a means of affirming "cultural identity and community in the face of the imposition of cultural dominance and oppression," that vernacular and academic discourses share large numbers of similarities, and that including vernacular discourse in writing pedagogy "would bring the African American experience from the margins to the center of the academic community where it belongs."

Coleman, Charles F. "Our Students Write with Accents—Oral Paradigms for ESD Students." *CCC* 48 (Dec. 1997): 486–500. Coleman provides important information for instructors on the practices that shape the writing of some English as a Second Dialect students.

"Commentary." *Black Caucus Notes*. Urbana: NCTE, 1997. This reprint of a document written twenty years ago carefully outlines the position of African American linguists and educators on the Ebonics issue.

Delpit, Lisa. *Other People's Children: Cultural Conflict in the Classroom.* New York: New P, 1995. An expansion of two influential essays that appeared in the *Harvard Educational Review*, this book offers an important reassessment of the "process movement" in composition. In it, Delpit argues that in some ways the methods employed in progressive education deny rather than give access to the skills that many African American students want and need.

Farr, Marcia, and Harvey Daniels. *Language Diversity and Writing Instruction.* Urbana: NCTE, 1986. This is an excellent discussion of variation and diversity in U.S. English. The authors argue that what we call "standard English" is really one particular variety of English, along with African American English vernacular, Hispanic-influenced English, and other ethnic and regional varieties. The book ends with concrete recommendations for teaching linguistically diverse students.

Ferguson, Charles A., and Shirley Brice Heath, eds. *Language in the USA.* Cambridge: Cambridge UP, 1981. Multiple varieties and dialects of English and the role that class, gender, race, occupation, and nationality play on such variety are covered by the authors.

Fu, Danling. *My Trouble Is My English: Asian Students and the American Dream.* Portsmouth: Boynton, 1995. This is a personal account of the writer's struggle to come to terms with the ways in which standard English helps both to empower and to oppress.

Galindo, D. Letticia. "Bilingualism and Language Variation among Chicanos in the Southwest." *Language Variation in North American English.* Ed. A. Wayne Glowka and Donald M. Lance. New York: MLA, 1993. 199–218.

Gilyard, Keith. *Let's Flip the Script: African American Discourses on Language, Literature, and Learning.* Detroit: Wayne State UP, 1996. This series of essays explores the politics of language teaching and the linguistic legacies of racism.

Heath, Shirley Brice, and Leslie Mangiola. *Children of Promise: Literate Activity in Linguistically and Culturally Diverse Classrooms.* Washington, DC: NEA, 1991.

Kachru, Braj B., ed. *The Other Tongue: English across Cultures.* 2nd ed. Urbana: U of Illinois P, 1992. This collection of essays on English in a global and multicultural context includes essays on nonnative Englishes, on American English, on culture and discourse, and on teaching world Englishes.

Kreiner, Leslie, and Alan Merikel. "The Bilingual Model: Encouraging Diversity in the Writing Classroom." *Teaching English in the Two Year College* 22 (Dec. 1995): 284–92.

Labov, William. *The Study of Nonstandard English.* Champaign: NCTE, 1970. A classic study in which Labov dispels a number of myths about nonstandard English and demonstrates that such nonstandard dialects are in fact self-contained and rule-governed systems worthy of serious study.

Lunsford, Andrea A. "Toward a Mestiza Rhetoric: Gloria Anzaldúa on Composition and Postcoloniality." *Journal of Advanced Composition* 18 (1998): 1–29. In this interview, Anzaldúa speaks at length about the importance of using a variety of languages (sometimes without translation) in her writing.

Marback, Richard. "Ebonics: Theorizing in Public Our Attitudes toward Literacy." *CCC* 53.1 (Sept. 2001): 11–32. Marback argues that responses to the Oakland Ebonics resolution miss the significance of the resolution; he focuses on attention to attitudes and literacy education in a racially divided democracy.

McKay, Sandra Lee, and Sau-Ling Cynthia Wong, eds. *Language Diversity: Problem or Resource?* Boston: Heinle, 1988. Following a discussion of historical perspective on language diversity, the authors of the essays in this collection focus on the language situations of Americans of Mexican, Puerto Rican, Cuban, Chinese, Filipino, Korean, and Vietnamese ancestry.

Moss, Beverly J., ed. *Literacy across Communities.* Cresskill: Hampton P, 1994. This collection includes five essays on literacy practices among Chicago Mexicanos, in Philadelphia's Hmong community, in Navajo print culture, among young African American males, and in African American churches, and a concluding reflection on broadening our understanding of nonmainstream literacies.

Pinker, Steven. *The Language Instinct.* New York: Harper, 1995.

Pough, Gwendolyn D. "Rhetoric: Black Students Writing Black Panthers." *CCC* 53.3 (Feb. 2002): 466–86. Pough examines black students' responses to Black Panther documents and how those documents moved the students toward change.

Smitherman, Geneva. *Talkin' and Testifyin': The Language of Black America.* Boston: Houghton, 1977.

Tannen, Deborah. "The Oral/Literate Continuum in Discourse." *Spoken and Written Language: Exploring Orality and Literacy.* Ed. Deborah Tannen. Norwood: Ablex, 1982.

———. *You Just Don't Understand: Women and Men in Conversation.* New York: Ballantine, 1990; *That's Not What I Meant! How Conversational Style Makes or Breaks Relationships.* New York: Ballantine, 1987; and *Talking from 9 to 5.* New York: Morrow, 1994. These books provide fascinating evidence of differences between the ways men and women converse and interact.

TuSmith, Bonnie. "The Englishes of Ethnic Folk." *CE* 58 (1996): 43–57. TuSmith argues that English instructors are responsible for teaching not only standard English but also other Englishes "without conveying the message that these systems are inferior." To illustrate one strategy for doing so, TuSmith looks closely at Milton Murayama's 1975 novel *All I Asking for Is My Body.*

Villanueva, Victor. *Bootstraps: From an American Academic of Color*. Urbana: NCTE, 1993. Villanueva discusses his own literacy histories and offers several insights about multilingual students in monolingual schools. Of special interest is Chapter 5, "*Inglés* in the Colleges."

Walters, Keith. "Dialects." *Encyclopedia of English and Language Arts*. Ed. Alan Purvec. Urbana: NCTE, 1994. Walters discusses the role of language variety on identity.

Wolfram, Walt. *Dialects and American English*. Englewood Cliffs: Prentice, 1991. Wolfram includes an extensive discussion of what dialects are and how they arise, and offers a thorough exploration of regional, social, ethnic, and gender-based variations in U.S. English; Chapters 10 and 11, "Standard English and Education" and "Dialect and Testing," are especially important for instructors of writing.

USEFUL WEB SITE

Center for Applied Linguistics

http://www.cal.org

This site offers links, an annotated bibliography, and multiple resources.

Word Choice and Spelling

22

The difference between the right word and the almost right word is really a large matter—'tis the difference between lightning and the lightning bug. —MARK TWAIN

What Mark Twain calls the difference between the "right" and the "almost right" word is a matter of *diction*, which derives from the Latin word for "say" and means literally how one says or expresses something. In speaking of someone you work with, for example, you might choose one or more of the following words: *accomplice, ally, associate, buddy, cohort, collaborator, colleague, comrade, co-worker, mate, partner, sidekick.* As these examples suggest, such choices of diction are always highly contingent on purpose, audience, and situation. Reconsidering these elements of every writer's rhetorical situation may be one good way to introduce a discussion of diction.

FOR TEACHING: Appropriate Formality (22a)

To give students practice in considering diction, have them write a paragraph about something they might want to do at school—change their major, spend their junior year abroad, take a semester off, or something else. Have them first use familiar words, assuming that their audience is someone close like their parents, a spouse, or a good friend. Then ask them to rewrite their paragraphs to address their academic adviser, using more formal diction. Finally, suggest that they analyze each paragraph to identify the elements that create familiar or formal diction.

On Slang and Colloquial Language (22a)

In "The Blab of the Pave," her *New York Times* book review of *The City in Slang*, Elizabeth Hawes tells us:

> Slang is by nature urban; it is "the blab of the pave" as Walt Whitman celebrated it, the informal language of reporters, policemen, songwriters and street

> kids—"hooligan," "plug ugly," "hooker," and "taxi." Like the city, it becomes richer with diversity.
>
> Technically, *slang*, a word that cropped up in the 18th century, can be distinguished from *cant*, the idiom of criminal and low life, and *argot*, the jargon of professional and social classes. But in practice, slang embraces all of these modes and is, by that fact, a cross-cultural, multi-ethnic distillation of voices. American slang, which diverged from British slang after independence, has its own special provenance. As H. L. Mencken concluded in his scholarly study *The American Language*, English slang seems to reside in doubling consonants or in the addition of "-er" to words, like "brekker" for breakfast, while its American counterpart concocts phrases like "lounge lizard" and "rubberneck." With the possible exception of the French, Americans have produced more slang than any other people and have put it to heavier daily use. And of all Americans, New Yorkers have waxed the most eloquent about metropolitan life.

More recently, linguist Steven Pinker says:

> As for slang, I'm all for it! Some people worry that slang will somehow "corrupt" the language. We should be so lucky. Most slang lexicons are preciously guarded by their subcultures as membership badges. When given a glimpse into one of these lexicons, no true language-lover can fail to be dazzled by the brilliant wordplay and wit: from medical students (*Zorro-belly*, *crispy critter*, *prune*), rappers (*jaw -jacking*, *dissing*), college students (*studmuffin*, *veg out*, *blow off*), surfers (*gnarlacious*, *geekified*), and hackers (*to flame*, *core-dump*, *crufty*). When the more passé terms get cast off and handed down to the mainstream, they often fill expressive gaps in the language beautifully. I don't know how I ever did without *to flame* (protest self-righteously), *to dis* (express disrespect for), and *to blow off* (dismiss an obligation), and there are thousands of now unexceptional English words like *clever*, *fun*, *sham*, *banter*, *mob*, *stingy*, *bully*, *junkie*, and *jazz* that began life as slang. It is especially hypocritical to oppose linguistic innovations reflexively and at the same time to decry the loss of distinctions like *lie* versus *lay* on the pretext of preserving expressive power. Vehicles for expressing thought are being created far more quickly than they are being lost.

FOR COLLABORATION: Slang and Colloquial Language (22a)

To help students recognize their own use of slang, and also to show how difficult it is for those not familiar with the terms to understand them, engage students in brainstorming the slang terms and phrases they use currently and have them work in pairs to check slang or urban online dictionaries to see if their favorite is among those listed and defined. If it is, ask them to determine if the definition is accurate; if their phrase is not listed, ask them to write their own definition. Put the pairs together and have the students discuss what they do and don't understand.

FOR TEACHING: Doublespeak (22a)

To combat the proliferation of public doublespeak, the National Council of Teachers of English published the *Quarterly Review of Doublespeak* from 1975–2002 and each year presented the Orwell Award (for honesty in public discourse) and the Doublespeak Award (for the most egregious example of doublespeak). The award winners are now available online at the NCTE Web site: www.ncte.org/about/awards/council/other/106868.htm.

The winner in 2004 was the entire Bush administration for the following examples of doublespeak:

> President George W. Bush, for the second year in a row, has set a high standard for his team by the inspired invention of the phrase "weapons of mass destruction–related program activities" to describe what has yet to be seen. Further he has made clear the principle of democratic discussion: "[A]s you know, these are open forums, you're able to come and listen to what I have to say." Bush also won for his creative use of language in public statements regarding the reasons why the United States needed to pursue war against Iraq—for unsubstantiated statements, for the lack of evidentiary support, and for the purported manipulation of intelligence data.
>
> Secretary of Defense Donald Rumsfeld's description of the widespread torture at Abu Ghraib as "the excesses of human nature that humanity suffers" was brilliantly mind-befuddling. The Secretary is well served by a Pentagon that erased terms like the Vietnam era "body bag" which became "human remains pouches" during the Gulf War and is now known as "transfer tubes," the transfer of which are to be kept from media sight.
>
> The Justice Department also deserves mention for its ingenious contributions to the cause of helping us not confront the shame of our government fostering torture. Jay S. Bybee, head of the Office of Legal Counsel, advised that, in order to be considered torture, the pain inflicted on a prisoner "must be equivalent in intensity to the pain accompanying serious physical injury, such as organ failure, impairment of bodily function, or even death." Leaving aside the problem of how to quantitatively measure human pain in this way, the memo advised that international laws against torture "may be unconstitutional if applied to interrogation" conducted against suspected terrorists.

We have too many high sounding words, and too few actions that correspond with them.
—Abigail Adams

FOR COLLABORATION: Pompous Language, Euphemisms, and Doublespeak (22a)

David Sprunger of Concordia College has created an entire Web site devoted to what he calls "Language Lite: A Gallery of Linguistic Trivia" at www.cord.edu/faculty/sprunger/e315/dbltk.html. Share with your students his page on Doublespeak Proverbs, reproduced below:

Doublespeak Proverbs

If you can translate these camouflaged (but familiar) witticisms, you have a talent for making clear writing out of mud.

Scintillate, scintillate asteroid minific.

Members of an avian species of identical plumage congregate.

Surveillance should precede saltitation.

It is fruitless to become lachrymose over precipitately departed lacteal fluid. Freedom from incrustrations of grime is contiguous to divinity.

The stylus is more potent than the claymore.

It is fruitless to indoctrinate a super-annuated canine with innovative maneuvers.

The temperature of the aqueous content of an unremittingly ogled cooking container does not reach 212 degrees Fahrenheit.

Male cadavers are incapable of yielding testimony.

Individuals who make their abode in vitreous edifices would be advised to refrain from catapulting petrous projectiles.

A plethora of individuals with expertise in culinary techniques vitiates the potable concoction produced by steeping comestibles.

Exclusive dedication to necessary chores without interludes of hedonistic diversion renders John a heptudinous fellow.

FOR TEACHING: Denotation and Connotation (22b)

Read aloud to students the following excerpt from *Dust Tracks on a Road*, Zora Neale Hurston's account of growing up in the South. As you read, your students may want to jot down the denotative and connotative language Hurston uses to describe the bittersweet flavor of being African American, being female, and being thrust ahead by a loving mother. After you have finished reading, ask your students to identify which of Hurston's phrases use academic language and which use her home language.

> [She] gave me my first glimmering of the universal female gospel that all good traits and leanings come from mother's side.
>
> Mama exhorted her children at every opportunity to "jump at de sun." We might not land on the sun, but at least we would get off the ground. Papa did not feel so hopeful. Let well enough alone. It did not do for Negroes to have too much spirit. He was always threatening to break mine or kill me in the attempt. My mother was always standing between us. She conceded that I was impudent and given to talking back, but she didn't want to "squinch my spirit" too much for fear that I would turn out to be a mealy-mouthed rag doll by the time I got grown. Papa always flew hot when Mama said that. I do not know whether he feared for my future, with the tendency I had to stand and give battle, or that he felt a personal reference in mama's observation. He predicted dire things for me. The white folks were not going to stand for it. I was going

> to be hung before I got grown. Somebody was going to blow me down for my sassy tongue. Mama was going to suck sorrow for not beating my temper out of me before it was too late. Posses with ropes and guns were going to drag me out sooner or later on account of that stiff neck I toted. I was going to tote a hungry belly by reason of my forward ways. My older sister was meek and mild. She would always get along. Why couldn't I be like her? Mama would keep right on with whatever she was doing and remark, "Zora is my young'un, and Sarah is yours. I'll be bound mine will come out more than conquer. You leave her alone. I'll tend to her when I figger she needs it." She meant by that that Sarah had a disposition like Papa's, while mine was like hers.

What words or phrases are most memorable? Are they academic or slang? specific or deliciously vague? In what ways does Hurston balance general and specific diction?

FOR COLLABORATION: Denotation and Connotation (22b)

To help students understand the distinction between denotation and connotation, ask each of them to write down their definition of "home." Then have them read their definitions aloud. Have a student record the similarities, but also note the differences, which provides an opportunity to discuss how connotative meanings are often cultural. Read a dictionary definition aloud to note how different or similar it might be to what students have written.

> **If I could fasten the mind of the reader upon words so firmly that he would forget words and be conscious only of his response, I felt that I would be in sight of knowing how to write narrative. I strove to master words, to make them disappear, to make them important by making them new, to make them melt into a rising spiral to emotional stimuli, each greater than the other, each feeding and reinforcing the other, and all ending in an emotional climax that would drench the reader with a sense of a new world. That was the single aim of my living.** —RICHARD WRIGHT

FOR COLLABORATION: General and Specific Language (22c)

Moving from general to specific language often involves describing something so that it can be seen, heard, felt, or experienced. Explain the concept of show versus tell in writing by brainstorming with students how they know when someone is *angry*. Write all the examples on the board. Then have them write a sentence that shows the reader someone who is angry without using the word *angry*. Then divide the class into groups, and ask them to expand each of the following brief sentences into a paragraph.

1. We had a good time.
2. We were bored and had nothing to do.

3. Their tiredness showed.
4. We weren't content to just sit there, frustrated, impatient, and annoyed.

Ask them to work on showing the reader the good time or the frustration and annoyance. Suggest questions such as the following to help them develop the sentences into concrete descriptions. For example, to develop *We had a good time*, you might have them ask:

> What were you doing? with whom?
> How did you do it? What did it involve?

You can also ask students to apply the same questions to *Their tiredness showed.*

FOR TEACHING: General and Specific Language (22c)

Introduce the concept of the "Ladder of Abstraction" to your students. Draw a ladder on the board—two vertical parallel lines with several horizontal lines. Write "abstract/general" at the top and "specifics/details" at the bottom. Have students "position" examples of their sentences on the ladder, and then ask them to make them either more general or more specific. Emphasize that strong writing contains sentences that go up and down the ladder, as staying in any one place makes for boring writing.

Another exercise is to ask students to read the following passage, from Joan Didion's "In Bed," carefully and identify the balance of abstract and concrete and of general and specific diction.

> Migraine is something more than the fancy of a neurotic imagination. It is an essentially hereditary complex of symptoms, the most frequently noted but by no means the most unpleasant of which is a vascular headache of blinding severity, suffered by a surprising number of women, a fair number of men (Thomas Jefferson had migraine, and so did Ulysses S. Grant, the day he accepted Lee's surrender), and by some unfortunate children as young as two years old. (I had my first when I was eight. It came on during a fire drill at the Columbia School in Colorado Springs, Colorado. I was taken first home and then to the infirmary at Peterson Field, where my father was stationed. The Air Corps doctor prescribed an enema.) Almost anything can trigger a specific attack of migraine: stress, allergy, fatigue, an abrupt change in barometric pressure, a contretemps over a parking ticket. A flashing light. A fire drill. One inherits, of course, only the predisposition. In other words I spent yesterday in bed with a headache not merely because of my bad attitudes, unpleasant tempers and wrongthink, but because both my grandmothers had migraine, my father has migraine and my mother has migraine.

FOR TEACHING: Figurative Language (22d)

To show your students that the use of figurative language occurs in our everyday reading and writing, encourage them to look at magazines, articles, and books that they read outside the classroom in their leisure time. For example, Roger Angell's *Season Ticket: A Baseball Companion*, a collection of essays that were originally published in the *New Yorker* between 1983 and 1987, contains wonderful examples of simile. Joel Conarroe, in a review in the *New York Times Book Review*, praises Angell: "This is a meticulous writer with an eye for the telling simile, the domestic image that can bring an observation vividly to life." Conarroe mentions Angell's description of "a slumping team" going through September "like an ember in a snowbank" and of Steve Carlton's three-quarter-speed slider that "drops out of the strike zone like a mouse behind the sink."

On Metaphors (22d)

The bare-bones definition of *metaphor* as an "implicit comparison" hardly does justice to this most important figure. In fact, many language theorists view metaphor as the very grounding of language, which is, in fact, always referring, always deferring. Even a concrete word like *chair* is metaphorical, standing in as it does for some specific object, "figuring" it in the mind of the hearer in certain ways. Students need to understand how deeply metaphorical all language is, and to understand the power of metaphor in shaping our thoughts. One good way to begin might be to take some examples from George Lakoff and Mark Johnson's now-classic 1980 study, *Metaphors We Live By*, which demonstrates in vivid detail how deeply metaphor is embedded in thinking.

FOR TEACHING: Metaphors and Slang (22d)

Share these metaphorical definitions of *slang* with your students. Ask them to decide which one they like best and why, and then to create their own metaphorical definitions of *slang* or of some other abstraction—*beauty*, *truth*, *justice*, *hunger*, and so on.

1. [Slang] is always strong. . . . Cut these words and they would bleed; they are vascular and alive; they walk and run. –RALPH WALDO EMERSON
2. Slang is the speech of him who rolls the literary garbage carts on their way to the dump. –AMBROSE BIERCE
3. Slang is language that takes off its coat, spits on its hands, and gets to work. –CARL SANDBURG
4. Slang: words with their shoes off. –PATRICK HARTWELL
5. Slang is adventure and experiment in words. –MARY AUGUSTA JORDAN
6. [Slang is] the grunt of the human hog (*Pignoramus intolerabilis*). –AMBROSE BIERCE
7. [Slang is] the poetry of everyday life. –S. I. HAYAKAWA

FOR MULTILINGUAL WRITERS: Analogies (22d)

For multilingual writers who may have a difficult time with the cultural nuances of diction, take time to review the following list of exaggerated analogies and the cultural connotations that produce the humor in each case. Read each sentence out loud, and then discuss what makes each analogy a parody.

- "The ballerina rose gracefully en pointe and extended one slender leg behind her, like a dog at a fire hydrant." (Jennifer Hart, Arlington)
- "The revelation that his marriage of thirty years had disintegrated because of his wife's infidelity came as a rude shock, like a surcharge at a formerly surcharge-free ATM." (Paul J. Kocak, Syracuse)
- "The dandelion swayed in the gentle breeze like an oscillating electric fan set on medium." (Ralph Scott, Washington)
- "It was an American tradition, like fathers chasing kids around with power tools." (Brian Broadus, Charlottesville)
- "He was deeply in love. When she spoke, he thought he heard bells, as if she were a garbage truck backing up." (Susan Reese, Arlington)
- "She was as easy as the *TV Guide* crossword." (Tom Witte, Gaithersburg)
- "She grew on him like she was a colony of *E. coli* and he was room-temperature Canadian beef." (Brian Broadus, Charlottesville)
- "The young fighter had a hungry look, the kind you get from not eating for a while." (Malcolm Fleschner, Arlington)

> I write out loud, hearing the music that gives writing meaning. I can write the first draft with the screen turned off. I write by ear. —DONALD M. MURRAY, *Boston Globe*

FOR TEACHING: Effective Similes, Metaphors, and Analogies (22d)

Ask your students to evaluate the effectiveness of similes, metaphors, and analogies in the following sentences and to revise any that are mixed metaphors or clichés.

1. These children were brought up to eat, drink, and sleep tennis.
2. In presenting his alibi, the defendant chose the alley he was going to bowl on—and the jury wouldn't swallow it.

3. The president's economic plan is about as useful as rearranging the deck chairs on the *Titanic.*
4. The narrative was heavy as lead—it just flowed on and on and on.
5. For as long as I can remember, my mother has been the backbone for my father's convictions.

You might have students work in groups to complete this exercise. In the case of identifying mixed metaphor and cliché especially, two (or more) heads are better than one. You also may want to ask students to write brief explanations of what they found wrong in the sentences and of how their revisions remedy the problems.

> Clichés are the last word in bad writing, and it's *a crying shame* to see all you *bright young things* spoiling your *deathless prose* with phrases *as old as the hills.* You must *keep your nose to the grindstone,* because the *sweet smell of success* only comes to those who *march to the tune of a different drummer.* —JANET BURROWAY

FOR COLLABORATION: Similes and Metaphors (22d)

Assign every student a partner for this activity. Working collaboratively, each pair should identify the similes and metaphors in the following passages, and decide how each contributes to an understanding of the passage it appears in. Next, students can try to write an imitation of one of these sentences, making sure to include an effective simile or metaphor. Have students bring all explanations and imitations to class for discussion.

1. John's mother, Mom Willie, who wore her Southern background like a magnolia corsage, eternally fresh, was robust and in her sixties.
   —MAYA ANGELOU, *The Heart of a Woman*
2. I was watching everyone else and didn't see the waitress standing quietly by. Her voice was deep and soft like water moving in a cavern.
   —WILLIAM LEAST HEAT-MOON, "In the Land of 'Coke-Cola'"
3. My horse, when he is in his stall or lounging about the pasture, has the same relationship to pain that I have when cuddling up with a good murder mystery—comfort and convenience have top priority.
   —VICKI HEARNE, "Horses in Partnership with Time"

> Language is not an abstract construction of the learned, or of dictionary-makers, but is something arising out of the work, needs, ties, joys, affections, tastes. . . . —WALT WHITMAN

TEACHING WITH TECHNOLOGY: Thinking Critically about Word Choice

Ask students to bring selections from their own work to class. Choose several to project from a computer onto a screen, and ask the class as a whole to discuss the diction of each piece. How would students describe the dominant impression given by the selection? How would they characterize its register? Which words seem most effective and memorable—and why? Are there any instances in which they might revise the diction for different effect?

Revise the selections collaboratively, using the keyboard and inputting students' suggestions.

> **Why shouldn't we quarrel about a word? What is the good of words if they aren't important enough to quarrel over? Why do we choose one word more than another if there isn't any difference between them?** —G. K. CHESTERTON

TEACHING WITH TECHNOLOGY: Thinking Critically about Word Choice

Since part of making effective word choices requires building a larger vocabulary, ask students to make a habit of visiting the Web site www.freerice.org. This site sets up multiple choice answers for definitions of words (synonyms); for every correct answer the Free Rice organization donates rice through the UN World Food Program to help end world hunger.

On Checking Spelling (22e)

Students ask us all the time—"Why do we need to attend so meticulously to spelling?" Our answer might be rooted in classical rhetoric, for what's at stake with spelling errors is the very ethos of the writer. As Larry Beason found out in his study of reader's impressions of orthographic errors, mistakes matter—immensely: "In the nonacademic workforce, errors can affect people and events in larger ways. . . . Whether we believe it to be the optimum situation or not, errors have an impact on the writer's image and communicability. Error avoidance, I submit, should have a presence in the composition curriculum—but without overpowering it" (60). Similarly, in research conducted for an earlier edition of *The Everyday Writer*, Andrea Lunsford and Robert Connors found that spelling errors were the most common mistakes made by student writers.

The public unfortunately believes that the majority of students are bad spellers, but in fact, the results of recent research contradict this notion. When Andrea Lunsford and Karen Lunsford replicated the Lunsford and Connor study twenty years later, they found that spelling errors had decreased dramatically. In that study spelling errors, including homonym errors, were the fifth most common error in student writing. Most of the misspellings found in the Lunsfords' study were those that spell checkers cannot identify—such as homonym errors, compound words incorrectly spelled as two separate words, and proper nouns. Encourage students to carefully proofread their work for these errors and to think critically about taking a spell checker's advice.

FOR TEACHING: Spell Checkers and Homonyms (22e)

In addition to using the spell-checker function of their word processing program, students should use the FIND function to check for homonym problems. Instruct them to search their drafts for homonyms and frequently confused words that they are unsure about (see the lists in 22e of *The Everyday Writer*). When the search stops at each instance of a word, students can double-check their use of it by consulting *The Everyday Writer* and a dictionary.

FOR COLLABORATION: Spell Checkers and Homonyms (22e)

To emphasize the danger of relying on spell checkers, distribute to pairs of students the excerpt from the following poem, "Candidate for a Pullet Surprise," by Mark Eckman and Jerrold H. Zar. Have them write the poem using the correct words, and for a challenge, ask students to define the unfamiliar words in the poem.

Eye halve a spelling chequer
It came with my pea sea
It plainly marques four my revue
Miss steaks eye kin knot sea.

Eye strike a key and type a word
And weight four it two say
Weather eye am wrong oar write
It shows me strait a weigh.

As soon as a mist ache is maid
It nose bee fore two long
And eye can put the error rite
Its rare lea ever wrong.

Eye have run this poem threw it
I am shore your pleased two no
Its letter perfect awl the weigh
My chequer tolled me sew.

On Homonyms (22e)

In the *Harper Dictionary of Contemporary Usage*, William and Mary Morris make an interesting distinction among homographs, homonyms, and homophones. *Homographs* are words spelled alike but pronounced differently (e.g., *tears* we shed and *tears* in a cloth). *Homonyms* are words spelled alike and pronounced alike (e.g., *bear* the animal, and *bear* meaning "carry"). *Homophones* are words spelled differently but pronounced alike (*peace* and *piece*). Normally, we just refer to all three under the label *homonym.*

FOR TEACHING: Spelling Rules (22f)

You can use the teaching of spelling rules to your advantage. Dorothy Thompson argues that short periods of spelling instruction are more effective than are longer periods. Ann Dobie suggests no more than fifteen or twenty minutes per class time.

Consider the following practice for each student's final draft:

1. Circle all misspelled words in the paper.
2. Ask the student to correct the misspellings.
3. Ask the student to bring in two other related words and identify the shared core.

Although spelling can be very important in the creation of ethos for the writer, too much emphasis on spelling in the classroom can eventually paralyze some writers. It is important to emphasize to your students that spelling correction is a late-draft revision activity rather than an early draft revision activity. Writers should not be concerned with spelling during early drafts that they know will be revised; they should get down on paper their ideas and the organization of those ideas before they address spelling. However, if student writers are bothered by the fact that they know some of the words are misspelled, between writing drafts they should go through the text of the last draft, marking all the words whose spellings they are unsure of. Then, before the next draft, they can look these words up and list them in their writing logs as troublesome words.

> **I could be typing *kifiu joew.mv jiw* and enjoy it as much as typing words that actually make sense.**
>
> **—Steve Martin**

FOR COLLABORATION: Spelling Rules (22f)

Many spelling errors are actually errors of proofreading—or the lack thereof. We all commit typos, but they indicate nothing more than our imperfect humanity, and they are easily corrected during spell checking and proofreading. Genuine spelling errors are, of course, a different story. But because the reader has no way to distinguish between the two, proofreading becomes a vitally important activity for the writer. To encourage students to proofread more carefully, you might consider the following practice.

Before taking up the final draft of the first paper, divide the class into pairs or groups of three. Have group members exchange papers and check for words that they think might be misspelled. On a separate sheet of paper, they should note the page number and paragraph number, the misspelled word, and what they believe is the correct spelling of that word. After the papers have been returned to the authors, allow students time to go through their papers and make the corrections. They should be aware that there is no guarantee that their proofreaders are correct 100 percent of the time. The writers themselves must make the final choice about the spelling. Along with the paper, the separate sheet with the proofreader's notes on the spelling should be handed in. When grading this first paper, don't count off for any corrected spelling, but do record the originally misspelled words pointed out by the proofreader.

Do the same for subsequent papers, but call special attention—whether through grading sanctions or by a reminder to the student—to misspellings that are repeated from their earlier work.

> **No doubt you are as alarmed as I by the tragic decline in America's language skills. If 10 people read the following sentence—"Two tanker trucks has just overturned in Alaska, spilling a totel of 10,000 gallons of beer onto a highway"—two would find an error in subject-verb agreement, two would find an error in spelling, and six would find a sponge and drive north.**
>
> **—MIKE NICHOLS**

USEFUL READINGS

Altick, Richard D., and Andrea A. Lunsford. *Preface to Critical Reading.* 6th ed. New York: Holt, 1984. See Chapter 1 for a discussion of the uses of connotation in advertising, political persuasion, and literature.

Beason, Larry. "Ethos and Error: How Business People React to Errors." *CCC* 53.1 (Sept. 2001): 33–64. Through quantitative research on fourteen businesspeople, Beason offers a rhetorical analysis of errors in terms of how textual transgressions lead readers to produce judgments of character and consequently construct "a negative ethos of the writer." An enlightening article for both teachers and students to read, Beason's research suggests that errors impede more than communication; they endanger a writer's credibility and character.

Coe, Richard M. "Beyond Diction: Using Burke to Empower Words—and Wordlings." *Rhetoric Review* 11.2 (Spring 1993): 368–77.

Corbett, Edward P. J., with Robert Connors. *Classical Rhetoric for the Modern Student.* 4th ed. New York: Oxford UP, 1999. Corbett's discussion of ethical and emotional appeals provides a sound rationale for the importance of diction.

Davis, Betty J. "Fanciful Spellings as a Reflection of Pronunciation in Advanced ESL Composition Students." *Journal of the American Society of Geolinguistics* 13 (1987): 107–23. Davis discusses spelling errors in relationship to pronunciation.

Dobie, Ann B. "Orthographical Theory and Practice, or How to Teach Spelling." *Journal of Basic Writing* 5 (1986): 41–48.

———. "Orthography Revisited: A Response to Kristen Anderson." *Journal of Basic Writing* 7 (1988): 82–83.

Heath, Shirley Brice. *Ways with Words.* Cambridge: Cambridge UP, 1983. See Chapter 9, "Learners as Ethnographers," for more information about students as "investigative reporters."

Herndon, Jeanne H. *A Survey of Modern Grammars.* New York: Holt, 1976. See pages 146–47 for a discussion of competence and performance, *la langue* and *la parole.*

Kidder, Ede, and Karl Taylor. "The Development of Spelling Skills from First Grade through Eighth Grade." *Written Communication* 5 (Apr. 1988): 222–44.

Lakoff, George, and Mark Johnson. *Metaphors We Live By.* Chicago: U of Chicago P, 1980.

Mencken, H. L. *The American Language.* 4th ed. New York: Knopf, 1999. See "The Expanding Vocabulary," "The Making of New Nouns," and "American Slang."

Olson, M. W., J. W. Logan, and T. P. Lindsey. "Early and Current Reading and Spelling Practices of Gifted Spellers." *Reading Psychology* 10 (1989): 189–201.

Orwell, George. "Politics and the English Language." *Shooting an Elephant and Other Essays.* New York: Harcourt, 1974. The essay provides a discussion of appropriate verbs and nouns, pretentious diction, and meaningless words.

Perry, Theresa, and Lisa Delpit, eds. *The Real Ebonics Debate: Power, Language, and the Education of African American Children*. Boston: Beacon, 1998. This collection of writings, by distinguished scholars and writers on the definitions and implications of Ebonics for the education of African American students, offers an insightful analysis of the complex and political nature of language as well as its inextricable relation to race and class in the United States.

Pinker, Steven. *The Language Instinct: How the Mind Creates Language*. New York: Harper, 1995.

Pyles, Thomas, and John Algeo. *The Origins and Development of the English Language*. 4th ed. New York: Harcourt, 1993. The fourth edition of this history of the language contains a good deal of information on spelling.

Shaughnessy, Mina. *Errors and Expectations*. New York: Oxford UP, 1977. See Chapter 5 on spelling.

Skorczewski, Dawn. "'Everybody Has Their Own Ideas': Responding to Cliché in Student Writing." *CCC* 52.2 (Dec. 2000): 220–39. While writing instructors often identify clichés as the weakest spots in student writing, Skorczewski argues that looking at students' uses of cliché in context can teach us about their knowledge base and ways of communicating.

Stark, Ryan J. "Clichés and Composition Theory." *Journal of Composition Theory* 19.3 (1999): 453–64. Stark makes the compelling case for the cliché as a rhetorical device to establish common ground.

Stevens, William J. "Obstacles to Spelling Reform." *English Journal* 54 (1965): 85–90.

Thompson, Dorothy. "Spelling's Day in the Sun." *Instructor* 85 (1976): 16.

Williams, Joseph M. *Origins of the English Language: A Social and Linguistic History*. New York: Macmillan, 1975. See pp. 204–7 for a discussion of slang as a source of change in word meaning. Williams cites interesting historical instances of slang.

23 Glossary of Usage

Conventions of usage might be called the "good manners" of discourse. Just as our notions of good manners vary from culture to culture and time to time, so do conventions of usage. The word *ain't*, for instance, now considered inappropriate in formal discourse, was once widely used by the most proper British speakers and is still used normally in some spoken American dialects. So matters of usage, like other choices writers must make, depend on a writer's purpose and on what is appropriate for a particular audience at a particular time. The Glossary of Usage provides, in brief form, a guide to generally accepted usage in college and professional writing, and a guide for distinguishing between words whose meanings are similar or that are easily confused.

USEFUL WEB SITES

The American Heritage Book of English Usage

http://www. bartleby.com/64/

This online version of the 1996 book aims to inform and help readers with current problems in English usage.

The Use of Clichés

http://www.nexus.edu.au/teachstud/dexed/docs/cliche.html

The account of an English teacher named Ms. English, with an ax to grind, who told her students to avoid clichés like the plague, this piece by Graeden Horsell claims that sometimes clichés are needed, and that one should never say "never."

yourDictionary.com

http://www.yourdictionary.com

This portal for language products and services advertises "the widest and deepest set of dictionaries on the Web." The site's 'Nyms & Such section offers links to many specialty dictionaries and databases, including an online homophone dictionary.

Sentence Style

Look: Wear your black some days, and wear your purple others. There is no other rule besides pulling it off.

—ZADIE SMITH

24 Coordination, Subordination, and Emphasis

It is when I struggle to be brief that I become obscure.

–HORACE

Current pedagogical theory—and popular lore—tends to value clarity and conciseness. Yet composition researchers tell us that complex sentences indicate a writer's syntactic maturity. Are we sending our students mixed messages, then? No. The two concepts are not necessarily contradictory: beginning writers often need practice in clarity and conciseness to make meaning; more mature writers can use those same qualities to form effective and more complex sentence structures.

The notion that subordination and complex sentence structures indicate sophistication of thought and language ability, or maturity in the writer, needs some qualification, if only historical. In Old and Middle English, subordination was not expected, nor was it used to measure a writer's skill. In *Classical Rhetoric for the Modern Student*, Edward P. J. Corbett and Robert J. Connors tell us that "the history of the prose style of most Western languages reveals a gradual evolution from a paratactic syntax—stringing together a series of coordinate structures without conjunctions—to the most sophisticated of sentence patterns, subordination."

In *Teaching English Grammar*, Robert C. Pooley cites passages from the King James Version (KJV) of the Bible as examples of the predominance of coordination over subordination in earlier English, but without acknowledging that that particular translation reflects the sentence structure of the original Hebrew, not English. John B. Gabel and Charles B. Wheeler tell us that "in general [Hebrew] lacks our great variety of words that indicate logical connections between clauses and phrases. In Hebrew, sentence units tend to string out one after another in boxcar fashion and to be hooked together by means of a single, all-purpose connective that is usually translated 'and' in the KJV" (*The Bible as Literature: An Introduction* [New York: Oxford UP, 1986]). For example, Genesis 19:1–3 repeats the connective seventeen times in Hebrew: in the KJV, it appears as "and" sixteen of those times.

> (1) And there came two angels to Sodom at even; and Lot sat in the gate of Sodom: and Lot seeing *them* rose up to meet them; and he bowed himself with his face toward the ground; (2) And he said, Behold now, my lords, turn in, I pray you, into your servant's house, and tarry all night, and wash your feet, and ye shall rise up early, and go on your ways. And they said, Nay; but we will abide in the street all night. (3) And he pressed upon them greatly; and they turned in unto him, and entered into his house; and he made them a feast, and did bake unleavened bread, and they did eat.

Additional exercises on coordination and subordination are available on *The Everyday Writer*'s companion Web site, **bedfordstmartins.com/everydaywriter**. Go to **Exercise Central** and click on **Coordination and Subordination**.

On Parataxis and Hypotaxis

Parataxis is Greek for "placing side by side." Paratactic clauses, phrases, or sentences are arranged independently (a coordinate, rather than a subordinate construction), often without the customary connectives. In the following passage from *A Farewell to Arms*, Ernest Hemingway leaves the causal connections up to the reader:

> There were wet dead leaves on the road from the rows of bare trees and men were working on the road, tamping stone in the ruts from piles of crushed stone along the side of the road between the trees.

Although many beginning writers use parataxis, few use it with Hemingway's skill. Hence, their prose, which balances overtly equal relationships, often elicits simple, spliced, or fused sentences.

Hypotaxis is Greek for "subjection." Hypotactic prose makes clear the dependent or subordinate relationships. In "Travail," H. L. Mencken makes clear causal and logical relationships:

> It is no wonder that schoolboys so often turn for stimulus from their teachers to their fellows. The fact, I believe, is largely to blame for the juvenile lawlessness that prevails in America, for it is the relatively daring and lawless boys who stand out from the mass, and so attract their weaker brethren. . . . On the female side they have the instincts of duennas, and on the male side they seldom rise above the levels of scoutmasters and Y.M.C.A. secretaries.

Students who write in paratactic style (and who are forming comma splices and fused sentences) are often thinking in hypotactic style. Ask them to make their connections aloud.

FOR TEACHING: Use Coordination to Relate Equal Ideas (24a)

Students tend to have little problem understanding coordination, dependent as many are on a few all-purpose connectors such as *and* or *but*. Because some students overuse coordination, you may want to emphasize the importance of striking a balance among coordinated, subordinated, and simple constructions.

In *Style: Ten Lessons in Clarity and Grace*, Joseph Williams cites another problem connected with coordination: lost connections. When the grammatical coordination of a sentence becomes too long, the reader cannot follow its internal connections. He uses the following sentence as an example:

> "Teachers should remember that students are vulnerable people, insecure and uncertain about those everyday, ego-bruising moments that adults ignore, *and that they do not understand that one day they* will become as confident and as secure as the adults that bruise them." (194)

According to Williams, placement of that italic clause is troublesome because it is not close enough to its source of coordination. And he offers two possible revisions: repetition of a key phrase or starting a new sentence. *Every teacher ought to remind himself daily that his students are vulnerable people, . . . and to remind himself that his students do not understand . . .* or . . . *adults no longer concern themselves with. Teachers should remind themselves that their students do not understand.* Note that the second revision uses nonsexist language.

FOR COLLABORATION: Use Coordination to Relate Equal Ideas (24a)

Ask students to work in groups to identify the coordinate elements in the following passage, taken from Joyce Carol Oates's *Black Water*. What is the effect of the coordinate elements? Each group might want to rewrite the passage, using subordination to create a different effect—from the point of view, perhaps, of the driver of the car, who had escaped watery death.

> He was her friend. He was no one she knew but he was her friend, *that* she knew. In another minute she would remember his name.
>
> It was a car that had trapped her, she was jammed somehow in the front seat of a car but the space was very small because the roof and the dashboard and the door beside her had buckled inward pinning her legs and crushing her right kneecap held as if in a vise and her ribs on that side were broken but the pain seemed to be held in suspension like a thought not yet fully acknowledged scarcely any sensation at all so she knew she would be all right so long as she could lift her head free of the seeping black water that smelled of raw sewage and was cold, colder than you could imagine on such a warm midsummer night.

On Subordination (24b)

In *Errors and Expectations*, Mina Shaughnessy describes subordination in terms of the demands it makes on the student writer:

> If the dependent unit comes first in the sentence, the writer must suspend the independent unit in his mind while he qualifies it (as with introductory adverbial phrases and clauses). If the dependent unit comes between the subject and predicate of the base sentence (as with a relative clause after the subject), the writer must hold the main subject in his mind while he writes out the subject and predicate of the qualifying clause, and then he must return to the predicate of the base sentence. These operations require a memory for written words and grammatical structures that the inexperienced writer may not have. He hears what he says easily enough, but he does not as easily recall what he has written once his hand has moved on to another part of the sentence, and unlike the experienced writer, he is not in the habit of reviewing what he has written but instead moves headlong, as a speaker might, toward the open line, often forgetting the constraints he has set for himself a few words back.

Students react to these demands in different ways, of course. Some will shy away from the complexity and rely as much as possible on simple and compound structures. Others, motivated by a perceived need to write academic-sounding discourse, will produce what Shaughnessy calls "ruptured" or garbled sentences. Shaughnessy offers several options for the instructor: drills and grammatical explanations, sentence-combining exercises, and other types of exercises. But she concludes that the most improvement may occur when students commit themselves to communicating with the reader, despite "the exasperating literalism of the medium" (89).

Traditionally, instructors have assumed that grammar reflected logical thinking—that use of subordination should include subordinate ideas, with the most important ideas going in the main clause, and that coordination juxtaposed two ideas of equal rank. Linguists, however, hold that grammar is not necessarily logical. In "Coordination (Faulty) and Subordination (Upside Down)," James Sledd writes that "the traditional theory of clauses is simply untenable." Subordinate ideas can and often do show up in main clauses, and main ideas can appear in subordinate clauses, as in the opening sentence of this note.

FOR TEACHING: Using Subordination to Distinguish Main Ideas (24b)

Have students combine each of the following sets of sentences into one sentence that uses subordination to signal the relationships among ideas. Here is an example:

I was looking over my books.
I noticed that *Burr* was missing.
This book is a favorite of my roommate's.

While I was looking over my books, I noticed that *Burr*, one of my roommate's favorite books, was missing.

1. I walked into the shelter.

   Men, women, and children were slumped against the wall.
   Shopping carts containing families' belongings lay on their sides.

2. Madonna announced her first concert tour in years.
   Ticket sales were advertised.

   Fans lined up as many as forty-eight hours in advance.

3. We had dug a seventy-foot ditch.

   My boss would pour gravel into the ditch.

   I would level the gravel with a shovel.

4. *Blink* was written by Malcolm Gladwell.
   It is a fascinating book.
   It explains how people make decisions in the "blink" of an eye.

5. The scenery there is beautiful.
   The mountains have caps of snow.
   The lakes are deep and full of fish.
   The pastures are green.
   It is an ideal spot to spend spring break.

Answers

1. Walking into the shelter, I saw men, women, and children slumped against the wall, their belongings lying in overturned shopping carts.

2. When ticket sales were advertised for Madonna's first concert tour in years, fans lined up as many as forty-eight hours in advance.

3. After my boss poured gravel into the seventy-foot-long ditch we had dug, I leveled the gravel with a shovel.

4. *Blink*, a fascinating book by Malcolm Gladwell, explains how people make decisions in the "blink" of an eye.

5. The snow-capped mountains, green pastures, and deep, fish-filled lakes make the park a beautiful and ideal spot to spend spring break.

FOR TEACHING: Use Closing and Opening Positions for Emphasis (24c)

Ask students to try their hand at imitating the sentences below to practice using openings that postpone the important information to the end of the sentence. Then duplicate some or all of them, read them aloud, and use them to stimulate class discussion of and appreciation for powerfully constructed sentences. You might also wish to ask students to match the imitations to the model, clause for clause, phrase for phrase, as a means of identifying structural elements in sentences. Focus class discussion on the opening and closing positions in the student's sentences.

1. On the pleasant shore of the French Riviera, about half way between Marseille and the Italian border, stands a large, proud, rose-colored hotel. (F. Scott Fitzgerald, *Tender Is the Night*, opening sentence)
2. *I* am an invisible man. No, *I* am not a spook like those who haunted Edgar Allan Poe; nor am *I* one of your Hollywood-movie ectoplasms. *I* am a man of substance, of flesh and bone, fiber and liquids—*and I might even be said* to possess a mind. *I* am invisible, understand, simply because people refuse to see me. (Ralph Ellison, *Invisible Man*, opening lines)

FOR COLLABORATION: Use Climactic Order to Emphasize Important Ideas (24c)

To demonstrate climactic order, ask the class to suggest a topic (such as the qualities of a good friend, a good car, or a popular campus restaurant). Brainstorm the topic, creating a list of associations on the board. Then ask students to write a one-sentence statement summarizing their ideas about the topic. Have students read their statements and comment on possible reasons for ordering their subtopics the way they did. You may want to take this opportunity to point out that climactic order reflects the relative importance the writer attaches to ideas.

FOR TEACHING: Use Climactic Order to Emphasize Important Ideas (24c)

Ask students to imitate the examples of effective and ineffective climactic form in 24c of *The Everyday Writer*. Then, after reading aloud the following sentences and examining their climactic order, ask students to write imitations.

1. I have in my own life a precious friend, a woman of 65 who has lived very hard, who is wise, who listens well, who has been where I am and can help me understand it; and who represents not only an ultimate ideal mother to me but also the person I'd like to be when I grow up. –JUDITH VIORST
2. To assign unanswered letters their proper weight, to free us from the expectations of others, to give us back to ourselves—here lies the great, the singular power of self-respect. –JOAN DIDION
3. She loved the flat, she loved her life, she loved Herbie. –DOROTHY PARKER

FOR COLLABORATION: Use Coordination and Subordination

Ask students to work in groups to revise the following paragraph using coordination and subordination where appropriate to clarify the relationships between ideas.

I stayed with my friend Louise. She owns a huge, mangy wolf. It is actually a seven-eighths wolf cross. The poor creature is allergic to everything. It looks like a shabby, moth-eaten exhibit of a stuffed wolf in a third-rate museum. Louise and Bill feed it rice and raw potatoes. It slavers all over everything. It never goes out of the house. It sleeps on the beds. They are covered with animal hair. It makes no sounds. It just looks at you with those sunken, wild eyes. It is not dangerous or ferocious. It is just completely miserable. This animal should never have been born. It's trying to tell you that with every twitch.

USEFUL READINGS

Corbett, Edward P. J., and Robert J. Connors. *Classical Rhetoric for the Modern Student*. 4th ed. New York: Oxford UP, 1999.

Lanham, Richard A. *Analyzing Prose*. 2nd ed. New York: Continuum, 2002. Lanham attacks the dominant theory of prose style, which values clarity, brevity, and sincerity. Instead, he calls for the use of a variety of different styles, depending on the desired rhetorical effects.

Pooley, Robert C. *Teaching English Grammar*. New York: Appleton-Century-Crofts, 1957.

Shaughnessy, Mina. *Errors and Expectations*. New York: Oxford UP, 1977.

Sledd, James. "Coordination (Faulty) and Subordination (Upside Down)." *CCC* 7 (1956): 181–87.

Traugott, Elizabeth Closs, and Mary Louise Pratt. *Linguistics for Students of Literature*. San Diego: Harcourt, 1980. See "Recursive Property of Language" for a transformational-linguistics perspective on coordination and subordination. Traugott and Pratt call subordination and coordination "linguistic creativity," or the ability to create complex sentences out of simple sentences by applying the generative principles of "recursiveness" (154–55).

Williams, Joseph M. *Style: Ten Lessons in Clarity and Grace*. 6th ed. New York: Addison-Wesley, 2002. Williams offers advice for the control of "sprawling" sentences, the result of a main clause connected to too many subordinate clauses.

Winterowd, Ross. "The Grammar of Coherence." *CE* 31 (1970): 328–35. Transformational grammar does not fully explain the coherence of units of discourse. Seven transitional relations account for coherence: coordinate expressed (*and*), obversive (*but*), causative (*for*), conclusive (*so*), alternative (*or*), inclusive (the colon), and sequential (*first . . . second*).

25 Consistency and Completeness

In “The Uses—and Limits—of Grammar,” Sarah D’Eloia explains “syntactically tangled sentences” as inconsistent and incomplete sentences that confuse the reader and that cannot be rhetorically justified in normal prose. Often these garbled sentences are the results of experiments in “logical and grammatical subordination, differential relation, and equivalence” (228), which students write for several reasons: (1) not knowing the “right” word or syntactic structure, the student may turn to the familiar (but inappropriate); (2) the student tries to juggle several subordinations at once; (3) unsure of the choice, the student may allow the alternatives to “contaminate” his or her decision; (4) the student lacks the academic self-confidence necessary to produce syntactically complex structures; (5) the student is unaware of the benefits that come with revision. Unfortunately, some of the most outgoing and sociable students lack confidence in academic situations: they do not believe their knowledge or opinions warrant development; their syntax is often tentative and qualifying. Worse, many of these students believe that “real” writers get it right the first time. When Mina Shaughnessy’s writing students saw the messy pages of Richard Wright’s novel *Native Son*, they concluded that Wright was not a good writer—he made too many mistakes.

If you ask students to listen carefully to the conversations around them, they will hear inconsistent and incomplete grammatical structures, particularly in lively or heated discussion. For instance:

> “The Cavs are . . . They must be the best team in . . . not in the league even . . . in the country.”
>
> “Wait till the Heat take them. Because you know Wade and Shaq, they make magic happen, in a SWEEP.”

In the flow of informal conversation, such structures pose few problems for speakers and listeners. But they do pose problems for writers.

Additional exercises on consistent and complete structures are available on the *The Everyday Writer*’s companion Web site, **bedfordstmartins.com/everydaywriter**. Go to **Exercise Central** and click on **Consistent and Complete Structures**.

FOR COLLABORATION: Revise Faulty Sentence Structure (25a)

We want our students to be able to produce clear and consistent texts, yet we ask them to appreciate texts—canonized essays and stories—that often do not incorporate those same qualities. Critically acclaimed writer Toni Cade Bambara, for instance, frequently uses sentence structures that resist classroom standards. Ask your students to listen for purpose and effect as you read aloud the following passage from "My Man Bovanne," a story of a woman and a blind man at a benefit dance. Then ask them to work in groups to revise the passage according to standard academic English. Did they improve the text? interfere with it? What were the specific effects of their revisions?

> But right away Joe Lee come up on us and frown for dancin so close to the man. My own son who knows what kind of warm I am about; and don't grown men all call me long distance and in the middle of the night for a little Mama comfort? But he frown. Which ain't right since Bovanne can't see and defend himself. Just a nice old man who fixes toasters and busted irons . . . and changes the lock on my door when my men friends get messy. Nice man. Which is not why they invited him. Grass roots you see. Me and Sister Taylor and the woman who does heads at Mamies and the man from the barber shop, we all there on account of we grass roots. And I ain't never been souther than Brooklyn Battery and no more country than the window box on my fire escape. And just yesterday my kids tellin me to take them countrified rags off my head and be cool. And now can't get Black enough to suit 'em. So everybody passin saying My Man Bovanne. . . . And him standin there with a smile ready case someone do speak he want to be ready. So that's how come I pull him on the dance floor and we dance. . . .

On Matching Up Subjects and Predicates (25b)

The mismatch of the linking verb *be* and clauses opening with *when* or *because* is often termed *faulty predication*. Linking verbs link a subject with a subjective complement, which renames or modifies the subject: *Sportsmanship is important to team players.* When a student uses *when* after *is*, he or she introduces an adverbial element, which no longer renames or modifies the subject, but modifies the verb: *Sportsmanship is when players treat one another with fairness and consideration.* Wilson Follett explains the construction of *the reason . . . is because* in *Modern American Usage*: when we make *reason* the subject of a sentence, we tend to substitute *because* for *that*; such a switch "besides being a breach of idiom, is an obvious redundancy: *because = for the reason that*" (275). Hence, *the reason is because* paraphrases as *the reason is for the reason that.*

On Using Elliptical Structures Carefully (25c)

Elliptical structures omit certain *understood* words. For instance, when your students ask you when you plan to pass back their papers and you answer "Tomorrow," you have left out the understood words, "I will pass back your papers." And when you say to them, "If in doubt about the comments I've made on your papers, please see me," you've left out the understood information: "If *you are* in doubt." One student may say to another, "You'll probably get an A, but I won't [get an A]." Although dependent on context, elliptical structures are the most convenient way to avoid repetition while providing conciseness and movement in speech and writing.

FOR TEACHING: Use Elliptical Structures Carefully (25c)

To better acquaint your students with the concept of ellipsis, you may want to turn to George Curmé's *English Grammar*, which provides a list of different kinds of ellipses—the stylistic and syntactic omission of key words and phrases. Curmé explains the following kinds of omissions:

Clauses of comparison

That teacher cares for her students as a mother (cares for) her children.

Conditional sentences

She could easily win the contest (if she tried).

Clauses of exception

Nobody knew her except/but I (knew her).

Imperatives

Heads, eyes front. (Turn your heads and eyes to the front.)

Independent propositions

He cooks better than you do (better than you cook).

FOR TEACHING: Make Comparisons Complete, Consistent, and Clear (25e)

Incomplete comparisons are common in spoken discourse. In practice, *A person who drives drunk is more dangerous* will probably make sense to most of your students. Context will supply the missing information, or students will effortlessly fill in the missing information. Ask students if they can create a context for the following incomplete comparisons:

1. Hybrid-electric cars operate more efficiently.
2. Does your sister seem any happier?
3. The equipment in our new warehouse is guaranteed to last longer.
4. The students liked science class better.
5. If you start studying a week before the test you will get a higher grade.

FOR COLLABORATION: Make Comparisons Consistent and Complete (25e)

Have students work in pairs to revise the following paragraph by making every sentence grammatically and logically consistent and complete. Students should bring their revisions to class and be prepared to explain them.

> The reason I believe the United States should have a military draft is because draft would make us better citizens. By requiring the same sacrifice from every young person would make everyone feel part of a common effort. In addition, a draft is fairer. When an army is made up of volunteers come mostly from the poor and minority groups. During the Persian Gulf War, news reports showed blacks were overrepresented among the troops, largely because their economic options were more limited than young whites and the military thus more attractive as a career. I also feel that women should be subject to the draft. A quality that the military needs is soldiers who are dedicated, and women soldiers have shown that they are more dedicated to their jobs than men. The requirements of a modern army also need skills that more women possess. Equality is when both sexes have equal responsibilities as well as equal opportunity.

USEFUL READINGS

Curmé, George O. *English Grammar.* 1947. New York: Harper, 1947. See Curmé's coverage of the ellipsis.

D'Eloia, Sarah. "The Uses—and Limits—of Grammar." *Journal of Basic Writing* 1 (Spring/Summer 1977): 1–20.

Follett, Wilson. *Modern American Usage.* New York: Hill, 1966.

26 Parallelism

All successful rhetoricians recognize the power of parallel structures. The rhetorician Gorgias (c. 420 BCE) was noted for his use of parallelism and antithesis. In his encomium (a formal expression of enthusiastic praise) to Helen, he declares:

> Speech is a powerful lord which by means of the finest and most invisible body effects the divinest words: it can stop fear and banish grief and create joy and nurture piety.

By contemporary standards, Gorgias's style is considered artificial and contrived—partially because of what we perceive as excessive parallelism.

In spite of the modern tendency to dislike excessive ornamentation of any kind, the appeal of parallel structures may be inherent in human psychology, or so argues Richard L. Graves in "Symmetrical Form and the Rhetoric of the Sentence." Graves notes that symmetry is everywhere—from our own physiology and self-expression to our art and architecture. Kenneth Burke, too, suggests that the concept of symmetry may be one of "the innate forms of the mind," along with comparison/contrast and repetition (46). Echoing tradition, Joseph Williams notes received wisdom: coordinate elements only of the same grammatical structure—clause and clause, predicate and predicate, prepositional phrase and prepositional phrase. Yet Williams concedes that the rule is often broken, on the grounds that clarity—not grammatical structure—measures the success or failure of parallel structures.

Parallelism involves more than initially meets the eye. For instance, instead of looking at *She is tall, tanned, and very handsome* as a set of parallel adjectives, we might regard it as a combination of three separate but parallel sentences: *She is tall. She is tanned. She is very handsome.* In combining these sentences, the writer suppresses the repeated subject verb cluster *She is*, expecting the reader to provide it mentally. When students see the source of parallel structures, they become more sensitive to their own parallel constructions.

Additional exercises on parallelism are available on *The Everyday Writer*'s companion Web site, **bedfordstmartins.com/everydaywriter**. Go to **Exercise Central** and click on **Parallelism**.

FOR TEACHING: Make Items in a Series Parallel (26a)

The following examples of parallel structures can be used to supplement those in the text:

> Why is second base so important? Because when an easy grounder or a high pop-up is hit to that position, and you kick it away, or misjudge it and let it bounce on your head, the whole team gets demoralized. The shortstop comes over and says, Too bad the school bus didn't clip you this morning. The first baseman slaps his leg and laughs. The pitcher gives you the finger in front of everybody.
>
> –LAURENCE SHEEHAN, "How to Play Second Base"

> The dog has got more fun out of Man than Man has got out of the dog, for the clearly demonstrable reason that Man is the more laughable of the two animals. The dog has long been bemused by the singular activities and the curious practices of men, cocking his head inquiringly to one side, intently watching and listening to the strangest goings-on in the world. He has seen men sing together and fight one another in the same evening. He has watched them go to bed when it is time to get up, and get up when it is time to go to bed. He has observed them destroying the soil in vast areas, and nurturing it in small patches. He has stood by while men built strong and solid houses for rest and quiet, and then filled them with lights and bells and machinery. His sensitive nose, which can detect what's cooking in the next township, has caught at one and the same time the bewildering smells of the hospital and the munitions factory. He has seen men raise up great cities to heaven and then blow them to hell.
>
> –JAMES THURBER, "A Dog's Eye View of Man"

As an additional example, ask students to consider the following passage from Barack Obama's speech on race. Read it aloud, and ask students to try to identify the parallel structures.

> Of course, the answer to the slavery question was already embedded within our Constitution—a Constitution that had at its very core the ideal of equal citizenship under the law; a Constitution that promised its people liberty, and justice, and a union that could be and should be perfected over time.
>
> And yet words on a parchment would not be enough to deliver slaves from bondage, or provide men and women of every color and creed their full rights and obligations as citizens of the United States. What would be needed were Americans in successive generations who were willing to do their part—through protests and struggle, on the streets and in the courts, through a civil war and civil disobedience and always at great risk—to narrow that gap between the promise of our ideals and the reality of their time.

What is the aural effect of the parallelism? Help your students break down each sentence into its root sentences, so they can see how beautifully those sentences are combined.

TEACHING WITH TECHNOLOGY: Make Items in a Series Parallel (26a)

Have students post a comment to your online discussion board concerning their analysis of the Obama passage. Then use the log entries as the basis for class discussion.

FOR COLLABORATION: Make Paired Ideas Parallel (26b)

Songwriters, like poets and other professional users of language, become exceptionally aware of the effects of parallelism (and of many other stylistic devices). In fact, a look at the songs from any generation will provide you with examples of parallelism. You might consider having students gather examples of various types of parallel structures that appear in pairs. Have them focus on songs, advertisements, and commercial jingles. Then use their findings for class discussion and for practice in creating parallel structures of their own.

FOR COLLABORATION: Parallel Structures

Have students work in pairs to revise the following paragraph for parallelism. They should supply all necessary words to maintain clarity and grammar in the parallel structures.

> Growing up in a large city provides a very different experience from a suburban childhood. Suburban children undoubtedly enjoy many advantages over those who live in a city, including lawns to play ball on, trees for climbing, and often the schools are better. However, in recent years many people raised in the suburbs but who moved to large cities as young adults are deciding to bring up their own children in an urban setting. Their reasons for doing so include what they consider the cultural advantages of the city, the feeling that they will be able to spend more time with their children if they do not have to commute so far to work, and also they want to expose the children to a greater diversity of social and economic groups than most suburbs offer. Just as their own parents left the city for the space and calm of suburbia, so crowds and excitement are why today's parents are returning to it. Wherever they bring up their children, though, parents have never nor will they ever find utopia.

USEFUL READINGS

Burke, Kenneth. "The Poetic Process." *Counter Statement.* 1931. Berkeley: U of California P, 1968.

Graves, Richard L. "Symmetrical Form and the Rhetoric of the Sentence." *Essays on Classical Rhetoric and Modern Discourse.* Ed. Robert J. Connors, Lisa S. Ede, and Andrea A. Lunsford. Carbondale: Southern Illinois UP, 1984. 170–78. Graves identifies four major categories of parallelism: the repetition of key words, the use of opposite words (antithesis), repetition of grammatical elements, and various combinations of these three categories.

Lindemann, Erika, and Daniel Anderson. *A Rhetoric for Writing Teachers.* 4th ed. New York: Oxford UP, 2001. See Chapter 10 on teaching sentences, especially the discussions of sentence combining, background for understanding syntactic parallelism, repetition, and reduction.

27 Shifts

The shifts that a speaker/writer makes—in language, dialect, grammar, punctuation, and spelling—can be thought of in several ways, from "merely an error" to practical social switching to accommodating a political agenda. In the most traditional sense, shifting is seen as an error, often not a very significant error. Currently, however, sociolinguists see shifts as changes in language that can be politically and rhetorically responsive to the setting and to the audience.

Isabella Halsted tells us that errors are simply mistakes that we are all capable of, given the wrong circumstances: lack of sleep, deadline pressure, unfamiliarity with formal standard English:

> Like the soot on the pane, Error is something that gets in the way of the clear vision. . . . Error on all levels is distracting, annoying, obstructive. Error is inexcusable ultimately, yes, [but] not because it is Wrong *per se*. . . . In plain pragmatic terms, the absence of Error is useful, but when our students take pains to avoid it—by writing short sentences, by sticking to one tense, by writing as little as possible—I doubt very much that they do so in order to better communicate with a reader, but rather to play safe, to avoid the red marks.

Errors in shift are relatively minor: they rarely obstruct communication, amounting to nothing more than stumbling blocks. Mina Shaughnessy says, for example, that pronoun shifts "usually go unnoticed by the writer until someone points them out" (113), for the writer usually believes the sentence is written correctly.

On the other hand, really dramatic or outrageous shifts are a staple of comedians and humor writers. Here is Stephen Colbert during his speech at the 2006 White House Correspondents' Dinner: "I believe in pulling yourself up by your own bootstraps. I believe it is possible. I saw this guy do it once in Cirque du Soleil. It was magical!" Part of Colbert's humor comes from his tendency to shift tone, from the serious (the American concept of the self-made man) to the banal (circus performances).

Additional exercises on shifts are available on *The Everyday Writer*'s companion Web site, **bedfordstmartins.com/everydaywriter**. Go to **Exercise Central** and click on **Shifts**.

FOR TEACHING: Revise Unnecessary Shifts

One way to approach errors like those described in this chapter is to have your students read about them, do exercises, and attempt to find them in their own work. Or you can wait until the error appears, then ask the student to read the erroneous sentence(s) aloud. In "The Study of Error," David Bartholomae suggests that students will often orally correct written errors without noticing the correction. Not only does the reading-aloud technique reveal their competence but it also allows you a dramatic way to reveal the error to them.

FOR COLLABORATION: Revise Unnecessary Shifts in Mood (27b)

Help your students identify mood by using the following passages from Martin Luther King Jr.'s "I Have a Dream" speech. Have students work in small groups to analyze each passage.

> *Indicative*: used in making a statement of fact
>
> It is obvious today that America has defaulted on this promissory note insofar as her citizens of color are concerned. Instead of honoring this sacred obligation, America has given the Negro people a bad check; a check which has come back marked "insufficient funds." But we refuse to believe that the bank of justice is bankrupt. We refuse to believe that there are insufficient funds in the great vaults of opportunity of this nation. So we have come to cash this check—a check that will give us upon demand the riches of freedom and the security of justice.
>
> *Imperative*: expresses a command or an entreaty
>
> Go back to Mississippi, go back to Alabama, go back to South Carolina, go back to Georgia, go back to Louisiana, go back to the slums and ghettos of our northern cities, knowing that somehow this situation can and will be changed. Let us not wallow in the valley of despair.
>
> *Subjunctive*: makes a conditional statement, expresses a wish, or indicates doubt and uncertainty
>
> I have a dream that one day every valley shall be exalted, every hill and mountain shall be made low, the rough places will be made plain, and the crooked places will be made straight, and the glory of the Lord shall be revealed, and all flesh shall see it together.

On Revising Unnecessary Shifts in Voice (27c)

Voice comes from the Latin *vox*, meaning "voice" or "sound." In 1382, John Wyclif became the first to use the term *voice* as a grammatical label in English. Students may need some extra help in understanding the grammatical sense of voice.

FOR TEACHING: Revise Unnecessary Shifts in Voice (27c)

To illustrate how shifts in person (and in tense) can be used effectively, read aloud Martin Luther King Jr.'s "I Have a Dream" speech. Make a special point of focusing on paragraphs 7, 8, and 11–18, discussing King's rhetorical purpose.

On Revising Unnecessary Shifts in Person and Number (27d)

Mina Shaughnessy suggests that problems in pronoun shifts stem from the writer's "unstable sense of the writer-audience relationship, with the shift to 'you' signifying a more direct sense of audience" (113). She identifies three additional general sources of pronoun-shift errors: students' tendency "to reduce complexity without impairing communication"; the problem of remembering which pronouns have been used; and the problem of learning the differences among descriptive, narrative, and analytic writing.

TEACHING WITH TECHNOLOGY: Revise Unnecessary Shifts in Person (27d)

Because many students have been told never to use I in their papers, they frequently alternate between *I* and *you* within a single piece of writing.

> *I* went to the fair and couldn't find any of *my* friends. So *I* was really bored. *You* want to be with *your* friends, but *you* can't find them, and *you* don't see anyone *you* know to ride the ferris wheel with. So *I* went to the beer garden, ordered a beer, sat down, and waited to see if *I* would see anybody *I* know.

To help make students aware of their shifts in pronoun, ask them to highlight or boldface all their uses of *I* and *you* in one of their essays. Then ask them to exchange essays and let their partner help them find appropriate alternatives to any shifts. Choose a few revisions to show to the entire class.

On Revising Unnecessary Shifts between Direct and Indirect Discourse (27e)

Indirect discourse is often preceded by the word *that*, and both pronouns and verb tenses are often different from those used in direct discourse.

Generally, if the introducing verb is in the past tense, it doesn't affect the verb in a direct quotation. However, a signal verb in the past tense will ordinarily shift the verbs in indirect discourse one step back into the past.

Direct discourse

The president said, "I have no knowledge of those events."

Indirect discourse

The president said that he had no knowledge of those events.

When questions appear in direct discourse, they are followed by a question mark (*The instructor confronted us, asking "What do you think you are doing?"*). When reported in indirect discourse, questions often include *who, if, why, whether, what,* or *how*—and they omit the question mark (*The instructor confronted us, asking what we thought we were doing.*).

On Revising Confusing Shifts in Tone and Word Choice (27f)

Tone denotes the way a writer's attitude toward a subject or audience comes across to an audience. Just as tone of voice in speaking may be irritating, harsh, or soothing, the tone of a piece of writing may be humorous, bitter, ironic, patronizing, passionate, or angry. Tone affects the attitude of readers just as tone affects listeners. A word like *terrific*, for example, can suggest enthusiasm, frustration, or sarcasm, depending on the speaker's tone.

Shifts in tone and diction can be effective. In the following excerpt of "Spring Bulletin," Woody Allen parodies the language of of college catalogs, and his diction shifts from formal, sometimes technical, language to much less formal, colloquial language, and finally to slang.

> Economic Theory: A systematic application and critical evaluation of the basic analytic concepts of economic theory, with an emphasis on money and why it's good. Fixed coefficient production functions, cost and supply curves and nonconvexity comprise the first semester, with the second semester concentrating on spending, making change, and keeping a neat wallet. The Federal Reserve System is analyzed, and advanced students are coached in the proper method of filling out a deposit slip. Other topics include: Inflation and Depression—how to dress for each. Loans, interest, welching.

FOR TEACHING: Revising Confusing Shifts in Tone and Word Choice (27f)

Read the following passage from Jessica Mitford's "Behind the Formaldehyde Curtain" to your class, and then ask students to write a short paragraph describing the tone and including specific references. Then ask students with differing opinions about the tone to read the passage aloud, demonstrating the tone they think suits the words. The drama begins to unfold with the arrival of the corpse at the mortuary.

> Alas, poor Yorick! How surprised he would be to see how his counterpart of today is whisked off to a funeral parlor and is in short order sprayed, sliced, pierced, pickled, trussed, trimmed, creamed, waxed, painted, rouged and neatly dressed—transformed from a common corpse into a Beautiful Memory Picture. This process is known in the trade as embalming and restorative art.

FOR COLLABORATION: Revising Shifts in Tone and Word Choice (27f)

To illustrate shifts in tone, you may want to provide your class with copies of both Lincoln's Gettysburg Address and Mencken's "Gettysburg Address in Vulgate." To highlight the changes in tone, read them aloud. Then ask the class to identify the phrases and words Mencken uses in place of Lincoln's terms. Discuss how the connotations of words control the "meaning" of a piece of writing.

To give students practice in identifying tone, break them into groups, asking each group to describe the characteristics of one Gettysburg Address. You can use Lincoln's version, Mencken's version, and the five variations reprinted in *Preface to Critical Reading*, sixth edition, by Richard D. Altick and Andrea A. Lunsford ([New York: Holt, 1984], 104–7).

FOR MULTILINGUAL WRITERS: Revising Shifts in Tone and Word Choice (27f)

Encourage students to record examples of shifts in tone and diction—including ones that are either intentionally or unintentionally humorous. Some students may enjoy fashioning deliberately humorous sentences containing such shifts, modeled after the preceding examples by Woody Allen and Stephen Colbert, and the example of Dave Barry in the opening paragraph of Chapter 27 of *The Everyday Writer*. Parodying the English language will help students learn faster.

USEFUL READINGS

Bartholomae, David. "The Study of Error." *CCC* 31 (1980): 253–69. Rpt. in *The Writing Teacher's Sourcebook*. 4th ed. Ed. Edward Corbett, Nancy Myers, and Gary Tate. New York: Oxford UP, 1999.

Berger, Mary I. *Speak Standard, Too—Add Mainstream English to Your Talking Style*. Chicago: Orchard, 1994.

Halsted, Isabella. "Putting Error in Its Place." *Journal of Basic Writing* 1 (Spring 1975): 72–86.

Mangelsdorf, Kate, Duane H. Roen, and Victoria Taylor. "ESL Students' Use of Audience." *A Sense of Audience in Written Communication*. Ed. Gesa Kirsch and Duane H. Roen. Newbury Park: Sage, 1990. 231–47. The authors consider the audience expectations of ESL writers/speakers and the ways that ESL students can come to reconsider the needs of their intended audience.

Shaughnessy, Mina. *Errors and Expectations*. New York: Oxford UP, 1977.

Smitherman, Geneva. *Talkin and Testifyin: The Language of Black America*. Detroit: Wayne State UP, 1986. See, especially, Chapter 6, "Where It's At: Black-White Language Attitudes."

28 Conciseness

Austen does more without words than most writers do with them.
—Patricia T. O'Conner

To demonstrate that being concise may not always be preferable, compare the opening paragraph of Charles Dickens's *A Tale of Two Cities* to the following revision, created by someone using the software program Workbench, a style and diction checker. Read both versions aloud, and then encourage the class to decide which makes the more effective opening for the novel.

> It was the best of times, it was the worst of times, it was the age of wisdom, it was the age of foolishness, it was the epoch of belief, it was the epoch of incredulity, it was the season of Light, it was the season of Darkness, it was the spring of hope, it was the winter of despair, we had everything before us, we had nothing before us, we were all going direct to Heaven, we were all going direct the other way—in short, the period was so far like the present period, that some of its noisiest authorities insisted on being received, for good or for evil, in the superlative degree of comparison only. —Charles Dickens

> The times were the best and worst, wise and foolish. The era was one of belief and disbelief, light and darkness, hope and despair. Before us lay everything and nothing. We were all going direct to heaven or straight to hell. The period was so much like today that its loudest critics could describe it only in superlatives.
> —Workbench

He can compress the most words into the smallest ideas of any man I ever met.
—Abraham Lincoln

FOR COLLABORATION: Eliminate Unnecessary, Redundant, and Empty Words (28a–c)

Ask students to work in small groups to read over the excerpt of Emily Lesk's essay in 10a of *The Everyday Writer* (or have them access the entire paper on the book companion Web site, under **Student Writing**

Models), paying attention to the sentences. Then have them choose a paragraph and evaluate its sentences in terms of emphasis and wordiness. Ask them to try to find a paragraph that they think might be made more emphatic or more concise and to revise accordingly. Finally, have each group report its findings to the whole class.

> If you would be pungent, be brief. —ROBERT SOUTHEY

FOR TEACHING: Simplify Sentence Structure (28e)

Read aloud the following paragraph from *In the Last Analysis*, a mystery novel by Amanda Cross (the heroine, Kate Fansler, is mapping out her mystery-solving plan), and then ask your students to revise the paragraph using the simplest grammatical structures. Finally, ask them to compare versions and to decide which ones they like best and why.

> She felt, nonetheless, as she stood indecisively in the hall, like a knight who has set off to slay the dragon but has neglected to ask in what part of the world the dragon may be found. It was all very well to decide upon action, but what action, after all, was she to take? As was her habit, she extracted notebook and pen and began to make a list: see Janet Harrison's room, and talk to people who knew her in dormitory; find out about ten and twelve o'clock patients; find out who person in picture Janet Harrison had was (lists always had a devastating effect on Kate's syntax).

FOR COLLABORATION: Clear and Concise Sentences

Students can implement the learning from this chapter by working collaboratively to make each of the following sentences clear and concise by eliminating unnecessary words and phrases. Ask students to come up with more than one revision whenever possible. Example:

summarize.
Let me ~~fill you in on the main points of the overall picture.~~
^

1. Many people have a tendency toward the expansion of their sentences by the superfluous addition of extra words that are not really needed for the meaning of the sentences.
2. One of the major problems that is faced at this point in time is that there is world hunger.
3. The tourist, who had come to New York for the first time and who was really proud of finishing the *Times* crossword puzzle on Monday, had no idea at all that Monday was the day of the week when the puzzle

is easiest in order to give everyone who tries it kind of a sense of accomplishment.

4. The stock market seems to be a source of anxiety to some investors due to the fact that they don't understand the very important principle of repetitive cycles.

FOR TEACHING: Clear and Concise Sentences

As your students begin their final revisions, challenge them to eliminate fifteen words from each paragraph. Use one of the students' papers to model this exercise and show how much stronger the writing is.

USEFUL READINGS

Burke, Kenneth. "Lexicon Rhetoricae." *Counter-Statement.* 1931. Berkeley: U of California P, 1968. 123–83. Burke explores the appeal to the reader of various categories of form.

Connors, Robert J. "The Erasure of the Sentence." *CCC* 52.1 (Sept. 2000): 96–128. Connors traces the history of sentence rhetorics, showing composition studies as a subfield of English and arguing that prior to 1980 studies indicate that sentence rhetorics were effective in producing "mature" writing. We have lost that benefit as a result of English theoretical perspectives on composition pedagogies.

Fowler, H. W. *A Dictionary of Modern English Usage.* 2nd ed. Rev. and ed. Sir Ernest Gowers. New York: Oxford UP, 1965.

Laib, Nevin. "Conciseness and Amplification." *CCC* 41 (1990): 443–59. Laib argues that carried to excess, conciseness can lead to "bluntness, opacity, and underdevelopment" and suggests that teachers of writing should encourage "profuseness" as well. According to Laib, "Elegant variation is an essential art of development, emphasis, and explanation."

Lanham, Richard. *Style: An Anti-Textbook.* New Haven: Yale UP, 1977. Lanham argues for the teaching of style, not of clarity. He writes that "instruction in composition builds on a single premise—clarity—and that premise is false."

O'Connor, Patricia T. *Words Fail Me: What Everyone Who Writes Should Know about Writing.* New York: Harvest, 2000. This humorous, practical guide to writing covers the basics of writing with stylistical sophistication through attention to strong sentences.

Williams, Joseph M. *Style: Ten Lessons in Clarity and Grace.* 6th ed. New York: Addison-Wesley, 2002. In "Managing Endings for Emphasis," Williams demonstrates ways of shifting emphasis to the end of sentences; in Lesson Ten he offers advice on how to achieve elegant structures.

Sentence Variety

29

All my books literally come to me in the form of a sentence, an original sentence which contains the entire book.

—RAYMOND FEDERMAN

Gifted writer, journalist, and literary, social, and political critic H. L. Mencken rarely limited his reviews to content: he enjoyed writing reviews of style as well. In 1921, Mencken wrote a column on former newspaper editor Warren G. Harding, making clear that not even the president of the United States was safe from Mencken's iconoclastic sensibilities.

Using the simplest of sentences and sustained repetition, Mencken writes a powerful and memorable review of Harding's style:

> He writes the worst English that I have ever encountered. It reminds me of a string of wet sponges; it reminds me of tattered washing on the line; it reminds me of stale bean soup, of college yells, of dogs barking idiotically through endless nights. It is so bad that a sort of grandeur creeps into it. It drags itself out of the dark abyss of pish, and crawls insanely up to the topmost pinnacle of posh. It is rumble and bumble. It is flap and doodle. It is balder and dash.

Student writers can take a cue from Mencken, trying their hands at a sustained insult—all in good fun, though!

On Varying Sentence Structures

Several techniques have been developed to help teach students to vary sentence structures, with sentence combining being perhaps the most well known and thoroughly studied. A lesser-known technique is Richard Larson's strategy of writing an essay on the board or overhead projector over several days, correcting and talking about the stylistic choices he makes as he writes. A third way to draw students' attention to varying sentence structures is Edward P. J. Corbett's method of stylistic analysis.

Whatever method you choose, remember that stylistic choices about sentence structures depend on the larger context of each individual sentence, the intended audience, and the purpose for writing.

FOR TEACHING: Vary Sentence Length (29a)

Very short "capsule" reviews usually contain varied sentence structures, perhaps to keep readers' attention with a snappy, fast-paced description. A review of the movie *The Dark Knight* in the *Boston Globe* included the following description of the Joker:

> We never find out where the Joker came from. Every time the character tells the story of how he got his smiling scars, the details are different, as though he were making himself up on the spot. The gambit works because Ledger reinvents the comic book super-villain as a wildly watchable Method nerd. The character's body movements are wobbly but controlled, the eyes darting with nervous energy as he calculates his next move. The tongue slithers.

The writer of this review varies sentence length by following three lengthy sentences with a three-word sentence and alternates openings as well, beginning one sentence not with the subject but with an adverbial clause. This variety helps make the review easy to read and remember.

Ask students to study some "capsule" reviews in a magazine or newspaper (or on television or a reputable blog or Web site like Amazon.com), noting the variety of sentences used and bringing a few examples to class to compare with those found by classmates. Together, try to draw conclusions about the effect of sentence variety on readers.

FOR COLLABORATION: Vary Sentence Length (29a)

Distribute the following paragraph taken from *Frankenstein*, by Mary Shelley. Ask half of your students to recast the information in the passage into a series of long sentences. Ask the other half to recast it into a string of short sentences. How do the revised paragraphs compare? Read the revisions aloud to help students "see" the difference.

> As I said this I suddenly beheld the figure of a man, at some distance, advancing towards me with superhuman speed. He bounded over the crevices in the ice, among which I had walked with caution; his stature, also, as he approached, seemed to exceed that of a man. I was troubled; a mist came over my eyes, and I felt a faintness seize me; but I was quickly restored by the cold gale of the mountains. I perceived, as the shape came nearer (sight tremendous and abhorred!) that it was the wretch whom I had created. I trembled with rage and horror, resolving to wait his approach and then close with him in mortal combat. He approached; his countenance bespoke bitter anguish, combined with disdain and malignity, while its unearthly ugliness rendered it almost too horrible for human eyes. But I scarcely observed this; rage and hatred had at first deprived me of utterance, and I recovered only to overwhelm him with words expressive of furious detestation and contempt.

FOR COLLABORATION: Vary Sentence Length (29a)

Have students, working in pairs or in groups of three, choose a topic of interest to all the members and then write passages of at least twenty-five short sentences (each shorter than twelve words). After they have traded passages with another group or pair, ask each group to combine some of the twenty-five sentences into longer sentences, while retaining some short sentences for emphasis.

Naturally, each group will combine sentences differently, so you might want to take an opportunity to explain their choices and reasons for combining some sentences while keeping others short.

TEACHING WITH TECHNOLOGY: Vary Sentence Length (29a)

Consider the following paragraphs from Maya Angelou's "Champion of the World" that include both long and short sentences used effectively. After your students have identified the variety of sentences according to length and type, ask them to post to your online discussion group an imitation of these paragraphs on a topic of their own, such as participating in sports, getting a first job, winning an award, or attending a concert. Then ask them to respond to two or three other posts and to comment on the variations in sentence length. You can also select several posts to project up on a computer screen for collaborative review and discussion.

> Champion of the world. A Black boy. Some Black mother's son. He was the strongest man in the world. People drank Coca-Colas like ambrosia and ate candy bars like Christmas. Some of the men went behind the Store and poured white lightning in their soft-drink bottles, and a few of the bigger boys followed them. Those who were not chased away came back blowing their breath in front of themselves like proud smokers.
>
> It would take an hour or more before the people would leave the Store and head for home. Those who lived too far had made arrangements to stay in town. It wouldn't do for a Black man and his family to be caught on a lonely country road on a night when Joe Louis had proved that we were the strongest people in the world.

On Sentence Openings (29b)

In *Classical Rhetoric for the Modern Student*, Edward P. J. Corbett lists eleven sentence openers—all of which any beginning writer can learn to use in effective combination.

1. Subject—*John* broke the window. *The high cost* of living will offset . . .
2. Expletives—*It* is plain that . . . *There* are ten Indians. Exclamations: *Alas*, *Oh*

3. Coordinating conjunction—*And, But, Or, Nor, For, Yet, So*
4. Adverb word—*First, Thus, Moreover, Nevertheless, Namely*
5. Conjunctive phrase—*On the other hand, As a consequence*
6. Prepositional phrase—*After the game, In the morning*
7. Verbal phrase—participial, gerundive, or infinitive phrase
8. Adjective phrase—*Tired but happy, we . . .*
9. Absolute phrase—*The ship having arrived, we . . .*
10. Adverb clause—*When the ship arrived, we . . .*
11. Front-shift (inverted word order)—*That expense we could not bear. Gone was the wind. Happy were they to be alive.*

FOR TEACHING: Vary Sentence Openings (29b)

Consider sharing with your students the following passage from Richard Rodriguez's "Aria: A Memoir of a Bilingual Childhood." Point out to them the ways Rodriguez varies his sentence openers, including his use of dependent clauses.

> Three months passed. Five. A half year. Unsmiling, ever watchful, my teachers noted my silence. They began to connect my behavior with the slow progress my brother and sisters were making. Until, one Saturday morning, three nuns arrived at the house to talk to our parents. Stiffly they sat on the blue living-room sofa. From the doorway of another room, spying on the visitors, I noticed the incongruity, the clash of two worlds, the faces and voices of school intruding upon the familiar setting of home. I overheard one voice gently wondering, "Do your children speak only Spanish at home, Mrs. Rodriguez?" While another voice added, "That Richard especially seems so timid and shy."

FOR COLLABORATION: Vary Sentence Openings (29b)

Ask your students to exchange their latest piece of writing in a peer-review group and analyze all the declarative sentences according to sentence openers. How many (and what percentage of) sentences begin with one of the eleven options in Corbett's preceding list? You might ask students to compare their use of sentence opening types to those of a professional essay.

FOR TEACHING: Vary Sentence Openings Using Dependent Clauses (29b)

Some students have considerable trouble punctuating dependent clauses, especially introductory dependent clauses. They often turn them into sentence fragments by separating them from the main clause with a period.

Outlined here is one possible method for helping students overcome this problem.

> I worked all summer at the car dealership. Although I really wanted to go to baseball camp.

1. You may want to point out the problem in meaning for the reader—the false or due expectation. (Coming after a period, the *Although I really wanted* clause makes us think that another sentence is coming.)
2. Then ask students to supply an alternative, relying on their competence to provide a solution. (They may want to erase the period and make the *A* of *Although* a lowercase letter. Or they may add more information to the *Although* clause: *Although I really wanted to go to baseball camp, I needed to earn money, not spend it.*)
3. You can use this opportunity to suggest other alternatives that clarify or reiterate the meaning conveyed by the kernel sentence [(1) *Although I really wanted to go to baseball camp, I worked all summer at the car dealership.* (2) *I worked all summer at the car dealership although I really wanted to go to baseball camp instead.* (3) *I worked all summer at the car dealership. Although I really wanted to go to baseball camp, I needed to earn money, not spend it.*]

FOR COLLABORATION: Sentence Variety

Ask students to choose two partners in order to complete this activity. Have each group analyze the following introductory paragraph carefully, noting each sentence for its length, its kind of opening, and its grammatical type. Then ask the groups to revise the paragraph to add variety in sentence length, sentence openings, and sentence types.

> When we arrived at the accident scene, I could tell that the injuries were not minor. I walked up to the car nearest me to check the injuries of the people inside. I looked through the driver's window and saw the woman's body entangled in the steering wheel. I told dispatch, via two-way radio, to send medics "code red, lights and siren." I then went to see how the passenger in the car was. The passenger appeared to be in shock and had a broken leg. The officer walked over and checked the other vehicle. The driver of the other vehicle had received no injuries at all.

USEFUL READINGS

Corbett, Edward P. J., and Robert J. Connors. *Classical Rhetoric for the Modern Student.* 4th ed. New York: Oxford UP, 1999. The author offers copious advice about analyzing sentence style.

Larson, Richard. "Back to the Board." *CCC* 29 (1978): 292–94. Larson offers further explanation of his composing technique.

Lindemann, Erika, and Daniel Anderson. *A Rhetoric for Writing Teachers*. 4th ed. New York: Oxford UP, 2001. See, especially, the historical survey of sentence-combining research—from Hunt and O'Hare to Daiker and Morenberg.

Sentence Grammar

Most of us don't know a gerund from a gerbil and don't care, but we'd like to speak and write as though we did.

—PATRICIA T. O'CONNER

30 Basic Grammar

. . . when the rules of Grammar are skillfully taught, any language can be more easily understood, more surely learnt, and longer kept in the memory. —CHRISTOPHER COOPER

Although closely related, rhetoric and grammar have traditionally maintained themselves as separate disciplines. Rhetoric, nearly as old as Greek culture itself, formed the basis of the *trivium*, the Greek educational system that also included grammar and dialectic (philosophical logic). For some 1,700 years, from late antiquity to the Middle Ages, the *trivium* remained the centerpiece of education, keeping grammar allied with rhetoric. But today, grammar is more closely connected with other fields of language study—with linguistics, composition studies, and stylistics—that make constant reference to grammatical terms. The relationship of grammar to composition studies has always been controversial: how to teach grammar in writing courses—indeed, whether to teach it at all—remains a topic much disputed. Few teachers have been willing to dispense entirely with instruction in grammar; most teach it without any conclusive evidence that teaching grammar in any way improves the writing of students. In his impressive meta-analysis, *Research on Written Composition*, George Hillocks reports that "[n]one of the studies reviewed . . . provides any support for teaching grammar as a means of improving composition skills" (138). Yet we continue to teach our students about grammar, perhaps because we feel that, to be the most effective writers, they need to learn certain grammatical conventions. As William Irmscher writes in *Teaching Expository Writing*, "The relation of grammar and writing is one of the enduring controversies of English studies" (16).

Additional grammar exercises are available on *The Everyday Writer*'s companion Web site, **bedfordstmartins.com/everydaywriter**. Go to **Exercise Central** and click on **Basic Grammar**.

Grammatically, *should of* is a predatory admonition; as such, it is always used as part of a herpetological phrase. —DAVE BARRY

On the Origins of Language and Its Grammar

The first Greek grammarian, Plato, debated theories of the origin of language and of the correlation between thought and language in the *Cratylus* (385 BCE). Moreover, he examined the concepts of *truth* and *falsehood* to see if they could be translated into and transmitted by any particular grammatical structure. For example, the following sentences are perfectly grammatical—and false:

> The Ohio State University football team likes to lose games.
>
> Condoleezza Rice is a doctor interested in health care reform.
>
> Learning to write is always easy.

Although Plato successfully and permanently separated judgments regarding grammatical structure and *truth*, using examples like the preceding ones, no grammarian has yet been able to dislodge the specious connection between grammatical correctness and morality. In *Grammar and Good Taste: Reforming the American Language*, Dennis E. Baron argues that the association of grammatical correctness with moral virtue and social prestige in the United States grew out of patriotic attempts during the post–Revolutionary period to distinguish American English from British English. He goes on to note that this association of grammar and morality fostered the anxiety over grammatical correctness that the public still feels today.

Plato's most important contribution to grammar, the division of the sentence into nominal (*onoma*) and verbal (*rheme*) components, has remained the primary grammatical distinction underlying syntactic analysis and word classification in all linguistic description; all grammatical approaches divide sentences into two parts, subject and verb. Later, in the *Rhetoric*, Aristotle added a third grammatical category of function words (*syndesmoi*) that includes conjunctions, articles, and pronouns. Plato's categories remain full parts of speech because they have meaning in isolation; Aristotle's function words, though, have only grammatical meaning.

On the Basic Grammar of Sentences (30a)

When students face grammar lessons, they often feel that their language has become suddenly foreign—that they don't know any grammar. Oh, but they do. They completely mastered the grammar of their native tongue long ago. They may be comforted to know that there is a difference between what they know about their language—their *competence*—and how they use their language—their linguistic *performance*. Unlike certain "speaking" animals, which can only imitate what they have heard before, your students know the rules for combining the elements of their native language—words, ideas, and sentences—and have the *competence* to say things that have never been said before and to create purposeful and meaningful discourse. If one of your students says, "Yesterday, I seen a horrible fight," you know exactly what she means. Her *competence* is perfect, though her *performance*—by the standards of academic English at least—may not be. She makes sense. But if she says, "A yesterday saw fight I horrible," you have trouble understanding her. The words themselves are correct, but not the grammar. Your student will be able to tell you that the second string of words is ungrammatical and that it doesn't make sense. Her *competence* with her language—her knowledge of grammar—gives her this ability.

> **Like everything metaphysical, the harmony between thought and reality is to be found in the grammar of language.**
> —LUDWIG WITTGENSTEIN

On the Parts of Speech: Verbs (30b)

A verb is the key to a sentence: the starting point for any translation, the pivot of action, the movement. We tend to emphasize verbs in our teaching because so few writers use them effectively, and writers who do master this skill produce lively, often powerful, prose. We usually begin to learn a language, however, by building up our repertoire of nouns—in much the way Helen Keller, who was blind and deaf, rose to a new level of consciousness when she learned her first word, a noun, with the help of Annie Sullivan. Read aloud to the class the following excerpt from *The Story of My Life* in which Keller relates that magical event, and then use it to lead a class discussion of the power of nouns and verbs:

> We walked down the path to the well-house, attracted by the fragrance of the honeysuckle with which it was covered. Someone was drawing water and my teacher placed my hand under the spout. As the cool stream gushed over one hand, she spelled into the other the word *water*, first slowly then rapidly. I stood still, my whole attention fixed upon the motion of her fingers. Suddenly I felt a misty consciousness as of something forgotten—a thrill of returning thought; and somehow the mystery of language was revealed to me. I knew then that "w-a-t-e-r" meant the wonderful cool something that was flowing over my hand. That living word awakened my soul, gave it light, hope, joy, set it free! . . . I left the well-house eager to learn. Everything had a name, and each name gave birth to a new thought. As we returned to the house every object which I touched seemed to quiver with life. That was because I saw everything with the strange, new sight that had come to me. . . . [*M*]*other, father, sister, teacher* were . . . words that were to make the world blossom for me. . . .

FOR COLLABORATION: Adjectives and Adverbs (30e–f)

Have students work in groups to transform the following ordinary statements into powerful messages—expanding them with adjectives and adverbs. Then have them share their messages with the rest of the class.

1. Candidates travel across the nation.
2. The spider went up the waterspout.
3. A stir was audible in the hall.
4. Fifi gets angry.
5. The prisoner dozed off and was wakened.
6. The boy entered the line.

On Prepositions (30g)

Besides connecting nouns and pronouns to other words, prepositions also have important semantic dimensions, serving as the most important words in certain sentences.

> Watch that crazed killer *behind* you.
>
> Tie that artery *below* his ear.

Until the late Middle Ages, relationships among words were indicated by inflectional endings. But by 1300, when only the possessive (*-'s*) and plural (*-s*) endings remained, prepositions were used to signal relationships. Chaucer was the first to use the preposition *during* (c. 1385), while the *Piers Plowman* poet was the first to use the prepositions *concerning* and *except* (c. 1377).

FOR TEACHING: Conjunctions (30h)

To give your students practice in thinking about the relationships between words and ideas, you may want to present them a conjunction-less passage, asking them to insert the appropriate conjunctions. With the italicized conjunctions left out, present the following passage from Toni Morrison's *The Bluest Eye*:

> *If* my mother was in a singing mood, it wasn't so bad. She would sing about hard times, bad times, *and* somebody-done-gone-and-left-me times. *But* her voice was so sweet *and* her singing-eyes so melty I found myself longing for those hard times, yearning to be grown without "a thin di-i-ime to my name." I looked forward to the delicious time *when* "my man" would leave me, *when* I would "hate to see that evening sun go down . . ." 'cause *then* I would know "my man has left this town." Misery colored by the greens *and* blues in my

mother's voice took all of the grief out of the words *and* left me with a conviction that pain was *not only* endurable, it was sweet.

Attempting to learn conjunctions by their grammatical categories can be confusing. Some students may respond better when they are presented with the following semantic categories of conjunctions (and transitional phrases):

1. *To express agreement between items*—and, also, likewise, both . . . and, similarly, not only . . . but also
2. *To express additional items*—besides, furthermore, moreover, and, also (in addition)
3. *To express disagreement between items*—but, yet, however, instead, anyway, nevertheless, still (in spite of that)
4. *To express alternative items*—or, nor, either . . . or, neither . . . nor
5. *To express causations*—for, so, since, because, therefore, thus
6. *To express various time relations*—when, often, before, while, as, until, finally, meanwhile, next, now, then
7. *To express certainty*—certainly, indeed, undoubtedly (to be certain, without a doubt)
8. *To express possibility or qualifications*—if, if . . . then, until, although, before, besides, unless, otherwise (on the other hand)
9. *To express parenthetically*—besides, incidentally
10. *To express specificity*—namely (that is to say)

On the Parts of a Sentence (30j–m)

In reaction to the purely formal, static quality of the terms *subject* and *predicate*, various linguists developed a theory linking the binary form of the sentence with the functions of those major divisions. William J. Van de Kopple describes this theory in "Something Old, Something New: Functional Sentence Perspective":

> In brief, for Functional Sentence Perspectivists a sentence conveys its message most effectively if its two major parts, the topic and comment, perform specific semantic and communicative tasks. In English, the topic usually includes the grammatical subject and its adjuncts. The comment usually includes the verb and objects or carries primary sentence stress.
>
> For each part the theorists posit slightly different but often corresponding communicative functions. They claim that the topic should express either the theme of the sentence, the elements with the least communicative dynamism

. . . the least important information, or the old information. They assert that the comment should express either information about the theme, the elements with the most communicative dynamism, the most important information, or the new information.

Never a day without a line. —HORACE

FOR TEACHING: Subjects and Predicates (30j–k)

Share the following poem with your students, asking them to identify the subject and predicate of each line and of the last two lines:

We'll begin with a box, and the plural is boxes.
But the plural of ox should be oxen, not oxes.
The one fowl is a goose, but two are called geese,
Yet the plural of moose should never be meese.
You may find a lone mouse or a whole set of mice,
Yet the plural of house is houses not hice.
If the plural of man is always called men,
Why shouldn't the plural of pan be called pen?
If I speak of a foot and you show me your feet,
And I give you a boot, would a pair be called beet?
If one is a tooth and a whole set is teeth,
Why should not the plural of booth be called beeth?
Then one may be that, and three would be those,
Yet hat in the plural wouldn't be hose.
And the plural of cat is cats and not cose.
We speak of a brother and also of brethren,
But though we say Mother, we never say Methren.
Then the masculine pronouns are he, his, and him,
But imagine the feminine she, shis, and shim.
So English, I fancy, you all will agree,
Is the funniest language you ever did see.

Clear in the poem are some of the inconsistencies of the English language, inconsistencies of plurality that have grown out of our long and colorful language history. Just as fashions inevitably change—more drastically and rapidly in some areas than others, over time, and because of foreign influences—so inevitably does language. Perhaps the most profound reflection of constant language change is the common assumption held by most of us that the language we speak is "standard," while that spoken by many others is "nonstandard."

The version of English found in most printed materials and spoken in most public arenas is often referred to as edited American English. But that is *not* to say that it is the one "standard" dialect. Speakers of American English offer many variations, many dialects, and many registers, which *The Everyday Writer* explores in Chapter 21.

FOR COLLABORATION: Subjects and Predicates (30j–k)

Have students bring to class a double-spaced copy of a paragraph from any current draft. For each sentence in their paragraph, they should identify the complete subject and predicate, the type of verb (linking, transitive, or intransitive), and all objects and complements. They may find it most productive to work in small groups to test their choices.

On Transitive and Intransitive Verbs (30k)

Verbs that take an object are *transitive*, from the Latin *transire*, "pass over." Transitive verbs cannot express their meaning without passing over to a complement.

We *bounced* our *ball* in Waterford Galley.

We *bounced* our *ideas* off one another.

We *bounced* the *pickpocket* out of the restaurant.

Intransitive—that is, "not passing over"—verbs are capable of expressing themselves without a complement to complete their meaning.

Oz has spoken.

Jorge slunk past the mission.

The ball bounced over my head.

Sometimes, transitive verbs take an indirect object as well as a direct object, as in:

Christiana gave Alfred [IO] a black eye [DO].

Aurelia sent Joe [IO] a Christmas card [DO].

These classifications, transitive and intransitive, vary from one sentence to another, depending on how a particular verb is used. A few words (*ignore*) are only transitive, while others (*reign, die*) are only intransitive. Dictionaries label verbs as *v.t.* (transitive verb) or *v.i.* (intransitive verb), according to use.

TEACHING WITH TECHNOLOGY: Phrases (30l)

Have students select any full page from a current draft and identify all the types of phrases (participial, gerund, infinitive, appositive, absolute, and prepositional) they have used. Then, on your course message board, have them post a description of the range and pattern of phrasal constructions they have employed and a plan to improve their use of phrases. Ask each student to post a response to one of their classmates' analyses.

FOR COLLABORATION: Phrases (30l)

Ask students to share the results of their survey of the kinds of phrases they use from the previous exercise. Then have students work together to incorporate new types of phrases into their drafts and to discuss the effects of these revisions.

FOR COLLABORATION: Phrases (30l)

For this exercise, which is meant to reinforce learning, ask students to work in pairs. Have them use prepositional, participial, gerund, infinitive, absolute, or appositive phrases to expand each of the following sentences. Example:

> *In response to my vigorous shake, the*
> ~~The~~ apples dropped from the limb.
> ^

Make sure students can explain how they expanded each sentence. When everyone is done, share the results as a class for comparison and discussion.

1. A man waited at the bottom of the escalator.
2. He quickly identified his blind date.
3. Tomas had lost almost all of his hair.
4. The Sunday afternoon dragged.
5. Zakiyyah looked at her mother.
6. The candidates shook hands with the voters.
7. The all-you-can-eat buffet was a bad idea.
8. I may move because my neighbor is too noisy.
9. The plants needed water desperately.
10. They lived in a trailer.

FOR TEACHING: Phrases (30l)

Consider using sentence-combining techniques to reinforce the effective compression that can be achieved with absolute and appositive phrases. For instance, *I jumped into the car and took off, the tires screeching in protest* combines at least three simpler sentences:

> I jumped; (I jumped) into the car.
>
> I took off.
>
> The tires were screeching in protest.

Write these sentences on the board and work with your students to delete repetitive elements and form a combined sentence with an absolute element. You can do the same exercise to achieve an appositive phrase:

> Maya Angelou will appear on campus tonight.
>
> Maya Angelou is a celebrated novelist and (Maya Angelou is a celebrated) essayist.

On Grammatical Classifications (30n)

In a series of essays, Francis Christensen demonstrated a way to map sentences and paragraphs according to levels of generality and modification. According to Christensen, *periodic* sentences are those that delay or postpone announcing the general main clause until the very end, leading into the topic with supporting or modifying details. This kind of sentence forces a reader to hold the subject in mind until the very end and keeps syntactic tension high. In the hands of skilled writers, periodic sentences can keep readers alert for what is to come and make the main idea, when it finally does appear, all the more impressive.

Although structures using various degrees of periodicity can be very effective in challenging and interesting readers, they do not constitute the most frequently used pattern in Modern English. Rather, the *cumulative* structure, which adds details after the main clause or announcement of the topic, is the more dominant. Christensen writes in "A Generative Rhetoric of the Sentence":

> The main clause, which may or may not have a sentence modifier before it, advances the discussion; but the additions move backwards, as in this clause, to modify the statement of the main clause or more often to explicate or exemplify it, so that the sentence has a flowing and ebbing movement, advancing to a new position and then pausing to consolidate it, leaping and lingering as the popular ballad does. (156)

Because the main clause is presented at or near the beginning of the sentence, cumulative structures do not require readers to hold the subject in suspense until the end. In one sense, then, these sentences may be easier to read than periodic ones, yet the skillful writer can position the most important piece of information at the end. But Christensen warns in *Notes toward a New Rhetoric* that "the cumulative sentence in unskilled hands is unsteady, allowing a writer to ramble on, adding modifier after modifier, until the reader is almost overwhelmed, because the writer's central idea is lost."

Using exclusively periodic or cumulative sentences, of course, would be very monotonous. And so the best writers mingle structures—short and long, periodic and cumulative—though never forgetting that the most important ideas naturally deserve the most prominent positions.

FOR TEACHING: Grammatical Classifications (30n)

Before your students turn in their work, ask them to classify by type each of the sentences in their papers. (You may want to review with them the definitions and constructions of each sentence type.) Then ask them to tally each type (simple, compound, complex, compound-complex). They should use the results to answer the following questions, possibly in their writing logs:

What kinds of sentences do you use most often?

Do you use all kinds of sentences or rely on just a couple?

What effect does your choice of sentence structures have on your prose?

Do you recognize or know how to construct all the sentence types?

If any students express interest in doing so, you may want to give them an opportunity to revise these papers before they hand them in.

FOR COLLABORATION: Revising Sentences

Ask students to work in groups on the following sentence-combining exercises. They should combine each group of sentences into a single sentence, transforming some individual sentences into phrases to expand and shape the basic sentence. Then they should try to produce at least two versions of each combined sentence. Example:

The paint is peeling.

The roof is leaking.

The house is in a crummy neighborhood. The house will never sell.

That paint-peeling, roof-leaking dump will never sell, especially in a crummy neighborhood.

With peeling paint and a leaking roof, that house in that crummy neighborhood will never sell.

1. It was a crisp morning in early spring.
   A man walked through the city park.
   He was alone.
   The trees and plants were newly budding.
2. We climbed a tree.
   The tree was gnarly.
   The cherries on the tree were sweet.
   The tree stood in Jess's backyard.
   We climbed all summer long.
3. Only two people were in the library.
   A man with gray hair was slightly sleepy.
   A young woman was in the library.
   She wore jeans.
4. Anna is a Snow Princess in the Marysville Winter Parade.
   Anna feels proud.
   Anna feels excited.
   The snow is falling furiously.
5. New York City is a great place to visit.
   New York City is a prohibitively expensive place to live.
6. Jaron was at the Easter egg hunt.
   Jaron found several eggs.
   The eggs were hidden.
   The eggs were tucked beneath a dogwood tree.

USEFUL READINGS

Baron, Dennis E. *Grammar and Good Taste: Reforming the American Language*. New Haven: Yale UP, 1982.

Christensen, Francis. "A Generative Rhetoric of the Sentence." *CCC* 14 (1963): 155–61. The idea for expanding sentences by adding and manipulating modifying phrases derives largely from Christensen, who maintains that students can achieve syntactic fluency by adding modifiers at the beginning, middle, and end of their sentences. He focuses on the cumulative sentence and demonstrates how writers can add final free modifiers to main clauses in order to expand sentences.

———. *Notes toward a New Rhetoric*. New York: Harper, 1978.

D'Eloia, Sarah. "The Uses—and Limits—of Grammar." *Journal of Basic Writing* 1 (Spring/Summer 1977): 1–20. In addition to her insights into the relationship between grammar and writing instruction, the author offers excellent classroom pedagogy.

Hartwell, Patrick. "Grammar, Grammars, and the Teaching of Grammar." *CE* 47 (1985): 105–27. Rpt. in *The St. Martin's Guide to Teaching Writing*. 5th ed. Hartwell examines the definitions and purposes of the various grammars.

Hillocks, George. *Research on Written Composition*. Urbana: NCTE, 1986.

Hunter, Susan, and Ray Wallace, eds. *The Place of Grammar in Writing Instruction: Past, Present, Future*. Portsmouth: Boynton, 1995. This compelling collection of essays provides what the editors describe as a reevaluation of grammar in terms of "discussions of 'standard' English and dialects, research on dialect-switching, attitudes toward error and students' right to their own language, academic discourse, and varieties of literacy, language acquisition, orality and literacy, and class struggle." See, especially, R. Baird Shuman's "Grammar for Writers: How Much Is Enough?" and Cheryl Glenn's "When Grammar Was a Language Art."

Irmscher, William. *Teaching Expository Writing*. New York: Holt, 1979.

Noguchi, Rei R. *Grammar and the Teaching of Writing: Limits and Possibilities*. Urbana: NCTE, 1991. Noguchi streamlines the teaching of grammar by focusing on the writing problems most responsive to grammar-based instruction; by drawing on students' unconscious understanding of their native language; and by relating grammar to style, content, and organization.

O'Hare, Frank. *Sentence Combining: Improving Student Writing without Formal Grammar Instruction*. Urbana: NCTE, 1973.

Pyles, Thomas, and John Algeo. *The Origins and Development of the English Language*. 4th ed. Boston: Heinle, 1993. Systematic and textbook-like, this book gives emphasis to American English.

Van de Kopple, William J. "Something Old, Something New: Functional Sentence Perspective." *Research in the Teaching of English* 17 (Feb. 1983): 85–99.

Weaver, Constance. *Grammar for Teachers: Perspectives and Definitions*. Urbana: NCTE, 1979. Although Weaver may be less confident about the use and importance of grammatical vocabulary for students, she claims that "the teacher needs a fairly solid background in grammar in order to work with students" (90).

Williams, Joseph M. *Style: Ten Lessons in Clarity and Grace*. 6th ed. New York: Addison-Wesley, 2002. Williams provides methods for both streamlining and enriching sentences.

31 Verbs

After the verb "to Love," "to Help" is the most beautiful verb in the world. – Bertha Von Suttner

English has the most varied and flexible verb forms of all the modern languages: its six tenses can fall in the indicative, subjunctive, or imperative mood; its verbs can be in active or passive voice, in present, continuous, or emphatic form, in completed or progressive aspect. English verbs can stand alone or work together, or they can transform themselves into nouns and adjectives.

Such plasticity arose from Scandinavian, German, and French influences. In fact, Old English verbs were Germanic in nature: they distinguished between only two simple tenses, present and past, and signified all other information (number, person, gender, mood, voice) by inflectional endings. Old English verbs were more often strong than weak, or more often *irregular* than *regular*: strong verbs (*sing, sang*; *bind, bound*; *choose, chosen*) have the power to indicate tense by transforming their medial vowels, not by merely adding a feeble *-ed* inflectional ending (*kick, kicked*).

The Norman Invasion greatly influenced Middle English, infusing it with the vocabulary and grammar of the French- and Latin-speaking ruling class. One significant influence was the linguistic regularization of the verbs: more than half of the strong (irregular) verbs became weak (regular), using *-ed* inflectional endings rather than internal transformation to indicate tense. This impulse to regularize verbs was checked by the rise of English on the social scale and the stabilizing effect of printing. Now, even the native-born English speaker must memorize the strong or irregular verb forms.

Additional exercises on verbs are available on *The Everyday Writer*'s companion Web site, **bedfordstmartins.com/everydaywriter**. Go to **Exercise Central** and click on **Verbs**.

Whenever the literary German dives into a sentence, that is the last you are going to see of him until he emerges on the other side of his Atlantic with his verb in his mouth.
– Mark Twain

On Verb Forms (31a)

By today's standards, even Shakespeare sometimes chose the "incorrect" verb form:

> Then, Brutus, I have much mistook your passion. –*Julius Caesar*
>
> Have you chose this man? –*Coriolanus*
>
> When they are fretten with the gusts of heaven. –*Merchant of Venice*

FOR TEACHING: Everyday Verb Forms (31a)

Restaurant menus are often a good source of verbs in action. The menu at a well-known eatery in Boston, for instance, offers to bake, broil, panfry, deep-fry, poach, sauté, fricassée, or scallop any of the available seafood entrées. To someone ordering—or cooking—at this restaurant, the important distinctions lie entirely in the verbs.

Have students discuss in groups some texts they read regularly, such as the sports section, a cookbook, or a piece of their own writing. Then ask them to look carefully at the text's use of verb forms, noting how a few examples model the power of everyday verbs at work.

FOR TEACHING: Forms of Verbs (31a)

Ask students to edit the following sentences so that all present-tense verb forms are appropriate for standard academic English. (Some of the sentences do not require any change.) Example:

> Although Joe ~~seem~~ *seems* in control, his actions ~~making~~ *make* me wonder.

1. When the dance begin, a man in costume appears.
2. The man have long fingernails and a mask.
3. All of the people in the village participate in the ceremony.
4. The doctor works two nights a week at a clinic.
5. A hot shower always relax me.
6. The thought of nuclear war be terrifying to most people.
7. New mothers often be suffering from depression.
8. He don't know whether to try again or to give up.
9. The deposit refunded if the customer don't buy the equipment.
10. Mayor Burns running for reelection this fall.

Answers

1. begin ~ begins
2. have ~ has
3. correct
4. correct
5. relax ~ relaxes
6. be ~ is
7. be suffering ~ suffer
8. don't ~ doesn't
9. is refunded; don't ~ doesn't
10. is running

On Auxiliary Verbs (31b)

The term *auxiliary* comes from the Latin *auxiliaris*, meaning "help." Hence, auxiliary verbs help to make some form of another verb. In *is eating*, the auxiliary verb *is* helps to make a form of the verb *eat*; in *have seen* and *will have brought*, the auxiliary verbs *have* and *will have* help to make forms of *see* and *bring*, respectively.

Your students should be aware that other words sometimes intervene between the auxiliary and the main verb, as in *I have already* <u>*given*</u> *you the money*.

TEACHING WITH TECHNOLOGY: Auxiliary Verbs (31b)

To practice and highlight the use of modals and auxiliaries, ask students to post an entry to your online discussion forum about hopes and dreams, a stream-of-consciousness list of what could or should be, or what could, should, or might have been.

The exercise will work best if students write on several hopes rather than focusing on just one. (By focusing, they may shift tenses and stop using the modal auxiliaries that you will soon be calling to their attention.) Then ask them to exchange their writing logs, read one another's entries, and mark the auxiliaries. Discuss their effective and their questionable uses of auxiliaries.

On *Shall* and *Will* (31b)

In the early seventeenth century, the rules of English usage were codified according to the Latin model by John Wallis, who prescribed that *shall* and *will* could not be considered synonymous. Simple future expectation was to be indicated by *shall* in first person and by *will* in second or third person.

> I *shall* meet Melinda in the morning, then we *shall* review his money-market account.
>
> Although you *will* gasp when you see her tattoo, Delphine *will* be delighted that you noticed.

According to Wallis (and all prescriptivists since), determination, desire, willfulness, or promise on the part of the speaker is represented by just the opposite paradigm—*will* in the first person and *shall* in second or third person:

> Tomorrow, I *will* return and defeat you.
>
> Of course, we *will* go to the funeral, whatever the weather. You *shall* remain in my will, no matter whom you marry.
>
> Before they return to the Republic of China, Meimei is determined that both she and Sheng *shall* finish medical school and their internships.

Despite the three-hundred-year crusade to establish this distinction, most English speakers have successfully expressed futurity and determination without it.

FOR TEACHING: Irregular Verb Forms (31c)

Because everyone has a tendency to regularize, or generalize, the English language, even native speakers need to memorize the irregular verb forms. Until we incorporate those irregular forms of our language, we overgeneralize the regular forms. As children, we overgeneralize both the plural form (*dogs*, *mouses*, and *sheeps*) and the verb form (*hummed*, *runned*, *shaked*, and *catched*). You may want to review these verb paradigms with your students. For additional review, write the present tense of ten or twelve irregular verbs on the chalkboard and call on volunteers to provide the past-tense and past-participle forms. Then, have students write entries in their writing logs, using only verbs from the list in 31c of *The Everyday Writer*. Ask several students to read their work aloud, noting the irregular forms they have used properly.

For a final class exercise using a recent piece of writing, ask students to identify the kinds of verbs they used: auxiliary, modal auxiliary, regular, and irregular. Then, in a portion of their text, have them make all verbs (except the verb *to be* and auxiliary verbs) monosyllabic and revise the piece by replacing all verbs with polysyllabic ones of similar meaning. As they read to themselves or aloud, can they hear a difference in style and tone, simply from the change in verbs? Is one version stuffier? clearer? more academic? reader friendly?

FOR COLLABORATION: Regular and Irregular Verb Forms (31c)

After dividing the class into groups, have students compose two sentences for each of twelve verbs—verbs of your own choosing or from the list in

31c of *The Everyday Writer*. In one sentence they should use the past-tense form; in the second they should use the past-participle form.

These exercises will help students recognize the comparative differences in usage and sense between the two forms. At the same time, students will also develop an ear for which auxiliaries sound best with which past participles.

Allow students time to share their sentences with the class so they can see the range of possible combinations.

FOR TEACHING: *Lie*, *Lay*; *Sit*, *Set*; *Rise*, *Raise* (31d)

As a mnemonic device, you might point out to students that, in each of these three troublesome pairs, the *i* word (l*i*e, s*i*t, r*i*se) is the intransitive one. For a quick review exercise, have students complete each of the following sentences with a form of either *raise* or *rise*:

1. She suddenly (*rose*) up and spoke.
2. Yeast causes bread to (*rise*).
3. We all know to (*raise*) our hand before we speak in class.
4. The tennis player (*raised*) the trophy to celebrate his victory.

On Verb Tenses (31e)

The concept of tense can be especially confusing to those students who try to correlate it directly with actual time. Grammatical tense gives us the mechanical forms of verbs, forms that follow definite rules of construction, but it does not always represent actual time in the past, present, or future.

For example, *present tense* can indicate an action or existence taking place in the present, past, or future:

His feet hurt. [taking place right now—present]

Water boils at 212°F. [a fact in the past, present, and future]

My roommate drinks iced tea every morning. [habitual action—past, present, future]

We are having turkey for Thanksgiving. [intended future action]

Huckleberry Finn is a resourceful, sensitive boy. [discussing a literary work—present]

I hear that Jaime spoke to the new students. [*hear* gives the past action a present connection]

In *Revising the Rules*, Brock Haussamen explains how the *aspect* of a verb enriches our understanding of its tense:

> The grouping of tenses in today's handbooks reflects the understanding of verbs as it stood at about the middle of the nineteenth century. Since that time,

while the handbook descriptions have remained frozen, linguists have broken away from the paradigm of past, present, and future and have taken the discussion of the meaning of verb forms into new realms. . . . Nineteenth-century linguists adopted the word *aspect* (from the Latin for the ways things appear from a certain point of view) to refer to such features of verbs as completion, duration, and repetition—and temporal features not related to past, present, or future, in other words. (35)

FOR MULTILINGUAL WRITERS: Verb Tenses (31e)

Because speakers of African American English Vernacular, Chinese, and Spanish often omit *-s*, *-ed*, and *-ing*, you may want to review the following chart with them:

I learn / am learning / learned
you learn / are learning / learned
s/he learns / is learning / learned
we learn / are learning / learned
you learn / are learning / learned
they learn / are learning / learned

FOR TEACHING: Sequence of Verb Tenses (31f)

The sequence-of-tense principle governs the relationship between the verbs in main and accompanying subordinate clauses.

Verbs in *natural sequence* indicate a natural, logical time relation between the actions they represent. In *Bob believes that you are telling the truth*, both actions take place simultaneously. Whereas in *Celia believes that you swiped her candlesticks*, the first verb reflects on a past-tense verb. And in *Tina guarantees that Mick will sing with her tonight*, the first and second verbs represent present and future tenses, respectively and naturally.

Verbs in *attracted sequence* harmonize without regard to the actual time represented. Main verbs in *past tense* and *past perfect tense* followed by indirect discourse and clauses of purpose call for attracted sequence:

Myra *said* that Rolf *was* slim and handsome. [He has not suddenly become fat and ugly.]

Myra *asked* if Rolf *was* also smart. [He remains brilliant.]

Adam *strangled* the serpent so that he *could live* without temptation. [purpose]

Eve *entered* an assertiveness training course so she *could learn* to be forceful. [purpose]

A main verb in any other tense followed by a clause of purpose attracts the present tense:

Helen *is joining* a health club so she *can get* in shape. [purpose]

She *will enter* the Chicago marathon so she *can compete*. [purpose]

Certain verbs (for example, *expect*, *suppose*, *thought*, *knew*) and predicate adjectives (*evident*, *certain*, *sure*) also call for attracted sequence:

We *expected/supposed/thought/knew* Chloë *would make* a grand entrance.

It was *evident* that Michele *was* happily pregnant.

Fritz was *sure/certain* you *would plead* innocent.

Ask students to look at their most recent piece of writing—an essay or a writing log entry—and note how they naturally balance the sequence of tenses in their prose.

FOR COLLABORATION: Active Voice and Passive Voice (31g)

With students working in groups of three, direct each group to find several pieces of writing that all group members particularly like, and to mark examples of the active voice and the passive voice in the writing. Have the groups convert these examples to the other voice, noting the effects of the revisions on emphasis and rhythm. Finally, ask the groups to bring the results of their work to class for discussion.

FOR TEACHING: Mood (31h)

In this passage from *A Room of One's Own*, Virginia Woolf employs the subjunctive mood:

> [I]t is unthinkable that any women in Shakespeare's day *should have had* Shakespeare's genius. For genius like Shakespeare's is not born among laboring, uneducated, servile people. It was not born in England among the Saxons and the Britons. It is not born today among the working classes. How, then, *could* it *have been* born among women whose work began, . . . almost before they were out of the nursery, who were forced to it by their parents and held to it by all the power of law and custom? Yet genius of a sort *must have existed* among women as it *must have existed* among the working classes.

Discuss how Woolf's use of the subjunctive affects the tone and meaning of this passage. How does mood help her make an ironic point?

FOR COLLABORATION: Tense, Voice, Mood (31e–h)

If the diversity of verbal forms (tense, voice, and mood) overwhelms your students, encourage them to appreciate how these forms help them convey meaning accurately and flexibly. Assure them that what the forms are called is less important than how they are used for specific purposes. Whenever possible, point out and discuss how their purpose in writing dictates the choice of a particular verbal treatment. For this practice session, divide the class into small groups and have students exchange recent essays or passages they have written. Can they identify the writer's use of tense, voice, and mood? You can move from group to group, helping students see these forms of verbs at work in their own writing.

FOR TEACHING: Reviewing Verbs

The following poem, Lewis Carroll's "Jabberwocky," is a famous example of nonsense verse that plays games with and freely invents words. Read the poem aloud to your students, and then ask them to identify all the verbs (whether or not the verbs are actual English words). Use this exercise as a way to judge what your students know about verbs.

'Twas brillig, and the slithy toves
  Did gyre and gimble in the wabe;
All mimsy were the borogoves,
  And the mome raths outgrabe.
"Beware the Jabberwock, my son!
  The jaws that bite, the claws that catch!
Beware the Jubjub bird, and shun
  The frumious Bandersnatch!"

He took his vorpal sword in hand:
  Long time the manxome foe he sought—
So rested he by the Tumtum tree,
  And stood awhile in thought.

And as in uffish thought he stood,
  The Jabberwock, with eyes of flame,
Came whiffling through the tulgey wood,
  And burbled as it came!

One, two! One, two! And through and through
  The vorpal blade went snicker-snack!
He left it dead, and with its head
  He went galumphing back.

"And hast thou slain the Jabberwock?
  Come to my arms, my beamish boy!
O frabjous day! Callooh! Callay!"
  He chortled in his joy.

'Twas brillig, and the slithy toves
  Did gyre and gimble in the wabe;
All mimsy were the borogoves,
  And the mome raths outgrabe.

USEFUL READINGS

Aitchison, Jean. *Language Change: Progress or Decay*. 3rd ed. Cambridge, Engl.: Cambridge UP, 2001. Written from a sociolinguist's perspective, this work explains the implementation, causes, and developmental features of language change. The entire discussion is accessible and straightforward. Chapter 3 specifically discusses verb forms.

Bailey, Guy. "A Perspective on African-American English." *American Dialect Research*. Ed. Dennis R. Preston. Philadelphia: John Benjamins, 1993. 287–318. A particularly informative discussion of verbs appears on pages 296–307.

Baugh, John. *Black Street Speech: Its History, Structure, and Survival*. Austin: U of Texas P, 1983. Baugh provides a useful discussion of invariant *be* and future perfective *be done*. See, especially, Chapter 6.

Chappell, Virginia A., and Judith Rodby. "Verb Tense and ESL Composition: A Discourse Level Approach." *On TESOL '82: Pacific Perspectives on Language Learning and Teaching; Teachers of English to Speakers of Other Languages*. Ed. Mark A. Clarke and Jean Handscombe. Washington, DC: TESOL Publications, 1983. 309–20.

Comrie, Bernard. *Aspect: An Introduction to the Study of Verbal Aspect and Related Problems*. Cambridge, Engl.: Cambridge UP, 1976. This is a study of aspect, which differs from tense in that it refers to the duration or continuation of an action in time, rather than its occurrence in relation to the present moment.

Fasold, Ralph W. *Tense Markings in Black English: A Linguistic and Social Analysis*. Washington, DC: Center for Applied Linguistics, 1978. The author offers a thorough explanation of verb forms in African American English Vernacular.

Haussamen, Brock. *Revising the Rules*. Dubuque: Kendall/Hunt, 1994. Haussamen uses descriptive linguistics to develop a rhetorical approach to describing grammar. He discusses verb tense, agreement, and punctuation.

Labov, William. *Language in the Inner-City: Studies in the Black English Vernacular*. Philadelphia: U of Pennsylvania P, 1972. This landmark work includes a discussion of verb forms in African American English Vernacular.

Smitherman, Geneva. *Talkin and Testifyin: The Language of Black America*. Detroit: Wayne State UP, 1986. This book contains a discussion of the aspectual verb system in African American English Vernacular. See, particularly, Chapter 2, "It Bees Dat Way Sometime."

Williams, Joseph M. *Origins of the English Language: A Social and Linguistic History*. New York: Free P, 1975. 265–74. Williams describes and traces the historical development of the two aspects: progressive and perfect.

———. *Style: Ten Lessons in Clarity and Grace*. 6th ed. New York: Addison-Wesley, 2002. The writer provides advanced discussion of the stylistic virtues of active and passive voice.

32 Subject-Verb Agreement

The subject always agrees with the verb, except on those occasions when the subject does not agree.
—GUSTAVE FLAUBERT

The English language, even in its earliest stages, is extremely redundant: such redundancy is a type of "agreement" in terms of person, number, gender, and tense. One needs only the most basic facility with language to make meaning out of the following passage, written in Modern English:

> The wolf stood in the pit, so hungry that he was crazy. He was really cursing the one who brought him there.

Look how much help we get with tense; *stood*, *was*, *was cursing*. We are provided with three times the information, the agreement, we need to know that this passage is in the past tense. Now, look at the information telling us that there is only one wolf: *wolf* has no plural marker (*-s*); the *was* and *was cursing* are in the third-person singular form; and the pronouns referring to the wolf are singular (*he* and *him*).

The preceding passage is adapted from *The Fox and the Wolf*, a text written in approximately 1200 CE. Even in the original Old English, we can see that redundancy or agreement wove a safety net for the reader:

> þe wolf in þe putte stod,
> A fingret so þat he ves wod.
> Inou he cursede þat þider him broute! (ll. 257–59)

Here, we are given the same three clues that the passage is in past tense from the verb forms that look vaguely familiar—*stod*, *ves*, *cursede*—and nearly the same information regarding the singleness of the wolf—*wolf* (without the plural marker *-s*) and the singular verb *ves*.

Additional exercises on subject-verb agreement are available on *The Everyday Writer*'s companion Web site, **bedfordstmartins.com/everydaywriter**. Go to **Exercise Central** and click on **Subject-Verb Agreement**.

On Agreement

In "Agreement," an important section of *Errors and Expectations*, master diagnostician Mina Shaughnessy writes:

> The idea of agreement—that is, of certain words in sentences being formally linked to others so as to reinforce or repeat some kinds of meaning rather than others—is common to many languages. What is arbitrary in each language is what that language chooses to reinforce. Standard English, for example, is laced by forms that reinforce number . . . a time frame . . . gender and person. (136)

One of the most common student errors—error of agreement—grows out of all the possibilities for agreement in our language. Shaughnessy saw such errors as "exercises in competence" and knew that students who have trouble with agreement need to become *habituated* in, to develop an "ear for," the conventions of their language.

If your students seem puzzled by the concept of agreement, or by the term itself, remind them that subjects and verbs are at work in almost every statement they make and that they make them "agree" effortlessly most of the time. Show them several sentences from a recent newspaper to illustrate agreement, such as these three from a sports page:

> *Guzman powers* another blistering ball over the plate.
>
> *The Yanks move* on to Milwaukee tomorrow.
>
> *The duel* of the no-hitters *continues* into the eighth.

Then ask students either to listen or to read for one day with special attention to subjects and verbs and to bring in a list of interesting sentences for a class discussion of agreement.

FOR MULTILINGUAL WRITERS: Subject-Verb Agreement

If your students speak languages in addition to English, ask them to explain the agreement necessary in those languages. Spanish, for example, extends agreement to the gender and number of adjectives. African American Vernacular English, French, and many other languages call for negative concord whereas English rejects it; Chinese languages do not use agreement, depending instead on word order to relate words in sentences.

FOR TEACHING: Agreement (32a–e)

Traditionally, sentence diagramming has been used to help students identify the subject and verb of a sentence. Although such close syntactical analysis will help *some* students determine subject-verb or pronoun-antecedent agreement, most of our students just don't have the technical command of grammar to diagram or parse a sentence.

To help your students develop an ear for agreement, ask them to bring in or create sentences that seem confusing. Then ask them to come up with ways of determining the information that separates the subject from the verb. For example, try these sentences orally with your students:

1. To see so many people here *is*/are gratifying.
2. The problems with the house is/*are* overwhelming.
3. Every one of the details *was*/were perfect.
4. It *is*/are the fault of the citizens.
5. Pizza with pepperoni, mushrooms, and green peppers *is*/are delicious.

The following sentences contain compound and collective-noun subjects. For additional practice, have students edit them for subject-verb agreement.

1. Every week, Sharma, Julio, and Richard attends/*attend* a group total of fifty hours of school.
2. Crosby, Stills, Nash, and Young *was*/were one of the hottest groups in the early seventies.
3. Neither the president nor his administration *claims*/claim to know anything about the wiretap.
4. Mike and his friends is/*are* going to decorate your yard with crepe paper after the game.
5. The composition class plan/*plans* to celebrate Valentine's Day at the professor's house.
6. The professor or her assistant *is*/are always in the office.
7. The couple vow/*vows* to have and to hold until death.

Here are three additional sets of exercises on agreement that will provide practice for your students. Have students edit the following sentences for subject-verb agreement:

1. The best thing about college *is*/are the vacations.
2. Panning up and down staircases *was*/were a frequent feature of Hitchcock's films.
3. In this context, the word *values* *is*/are vague.
4. *The Letters of Henry James* provide/*provides* interesting and important, if sometimes ambiguous, information about the nineteenth-century author.

5. It *is*/are a melancholy object to those who *walk*/walks through this great town or *travel*/travels in the country, when they *see*/sees in the streets, the road, and cabin doors, crowded with beggars of the female sex, followed by three, four, or six children, all in rags and importuning every passenger for an alms. These mothers, instead of being able to work for their honest livelihood, is/*are* forced to employ all their time in strolling to beg sustenance for their helpless infants, who, as they *grow*/grows up, either *turn*/turns thieves for want of work, or leaves/*leave* their dear country to fight for the Pretender of Spain, or *sell*/sells themselves to the Barbados. –JONATHAN SWIFT, "A Modest Proposal"

Have students edit the following sentences for verb agreement. In addition, ask them to note carefully linking verbs, inverted-word order, and titles.

1. You need to know that both of them *appeal*/appeals to me.
2. Everybody in both classes *was*/were ready.
3. Some is/*are* here; others is/*are* not.
4. Every one of the details *was*/were perfect.
5. I like instructors who *smile*/smiles.
6. *The 39 Steps* demand/*demands* moviegoers' rapt attention.

Have students underline the appropriate verbs in parentheses in the following passage from "The Iks" by Lewis Thomas, a piece about a tribe in Uganda.

> The solitary Ik, isolated in the ruins of an exploded culture, (*has*/have) built a new defense for himself. If you (lives/*live*) in an unworkable society, you can make up one of your own, and this (*is*/are) what the Iks (has/*have*) done. Each Ik (*has*/have) become a one-man tribe on its own, a constituency. Now everything (*falls*/fall) into place. This is why they do (seems/*seem*), after all, vaguely familiar to all of us. We've seen them before. This is precisely the way groups of one size or another, ranging from committee to nations, (behaves/*behave*). It is, of course, this aspect of humanity that (*has*/have) lagged behind the rest of evolution, and this is why the Ik (*seems*/seem) so primitive. In his absolute selfishness, his incapacity to give anything away, no matter what, he (*is*/are) a successful committee.

FOR TEACHING: Collective-Nouns Subjects (32d)

Encourage students to think critically about collective nouns as wholes or parts. Write this topic sentence on the board: *The jury disagree/disagrees on several details*. Then ask students to decide whether to treat *jury* as singular or plural, according to the following context:

After examining both sides of the case for over seven hours, only one member thinks for certain that the defendant is not guilty. Three other jurors, however, cannot decide at all. In view of this stand-off, the jury leader has no choice but to insist that the entire jury review the case and evidence yet one more time.

FOR COLLABORATION: Subject-Verb Agreement

Working in pairs, students should write a paragraph about a specific movie, making sure to use the present tense as they describe some of the actions, special effects, or other elements of the film that they admire. Students should then go through their paragraph, identifying every subject and its verb. Ask them to use the guidelines in Chapter 32 of *The Everyday Writer* to make sure all subjects and verbs agree. Students can read their final paragraphs aloud in class.

USEFUL READINGS

Kolln, Martha. *Rhetorical Grammar*. 4th ed. New York: Longman, 2001.

Shaughnessy, Mina. *Errors and Expectations*. New York: Oxford UP, 1977.

Pronouns

33

A kind of duet—she as oboe, he as contrabassoon, and full of obbligato digressions. –RICHARD EDER

When a pronoun follows a pronoun's nature, a pronoun substitutes for a noun; the noun then becomes the pronoun's antecedent.

Thanks to the existence of pronouns, we are able to avoid such redundancy and write, instead:

When a pronoun follows its nature, it substitutes for a noun that becomes its antecedent.

The most highly inflected parts of speech in present-day English, pronouns are nearly as complex and informational as their Latinate counterparts. Compare:

As Dennis delivered Dennis's inaugural address, Dennis nervously looked out into the freezing crowd only to see Dennis's mother smiling beatifically at Dennis.

As *he* delivered *his* inaugural address, Dennis nervously looked out into the freezing crowd only to see *his* mother smiling beatifically at *him*.

Although *Dennis* is the antecedent of *he*, *his*, and *him*, the pronoun form changes. English pronouns are specific in terms of person, gender, and number. In fact, our pronouns often carry as much information as their antecedents. *I*, *you*, and *he* tell us about person; *he*, *she*, and *it* tell us about gender; *I*, *we*, *she*, and *they* tell us about number.

Additional exercises on pronouns are available on *The Everyday Writer*'s companion Web site, **bedfordstmartins.com/everydaywriter**. Go to **Exercise Central** and click on **Pronouns**.

On Pronouns

In their study *Frequency Analysis of English Usage*, W. Nelson Francis and Henry Kucera note the frequency with which words appear in edited

American English. Pronouns are among the most frequently used words, as the following chart indicates:

Word	Rank
he	7
it	11
they	13
I	15
we	23
she	24
you	30
who	35

The authors also note that personal, reflexive, singular pronouns (*myself, herself, himself*) occur much more frequently in imaginative prose than in informative prose. Conversely, plural forms of these reflexive personal pronouns (*ourselves, themselves*) occur much more frequently in informative prose than in imaginative prose. While Francis and Kucera offer no explanation for this relationship, pronoun use seems to indicate that imaginative prose tends to focus on individuals, while transactional or informative prose tends to focus on groups of people.

FOR MULTILINGUAL WRITERS: Case, Number, and Gender of Pronouns

If you have students who speak languages other than English, ask them to explain the pronoun system of those languages, in terms of case, number, and gender.

FOR COLLABORATION: Pronoun Case (33a)

The following passage comes from "University Days," James Thurber's classic essay about his years as a student at Ohio State University. Most of its pronouns have been removed. Have students work together to put a correct pronoun in each blank. (You may also have them label each pronoun as subjective, objective, or possessive case.)

> Another course that I didn't like, but somehow managed to pass, was economics. _____ went to that class straight from the botany class, which didn't help _____ to understand either subject. _____ used to get them mixed up. But not as mixed up as another student in _____ economics class who came there direct from a physics laboratory. _____ was a tackle on the football team, named Bolenciecwcz. At that time Ohio State University had one of the best football teams in the country, and Bolenciecwcz was one of _____ outstanding stars. In

order to be eligible to play it was necessary for _____ to keep up in _____ studies, a very difficult matter, for while _____ was not dumber than an ox _____ was not any smarter. Most of _____ professors were lenient and helped _____ along. None gave _____ more hints in answering questions or asked _____ simpler ones than the economics professor, a thin, timid man named Bassum. One day when _____ were on the subject of transportation and distribution, it came Bolenciecwcz's turn to answer a question. "Name one means of transportation," the professor said to _____. No light came into the big tackle's eyes. "Just any means of transportation" said the professor. Bolenciecwcz sat staring at _____. "That is," pursued the professor, "any medium, agency, or method of going from one place to another." Bolenciecwcz had the look of a man _____ is being led into a trap. "You may choose among steam, horse-drawn, or electrically propelled vehicles," said the instructor. "I might suggest the one which _____ commonly take in making long journeys across land." There was a profound silence in which everybody stirred uneasily, including Bolenciecwcz and Mr. Bassum. Mr. Bassum abruptly broke this silence in an amazing manner. "Choo-choo-choo," _____ said, in a low voice, and turned instantly scarlet. _____ glanced appealingly around the room. All of _____, of course, shared Mr. Bassum's desire that Bolenciecwcz should stay abreast of the class in economics, for the Illinois game, one of the hardest and most important of the season, was only a week off. "Toot, toot, too-tooooooot!" some student with a deep voice moaned, and _____ all looked encouragingly at Bolenciecwcz. Somebody else gave a fine imitation of a locomotive letting off steam. Mr. Bassum himself rounded off the little show. "Ding, dong, ding, dong," _____ said, hopefully. Bolenciecwcz was staring at the floor now, trying to think, _____ great brow furrowed, _____ huge hands rubbing together, _____ face red.

Answers

(Besides the unkind stereotypes of student athletes, Thurber also resorts to generalizations about the student's ethnicity, acceptable fodder for humor some fifty years ago.)

Another course that I didn't like, but somehow managed to pass, was economics. *I* went to that class straight from the botany class, which didn't help *me* to understand either subject. *I* used to get them mixed up. But not as mixed up as another student in *my* economics class who came there direct from a physics laboratory. *He* was a tackle on the football team, named Bolenciecwcz. At that time Ohio State University had one of the best football teams in the country, and Bolenciecwcz was one of *its* outstanding stars. In order to be eligible to play it was necessary for *him* to keep up in *his* studies, a very difficult matter, for while *he* was not dumber than an ox *he* was not any smarter. Most of *his* professors were lenient and helped *him* along. None gave *him* more hints in answering questions or asked *him* simpler ones than the economics professor, a thin, timid man named Bassum. One day when *we* were on the subject of transportation and distribution, it came Bolenciecwcz's turn to answer a question. "Name one means of transportation," the professor said to *him*. No light came into the big tackle's eyes. "Just any means of transportation," said the professor. Bolenciecwcz sat staring at *him*. "That is," pursued the professor, "any medium, agency, or method of going from one place to another." Bolenciecwcz had the look of a man *who* is being led into a trap. "You may choose among steam, horse-drawn, or electrically propelled vehicles," said the instructor. "I might suggest the one which *we* commonly take in making long journeys across land." There was a profound silence in which everybody stirred uneasily, including Bolenciecwcz and Mr. Bassum. Mr. Bassum abruptly broke this silence in an amazing manner. "Choo-choo-choo," *he* said, in a low voice, and turned instantly scarlet. *He* glanced appealingly around the room. All of *us*, of course, shared Mr. Bassum's desire that Bolenciecwcz should stay abreast of the class in economics, for the Illinois game, one of the hardest and most important of the season, was just a week off. "Toot, toot, too-tooooooot!" some student with a deep voice moaned, and *we* all looked encouragingly at Bolenciecwcz. Somebody else gave a fine imitation of a locomotive letting off steam. Mr. Bassum himself rounded off the little show. "Ding, dong, ding, dong," *he* said, hopefully. Bolenciecwcz was staring at the floor now, trying to think, *his* great brow furrowed, *his* huge hands rubbing together, *his* face red.

FOR TEACHING: Second-Person Pronouns (33a)

The pronoun *you* gives no information other than number—second person. Except for context, there is no way to tell if *you* is singular or plural, masculine or feminine. Such was not always the case. Until the thirteenth century, English used different forms of second-person pronouns: the *th*-forms, indicating singular (*thee*, *thy*, *thou*); and the *y*-forms, indicating plural (*ye*, *you*, *your*).

With the influence of the French language, the *th*-forms came to denote intimacy and were used with close friends, family, and children; the *y*-forms, to denote a measure of formality or respect, were used with everyone else. These two forms corresponded with the *tu* and *vous* forms of French.

Who would succeed in the world should be wise in the use of pronouns. Utter the You twenty times, when you once utter the I.
—JOHN HAY

FOR TEACHING: Possessive Case (33a)

Ask students to insert the correct possessive pronoun in the blank in each sentence. Example:

<u>My</u> eyes ached after studying for ten hours.

1. Your parents must be pleased about _____ going back to college.
2. Ken's dinner arrived quickly, but Rose waited an hour for _____.
3. We agreed to pool _____ knowledge.

4. Even many supporters of Lincoln opposed _____ freeing the slaves.
5. _____ responsibility should it be to teach moral values?

Answers

1. your
2. hers
3. our
4. his
5. Whose

> I, *pro.* In grammar it is a pronoun of the first person and singular number. Its plural is said to be *We*, but how there can be more than one myself is doubtless clearer to the grammarians than it is to the author of this incomparable dictionary.
>
> ME, *pro.* The objectionable case of I. The personal pronoun in English has three cases, the dominative, the objectionable and the oppressive. Each is all three.
>
> —AMBROSE BIERCE, *The Devil's Dictionary*, 1911

FOR COLLABORATION: Pronoun Case (33a)

Have students work with a classmate to edit the following sentences for errors in pronoun case. (Some sentences are correct as written.) Example:

> *she*
> Of the group, only ~~her~~ and I finished the race.

Have the groups prepare to present their edited sentences to the class and explain why they made each change as well as why they left some sentences as written.

1. Waiting for the train, her and him began to talk.
2. If you have any questions, ask Steve or I.
3. The people who Jay worked with were very cold and unsociable.
4. Who would have thought that twenty years later he would be king?
5. One waitress told that customer that she was tired of him forgetting to leave a tip.
6. Only him, a few cabinet members, and several military leaders were aware of the steady advance Japan was making toward Pearl Harbor.
7. No one could feel worse than me about missing your party.
8. Except for Alyssa and her, everyone was on a diet.

9. I never got to play that role in front of an audience, but I am one of the few performers who really did break a leg.
10. Connor always lent money to whomever asked him for it.

On *Who*, *Whoever*, *Whom*, and *Whomever* (33b)

Students may enjoy H. L. Mencken's discussion of the "shadowy line" between sound usage and barbarism in *The American Language*:

> The schoolmarm . . . continues the heroic task of trying to make her young charges grasp the difference between *who* and *whom*. Here, alas, the speechways of the American people seem to be again against her. The two forms of the pronoun are confused magnificently in the debates in Congress, and in most newspaper writing, and in ordinary discourse the great majority of Americans avoid *whom* diligently, as a word full of snares. When they employ it, it is often incorrectly, as in "*Whom* is your father?" and "*Whom* spoke to me?" Noah Webster, always the pragmatic reformer, denounced it as usually useless so long ago as 1783. Common sense, he argued, was on the side of "*Who* did he marry?" Today such a form as "*Whom* are you talking to?" would seem very affected to most Americans; they might write it, but they would never speak it. . . . A shadowy line often separates what is currently coming into sound usage from what is still regarded as barbarous.

On Pronoun-Antecedent Agreement (33f)

The use of a plural pronoun with an indefinite antecedent has a long history in educated usage:

> Everyone in the house were in their beds. —HENRY FIELDING
>
> A person can't help their birth. —WILLIAM THACKERAY
>
> It's enough to drive anyone out of their senses. —GEORGE BERNARD SHAW

This lineage notwithstanding, such usage is now apt to be considered incorrect by many readers. However, because it provides a simple solution to many problems of sexist usage, it is becoming more and more widely accepted in academic and formal writing.

The adjectives *every* and *each* and the pronouns *everyone*, *no one*, *anyone*, and *anybody* are generally regarded as singular, regardless of the sentence construction. These words cause difficulty for students, not so much because of their indefiniteness, but because of the agreement problem inherent in third-person singular nouns and verbs: should agreement be reached in number or gender?

In the following sentence, should you pair *every* with *his* and perpetuate sexist language? Or should you pair the singular *every* with the plural *their*, a practice that is falling into general usage?

Every driver takes *his/her/its/their* lives into *his/her/its/their* own hands.

Or should you recast the entire sentence into the plural?

All drivers take *their* lives into *their* own hands.

Current convention prefers the singular for *everybody* even when a contextual and commonsense analysis shows that *everybody* refers to more than one person.

On Saturday mornings, *everybody* meets at Shauna's place before heading to the baseball field. Beth, Cindi, and Robert always show up first. Aneil and Matt usually arrive last.

> **There is nothing more likely to start disagreement among people or countries than an agreement.**
> **—E. B. WHITE**

FOR TEACHING: Pronoun-Antecedent Agreement (33f)

Ask students to think for a moment of a memorable object—a toy, a favorite children's book, anything they can remember well—and to write a paragraph or two describing the object: what it looks like, how they used it, how they feel about it. Then ask them to look over the descriptions, identifying all pronouns. Finally, ask them (in small groups, perhaps) to check to see that each pronoun has a clear antecedent.

FOR TEACHING: Pronoun-Antecedent Agreement (33f)

Ask students to spend five minutes interviewing two friends or classmates about the courses they are currently taking. Have them take notes and try to transcribe the interviewees' exact words. Then ask them to write a brief summary of their interviews and to note how they use pronouns in the summary. Remind them to check that each pronoun refers accurately to the intended person.

FOR TEACHING: Sexist Pronouns (33f)

Ask students to look in newspapers, in magazines, or on the Web for examples of pronouns that refer to both men and women, using the examples in the At a Glance box, "Editing Out Sexist Pronouns," in 33f of *The Everyday Writer* as guides. Suggest that they collect both sexist and nonsexist examples for small-group analysis and in-class discussion. You might want to read a few examples aloud and then put one sexist example on the board for the class to revise.

> Long afterward, Oedipus, old and blinded, walked the roads. He smelled a familiar smell. It was the Sphinx. Oedipus said, "I want to ask one question. Why didn't I recognize my mother?" "You gave the wrong answer," said the Sphinx. "But that was what made everything possible," said Oedipus. "No," she said. "When I asked, What walks on four legs in the morning, two at noon, and three in the evening, you answered, Man. You didn't say anything about woman." "When you say Man," said Oedipus, "you include women too. Everyone knows that." She said, "That's what you think."
>
> —MURIEL RUKEYSER

FOR TEACHING: Clear Pronoun Reference (33g)

If your students are not familiar with the term *pronoun reference*, remind them that they use the concept every day, particularly in conversation. In fact, speakers of English rely constantly on clear pronoun reference, as this conversation between a driver and a mechanic illustrates:

Mechanic: So what's the problem?

Driver: On rainy days, it really acts weird.

Mechanic: It won't start on rainy days?

Driver: Sometimes it won't start. But there are other problems, too. All those little lights on the dashboard light up at once. That white needle goes all the way over, and the little gauge there jiggles around nervously.

Mechanic: Hmmm. Does it crank?

Driver: The little gauge?

Mechanic: The car. The engine.

This conversation shows pronoun reference in use. The one breakdown in communication occurs because the driver assumes that the mechanic's question—"Does it crank?"—refers to the last thing the driver mentioned—"the little gauge." The mechanic, however, is using *it* to refer to *the car*, not the gauge. Have students think of times when unclear pronoun reference has made for confusion.

FOR COLLABORATION: Pronouns

Ask students to work in groups of three for this exercise. One student should read the following poem aloud, while the other two students try to figure out the poem's two-word title. Then, ask students how the group members knew what the title should be. Next, have each member of the group write a similar poem of three or four verses, using pronouns and other words to give clues to the title. Ask one member from each group to read the poems aloud. Can group members guess the titles? Review the results of this collaboration in class, and discuss the importance of clear pronoun references and agreement using their poems as examples.

His art is eccentricity, his aim
How not to hit the mark he seems to aim at,
His passion how to avoid the obvious,
His technique how to vary the avoidance.
The others throw to be comprehended. He
Throws to be a moment misunderstood.
Yet not too much. Not too errant, arrant, wild,
But every seeming aberration willed.
Not to, yet still, still to communicate
Making the batter understand too late.

—ROBERT FRANCIS, "The Pitcher"

USEFUL READINGS

Baron, Dennis. *Grammar and Gender*. New Haven: Yale UP, 1986. Baron offers a critical history of the relationship between sexism and the development of the English language; Chapter 10 focuses on attempts to solve the problem of pronoun agreement with the third-person singular.

Francis, W. Nelson, and Henry Kucera. *Frequency Analysis of English Usage*. Boston: Houghton, 1982. Nelson and Kucera provide a study of word usage frequency in English, as well as some statistical analysis.

Haussamen, Brock. *Revising the Rules: Traditional Grammar and Modern Linguistics*. Dubuque: Kendell/Hunt, 1994. See Chapters 6–8 for more on "Pronoun Agreement," "Pronoun Case and Restrictiveness," and "He and They," respectively.

Hayes, Christopher G. "A Brief Writing Assignment for Introducing Non-Sexist Pronoun Usage." *TETYC* 28.1 (Sept. 2000): 74–77. Hayes describes a narrative writing assignment that helps demonstrate to students how and why sexist language usage can limit thinking, sometimes injuriously.

Nilsen, Aileen Pace. "Winning the Great 'He'/'She' Battle." *CE* 46 (1984): 151–57. Nilsen uses an examination of manuscripts submitted to *English Journal* to demonstrate the complexities of using "sex-fair" language. She then offers four principles intended to guide such usage.

Schwartz, Marilyn. *Report of the Task Force on Bias-Free Language of the Association of American University Presses*. Bloomington: Indiana UP, 1995. This AAUP report gives the association's official recommendations on how to produce "biasfree" writing, paying special attention to nonsexist discourse.

Traugott, Elizabeth, and Mary Louise Pratt. *Linguistics for Students of Literature*. San Diego: Harcourt, 1980.

Williams, Joseph M. *Style: Ten Lessons in Clarity and Grace*. 6th ed. New York: Addison-Wesley, 2002.

34 Adjectives and Adverbs

The adjective is the banana peel of the parts of speech.
–Clifton Paul Fadiman

In early English, many adverbs were formed from adjectives by adding *e*: *bright*, the adjective, became *brighte*, the adverb. In time, the *e* was dropped, but the adverbial use was kept. Hence by analogy, many adjectives (such as *excellent*) that could not form adverbs by adding *e* were simply used as adverbs. Shakespeare freely used such constructions:

Which the false man does *easy*. –*Macbeth* 2.3.143

Thou didst it *excellent*. –*Taming of the Shrew* 1.1.89

Grow not *instant* old. –*Hamlet* 1.5.94

'Tis *noble* spoken. –*Antony and Cleopatra* 2.2.99

And he used both forms of the adverb side by side:

She was *new* lodged and *newly* deified. –*Lover's Complaint* 84

In function, adjectives and adverbs alike modify other parts of speech, and their differences in spelling and pronunciation have been conflated in the linguistic tendency toward regularization. Like the English of Shakespeare's day, many informal varieties of English often make no distinction between an adjective and an adverb in constructions such as *Come quick!* and *The moon shines bright* that omit the *-ly* adverb suffix. In their enthusiasm to use standard academic or "correct" English, some speakers even add the *-ly* suffix to words that function as adjectives, such as in *I feel badly that you've lost your job*. Since *feel* is a linking verb, the speaker should use the adjective *bad* rather than the adverb *badly*.

Additional exercises on adjectives and adverbs are available on *The Everyday Writer*'s companion Web site, **bedfordstmartins.com/everydaywriter**. Go to **Exercise Central** and click on **Adjectives and Adverbs**.

On Overusing Adjectives and Adverbs

Many well-known writers on style, heirs of Hemingway and Orwell, counsel in the strictest terms against any but the most "necessary" adjectives and adverbs. William Zinsser calls the overuse of modifiers "clutter" and advises writers to "strip every sentence to its cleanest components":

> . . . Every word that serves no function . . . [and] every adverb that carries the same meaning that's already in the verb, . . . weaken the strength of a sentence.

According to Zinsser in *On Writing Well*, carefully chosen nouns and verbs resonate with connotative meaning. These words rarely need modifiers: *friend* does not need *personal*; *mope* does not need *dejectedly*. On the other hand, Francis Christensen, in "A Generative Rhetoric of the Sentence," argues that a mature and interesting prose style lies in the use of adjectives and adverbs, which enables students to express complicated thoughts in complicated ways.

And on still *another* hand, in her chapter on "Vocabulary" in *Errors and Expectations*, Mina Shaughnessy describes the vocabulary features of three groups of writers (basic, intermediate, and advanced), including their use of adjectives and adverbs. Basic writers commonly use only a few, already overused adverbs (*too*, *very*, *really*, *quite*, *hardly*) and just twenty-one or so adjectives. Intermediate writers, she claims, use *-ly* adverbs (*adequately*, *fluently*, for example). Their adjectives are more "informative" than *good*, *bad*, *important*; these include *hostile*, *honest*, *monstrous*, *impatient*. Shaughnessy encourages instructors to work with writers of all levels, building their academic vocabulary in three ways: learning about words, learning words, and learning a sensitivity to words.

Adjectives often carry indispensable shades of meaning. In basketball, for example, there's an important difference between a *slam dunk* and an *alley-oop dunk*, a *flagrant foul* and a *technical foul*, a *layup* and a *reverse layup*. Consider as well the distinction between *talk* and *trash talk*, or *color commentary* and *play-by-play commentary*. In each case, the difference is in the adjectives. Ask your students to look in the newspaper for examples of adjectives that carry significant meaning in a sport or other activity that they know well. Of the adjectives they find, ask them to identify which ones add vividness to the writing and which ones add essential information.

FOR COLLABORATION: Adjectives (34a–b)

The following sentence, from Truman Capote's *Other Voices, Other Rooms*, uses adjectives effectively to paint a picture of beauty in motion:

> *Tall, powerful, barefoot, graceful, soundless,* Missouri Fever was like a *supple black* cat as she paraded serenely about the kitchen, the *casual* flow of *her* walk beautifully *sensuous* and *haughty.*

Have students break into groups and write imitations of Capote's sentence, using as the focus of their descriptions a pet, a person they know, or a performing artist (dancer, musician, or actor) they have seen. Have them compare sentences among their groups and then select one they find particularly powerful to share with the class.

By using Capote's sentence as a model, they will be able to internalize his syntax while they experiment and discover the semantic possibilities of adjectives.

> **Anything that needs an adjective, be it civics education, or socialist education, or Christian education, or whatever-you-like education, is not education, and it has some different goal. The very existence of modified "educations" is testimony to the fact that their proponents cannot bring about what they want in a mind that is free. An "education" that cannot do its work in a free mind, and so must "teach" by homily and precept in the service of these feelings and attitudes and beliefs rather than those, is pure and unmistakable tyranny.**
>
> **—Richard Mitchell**

TEACHING WITH TECHNOLOGY: Adjectives (34a–b)

Suggest that students do a version of the preceding For Collaboration exercise on their own. Have them locate two or three other sentences that use adjectives effectively—perhaps from song lyrics or films they know well—and post them on your course's electronic bulletin board. Then have them try generating their own sentences using the quotes as models.

On *Well* and *Good* (34b)

The use of *well* and *good* to describe physical health is confusing, especially since many English speakers consider the two words synonymous: "Don't you feel good?" "Don't you feel well?"

Used as an adjective, *well* expresses relief from sickness, while the adjective *good* expresses a more general sense of well-being. When *good* is used after such linking verbs as *be, feel, seem, smell, sound,* and *taste,* it qualifies the subject of the verb.

On Comparatives and Superlatives (34c)

Not the product of a set of rules, the common irregular adjectives and adverbs originated from different Old English words. For example, *good* came from the Old English *god*, which is related to the German *gut*. Both words are derived from the Indo-European root *ghedh-*, "unite, join together, be suitable." *Better* and *best* come from the Old English *betera* and *betst*, both of which are derived from the Indo-European *bhad-*, "good."

Bad is not derived from the Old English word for bad or evil, *yfel*. Instead, it comes from the Old English *baedan*, "compel, afflict." *Worse* and *worst* come from their Old English synonyms, *wiersa* and *wyrsta*.

On Double Comparatives (34c)

In *The American Language*, H. L. Mencken points out that some double comparatives may actually have a logic to their usage: "more better," for instance (463). One day we feel better than the day before; the next day, we feel completely well. Hence, we can report that we are "even better" or "still better" or, colloquially, "more better."

FOR TEACHING: Incomplete Comparisons (34c)

Ask students to rewrite the following incomplete comparisons, making them clear and explicit by providing a situation and a revised, complex form:

1. You're taller!
2. No, you're more than I am.
3. She's happier.
4. They cheat more.
5. Mine are the most.
6. Mostly red ones.

FOR COLLABORATION: Reviewing Adjectives and Adverbs

Have students identify all of the adjectives and adverbs in the following passage from Mary Helen Washington's "Taming All That Anger Down." Ask them to comment on what these words add to the writing. What would be lost if they were removed?

> Gwendolyn Brooks "describes the 'graceful life' as one where people glide over floors in softly glowing rooms, smile correctly over trays of silver, cinnamon, and cream, and retire in quiet elegance."

Display students' responses on the board, and ask them to share their thoughts about what the adjectives and adverbs add in each case. Ask students to suggest synonyms and to consider the effectiveness of the different versions. Try removing the adjectives and adverbs altogether, and consider the result. Finally, ask students which version they prefer—and why.

USEFUL READINGS

Christensen, Francis. "A Generative Rhetoric of the Paragraph." *CCC* 16 (Oct. 1965): 144–56.

———. "A Generative Rhetoric of the Sentence." *CCC* 14 (1963): 155–61. Rpt. in Donald W. Lee, ed. *English Language Reader: Introductory Essays and Exercises*. New York: Dodd, 1963. This collection includes essays on grammar, history of the language, dictionaries, and other language-related topics. The final section discusses the various definitions of *adjective*.

Curmé, George O. *English Grammar*. 1947. New York: Harper, 1991. This book contains a traditional grammarian's explanations and examples of the common kinds and forms of adjectives and adverbs.

Mencken, H. L. *The American Language*. 2nd ed. New York: Knopf, 1921.

Shaughnessy, Mina P. *Errors and Expectations*. New York: Oxford UP, 1977. See Chapter 6, "Vocabulary."

Williams, Joseph M. *Style: Ten Lessons in Clarity and Grace*. 6th ed. New York: Addison-Wesley, 2002.

Wolfram, Walt. *Dialects and American English*. Englewood Cliffs: Prentice, 1991. See, especially, Chapter 4, "Regional Dialects."

Zinsser, William. *On Writing Well: An Informal Guide to Writing Nonfiction*. 5th ed. New York: HarperCollins, 1995.

Modifier Placement

35

Modifiers—adjectives, adverbs, and the various kinds of phrases and clauses used as adjectives and adverbs—enrich writing by making it more concrete, vivid, and memorable. Writers want to take full advantage of them, as Ann Petry does in the following sentence from *The Narrows*:

> She wore the kind of clothes he liked, simple, unadorned and yet completely feminine, white gloves on Sundays, small black leather pocketbooks, carefully polished shoes, pretty small hats, a feather the only gay note on her best felt hat, and the seams in her stockings always straight.

You might point out to students that this sentence could have stopped after the first clause: "She wore the kind of clothes he liked." Everything that follows is built on modifiers; they bring the sentence to life and help readers picture the clothes she wore.

Note also, perhaps, that modifiers must be carefully placed and must refer clearly and unambiguously to some word or words in the sentence. In the preceding sentence, for example, *completely* modifies *feminine*. If it were placed elsewhere in the sentence, we would have a different statement: "completely unadorned and yet feminine," perhaps. And look at the difference if *only* were placed somewhere else: white gloves "only on Sundays," for instance, or "only white gloves on Sundays"!

Additional exercises on modifier placement are available on *The Everyday Writer*'s companion Web site, **bedfordstmartins.com/everydaywriter**. Go to **Exercise Central** and click on **Modifier Placement**.

FOR TEACHING: Identifying Modifiers (35a–c)

Ask students to study the following paragraph from *Singin' and Swingin' and Getting' Merry Like Christmas*, in which Maya Angelou relies heavily on modifiers to describe herself at an awkward age:

> I was too tall and raw-skinny. My large extroverted teeth protruded in an excitement to be seen, and I, attempting to thwart their success, rarely smiled. Although I lathered Dixie Peach in my hair, the thick black mass crinkled and

kinked and resisted the smothering pomade to burst free around my head like a cloud of angry bees.

Then ask students to think for a few minutes about some of the awkward stages they remember going through, brainstorming a bit by completing these thoughts: *I was too . . .* or *What I remember most about being fifteen was. . . .* Have them spend ten minutes or so writing a brief description about themselves, underlining the words they recognize as modifiers and then revising the passage by eliminating them all. Finally, ask students, in comparing the two versions, to think about what modifiers add to their writing.

On Placing Modifiers Appropriately: *Only* (35a)

Columnist James J. Kilpatrick offers this humorous and enlightening demonstration of just how many ways the modifier *only* could be placed. He starts with the sentence "She told me that she loved me."

> Let us count the ways:
>
> *Only she told me that she loved me.* No one else has told me that.
>
> *She only told me that she loved me.* She did not provide any evidence of her love—she only told me about it.
>
> *She told only me that she loved me.* Not the gabby type.
>
> *She told me only that she loved me.* Pretty closemouthed. She had nothing more to say.
>
> *She told me that only she loved me.* The lady is claiming exclusive rights.
>
> *She told me that she only loved me.* She doesn't adore me, worship me, idolize me. She only loves me.
>
> *She told me that she loved me only.* Ahhhh!

Parade Magazine received a letter from a reader, "Gloria J." from Salt Lake City, Utah, asking the following question—and providing her own answer:

> There's only one word that can be placed successfully in any of the 10 numbered positions in this sentence to produce 10 sentences of different meaning (each sentence has 10 words): (1) *I* (2) *helped* (3) *my* (4) *dog* (5) *carry* (6) *my* (7) *husband's* (8) *slippers* (9) *yesterday* (10).
>
> What is that word?

The word is "only," which makes the following ten sentences:

1. Only *I* helped my dog carry my husband's slippers yesterday. (Usually the cat helps too, but she was busy with a mouse.)
2. I only *helped* my dog carry my husband's slippers yesterday. (The dog wanted me to carry them all by myself, but I refused.)

3. I helped only *my* dog carry my husband's slippers yesterday. (I was too busy to help my neighbor's dog when he carried them.)
4. I helped my only *dog* carry my husband's slippers yesterday. (I considered getting another dog, but the cat disapproved.)
5. I helped my dog only *carry* my husband's slippers yesterday. (I didn't help the dog eat them; I usually let the cat do that.)
6. I helped my dog carry only *my* husband's slippers yesterday. (My dog and I didn't have time to help my neighbor's husband.)
7. I helped my dog carry my only *husband's* slippers yesterday. (I considered getting another husband, but one is enough.)
8. I helped my dog carry my husband's only *slippers* yesterday. (My husband had two pairs of slippers, but the cat ate one pair.)
9. I helped my dog carry my husband's slippers only *yesterday*. (And now the dog wants help again; I wish he'd ask the cat.)
10. I helped my dog carry my husband's slippers yesterday only. (And believe me, once was enough—they tasted *terrible*.)

Finally, here is James Thurber's take on *only* in *Ladies' and Gentlemen's Guide to Modern English Usage*:

> Where to use *only* in a sentence is a moot question, one of the mootest questions in all rhetoric. The purist will say the expression "He only died last week" is incorrect, and that it should be "He died only last week." The purist's contention is that the first sentence, if carried out to a natural conclusion, would give us something like this: "He only died last week; he didn't do anything else; that's all he did." It isn't a natural conclusion, however, because nobody would say that. . . . The best way is often to omit *only* and use some other expression. Thus . . . one could say: "It was no longer ago than last Thursday that George L. Wodolgoffing became an angel."

On Misplaced Modifiers (35a)

Although misplaced, disruptive, and dangling modifiers affect the reader differently, they all create ambiguity within a sentence. Misplaced and disruptive modifiers often lead to confusing or garbled sentences. Dangling modifiers leave the reader guessing to which word or phrase the modifier belongs.

For many, clarity is an unchallenged ideal. Indeed, when assembling a new barbecue grill or mountain bike we want clear, unambiguous instructions. Many advertisements, however, *deliberately* create ambiguity, conflating the product being advertised with another desirable image. For example, an advertisement for a television set that uses the caption "PLAY TIME" suggests vigorous physical activity, while in fact promoting an activity—watching television—that is anything but physical or vigorous. The ambiguous use of the word *play* evokes both the physical activity and the programs that will play on the television itself. And the reader has little trouble understanding and synthesizing that ambiguity—indeed, the reader probably doesn't even notice it.

Although it is most clear to place a modifier either directly before or after the words it modifies, there are exceptions. For an example, see the sample sentences on limiting modifiers in 35a of *The Everyday Writer*. Sometimes the writer's *emphasis* or *sense of rhythm* or *intention* determines the syntactic placement of the modifier in a sentence.

Misplaced modifiers usually lead to confusion, but sometimes they lead to amusing double entendres as well. Consider, for example, the following Associated Press description of England's Prince Andrew as "the son of Queen Elizabeth and a Royal Navy helicopter pilot." Whether deliberate (for effect) or inadvertent, these little beauties crop up from time to time. Several months later, the AP reported that Princess Anne was the daughter of Queen Elizabeth and a noted equestrian performer. A Florida newspaper reported that the "37-year-old daughter of Queen Elizabeth II and her horse finished fourth in the National Hunt at Hereford."

FOR TEACHING: Misplaced, Disruptive, and Dangling Modifiers (35a–c)

You may want to share the following examples of misplaced, disruptive, and dangling modifiers with your students:

1. Retrieving the duck, Kevin knew he could become a trainer.
2. I ate a hamburger wearing my tuxedo.
3. Soft and mushy, Albert baked a banana cake.
4. Big and noisy, Tom ran for his life away from the street gang.
5. Hanging from the telephone pole, Sally could not retrieve her kite.
6. Big after-Christmas shirt sale for men with sixteen necks.

You might also have students work in small groups to see if they can deliberately generate some funny or ludicrous examples of their own.

On Dangling Modifiers (35c)

We have not always been so strict about enforcing the incorrectness of dangling modifiers. In *Modern American Usage*, Wilson Follett points out that in the eighteenth century, any modifier was acceptable as long as it referred to a noun either present or implied in the sentence. Follett quotes from the *Old Farmer's Almanac*:

> Sheridan was once staying at the house of an elderly maiden lady who wanted more of his company than he was willing to give. Proposing, one day, to take a stroll with him, he excused himself on account of the badness of the weather. (117)

Follett tells us that "it was the maiden lady that did the proposing; she is present only in the preceding sentence, and only in a very subordinate construction. But the passage does not violate the canons of Sheridan's generation or the next." He goes on to explain that after around 1880, such constructions began to be cited as errors, as they are today. Nevertheless, experienced adult writers continue to use, and to get by with using, such constructions. Although "dangling" remains the most common label for these constructions, Follett believes it to be a misnomer, indicating an attachment that is not really there. He would have us use, instead, a word such as *adrift, unanchored, unmoored, unlinked, floating, disconnected, loose,* or *unattached.*

Cornelia and Bergen Evans tell us that the rule against the dangling modifier must sometimes be broken. In *A Dictionary of Contemporary American Usage*, they discuss two types of participial phrases that are exceptions. First of all, some participles are often used independently either as prepositions or conjunctions: *concerning, regarding, providing, owing to, excepting,* and *failing.* Frequently, an unattached participle is meant to apply indefinitely to anyone or everyone, as in *Facing north, there is a large mountain on the right* and *Looking at the subject dispassionately, what evidence is there?* Constructed any other way, these idiomatic statements would seem unnatural and cumbersome.

TEACHING WITH TECHNOLOGY: Dangling Modifiers (35c)

In your computer classroom, have students revise each of the following sentences to eliminate the dangler by (1) providing a subject that tells who or what is being modified, and (2) rewording the sentences. (Sentence 3 is correct.)

1. Diving into the lake, Bev's head struck the raft.
2. To be considered for a teaching job, your references must be top-notch.
3. Listening to the CD, we forgot our worries.
4. Found guilty, the judge dismissed him.
5. At the age of two, my dad took me and my mom with him to Texas.

FOR TEACHING: Revising Modifiers (35a–c)

Ask students to revise the following passage to eliminate any misplaced, disruptive, or dangling modifiers.

> One day last December, before going to class, a blizzard forced the administration to, for the first time anyone could remember, announce that all classes would be until further notice suspended. After leaving the dorm, the first thing that we noticed was the silence. The snow that had been falling all night steadily covered the ground. Being the last day of the semester, we weren't very worried about classes, so we "arranged," with another dormitory, a snowball fight. While building up a stock of good snowballs near Lord Hall, our jackets began to get oppressively warm. Eventually, we peeled down to shirt sleeves, ready for a fight. The central lawn became the battleground for the great Stoke-Lord Snowball Fight, where the Stoke Hall people finally set up their forts. Our piles of snowballs almost reached the tops of our forts, which were well-packed and handy to be picked up and thrown. At last both sides were ready, and the first snowball flew through the air from the "Stoke stack." The bombardment was for a while fierce and deadly. I learned that when throwing a snowball, the standing position is very risky, getting a hard one in the mouth. Finally, having almost thrown all of our snowballs, the Stoke charge was met and resisted. The timing was measured with great accuracy, being sure not to countercharge until we saw that Stoke was low on snowballs. Then we all ran toward the enemy carrying three or four snowballs each and routed them.

USEFUL READINGS

Evans, Cornelia, and Bergan Evans. *A Dictionary of Contemporary American Usage*. New York: Random, 1957. 354–55.

Follett, Wilson. *Modern American Usage*. New York: Hill, 1966.

Williams, Joseph M. *Style: Ten Lessons in Clarity and Grace*. 6th ed. New York: Addison-Wesley, 2002. See, especially, "Some Problems with Modifiers," in which Williams discusses dangling and misplaced modifiers.

36 Comma Splices and Fused Sentences

While we certainly pause as we speak in order to mark off our thoughts or to add emphasis, we do not "speak" punctuation. In fact, excited conversation usually contains "comma splices," which then appear in dialogue to represent the rhythms of speech. Take this excerpt from Thomas Rockwell's *How to Eat Fried Worms*, for example:

> "What about Tom?"
>
> "We can tell your father and Billy that Tom's mother called, he was sick, his grandmother died, anything, just so we don't have to bring him with us."

The comma splices in this dialogue are effective because they convey the speech patterns of two ten-year-old boys.

As this example suggests, comma splices and fused sentences appear frequently in literary and journalistic writing, for, like many other structures commonly identified as "errors," each can be used to powerful effect. In the following passage, written by Anne Cameron, the comma splices create momentum and build to a climax:

> Golden eagles sit in every tree and watch us watch them watch us, although there are bird experts who will tell you in all seriousness that there are NO golden eagles here. Bald eagles are common, ospreys abound, we have herons and mergansers and kingfishers, we have logging with percherons and belgians, we have park land and nature trails, we have enough oddballs, weirdos, and loons to satisfy anybody.

In the second sentence, six independent clauses are spliced together with commas. The effect is a rush of details, from the rather oddball birds to the oddball people and finally to the "loons," a word that can apply to either birds or people.

In their attempts to recapture the "stream of consciousness," both James Joyce and William Faulkner experimented freely with comma splices and fused sentences. Molly's soliloquy in Joyce's *Ulysses* is one of the most famous of these attempts:

why cant you kiss a man without going and marrying him first you sometimes love to wildly when you feel that way so nice all over you you cant help yourself I wish some man or other would take me sometime when hes there and kiss me in his arms theres nothing like a kiss long and hot down to your soul almost paralyses you[.]

Joyce deliberately used comma splices and fused sentences for purpose and effect.

When student writers use comma splices or fused sentences (which are almost never appropriate in academic writing), they usually do so unknowingly. When they combine two independent clauses without appropriately signaling the combination, they produce a *comma splice* (often called a *comma fault*) or a *fused sentence* (often called a *run-on sentence*). Student writers often defend their *comma splices* in terms of their closely connected ideas or logical progression.

Anna came in from the tennis court absolutely famished, she opened the freezer, took out the chocolate mocha ice cream, and dug in.

Because it indicates how the two independent clauses are to be separated, the *comma splice* above is easier to read than the following *fused sentence*:

Anna came into her room to find her cat prancing around on her dresser her jewelry box was lying sideways on the floor her jewelry all sprawled out.

Although these sentence-level "errors" often indicate closely connected ideas, they just as often reflect hurried writing or typing and little or no proofreading.

Additional exercises on comma splices and fused sentences are available on *The Everyday Writer*'s companion Web site, **bedfordstmartins.com/everydaywriter**. Go to **Exercise Central** and click on **Comma Splices and Fused Sentences**.

FOR TEACHING: Separate the Clauses into Two Sentences (36a)

If you provide students with practice in differentiating conjunctions, they will be better able to write effective and meaningful sentences. Supply them with the following fused sentences, and ask them to make revisions:

The apple cider was steaming hot, we sipped it eagerly, it took the chill out of us.

They will likely come up with revisions like these:

1. Because/Although/Even though the apple cider was steaming hot, we sipped it eagerly. It took the chill out of us.

2. The apple cider was steaming hot. Even so, we sipped it eagerly because it took the chill out of us.
3. The apple cider was steaming hot, but/yet/and we sipped it eagerly for it took the chill out of us.

Each of these combinations results from and indicates a particular meaning.

FOR TEACHING: Link the Clauses with a Comma and a Coordinating Conjunction (36b)

Give students the following sentences for revision. Ask them to explain their revision choices, carefully accounting for the context of each revision.

> The clock struck 2:00 AM. We continued talking.

FOR TEACHING: Link the Clauses with a Semicolon (36c)

Ask students to revise the following passage adapted from Jessica Mitford's "Behind the Formaldehyde Curtain" to eliminate sentence-level errors by using the semicolon:

> The religious service may be held in a church, it may be held in the chapel of the funeral home, the funeral director vastly prefers the latter arrangement. Not only is it more convenient for him but it affords him the opportunity to show off his beautiful facilities to the gathered mourners. After the clergyman has had his way, the mourners queue up to file past the casket for a last look at the deceased, the family is never asked whether they want an open-casket ceremony, in the absence of their instruction to the contrary, this is taken for granted, well over 90 per cent of all American funerals feature the open casket—a custom unknown in other parts of the world, foreigners are astonished by it.

FOR COLLABORATION: Reading with an Eye for Special Effects

Ask students to read this passage by Gertrude Stein and write a short paragraph describing the effects Stein achieves with comma splices. As a class, share your insights in a discussion. Then ask students to rewrite the passage to achieve a different effect, such as short, choppy sentences or a stream-of-consciousness narration.

> Think of all the detective stories everybody reads. The kind of crime is the same, and the idea of the story is very often the same, take for example a man like Wallace, he always has the same theme, take a man like Fletcher he always

has the same theme, take any American ones, they too always have the scene, the same scene, the kind of invention that is necessary to make a general scene is very limited in everybody's experience, every time one of the hundreds of times a newspaper man makes fun of my writing and of my repetition he always has the same theme, always having the same theme, that is, if you like, repetition, that is if you like repeating that is the same thing, but once started expressing this thing, expressing any thing there can be no repetition because the essence of that expression is insistence, and if you insist you must each time use emphasis and if you use emphasis it is not possible while anybody is alive that they should use exactly the same emphasis.

FOR TEACHING: Reading with an Eye for Special Effects

To help students better understand the role of context in determining the acceptability of comma splices or fused sentences, bring in texts from outside the classroom as sources of exercises. Advertisements, for example, are a prime source of comma splices and sentence fragments, though ideas are rarely left without closure long enough to become fused sentences. Song lyrics are another good source. Ask students to identify and revise the sentence-level errors in the advertisements or lyrics, and discuss the lack of punctuation. (Ads and song lyrics do not need to be punctuated according to academic standards; often, the function of the advertisement is to present images rather than explanations; lyrics often depend on tone, pitch, rhythm, and stress to achieve meaning.)

FOR COLLABORATION: Revising Comma Splices and Fused Sentences

Have students work in pairs to revise the following paragraph, eliminating the comma splices and fused sentences by using one of the six methods discussed in the At a Glance box in Chapter 36. Then, have the groups revise the paragraph again by using a different method. Ask them to write a response about which paragraph they feel is more effective—and why. Finally, request that students compare their preferred revision to those of the other groups in class. As a class, discuss how the versions differ in meaning.

Gardening can be very satisfying, it is also hard work people who just see the pretty flowers may not realize this. My mother spends long hours every spring tilling the soil, she moves many wheelbarrow-loads of disgusting cow manure and chicken droppings, in fact, the whole early part of gardening is nauseating. The whole garden area has to be rototilled every year, this process is not much like the ad showing people walking quietly behind the rototiller, on the contrary, my father has to fight that machine every inch of the way, sweating so much he looks like Hulk Hogan after a hard bout. Then the planting all must be done by hand, my back aches, my hands get raw, my skin gets sunburned. I get filthy whenever I go near that garden my mother always asks me to help, though. When harvest time comes the effort is almost worth it, however, there are always extra zucchinis I give away at school everybody else is trying to give away zucchinis, too. We also have tomatoes, lettuce, there is always more than we need and we feel bad wasting it wouldn't you like this nice bag of cucumbers?

USEFUL READING

Weathers, Winston. "Grammars of Style: New Options in Composition." *Freshman English News* 4 (Winter 1976): 1–4. Weathers points out that although instructors think they are giving students a wide range of stylistic options, they are, in fact, subscribing to a rather limited "grammar of style." He offers a description of marginalized styles that teachers should consider, including a style he calls the "labyrinthine sentence."

37 Sentence Fragments

Many instructors simply ban fragments outright. However, certain students will discover in their reading and writing just how effectively fragments can be used. In their research, Charles R. Kline Jr. and W. Dean Memering quote fragments from several "formal" writings:

> "They then determined the number of these unrelated words and the sequence of words. 'The more words recalled, the less memory used to store the sentence. The fewer words recalled, the more memory used to store the sentence.'"
>
> –NOAM CHOMSKY, "Language and Mind"

> "Emily Dickinson's poems . . . are more authentically in the metaphysical tradition than Emerson's are. Not, however, that many of his values were not hers also—especially where they concerned the integrity of the mind and the sufficiency of inner resources." –F. O. MATTHIESEN, *American Renaissance*

Here is another example, this one from Virginia Woolf's "Women and Literature":

> The history of England is the history of the male line, not of the female. Of our fathers we know always some fact, some distinction. They were soldiers or they were sailors; they filled that office or they made that law. But of our mothers, our grandmothers, our great-grandmothers, what remains? *Nothing but a tradition.* One was beautiful; one was red-haired; one was kissed by a Queen. We know nothing of them except their names and the dates of their marriages and the number of children they bore.

"Nothing but a tradition." This fragment brings drama to Woolf's statement, arresting readers' attention in a way that a complete sentence would not, giving added emphasis to the word *nothing* and thus to Woolf's point.

What distinguishes these "professional" fragments from those of our students? Often nothing. Consider viewing student papers as professional texts in the making. Allow that fragments can be acceptable on rhetorical or stylistic grounds. Unacceptable fragments are those that (1) lack a close relationship to other sentences, (2) create noncontinuous thought, or (3) confuse the reader.

Additional exercises on sentence fragments are available on *The Everyday Writer*'s companion Web site, **bedfordstmartins.com/everydaywriter**. Go to **Exercise Central** and click on **Sentence Fragments**.

> **A writer is not someone who expresses his thoughts, his passion or his imagination in sentences but someone who thinks sentences. A Sentence-Thinker.**
>
> —ROLAND BARTHES

FOR TEACHING: Phrase Fragments (37a)

As rhetorical devices, sentence fragments should not be overused lest they lose their effect. But, first of all, students need to be able to recognize unacceptable sentence fragments, those discontinuous ones that confuse the reader. Introduce the ineffective fragment by speaking to students in fragments: "Today. Chapter 37. Frequently used. Understand?" Naturally, your students won't know what you mean and will try to get more information from you. Write what you said on the board. Eventually, your students will tell you that your statements are incomplete. Then drop your mask and announce that they've just given you the definition of *sentence fragment*. Ask them to complete your statements. Once students demonstrate their ability to recognize and revise unacceptable fragments, introduce the concept of acceptable "nonsentences."

On the board, write this famous quote from Mark Twain: "Man is the only animal that blushes. Or needs to." Ask your students to "correct" this fragment, no doubt an easy task for them: "Man is the only animal that blushes or needs to." Some of your students may be bothered by this revision and may suggest other forms of punctuation in an attempt to recapture the emphasis lost in the revision, while others may be content with the revised version. You might want to ask students to point out what is "wrong" with the original. Is it confusing? Does the second part connect with the preceding sentence? Were they bothered or confused when they first read it?

From here, you can explain the difference between acceptable and unacceptable fragments, emphasizing the criteria of clarity and continuity. Point out that fragments of any kind should be used rarely and that acceptable fragments do not validate those that should be corrected.

FOR TEACHING: Identifying Fragments (37a–c)

Sentence fragments can be particularly effective not only in narrative, where they call up the rhythms of speech, but also in description. Note the following passage from Keith Gilyard's *Voices of the Self: A Study of Language Competence*. In this passage, Gilyard uses verbal and noun phrase fragments to describe both his route to church on Sundays as well as the church itself:

> On Sundays, for religion, we went up the hill. Skipping along the hexagon-shaped hill in Colonial Park. . . . Leaning forward for leverage to finish the climb up to the church. I was always impressed by this particular house of the Lord. Tremendous gray and white cinder blocks. Polished maple pews in the main service room. Red carpet, stained windows, and gigantic organ pipes. . . . And Pops was up in the front row with the rest of the deacons. A broad-shouldered frame in a gray or blue suit. (24)

Ask students to bring in similar examples of fragments and identify their type (and purpose); this additional practice will help them better identify these structures.

FOR TEACHING: Identifying Fragments (37a–c)

Have those students who have a pattern of writing sentence fragments use the following "sentence machine": in front of the sentence, have the student say aloud, "They refused to believe the idea that" [student's sentence goes here]. If the student's own sentence is complete, this entire sentence makes sense. If the student's own sentence is a fragment, then this entire sentence doesn't make sense.

FOR COLLABORATION: Revising Fragments (37a–c)

Ask students to bring to class any essays in which they find fragments. Choose several fragments to display on the board for class discussion. Ask students to identify the missing element in each fragment and, after supplying necessary context from the essay, to decide on the best means of revision.

USEFUL READINGS

Gilyard, Keith. *Voices of the Self: A Study of Language Competence*. Detroit: Wayne State UP, 1991.

Kline, Charles R., Jr., and W. Dean Memering. "Formal Fragments: The English Minor Sentence." *Research in the Teaching of English* 11 (Fall 1977): 97–110. Rpt. in *Rhetoric and Composition: A Sourcebook for Teachers and Writers*. Ed. Richard L. Graves. Upper Montclair: Boynton, 1984. 148–61. Kline and Memering report that in their analysis of fifty books and magazines representing educated adult writers, they found a wide variety of sentence fragments—none of which resulted in confusing or incoherent prose. They conclude that fragments that function effectively should be considered "minor sentences," and they offer a few general rules for the use of such sentences.

Noguchi, Rei R. *Grammar and the Teaching of Writing: Limits and Possibilities*. Urbana: NCTE, 1991. Noguchi streamlines the teaching of grammar by focusing only on those problems that are amenable to instruction and by taking advantage of what all native speakers of English already know; Chapter 5 deals specifically with fragments.

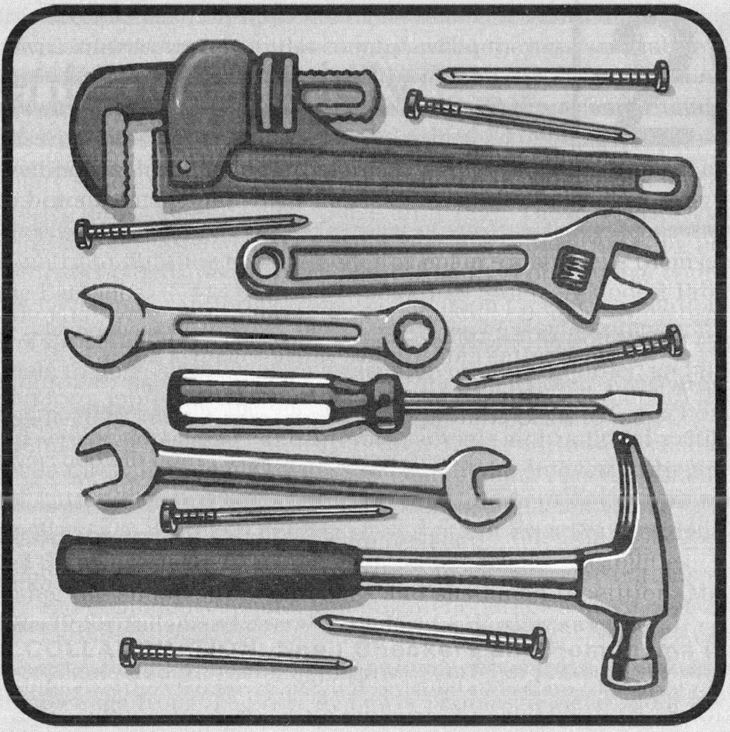

Punctuation and Mechanics

You can show a lot with a look. . . . It's punctuation.

—CLINT EASTWOOD

38 Commas

The commas are the most useful and usable of all the stops. It is highly important to put them in place as you go along. If you try to come back after doing a paragraph and stick them in the various spots that tempt you you will discover that they tend to swarm like minnows into all sorts of crevices whose existence you hadn't realized and before you know it the whole long sentence becomes immobilized and lashed up squirming in commas. Better to use them sparingly, and with affection, precisely when the need for each one arises, nicely, by itself. –LEWIS THOMAS

The first system of punctuation was introduced circa 260 BCE by a librarian in Alexandria named Aristophanes. His system can be considered a forerunner of our own, but it was ignored in his own time, and Greek and Latin generally observed no punctuation at all until about the ninth century CE. Aristophanes' system used three marks: the *periodos* (a dot set high on the line), the *kolon* (a dot set on the line), and the *komma* (a dot set halfway between the top and bottom of letters). Ancient Greece was, of course, preeminently an oral culture, and these marks signaled not grammatical units but places for the speaker to breathe. Punctuation took on grammatical functions, as opposed to performative ones, as a part of the emergence of a print culture. In "Historical Backgrounds of Elizabethan and Jacobean Punctuation Theory," Walter Ong notes that medieval grammarians

> *never* refer to the position of a punctuation mark in terms of grammatical structure. For the most part, they are content to indicate where a *distinctio* [period] may (not where it must or must not) occur, and if one wishes to breathe oftener than would be usual, there is no objection, apparently, to inserting the marks 'ex abundanti.' (351)

The concept of punctuation as breathing marks continued through the sixteenth and seventeenth centuries. Today, most handbooks define the proper uses of commas in grammatical terms, although this chapter does note the stylistic uses of commas (for rhythm, emphasis, and clarity).

Additional exercises on commas are available on *The Everyday Writer*'s companion Web site, **bedfordstmartins.com/everydaywriter**. Go to **Exercise Central** and click on **Commas**.

> **A world that has only periods is a world without inflections. It is a world without shade. It has a music without sharps and flats. It is a martial music. It has a jackboot rhythm. Words cannot bend and curve. A comma, by comparison, catches the gentle drift of the mind in thought, turning in on itself and back on itself, reversing, redoubling and returning along the course of its own sweet river music while the semicolon brings clauses and thoughts together with all the silent discretion of a hostess arranging guests around her dinner table.**
>
> **—Pico Iyer**

FOR TEACHING: Comma Choices

The following paragraph from "Homeless" by Anna Quindlen is reproduced without any of the commas Quindlen used. Ask students to add commas where they think they're necessary or would be helpful. Then have them look through Chapter 38 of *The Everyday Writer* to see if their choices are appropriate. Do they use any unnecessary commas? Can they see places where they need to add any? Use their findings for class discussion.

> They were not pictures of family or friends or even a dog or cat its eyes brown-red in the flashbulb's light. They were pictures of a house. It was like a thousand houses in a hundred towns not suburb not city but somewhere in between with aluminum siding and a chain-link fence a narrow driveway running up to a one-car garage and a patch of backyard. The house was yellow. I looked on the back for a date or a name but neither was there. There was no need for discussion. I knew what she was trying to tell me for it was something I had often felt. She was not adrift alone anonymous although her bags and her raincoat with the grime shadowing its creases had made me believe she was. She had a house or at least once upon a time had had one. Inside were curtains a couch a stove potholders. You are where you live. She was somebody.

FOR TEACHING: Using Commas to Set Off Introductory Elements (38a)

Ask students to bring in examples of sentences with introductory elements. Have them look for sentences in which introductory elements are set off by commas as well as ones in which they're *not* set off by commas. Put several examples up for discussion of how the comma (or the lack of a comma) affects readers' understanding of an author's intended meaning. You might also try repunctuating the examples, adding or deleting commas, and then considering the difference a comma makes.

> **The comma, the most ubiquitous and flexible, not to say slippery, of all stops, is the least susceptible to hard and fast rules.** —G. V. Carey

FOR TEACHING: Use Commas to Separate Items in a Series (38d)

Consider using sentence-combining exercises like the following one to help students practice using commas.

> Erin gathered the blocks.
>
> She took careful aim.
>
> She flung handful after handful at her little brother. She finally relented.
>
> Erin gathered the blocks, took careful aim, and flung handful after handful at her little brother before finally relenting.

To further develop your students' skills with commas in a series, challenge them to construct long sentences with multiple modifiers. Francis Christensen's analysis of cumulative sentences in "A Generative Rhetoric of the Sentence" contains some good models for students to imitate, including this one by William Faulkner:

> Calico-coated, small-bodied, with delicate legs and pink faces in which their mismatched eyes rolled wild and subdued, they huddled, gaudy motionless and alert, wild as deer, deadly as rattlesnakes, quiet as doves.

You might give your students a few simple sentences—for example, *They huddled*—and ask them to expand them, either individually or collaboratively, into sentences like Faulkner's, paying close attention to punctuation as they go.

FOR COLLABORATION: Commas and Style

Consider sharing the following passage from Mark Twain's *Roughing It* with your students, asking them to work together in groups to identify the grammatical reasons for Twain's commas. Then ask the groups to rewrite some or all of the passage, combining sentences or eliminating commas by shortening sentences. Finally, discuss Twain's stylistic reasons for punctuating this passage as he does. What effects have your students achieved by punctuating the passage differently?

> The bull started up, and got along well for about ten feet, then slipped and slid back. I breathed easier. He tried it again—got a little higher—slipped again. But he came at it once more, and this time he was careful. He got gradually higher and higher, and my spirits went down more and more. Up he came—an inch at a time—with his eyes hot, and his tongue hanging out.

Higher and higher—hitched his foot over the stump of a limb, and looked up, as much as to say, "You are my meat, friend." Up again—higher and higher, and getting more excited the higher he got. He was within ten feet of me! I took a long breath—and then said I, "It is now or never." I had the coil of the lariat all ready; I paid it out slowly, till it hung right over his head; all of a sudden I let go of the slack, and the slip noose fell fairly round his neck! Quicker than lightning I out with the allen and let him have it in the face. It was an awful roar, and must have scared the bull out of his senses. When the smoke cleared away, there he was, dangling in the air, twenty foot from the ground, and going out of one convulsion into another faster than you could count! I didn't stop to count, anyhow—I shinned down the tree and shot for home.

Popping in a comma can be like slipping on the necklace that gives an outfit quiet elegance, or like catching the sound of running water that complements, as it completes, the silence of a Japanese landscape.
—Pico Iyer

TEACHING WITH TECHNOLOGY: Use Commas to Prevent Confusion (38l)

To show your students how significantly commas facilitate our understanding of texts, post the following sentence on your class electronic bulletin board and ask students to supply the proper punctuation:

> woman without her man is nothing

Many professors of English using this exercise find that, consistently and over time, the men write "Woman, without her man, is nothing," whereas the women write "Woman! Without her, man is nothing." Discuss these differences with your students.

FOR TEACHING: Revise Unnecessary Commas (38j)

Students often punctuate with commas in a way that reflects regular speaking patterns. For this reason, they may find it difficult to determine when commas are unnecessary. To help them learn how to check for unnecessary commas, use a little humor. Share with your students the following passage from a Dave Barry humor column titled "Grammar Tends to Slip after Drinking a Giraffe":

> We shall commence today's column right at the outset with a "punctuation" question:
>
> Q. I, am never sure, when, to use, commas.
> A. You should use a comma whenever you have a need to pause in a sentence.
>
> EXAMPLE: "So me and Tiffany were at the mall and she ate like four of those big fudge squares which is why her butt is the size of a Volkswagen

Jetta I don't know WHAT Jason sees in, wait a minute I'm getting another call."

To indicate a longer pause, use more commas:

EXAMPLE: "Then the earth,,,,,,,,,, cooled off."

FOR COLLABORATION: Revise Unnecessary Commas (38j)

Have students work in pairs in class to revise each of the following sentences. Ask them to delete unnecessary commas and prepare an explanation for every change they make.

1. Awards are given for, best actor, best actress, best supporting actor, and best supporting actress, every year.
2. Observers watch facial expressions and gestures, and interpret them.
3. We could see nothing, except jagged peaks, for miles around.
4. Everyone in the high school auditorium that night, felt strongly about the proposed zoning changes.
5. Clothes, that had to be ironed, were too much trouble.
6. Before we got into the sun-baked car, we opened the doors, and waited for a few minutes.
7. Students, with high scores on standardized tests, do not necessarily get high grades in college.
8. The photographer, Edward Curtis, is known for his depiction of the West.
9. We all took panicked, hasty, looks at our notebooks.
10. An invitation to buy prescription drugs online, and an offer for golf balls, were two of the junk email messages waiting in my computer's mailbox.

FOR TEACHING: Thinking Critically about Commas

Ask students to read the following passage from Richard Wright's "The Library Card" aloud, listening for the use of commas. Then have them read it again, mentally deleting the commas and noting how their absence affects meaning and rhythm. Finally, have them choose two of the sentences to use as models for creating a similar pair of sentences of their own.

> I ran across many words whose meanings I did not know, and I either looked them up in a dictionary or, before I had a chance to do that, encountered the word in a context that made its meaning clear. But what strange world was this? I concluded the book with the conviction that I had somehow overlooked

something terribly important in life. I had once tried to write, had once reveled in feeling, had let my crude imagination roam, but the impulse to dream had been slowly beaten out of me by experience. Now it surged up again and I hungered for books, new ways of looking and seeing. It was not a matter of believing or disbelieving what I read, but of feeling something new, of being affected by something that made the look of the world different.

The most important fact about a comma is that there are places where it must not be used. That is, there are places where a comma alters the meaning of a statement. Max Beerbohm was being witty when he used a comma in writing about Frank Harris, and many good writers. —Bergen Evans and Cornelia Evans

USEFUL READINGS

Barry, Dave. "Grammar Tends to Slip after Drinking a Giraffe." *Miami Herald* 25 Feb. 2001.

Christensen, Francis. "A Generative Rhetoric of the Sentence." *Rhetoric and Composition.* Ed. Richard Graves. Upper Montclair: Boynton, 1984.

Dawkins, John. "Teaching Punctuation as a Rhetorical Tool." *CCC* 46 (1995): 533–48. Dawkins argues that punctuation choices are always *rhetorical* choices and proposes a method for teaching students to recognize subtle rhetorical effects and to make good choices by "analyz[ing] their semantic and rhetorical intentions and then matching those intentions to readers' needs."

Ong, Walter. "Historical Backgrounds of Elizabethan and Jacobean Punctuation Theory." *PMLA* 59 (1944): 349–60. Despite the title, both the history of punctuation and Renaissance attitudes are treated equally.

Period Styles: A History of Punctuation. New York: Herb Lubalin Study Center of Design and Typography, Cooper Union for the Advancement of Science and Art, 1988. See the first essay, "Period Styles: A Punctuated History."

Shaughnessy, Mina. *Errors and Expectations.* New York: Oxford UP, 1977. See "Handwriting and Punctuation," particularly pages 18–24, for a discussion of how basic writers use commas and periods.

Thomas, Lewis. "Notes on Punctuation." *New England Journal of Medicine* 296 (1977): 1103–5. This witty personal essay is remarkable for its erudition—perhaps more so because it was written by a medical researcher (turned essayist) and originally published in a medical journal.

Williams, Joseph M. *Style: Ten Lessons in Style and Grace.* 6th ed. New York: Addison-Wesley, 2002. Williams groups nonrestrictive modifiers under the heading "loose or nonspecifying commentary."

39 Semicolons

> *Among punctuation marks, the semicolon is a relative latecomer, lagging behind the comma, colon and period, most linguists agree. Of course, punctuation itself did not become a standard part of written discourse until the late 18th century. Composition had been a haphazard enterprise at best, with writers employing punctuation marks when and how they chose.* –JULIA KELLER, "Secrets of the Semicolon"

In classical Greek, groups of words comparable to what we call sentences were set off and called *colons*. A semicolon, therefore, is literally half a colon, or half of a sentence divided by the punctuation mark we call a *semicolon*. Lewis Thomas demonstrates effective use of the semicolon as he defines it in "Notes on Punctuation," noting the following:

> The semicolon tells you that there is still some question about the preceding full sentence; something needs to be added. . . . It is almost always a greater pleasure to come across a semicolon than a period. The period tells you that is that; if you didn't get all the meaning you wanted or expected, you got all the writer intended to parcel out and now you have to move along. But with a semicolon there you get a pleasant little feeling of expectancy; there is more to come; read on; it will get clearer.

As Thomas suggests, semicolons have the effect of creating a pause stronger than that of a comma but not as strong as the full pause of a period. Their primary uses are to link coordinate independent clauses and to separate items in a series.

The semicolon as we know it today was introduced in the seventh century CE. During the eighth century, an inverted semicolon was used to indicate a vocal pause halfway between the comma and the semicolon. By the fifteenth century, however, the inverted semicolon had fallen out of favor.

Additional exercises on semicolons are available on *The Everyday Writer*'s companion Web site, **bedfordstmartins.com/everydaywriter**. Go to **Exercise Central** and click on **Semicolons**.

> The distinction between the Greek semicolon [·], a raised point whose aim is to keep the voice from being lowered, and the German one, which accomplishes the lowering with its period and its hanging lower part and yet keeps the voice suspended by incorporating the comma—truly a dialectical image—seems to reproduce the distinction between classical antiquity and the Christian Era, finitude refracted through the infinite. . . .
>
> History has left its residue in punctuation marks, and it is history, far more than meaning or grammatical function, that looks out at us, rigidified and trembling slightly, from every mark of punctuation. —ADORNO

On Semicolons and Academic Discourse

Bergen and Cornelia Evans claim that the semicolon is most appropriate for formal writing. "If a writer wishes to use an informal narrative style he should avoid semicolons as much as possible" (440). However, George Summey Jr., in *American Punctuation*, argues against thinking of the semicolon as "a stiff and formal mark that ought to be seldom used": "It is actually used by good current writers today and might well be used oftener if our writers would take the trouble to drop some of their *and*'s and *but*'s and use patterns that take a semicolon and no conjunction." The problem is not with the semicolon, Summey says, but with the "awkward patterns" and "stiff wording" with which it has been associated (98).

William and Mary Morris suggest that one reason for the lack of use of the semicolon is "the trend toward short, trenchant sentences" in journalism (547). But, in fact, the absence of the semicolon in less formal writing is changing. Still, the tendency to use the semicolon remains a stylistic choice. Some writers like Annie Dillard, whose *Pilgrim at Tinker Creek* is definitely not a formal piece, seem fond of the semicolon, while other writers, like John McPhee, rarely use it. Donald Barthelme's short story "Sentence" consists of one long sentence (or actually, of a part of one sentence). While it includes numerous instances of dashes, parentheses, quotation marks, question marks, exclamation points, and commas, it has only one semicolon. The reason might be that the semicolon seems too close to being end punctuation, and the story is meant to give us the feeling of continuousness and endlessness. The period, incidentally, doesn't appear at all.

FOR TEACHING: Use Semicolons to Link Independent Clauses (39a)

Phyllis Rose chose not to use any semicolons in the following paragraph from "Shopping and Other Spiritual Adventures," although there are several places where she might have. Ask students to read the paragraph carefully to find at least two such places and then decide whether they would have used a semicolon.

> It is appropriate, I think, that Bob's Surplus has a communal dressing room. I used to shop only in places where I could count on a private dressing room with a mirror inside. My impulse then was to hide my weaknesses. Now I believe in sharing them. There are other women in the dressing room at Bob's Surplus trying on blue jeans who look as bad as I do. We take comfort from one another. Sometimes a woman will ask me which of two items looks better. I always give a definite answer. It's the least I can do. I figure we are all in this together, and I emerge from the dressing room not only with a new pair of jeans but with a renewed sense of belonging to a human community.

> **Theodor Haeker was rightfully alarmed by the fact that the semicolon is dying out; this told him that no one can write a period, a sentence containing several balanced clauses, any more. Part of this incapacity is the fear of page-long paragraphs, a fear created by the marketplace—by the consumer who does not want to tax himself and to whom first editors and then writers accommodated for the sake of their incomes. . . . It starts with the loss of the semicolon; it ends with the ratification of imbecility by a reasonableness purged of all admixtures.**
>
> **—Adorno**

On Revising Misused Semicolons (39c)

One can imagine writers getting away with never using semicolons, except perhaps the rare use with a series of items. From this perspective, the semicolon becomes more a stylistic device than a grammatical one, which is not something you can say about the period, for instance. Clearly, then, the choice of a semicolon over another punctuation mark is often a rhetorical choice. George Summey Jr. offers these flexible guidelines for when to choose the semicolon:

> What mark should be used in a given case—comma or semicolon, semicolon or period—will depend only in part on the length of the groups. Circumstances that may make the semicolon preferable to the comma are length and complexity of the groups, the absence of a connective, or a shift of grammatical subject. And any of these same circumstances may make the period better than the semicolon. Each case must be settled by the writer according to the immediate situation. The more important a group is in its context, the more reason for preferring semicolon to comma or period to semicolon. (99)

FOR COLLABORATION: Revise Misused Semicolons (39c)

In "Secrets of the Semicolon" Julia Keller gives a brief history and user's guide to the semicolon. Read the following passage to your students:

> Once dismissed as a fussy, somewhat effete affectation, the white-gloved cousin to the calloused, workaholic comma or brutally abrupt period, the semicolon may be coming into its own. Most people, truth to tell, still seem somewhat intimidated by the semicolon; it smacks of deep thoughts and booklined studies, of long pauses accompanied by rhythmic strokes of the chin. Semicolons function several ways in sentences. They can divide coordinate clauses that are complete in themselves; they can replace commas, indicating a longer pause; they can separate items in a list. But semicolons historically were deftly avoided. They were the fine china of the punctuation world, when plastic forks would do.

When you are done, ask your students to keep these guidelines in mind and look over the passage in groups, checking for overused and misused semicolons. Finally, have them work in peer-review groups to assess one another's writing.

> . . . only a person who can perceive the different weights of strong and weak phrasings in musical form can really feel the distinction between the comma and the semicolon.
>
> —ADORNO

On Revising Overused Semicolons (39c)

Mina Shaughnessy notes that semicolons are rarely used by beginning writers, who typically read little and so are unfamiliar with the form. They sometimes "strain the resources of the comma" to cover situations requiring other marks, including semicolons. Thus, comma splices may result (23, 33–34).

The opposite problem can occur once students have been introduced to semicolons; they may begin to overuse them. Part of the problem is the power of the semicolon itself. Shaughnessy notes that "as its form suggests, it has the linking power of a comma and the terminating authority of a period. Given the difficulties of the unpracticed writer with both linking and sustaining sentences, the semicolon must appear as something of a bargain" (34). Punctuation marks produce different psychological effects—on the writer as well as the reader. If the writer resists putting an end to a sentence because he or she fears having to start another, the instructor may see an overuse of semicolons.

Ultimately, the writer must get a feel for when to use semicolons to link ideas. Shaughnessy goes on to note that use of the semicolon, unlike the period and the comma, depends on the situation, on the relationships of ideas as much as on conventional formal requirements. George Summey Jr. states that the semicolon is "the most clearly specialized balancing and coordinating mark" and is "not a general-purpose mark like the comma" (97).

Sometimes a semicolon marks the frontier between a thought and a triviality.
—Erich Heller, commenting on the thought of Wittgenstein

FOR TEACHING: Semicolons and Parallelism

Semicolons often work well in creating a strong sense of parallelism, as in this review by Jeff Jarvis:

> Last season, I liked *Frasier*; this season, I love it. But it's not my opinion that has changed. It's the show. Last year, *Frasier* was good; this year, it's getting great.

Ask students to take a piece of writing they are working on and look for a passage that could be emphasized by using semicolons to create parallelism. Then ask them to bring their experiments to class for discussion about the rhetorical effects semicolons can create.

Semicolons function several ways in sentences. They can divide coordinate clauses that are complete in themselves; they can replace commas, indicating a longer pause; they can separate items in a list. **—Julia Keller**

USEFUL READINGS

Baker, Nicholson. "The History of Punctuation." *The Size of Thoughts*. New York: Vantage, 1997.

Barthelme, Donald. "Sentence." *City Life*. New York: Farrar, 1970.

Evans, Cornelia, and Bergen Evans. *A Dictionary of Contemporary English Usage*. New York: Random, 1957.

Keller, Julia. "Secrets of the Semicolon." *Chicago Tribune* 12 May 1999: 1.

Morris, William, and Mary Morris. *Harper Dictionary of Contemporary Usage*. New York: Harper, 1975.

Shaughnessy, Mina. *Errors and Expectations*. New York: Oxford UP, 1977.

Summey, George, Jr. *American Punctuation*. New York: Ronald, 1949.

Thomas, Lewis. "Notes on Punctuation." *The Medusa and the Snail*. New York: Penguin, 1995.

End Punctuation

40

Punctuation has long been considered the stronghold of inflexible and prescriptive rules. This tradition is unfortunate. To a great degree, punctuation is variable, flexible, and even imaginative. – WILLIAM D. DRAKE

End punctuation—a period, question mark, or exclamation point—tells readers they have reached the end of one unit of thought and can pause and take a mental breath before moving on to the next one. Student writers need to be guided by meaning in their choice of end punctuation, understanding, however, that they can sometimes use it for special effect. Ask them to look, for instance, at the way end punctuation guides readers in the following three sentences:

Am I tired.

Am I tired?

Am I tired!

The end punctuation tells how to read each sentence: the first as a dry, matter-of-fact statement; the second as a puzzled or perhaps ironic query; the last as a note of exasperation.

In order to use end punctuation of any kind, of course, the student must first have a sense of what a traditionally punctuated sentence is. As Mina Shaughnessy points out in *Errors and Expectations*, end punctuation requires "a familiarity with the sentence as a grammatical unit and with the process whereby simple sentences are enlarged so as to include various types of subordinate structures" (27). Beginning writers will have been producing sentences orally for a long time before they come to produce them in writing, but writing is an abstract operation, not a natural operation like speaking. We speak, producing whole thoughts in subjects and predicates, without reflection; writing requires a great deal of reflecting on what we are doing. Thus you may want to review *The Everyday Writer* chapter on basic grammar (Chapter 30).

You may also encounter "a psychological resistance to the period" (Shaughnessy 18). The period imposes an end to the thought that the student may have had difficulty in beginning. The period tells the writer that he or she must begin again, a task that the inexperienced writer may find fearful. Also, students sometimes become overly concerned with end punctuation. Shaughnessy believes that such concern suggests a perception of the sentence as a whole unit that ought not to be divided or modified in any way.

Additional exercises on end punctuation are available on *The Everyday Writer*'s companion Web site, **bedfordstmartins.com/everyday writer**. Go to **Exercise Central** and click on **End Punctuation**.

> For many beginning writers, the need to mark off sentences inhibits the progress of their thoughts. In speech, they can produce sentences as easily and unconsciously as they can walk; in writing, they must stop to deliberate over what is and what is not a sentence.
>
> –MINA SHAUGHNESSY

FOR MULTILINGUAL WRITERS: Using End Punctuation

Because the European system of punctuation marks can differ markedly from those in other cultures, multilingual writers need to memorize which punctuation marks can *begin* a line—and which cannot.

End punctuation, including ['!:").?;] cannot begin a line, but some punctuation can [("]. As a result multilingual writers will want to look carefully at the ways English texts are punctuated on the page.

FOR COLLABORATION: Understanding End Punctuation (40a–c)

Ask students to work in small groups, imagining that they work for a company that is preparing to launch a new product. First, they should decide what the product is—some sort of food or drink, an automobile, the latest laptop, or something else—and what its name should be. Then they should write a headline and some copy for the product's first advertisement.

Finally, ask students to note how they have used end punctuation—where they have placed periods, question marks, and exclamation points—and to compare their advertisement with those of several other groups. Use their findings to begin a class discussion on the rhetorical effects of end punctuation.

On Question Marks (40b)

The question mark appeared in the eighth century. Lewis Thomas, in his "Notes on Punctuation," claims the question mark is not, "strictly speaking," a stop, but rather an "indicator of tone." Yet question marks also indicate grammatical meaning. A sentence like *Joseph danced the boogaloo* may be either declarative or interrogative, depending on the context.

> Joseph danced the boogaloo.
>
> Joseph danced the boogaloo?

John Wilson Jr., in *The Elements of Punctuation*, describes the dual function of the question mark, along with the exclamation point, parenthesis, and dash:

> They are rhetorical, so far as they help to exhibit the force and intensity of a style which is rhetorical in its structure; but they are also grammatical, because they often serve to indicate, in connection with other marks, the nature, construction, and sense of the passages in which they occur. (92)

> **The exclamation point has been variously called the note of admiration, the shriek of surprise, the astonisher or paralyzer, the period that blew its top. —George Summey Jr.**

On Exclamation Points (40c)

The exclamation point was rarely used before the Renaissance. It differs fundamentally from the other two end punctuation marks. While the period and the question mark function grammatically (as well as "rhetorically"—that is, phonologically—in the case of the question mark), the exclamation point functions almost entirely to indicate a change in voice. While it does mark the end of a sentence, it could be replaced with a period or question mark.

Attitudes toward the exclamation point have ranged from disgust to simple tolerance. Rarely has anyone exclaimed the praises of the exclamation point. At best, commentators describe it neutrally, as did the author of *A Treatise of Stops, Points, or Pauses* in 1680, calling it "a Note of Admiration, wondering, or crying out." Typically, we encounter descriptions like that of George Summey Jr. who notes that, at the time he was writing *American Punctuation* (1949), typewriters did not possess exclamation point keys. Instead, the mark was made by striking a period, backspacing, and then striking an apostrophe. Summey calls this procedure "more trouble than the mark is likely to be worth" (90).

USEFUL READINGS

Shaughnessy, Mina. *Errors and Expectations*. New York: Oxford UP, 1977. Chapter 2, "Handwriting and Punctuation," focuses on end punctuation.

Summey, George, Jr. *American Punctuation*. New York: Ronald, 1949.

Thomas, Lewis. "Notes on Punctuation." *New England Journal of Medicine* 296 (1977): 1103–5. This witty personal essay is remarkable for its erudition—perhaps more so because it was written by a medical researcher (turned essayist) and originally published in a medical journal.

Wilson, John, Jr. *The Elements of Punctuation*. Boston: Crosby, Nichols, and Company, 1856.

Apostrophes

41

As a mark of the possessive case, the apostrophe has an unusual history. In Old English, the endings of nouns changed according to the noun's grammatical function—a noun used as a subject, for example, had a different ending from one used as a direct object. By the fourteenth century, Middle English had dropped most of this complicated system, yet possessive and plural endings remained: *Haroldes sword* was still used to mean "the sword of Harold." Then in the sixteenth century, scholars concluded that the ending *-es* and its variants were actually contractions of *his*. Believing that *Haroldes sword* meant "Harold his sword," they began using an apostrophe instead of the *e*: *Harold's sword.*

Even though this theory was later discredited, the possessive ending retained the apostrophe because it was a useful way to distinguish between possessive and plural forms in writing. Today we use the apostrophe primarily to signal possessive case, contractions and other omissions of words and letters, and certain plural forms.

One of the special difficulties in teaching today's students to use apostrophes is tied to the differences between speaking and writing. Our students will often omit apostrophes in writing because they do not hear them in oral discourse. Though it can be argued that indeed we *do* hear some punctuation (through intonation, rhythm, pauses, and breathing), the apostrophe is decidedly "silent"; based on sound alone, there is no way to distinguish *cant* from *can't*, *isnt* from *isn't*, *Joes* from *Joe's*. A student may be very adept at spoken discourse (as most are), but less practiced with the conventions of written English and, hence, have difficulty remembering to insert apostrophes. Indeed, some linguists suggest that English, with its tendency to rely on word order and to drop inflections, may someday be *without* apostrophes.

Additional exercises on apostrophes are available on *The Everyday Writer*'s companion Web site, **bedfordstmartins.com/everydaywriter**. Go to **Exercise Central** and click on **Apostrophes**.

On Apostrophes and the Possessive Case (41a)

Although there is some disagreement over adding just an apostrophe rather than an apostrophe and *-s* to singular nouns ending in *-s*, the most authoritative sources on usage recommend using an apostrophe and an *-s* with all singular nouns, including those words ending with *-s*. Here are some additional examples:

Nogales's hot and dry summers

Cass's research into the squash melon

the *princess's* last visit

Exceptions, however, are proper names that end in an "eez" sound—often Greek or hellenized names.

Aristophanes' comedies

B. F. Yerkes' research

On Apostrophes for Contractions (41b)

Typically, contractions have a less formal tone than the combined words written out in full. As a general rule, writers are probably wise to limit the use of contractions in formal settings, including letters of application, business letters, legal documents, and papers for college courses. Yet even in formal contexts, contractions may sometimes be appropriate where the alternative would sound overly contrived. The rhetorical considerations of purpose, content, context, and audience should guide the writer's use of contractions. Fred Astaire would have sounded somewhat stiff singing "Is it not romantic?" while Abraham Lincoln would have struck an incongruously chatty tone had he said, "With firmness in the right, as God gives us to see the right, let's strive on to finish the work we're in."

FOR COLLABORATION: Use Apostrophes

All apostrophes have been deleted from the following sentences. Ask students to review the sentences by working with a classmate. They should insert apostrophes where appropriate and bring their work to class for comparison with others. Example:

Who's
~~Whos~~ in charge here?
^

1. His Great-Uncle Rays contribution helped him pay off his auto loan.
2. Zillah couldnt finish painting the garage before dark.

3. Each of the dogs in the shelter has its own charm, but theres no way to find a home for every one.
4. If you went to Hollywood, youd have to forget about how difficult itd be to get a job in the film industry.
5. Its late; lets go out for pizza instead of making supper.

Answers

1. His Great-Uncle Ray's contribution helped him pay off his auto loan.
2. Zillah couldn't finish painting the garage before dark.
3. Each of the dogs in the shelter has its own charm, but there's no way to find a home for every one.
4. If you went to Hollywood, you'd have to forget about how difficult it'd be to get a job in the film industry.
5. It's late; let's go out for pizza instead of making supper.

USEFUL READINGS

Flesch, Rudolf. *The ABC of Style: A Guide to Plain English.* New York: Harper, 1964. See pages 29–30 on the use of contractions in writing.

Hashimoto, Irwin. "Pain and Suffering: Apostrophes and Academic Life." *Journal of Basic Writing* 7.2 (1988): 91–98. Hashimoto humorously discusses students' frequent problems with apostrophes. He places "a large chunk of the blame" on a handbook tradition that leads us to look for simple, clear rules and overlook "the ugly truth" that the rules for apostrophes are really quite messy.

42 Quotation Marks

By necessity, by proclivity, and by delight, we all quote.
–Ralph Waldo Emerson

Before the seventeenth century, there was no regulated punctuation mark to indicate quotations. In ancient Greek texts, the *paragraphos* (a short horizontal line used to divide texts into units) was used to indicate changes in dialogue. Quotations and direct speech were simply introduced with phrases like *he said*, without any punctuation. During Shakespeare's time, however, commas and inverted commas were generally placed at the start of a passage. Shakespeare scholar Margreta de Grazia tells us that these commas were used interchangeably with the pointing index finger (~) directing the reader's eye to passages of special note. According to Grazia, both signals—commas and (~)—appeared in the margin, the place where aids to the reader were supplied. Such signals never appeared within the text itself. And these signals primarily indicated to the reader that a passage was important—not that it originated elsewhere.

Although quotation marks now are exclusionary, marking off private property, during Shakespeare's time, they signaled communal ground or commonplaces. They marked material to be copied by each reader in his copybook or commonplace book, thereby assuring that the commonplaces would become more common still. By simply perusing the margins of a text, readers might lift material for their own personalized storehouse of wise and therefore widely applicable sayings.

By the mid-seventeenth century, the double comma was placed within the text, before a sentence to indicate its importance: ,, *The time to act is now.* The double comma was later used to enclose quotations, and printers began to edge both margins of quoted materials with double commas.

Inverted commas is the British label for *quotation marks*, a label that indeed recalls the origin of the marks in the seventeenth century. However, Wilson Follett points out that, although either expression is acceptable, *inverted commas* is an inaccurate label:

> The opening signs (' ") consist of commas both inverted and reversed; the closing signs (' ") are neither inverted nor reversed, but merely superior—i.e., above the line. (186)

Today theorists are questioning the ideologies surrounding practices of quotation. An early critique of such practices appears in the work of Bakhtin and Volosinov, who question the ways in which quotation perpetuates a view of language as the property of a radically unique individual rather than as a set of socially constructed systems.

Additional exercises on quotation marks are available on *The Everyday Writer*'s companion Web site, **bedfordstmartins.com/everydaywriter**. Go to **Exercise Central** and click on **Quotation Marks**.

On Direct Quotations (42a)

As a general rule, a writer can decide whether or not to use a comma or colon before a quotation by reading aloud the sentence or passage containing the quotation. If the quotation follows smoothly from the text that precedes it, no comma or colon is necessary. For instance, the quotation in the following sentence needs no comma or colon:

> Mannes argues that television commercials "contribute to the diminution of human worth and the fragmenting of our psyches."

However, if the quoted words do not fit syntactically into the larger sentence, then they should be preceded by a comma or colon, as in the following sentence:

> When Ralph Waldo Emerson was asked to take part in directly promoting abolition, he said: "I have my own spirits in prison—spirits in deeper prisons—whom no man visits if I do not."

FOR TEACHING: Use Quotation Marks (42a–e)

Divide the class into groups of three, and ask each group to compose a one- or two-page passage that includes as many of the following as possible: direct quotations, quotations within quotations, dialogue, titles, definitions, and special-emphasis words or phrases. Then ask groups to trade pieces and evaluate the paragraphs' use of quotation marks: Are they used accurately throughout? Are any uses of quotation marks confusing or unclear? What suggestions could they give each other for revision?

FOR COLLABORATION: Direct Quotation (42a)

Divide the class into groups of three. Using one of the following sentences as an opener, have two members of each group take on the roles involved and produce a dialogue. The third person of the group records the dialogue, and afterward, the group members decide on how it should be punctuated.

1. One roommate asks the other, “What should we do tonight?”
2. One sibling says to the other, “Oh no you don’t.”
3. As I turned the corner, I heard someone say “Stop right there.”

On Misused Quotation Marks (42g)

Lewis Thomas offers the following advice for using quotation marks: (1) quote exact words; (2) do not string together thoughts that the author did not intend to be connected; (3) do not use quotation marks to qualify ideas that you would like to disown; (4) do not put them around clichés to avoid your responsibility in using them.

FOR COLLABORATION: Revising Quotation Marks (42a-g)

Have students collaborate with a classmate to revise the following paragraph. Each group should try to use quotation marks appropriately.

> An article called Their Game, Their Gold appeared in the *New York Times* the morning after Canada won the gold medal in men’s hockey at the 2002 Winter Olympics in Park City, Utah. Sportswriter George Vecsey described the final match as ‘so fast, so furious, so full of skill that it will live in the memories of all who witnessed it’ and noted, “The game itself deserved a gold medal”. The Canadian men’s hockey team had not won a gold medal at the Olympics since 1952, fifty years “to the day” before their winning match in Utah. Wayne Gretzky, one of the “all-time greats” of the sport and the executive director of the winning team, said that “his country desperately needed to win this tournament.”

FOR TEACHING: Revising Quotation Marks (42a–g)

Ask students to read each of the following sentences, deleting quotation marks used inappropriately, moving those placed incorrectly, and using more formal language in place of slang expressions in quotation marks.

> In “Bartleby the Scrivener,” Bartleby states time and again, “I would prefer not to”.

1. The grandmother in O’Connor’s story shows she is still misguided when she says, “You’ve got good blood! I know you wouldn’t shoot a lady”!
2. What is Hawthorne telling the readers in “Rappaccini’s Daughter?”

3. Very quietly, Chun Lee said, "I know the answer".
4. This "typical American" is Ruby Turpin, who in the course of the story receives a "message" that brings about a "change" in her life.
5. Being "overweight" is a problem because "excess pounds" are hard to lose and can be "dangerous" to a person's health.
6. One of Joyce Carol Oates's most shocking stories is "The Bingo Master;" the triumph of brutality is devastating.
7. Macbeth "bumps off" Duncan to gain the throne for himself.
8. In his article "The Death of Broadway", Thomas M. Disch writes that "choreographers are, literally, a dying breed[1]".
9. "Know thyself—" this is the quest of the main characters in both Ibsen's *Peer Gynt* and Lewis's *Till We Have Faces*.
10. One thought flashed through my mind as I finished *"In Search of Our Mothers' Gardens:"* I want to read more of this writer's books.

Answers

1. The grandmother in O'Connor's story shows she is still misguided when she says, "You've got good blood! I know you wouldn't shoot a lady!"
2. What is Hawthorne telling the readers in "Rappaccini's Daughter"?
3. Very quietly, Chun Lee said, "I know the answer."
4. This "typical American" is Ruby Turpin, who in the course of the story receives a message that brings about a change in her life.
5. Being overweight is a problem because excess pounds are hard to lose and can be dangerous to a person's health.
6. One of Joyce Carol Oates's most shocking stories is "The Bingo Master"; the triumph of brutality is devastating.
7. Macbeth murders Duncan to gain the throne for himself.
8. In his article "The Death of Broadway," Thomas M. Disch writes that "choreographers are, literally, a dying breed."[1]
9. "Know thyself"—this is the quest of the main characters in both Ibsen's *Peer Gynt* and Lewis's *Till We Have Faces*.
10. One thought flashed through my mind as I finished *In Search of Our Mothers' Gardens*: "I want to read more of this writer's books."

> Quotation marks should be used only when something is quoted and if need be when the text wants to distance itself from a word it is referring to. They are to be rejected as an ironic device. For they exempt the writer from the spirit whose claim is inherent in irony, and they violate the very concept of irony by separating it from the matter at hand and presenting a predetermined judgment on the subject. —ADORNO

USEFUL READINGS

Follett, Wilson. *Modern American Usage*. New York: Hill, 1966.

Shaughnessy, Mina. *Errors and Expectations*. New York: Oxford UP, 1977. See Chapter 2 for an insightful discussion of punctuation. In particular, Shaughnessy claims that basic writers rarely use quotation marks.

Thomas, Lewis. "Notes on Punctuation." *New England Journal of Medicine* 296 (1977): 1103–5.

Volosinov, Valentin N. "Exposition of the Problem of Reported Speech." *Marxism and the Philosophy of Language*. Cambridge: Harvard UP, 1973. Here Volosinov mounts a powerful critique of quotation practices, revealing the ways they are inevitably embedded in ideology.

Other Punctuation Marks

43

To say that no two persons punctuate exactly alike would no doubt be an exaggeration, but most people would probably agree that punctuation is a matter not only of rules but of personal taste. . . . I should define punctuation as being governed two-thirds by rule and one-third by personal taste.

–G. V. Carey

Parentheses, brackets, dashes, and slashes developed well after the technology of the written word first appeared, but the colon was one of the first punctuation marks used. Since most discourse was oral rather than written, punctuation evolved to mark places where speakers paused or breathed rather than as grammatical units. The first system of punctuation, created by Aristophanes in the second century BCE, used only three marks: the period, colon, and comma. Six centuries later, St. Jerome (400 CE) punctuated his translation of the Vulgate Bible using a rhetorical system of colons and commas to mark breathing points. The elocutionary nature of punctuation developed further during the tenth to thirteenth centuries with the addition of marks to denote places where the speakers should raise their voices (the *punctus elevatus*, *punctus interrogativus*, and *punctus circumflexus*) and confirmed the use of the colon as a breathing stop, particularly between verses of the Psalms. However, over time, written discourse became less connected to oral discourse, especially after the invention of printing, and punctuation began to take on more rhetorical or grammatical functions. Parentheses, brackets, dashes, and slashes functioned primarily to indicate grammatical divisions. Parentheses began to appear around 1500, and dashes by 1700, but the slash (also called a virgule or solidus) has been with us a little longer. Virgules first appeared in the thirteenth and fourteenth centuries as a form of light stop; after about 1450 the virgule, which was originally placed high, began to appear on the base line and developed a curve. Today we know this mark as a comma.

Additional exercises on punctuation are available on *The Everyday Writer*'s companion Web site, **bedfordstmartins.com/everydaywriter**. Go to **Exercise Central** and click on **Other Punctuation**.

> **for life's not a paragraph and death I think is no parenthesis.** —E. E. CUMMINGS

On Parentheses (43a)

The term *parentheses* derives from the classical Greek figure of speech *parenthesis*, which denotes the act of inserting a verbal unit (a word, phrase, or sentence) into a position that interrupts the sentence flow. Such material can be punctuated with dashes or commas as well as with parentheses.

> **A parenthesis is a convenient device, but a writer indulges his own convenience at the expense of his readers' if his parenthesis is so long that a reader, when he comes to the end of it, has little chance of remembering where he was when it began.**
>
> —H. W. FOWLER

On Dashes (43c)

You may want to share Adorno's thoughts on dashes with students. Ask them to write up a brief explanation of what *they* think the dash is used for.

> In the dash, thought becomes aware of its fragmentary character. It is no accident that in the era of the progressive degeneration of language, this mark of punctuation is neglected precisely insofar as it fulfills its function: when it separates things that feign a connection. All the dash claims to do now is to prepare us in a foolish way for surprises that by that very token are no longer surprising.
>
> The test of a writer's sensitivity in punctuating is the way he handles parenthetical material. The cautious writer will tend to place that material between dashes and not in round brackets [i.e., what is commonly called parentheses, ( )], for brackets take the parenthesis completely out of the sentence, creating enclaves, as it were, whereas nothing in good prose should be unnecessary to the overall structure. By admitting such superfluousness, brackets implicitly renounce the claim to the integrity of the linguistic form. . . . Dashes, in contrast, which block off the parenthetical material from the flow of the sentence without shutting it up in a prison, capture both connection and detachment.

> **Undiluted dashiness has become the mark of the slapdash writer who fails to take the trouble to differentiate among the pauses of punctuation.** —WILLIAM SAFIRE

FOR TEACHING: Dashes (43c)

Emily Dickinson published very few poems during her lifetime. But privately, she bound her manuscripts into packets or "fascicles," folded sheets of paper sewn together by hand, which give the impression of being little books, meant to be read by others. Her capitalization and punctuation were very unconventional. Especially curious is her use of dashes as an almost universal punctuation mark, sometimes occurring in places that break up sentences into ungrammatical units.

The first editor of Dickinson's work systematically eliminated the dashes, and in fact, until the middle of the twentieth century, editors always normalized her mechanics. In 1950, Edith Perry Stamm proposed a theory to explain Dickinson's dashes. She claims that Dickinson's system of dashes indicated various spoken intonations. Most experts discount Stamm's theory, because it seems likely that if Dickinson had wanted to indicate intonation, she would have made her marks clearer to distinguish.

Ask students to read the following brief Emily Dickinson poem—with her original dashes restored—at least twice, first ignoring the dashes and then using them to guide their reading. Then ask students to work in small groups to decide what effect the final dash has. Finally, ask them to try composing a four-line poem that uses dashes to guide reading and meaning.

> Much Madness is divinest Sense—
> To a discerning Eye—
> Much Sense—the starkest Madness—
> 'Tis the Majority
> In this, as All, prevail—
> Assent—and you are sane—
> Demur—you're straightway dangerous—
> And handled with a Chain—

For additional practice, ask students to read some other poems with dashes and study the effects they bring to the poems. They might even try to repunctuate a poem, replacing dashes with colons or parentheses to appreciate the difference. Other poems with dashes you might suggest include:

"Birches" and "Mending Wall," Robert Frost

"The Love Song of J. Alfred Prufrock," T. S. Eliot

"The Ruined Maid," Thomas Hardy

"Daddy," Sylvia Plath

> **The dash is a handy device, informal and essentially playful, telling you that you're about to take off on a different tack but still in some way connected to the present course—only you have to remember that the dash is there, and either put in a second dash at the end of the notion to let the reader know that he's back on course, or else end the sentence, as here, with a period.** —LEWIS THOMAS

On Colons (43d)

In Greek, the word *colon* denoted a unit of prose with certain rhythmical qualities, linking it to oral delivery. But today, colons function primarily to indicate a kind of grammatical equality or identification between the material located on one side and that on the other side. One of the benefits of the colon is the leisure it allows the writer to explain without having to write full sentences.

> **The stately colon, the confiding parenthesis and the gently pausing comma demand to know: what's behind today's big dash to the dash? Why has this lingua interruptus—expressing uncertainty, jerking the reader around, setting up startling conclusions, imitating patterns of speech—come to dominate our prose?** —WILLIAM SAFIRE

On Ellipses (43f)

Ellipses are purely rhetorical or grammatical in function. They derive from the classical Greek scheme *ellipsis*, which refers to the omission of a word or words from a text. Classical rhetoricians had in mind a conscious omission that would be implied by the context:

> And he to England shall along with you. —*Hamlet*

> So let the class invent its own assignments. If it wants more sophistication, fine. —PETER ELBOW

Have students quote parts of the preceding excerpts in sentences indicating omissions, as explained in 43f of *The Everyday Writer*. Teach your students how to recognize the use of ellipses by sharing with them a variety of examples and pointing out instances in their own writing.

FOR COLLABORATION: Punctuation

Ask students to form groups for this activity. Each group should read the following paragraph carefully, noting how it uses many parentheses and dashes. Then ask students to use the guidelines in this chapter to revise the paragraph, making it flow more smoothly. They should emphasize appropriate elements by deleting some of the parentheses and dashes, replacing one with the other, or substituting other punctuation. When all the groups are finished, discuss the changes to help students recognize how best to use parentheses and dashes.

> By the time we reached Geneva, we had been traveling more than seven weeks—it seemed like seven months!—and were getting rather tired of one another's company. (We had been only casual acquaintances before the trip.) Since there was not a great deal to see in the city—especially on Sunday—we decided to take the train to Chamonix (France) to see Mont Blanc—Europe's second-highest mountain (a decision that proved to be a disaster). After an argument about the map (the kind of argument we were having more and more often), we wandered around endlessly before finding the train station, only to discover that it was the wrong one. So we had to walk even farther—back to the other train station. Despite an exhausting pace, we just missed the train—or so we thought—until we learned that there was no train to Chamonix that day—because it was Sunday. I have never (for obvious reasons) gone back to Geneva.

USEFUL READINGS

Baker, Nicholson. "The History of Punctuation." *The Size of Thoughts.* New York: Vantage, 1997. 70–88. Baker remarks on "newer forms of emotional punctuation called 'smileys' or 'emoticons.'"

The Chicago Manual of Style. 15th ed. Chicago: U of Chicago P, 2003. See Chapter 6, "Punctuation," which discusses colons, dashes, parentheses, brackets, hyphens, and other marks of punctuation.

Hale, Constance, ed. *Wired Style: Principles of English Usage in the Digital Age.* New York: Broadway, 1999.

Harmon, Mark D. "Crossing a Question Mark with an Exclamation Point." *Chronicle of Higher Education* 28 July 2000: B7.

Palacas, Arthur L. "Parentheticals and Personal Voice." *Written Communication* 6 (1989): 506–27. Based on a sample of professional writing, Palacas argues that one clear source of "voice" is appositive and parenthetical structures.

44 Capital Letters

In early texts, a large letter usually marked the beginning of a sentence, and that letter could be either uppercase or lowercase. The *Codex Alexandrinus* (a fifth-century copy of the Bible) is one of the first documents that uses this system. A full lowercase set of characters existed as early as 510 CE, and the mixing of lowercase and uppercase characters developed from this date. By the time printing became established (in the mid-1500s), capital letters always signaled the start of a sentence (as in the Gutenberg Bible), but they were also liberally scattered throughout manuscripts at the printer's discretion. By the seventeenth century, the use of capital letters had become more or less standardized; they were used at the beginning of sentences and for proper names and titles. The *Encyclopaedia Britannica* (1975) notes that standardizing the usage of uppercase and lowercase letters was a crucial development:

> Three of the most important components [of a system of punctuation] are the space left blank between words; the identification of the first line of a new paragraph; and the uppercase, or capital, letter written at the beginning of a sentence and at the beginning of a proper name or a title.

Today, we take blank space and paragraph indentation for granted. However, our elaborate conventions for the use of capital letters—especially in online discourse—take more time and effort for students to recognize and adhere to.

Additional exercises on using capitalization are available on *The Everyday Writer*'s companion Web site, **bedfordstmartins.com/everyday writer**. Go to **Exercise Central** and click on **Capitalization**.

On the Rhetorical Function of Capital Letters

The use of capitals may seem simply conventional, but the conventions involved have rhetorical functions. In Modern Punctuation, George Summey Jr. lists three general functions of capitalization:

1. "As an aid to clearness." (Capitalizing proper nouns to distinguish them from common nouns and capitalizing the first letter of a sentence aid the logos of the writer's work.)
2. "For courtesy or reverence." (Capitalizing names and titles aids the writer's ethos.)
3. "For emphasis." (Although generally out of fashion nowadays, capitalizing words such as *nature* can possibly aid a writer's logos or pathos.) (165)

FOR MULTILINGUAL WRITERS: Differences in Capitalization Styles

It is important to recognize and discuss with students that rules for capitalization (as well as punctuation and mechanics in general) are conventions, agreements between readers and writers. These rules may differ from publisher to publisher, between disciplines such as English and psychology, and from instructor to instructor. Students need to know the conventions they are asked to write in. To work from a position of strength, students should become familiar with the basic rules that have achieved the consensus in standard academic English (the rules summarized in *The Everyday Writer*), and then find out how those rules differ in other disciplines or from one instructor to another.

FOR TEACHING: Capitalize the First Word of a Line of Poetry (44a)

Use poetry as a way to discuss the rules of capitalization and how playing with those rules can change meaning by having students compare the work of two poets who take different approaches to capitalization. You might have them read e. e. cummings' "since feeling is first" and "as freedom is a breakfastfood" (discussed in Bonnie Sillay's paper in 61c) alongside Emily Dickinson's "A little Madness in the Spring." Discuss how cummings's placement of capitals helps readers understand the poems. How do Dickinson's choices differ? How does this affect meaning?

On Proper Nouns (44b)

The eighteenth century saw a movement to begin proper nouns with lowercase letters. In a letter to his son, dated April 13, 1752, Lord Chesterfield denounced the fashion:

> It offends my eyes to see *rome, france, caesar, henry the fourth*, etc. begin with small letters; and I do not conceive that there can be any reason for doing it half so strong as the reason of long usage to the contrary. This is an affectation of Voltaire.

However, in the first draft of the Declaration of Independence, Thomas Jefferson did not capitalize words that usually received capitalization in the eighteenth century, including *nature*, *creator*, and even *god*.

FOR TEACHING: Capitalize Titles of Works (44c)

Consider encouraging your students to act as researchers by asking them to bring to class examples of how capitalization rules are used for titles. Direct them to student newspapers, print advertisements, labels on bottles and cans, and billboards for examples, and ask them to determine what they feel are appropriate and inappropriate uses (when capitals *should* be used), and effective and ineffective uses (when capitals help focus attention). Try to direct attention to the context of language use; what may be appropriate in an advertisement may be inappropriate in a formal paper for your class.

FOR TEACHING: Revise Unnecessary Capitalization (44d)

For stylistic purposes, writers might deliberately capitalize words or even whole passages to add a special emphasis (WOW! ZAP!). The writer Dave Barry uses this technique in his humorous newspaper columns: "Today, I saw a chicken driving a car. (I AM NOT MAKING THIS UP.)" The capital letters are mechanically not necessary, but they add special emphasis to Barry's prose.

For an example of how a writer of serious intentions may use capitalization for different kinds of emphasis, show them the following excerpt from Cynthia Ozick's "We Are the Crazy Lady":

> There were four big tables arranged in a square, with everyone's feet sticking out into the open middle of the square. You could tell who was nervous, and how much, by watching the pairs of feet twist around each other. The Great Man presided awesomely from the high bar of the square. His head was a maestic granite-gray, like a centurion in command; he *looked* famous. His clean shoes twitched only slightly, and only when he was angry.
>
> It turned out he was angry at me a lot of the time. He was angry because he thought me a disrupter, a rioter, a provocateur, and a fool; also crazy. And this was twenty years ago, before these things were *de rigueur* in the universities. Everything was very quiet in those days: there were only the Cold War and Korea and Joe McCarthy and the Old Old Nixon, and the only revolutionaries around were in Henry James's *The Princess Casamassima*.

After reviewing these examples, ask students to look through the local newspaper, noting instances of capital letters used for emphasis. Have students bring some examples to class for comparison with those found by classmates.

USEFUL READINGS

The Chicago Manual of Style. 15th ed. Chicago: U of Chicago P, 2003. See Chapter 8, "Names and Terms," for a discussion of when to use capital letters.

Period Styles: A History of Punctuation. New York: Herb Lubalin Study Center of Design and Typography in the Cooper Union for the Advancement of Science and Art, 1988. See the first essay, "Period Styles: A Punctuated History."

Summey, George, Jr. *Modern Punctuation*. New York: Oxford UP, 1919.

45 Abbreviations and Numbers

As the opening to Chapter 45 in *The Everyday Writer* suggests, students may be most familiar with the numbers and abbreviations they find in the phone book (or on the Internet or in the *TV Guide* listings). Point out to them the way both abbreviations and numbers function in the following excerpt, and then ask them to jot down the major places in which they ordinarily encounter abbreviations and numbers.

AAA—CHICAGO MOTOR CLUB
Emergency 24 Hr. Road Service
Toll Free......... 800-262-6327 Membership Services and Insurance
68 E. Wacker Pl....................... 372-1818

Additional exercises on using abbreviations and numbers are available on *The Everyday Writer*'s companion Web site, **bedford stmartins.com/everydaywriter**. Go to **Exercise Central** and click on **Abbreviations**.

On Abbreviations (45a–e)

The controversy over whether to abbreviate or spell out a word can become heated. On the one hand, commentators William and Mary Morris take the conservative approach: "Generally speaking, *abbreviations* are to be avoided in formal writing" (2). On the other hand, commentators like Rudolf Flesch take a different view: "It's a superstition that abbreviations shouldn't be used in serious writing and that it's good style to spell everything out. Nonsense: use abbreviations whenever they are customary and won't attract the attention of the reader" (3).

Flesch's statement points to an important aspect of abbreviation usage: choosing whether to use abbreviations or spell out the words is a rhetorical decision. As the authors of *Words into Type* note, "An abbreviation that can be used in certain branches of writing might be poor form in others" (100). For instance, *vs.* for *versus* is acceptable in legal writing, but not, to conservative taste, in some other formal writing. The writer must once again recognize and evaluate her or his audience. One rule of thumb, however, does apply across disciplines: when in doubt, spell it out. Today, writers find abbreviations in many Web site URLs and the conventions surrounding these uses of abbreviations are still very much in flux.

On the History of Abbreviations

Writers have always used abbreviations, whether on stone, paper, or computer screens. *SPQR*, *Senatus Populusque Romanus*, the insignia of Rome, was the most famous abbreviation of Western antiquity. For the several centuries preceding our own, the use of abbreviations declined, but since World War II, we have experienced a veritable flood of abbreviated words, especially in the United States. Just looking at the way some companies and products are spelled will indicate the extent to which people in the United States abbreviate:

EZ for *easy* as in EZ Sleep Motel

X for *ex-* as in X-cel Optical Co.

Hi for *high* as in Hi-Lo Oil Co.

Also, our abbreviations, taking the general meaning of that word, involve much more than this chapter suggests. *Laser*, *radar*, *scuba*, *snafu*, and *sonar* are among the acronyms that are now integral parts of the English lexicon. Abbreviations as well as acronyms can become pronounceable words themselves. Abbreviating has become an important way of coining new words: *ad* for *advertisement*; *auto* for *automobile*; *bra* for *brassiere*; *exam* for *examination*; *lab* for *laboratory*; *phone* for *telephone*; *photo* for *photograph*.

Ask your students to compile a list of all the new computer-related abbreviations they can think of.

On Abbreviations with Years: BC, BCE, and AD (45b)

Most of us don't always remember that while BCE and BC follow a date, AD precedes it. Even columnist and conservative grammarian William Safire admits an infamous mistake regarding the use of AD. As a speechwriter at the White House, he approved the wording of the plaque left on the moon by the first American astronauts to land there. It reads "July 1969, AD." Safire expresses the wish that "some descendant of mine will take a sharp stylus on some weekend rocket to the moon and, while awaiting a transfer rocket to Mars, will draw a little arrow placing it in front of the word *July*. This will show that human beings in the early days of space were grammatically fallible; that mankind . . . is forever editing, and that a little precision is a dangerous thing."

On Latin Abbreviations: *i.e.* and *e.g.* (45e)

Two Latin abbreviations, *e.g.* and *i.e.*, can easily be confused, although their meanings are rarely interchangeable. *E.g.* means "for example" (from the Latin *exempli gratia*). It introduces an instance or example of that to which it refers. *I.e.* means "that is" (from the Latin *id est*). It introduces a repetition in different words, a restatement or amplification of ideas just preceding it.

FOR TEACHING: Spell Out Numbers (45h)

You might be asked to specify relatedness as a factor in deciding whether to use a numeral or spell out the number. *The Chicago Manual of Style* states:

> Where many numbers occur within a paragraph or a series of paragraphs, maintain consistency in the immediate context. If according to rule you must use numerals for one of the numbers in a given category, use them for all that category. In the same sentence or paragraph, however, items in one category may be given as numerals and items in another spelled out. (381)

Here is an example:

> The English Department has 75 graduate students in six major areas: 29 in literature; 25 in rhetoric and composition; 8 in literary theory; 6 in linguistics; 4 in folklore; and 3 in film.

In this sentence, all the numerals relate to student population. However, the spelled-out number (*six*) relates to *major areas*. Therefore, the writer is permitted to spell out numbers and use numerals in the same sentence. The key factor in deciding whether to spell it out or not is rhetorical: which way would cause less confusion? Spelling out the one number that is unrelated to the seven other numbers distinguishes it so that the reader will not confuse it with the others.

USEFUL READINGS

The Chicago Manual of Style. 15th ed. Chicago: U of Chicago P, 2003. The *Manual* provides complete information on the standard form and punctuation of abbreviations.

Flesch, Rudolf. *The ABC of Style*. New York: Harper, 1964.

Mencken, H. L. *The American Language*. 5th ed. New York: Knopf, 1999. The author provides a readable discussion of abbreviations.

Morris, William, and Mary Morris. *Harper Dictionary of Contemporary Usage*. New York: Harper, 1975. This usage guide differs somewhat from others by relying on a panel of writers to discuss problems of usage.

Skillin, Marjorie E., and Robert Malcolm Gay. *Words into Type*. 3rd ed. Englewood Cliffs: Prentice, 1974.

46 Italics

Italic is one of the three families of type that have dominated Western typography since the invention of printing. The other two are roman (the type used here) and **black letter** (also referred to as Old English or Gothic but not to be confused with newer Gothic typefaces). Black letter type is used today almost exclusively for decoration. Roman is the name for the kind of type that is used predominantly in printing in the West today. Italic falls in between, having both technical uses (to indicate titles, etc.) and rhetorical uses (to indicate emphasis). Each of the three major types has its origins in calligraphy.

Black letter type developed out of decorative handwriting usually associated with Germany and England. Roman letters developed first as capitals—in Rome, of course. Italic letters were based on the cursive writing used by chancery scribes in Italy to speed up their work.

The preferred type of the earliest printers was black letter. However, the first printers in Italy, Konrad Sweynheim and Arnold Pannartz, found it inappropriate for the Humanist movement that was sweeping fifteenth century Italy. They searched calligraphic history for a more "Humanistic" type and developed what they called "Antiqua." In time, Antiqua became what we know of as roman. For many years, black letter continued to be used for non-Humanist texts, ecclesiastical writings, and legal works.

The first printer to use italic type was Aldus Manutius, who worked in Venice in the late fifteenth century. His type designer, Francesco Griffo of Bologna, modeled his italic design on the cursive letters used in the papal chanceries of the time. Italic type first appeared in a series of Latin pocketbook-size texts, aimed at the new audience of Renaissance readers who had the Humanist love for Latin writers. The series succeeded immediately. The first volume, the "Aldine Virgil," appeared in 1501.

Today, word processors and some email programs allow for italics. If your students *don't* have access to such programs, they can still indicate italics by <u>underlining</u>.

Additional exercises on using italics are available on *The Everyday Writer*'s companion Web site, **bedfordstmartins.com/everydaywriter**. Go to **Exercise Central** and click on **Italics**.

On the History of Print Types

Printing was introduced into England in 1474 by William Caxton, who used a rather striking black letter type. His assistant and eventual successor, Wynkyn de Worde, introduced italic type to England in 1524.

The French, however, were to be the most influential printers in England, establishing the dominance of roman type. As early as 1518, Richard Pinson, a Norman, introduced roman type into England and established a forty-year printing career that issued more than four hundred printed works. In 1540, Claude Garamond, the first commercial typefounder, designed and cut a roman type, referred to as the Garamond type. It quickly displaced most of the other types used in Europe. However, in 1672, when King Louis XIV ordered the creation of a new type based on "scientific principles," typecutter Philippe Grandjean designed *Roman du Roi*, which immediately overtook Garamond as the preferred type.

In 1734, William Caslon introduced a refined version of the Garamond type, which became what we think of as the traditional roman type. The Caslon type won wide acceptance and was introduced into the American colonies by Benjamin Franklin. The official copies of the Declaration of Independence were printed in Caslon's roman type.

On Italics for Titles (46a)

Newspapers provide an inexpensive, always available source of writing on which students can model much of their own use of conventions. However, in some cases, a newspaper may not be a good resource for models of italics usage. Traditionally, they have used quotation marks in place of italics. Today, many major newspapers, including the *New York Times*, *Washington Post*, *Chicago Tribune*, and *Los Angeles Times*, italicize their headlines. They use several different typefaces in order to produce variety, especially on front pages, which are full of different news stories. However, they continue to use quotation marks to indicate any titles, including those of books, plays, and magazines, despite style manuals that say these titles ought to be italicized.

On Italics for Special Emphasis

Writers may want to use italics to emphasize parts of a work for a variety of different reasons. Fowler suggests several:

1. To emphasize the main point of the phrase or clause or sentence.
2. To stress a contrast with reader expectations (and, of course, reveal the writer's awareness of the contrast).

3. To stress a contrast with another word, phrase, etc., within proximity (with both words, phrases, etc., usually italicized).
4. To suggest a stress upon a word or phrase, if it were spoken aloud.
5. To suggest that that which is being emphasized deserves more consideration or "thinking over" than the reader would normally give it: "They [italics] pull up the reader and tell him not to read on, or he will miss some peculiarity in the italicized word. The particular point he is to notice is left to his own discernment. . . ." (313)

Whether or not to use italics for emphasis is still being debated and probably will continue to be debated as long as some writers feel the need for that special emphasis. Fowler calls it "a primitive way of soliciting attention" (313). Yet, as *The Chicago Manual of Style* states, sometimes "emphasis would be lost without the italics" (290).

USEFUL READINGS

The Chicago Manual of Style. 15th ed. Chicago: U of Chicago P, 2003. The *Manual* provides full guidance in the use of italics.

Fowler, Henry. *A Dictionary of Modern English Usage*. 2nd ed. New York: Oxford UP, 1965.

"Printing, Typography, and Photoengraving." *The New Encyclopaedia Britannica: Macropaedia*. 1987. This article provides a brief history and discussion of the nature of typography.

Hyphens

47

. . . *the lady, whose odd smile is the merest hyphen.*
—KARL SHAPIRO

The "merest" hyphen is used to divide words at the end of a line and to link words or word parts (such as *hand-me-down* or *bye-bye*). As such, it serves purposes both mechanical and rhetorical. Its mechanical uses are fairly straightforward, with simple rules that tell us when and where we can divide a word at the end of a line. The rhetorical ones, however, are somewhat more complicated, for though they are governed in some cases by rules, they are defined in other cases by the needs of readers. You can use the following anecdote from Stewart Beach to point out the rhetorical usefulness of a hyphen:

> I came across a word I thought was a series of typos for *collaborators*. Reading it again, I realized the word was *colaborers*. But a hyphen would have [prevented] all the confusion.

Indeed, had the word included a hyphen—*co-laborers*—its meaning would have been instantly clear.

Additional exercises on using hyphens are available on *The Everyday Writer*'s companion Web site, **bedfordstmartins.com/everydaywriter**. Go to **Exercise Central** and click on **Hyphens**.

Hooray for the hyphen! Or, rather, Hoo-ray! —GEORGE PLIMPTON

On the History of Hyphens

Early Greek grammarians placed a short line *under* a compound to indicate that it was not to be read as two words. This sign did not appear *within* the line because paper was so scarce, the same reason that most Greek and early Latin manuscripts appear with no spaces between words. But even after spacing had been introduced, it was haphazard at best.

Greek manuscripts never perfectly divided text into words, and it was only in the eleventh century that hyphens began appearing in Latin manuscripts. As A. C. Partridge reminds us, though, the use of the hyphen did not become systematic until the twelfth century, and even then, the hyphen was sometimes repeated at the beginning of the next line (58). By the sixteenth century, hyphens were commonplace and used for the same purposes that we use them today, although they appeared in manuscripts doubled, like an equal sign (=), and slanted.

FOR COLLABORATION: Use Hyphens with Compound Words (47a)

Consider the following excerpt from a modern translation of *Beowulf*. Read it aloud to the class, and then ask students to suggest synonyms for the compounded terms. Finally, read both the excerpt and the version with their synonyms, and attempt to describe the difference in tone that results.

> There was stone paving on the path that brought
> the war-band on its way. The war-coats shone
> and the links of hard hand-locked iron
> sang in their harness as they stepped along
> in their gear of grim aspect, going to the hall.
> Sea-wearied, they then set against the wall
> their broad shields of special temper,
> and bowed to bench, battle-shirts clinking,
> the war-dress of warriors. The weapons of the
> seamen stood in the spear-rack, stacked together,
> an ash-wood grey-tipped. These iron-shirted
> men were handsomely armed.

FOR TEACHING: Use Hyphens with Compound Words (47a)

Consider reading Paul Fussell's "Notes on Class" with your class, focusing on the way he uses hyphenated compounds to name social classes. Because the topic of his essay—class divisions in society—is "a dirty little secret," no names exist to designate the distinctions Fussell wishes to make:

Top Out-of-Sight
Upper Class
Upper-Middle-Class
Middle Class
High-Proletarian
Mid-Proletarian
Low-Proletarian
Destitute
Bottom Out-of-Sight

Fussell also uses hyphens to create compound words to express his ideas: pseudo-genteel, shape-change, quasi-official, and dark-suited first-generation aspirants ("Notes on Class," from *The Boy Scout Handbook and Other Observations* [New York: Oxford UP, 1982]).

More recently, English has been absorbing large numbers of compounds derived from the computer industry. *Wired Style*, edited by Constance Hale, offers good advice on how to deal with hyphenating (or *not* hyphenating) these new terms.

FOR TEACHING: Use Hyphens to Divide Words at the End of a Line (47c)

After reviewing the rules in 47c of *The Everyday Writer*, share with your students the following amusing anecdote by Dave Barry about using hyphens to divide words at the end of a line:

> According to a *Washington Post* news item concerning an internal memo distributed by IRS deputy chief counsel, Marlene Gross, Gross "does not want to receive any memorandums, letters, etc. with hyphenated words." A second memo stated that Gross "does not want hyphenated words in letters, memos, unless it is at the end of the sentence." The *Post* does not say why Gross feels so strongly about hyphens. But it's quite common for people to develop hostility toward punctuation. I myself fly into a homicidal rage when I see business names featuring apostrophes on either side of the letter 'n,' such as "The Chew 'n' Swallow Café."

FOR COLLABORATION: Using Hyphens

Have students work in groups of two to insert hyphens in the following items as needed. Make sure each group has access to a dictionary.

1. antiinflammatory
2. pre Industrial Revolution
3. pro and anti handgun lobbyists
4. happily married couple
5. a "what me worry" look
6. self important
7. bride to be
8. seven hundred thirty three
9. bumper to bumper traffic
10. a politician who is fast talking

Answers

1. anti-inflammatory
2. pre-Industrial Revolution
3. pro- and anti-handgun lobbyists
4. happily married couple
5. a "what-me-worry" look
6. self-important
7. bride-to-be
8. seven hundred thirty-three
9. bumper-to-bumper traffic
10. a politician who is fast talking

USEFUL READINGS

Hale, Constance, ed. *Wired Style: Principles of English Usage in the Digital Age*. San Francisco: Hardwired, 1996.

Partridge, A. C. *Orthography in Shakespeare and Elizabethan Drama*. Lincoln: U of Nebraska P, 1964. For a concise and informative discussion of how the major punctuation marks evolved, see Appendix 8, "The Historical Development of Punctuation Marks."

Teall, Edward N. *Meet Mr. Hyphen and Put Him in His Place*. New York: Funk, 1937. See Chapter 1 for a short history of hyphens.

Webb, Robert A. *The* Washington Post *Deskbook on Style*. 2nd ed. New York: McGraw, 1989. See the entry under "hyphens" for rules and illustrative examples.

MLA Documentation

Careful citation shows your reader that you've done your homework. . . . It amounts to laying your intellectual cards on the table.

—JACK LYNCH

48–51 MLA Documentation

> *The style recommended by the association for preparing scholarly manuscripts and student research papers concerns itself with the mechanics of writing, such as punctuation, quotation, and documentation of sources. MLA style has been widely adopted by schools, academic departments, and instructors for nearly half a century.* –MLA WEB SITE

In "The Rhetoric of Citations Systems," Robert Connors traces the origins of contemporary citation forms to manuscript annotation practices, which go all the way back to the beginnings of alphabetical literacy. With the development of movable type in the mid-fifteenth century, however, printers and authors began to develop the formal structures that are now familiar to us as notes and citations. Before 1580, the two familiar kinds of notes, dialogic and reference notes, had become standard. Scholars argued over which notes and what kinds of content were appropriate, but recognizable modern marginal notes had evolved by 1690, and the first footnotes began to appear soon after. During the eighteenth century, citation systems were refined and brought to a high development by such historians as David Hume and, most famously, Edward Gibbon, whose *Decline and Fall of the Roman Empire* remains a touchstone of expert use of both dialogic and reference notes. In the nineteenth century, citation structures evolved further, especially in the sciences, which use annotations for slightly different purposes than do the humanities. It was during this time that the first citation-style books and pamphlets for authors appeared. Finally, in 1951, the Modern Language Association (MLA) published its first official manual.

Today, citation styles are important to the self-definition of many disciplines, and their forms reflect serious choices for writers and publishers. Indeed, the ideology of citation practices and styles is hotly debated. We suggest that student writers think about the implications of citation styles, what they foreground, and what they erase.

Additional coverage of MLA documentation is available on *The Everyday Writer*'s companion Web site, **bedfordstmartins.com/everydaywriter**. Go to **Documenting Sources**.

On the Reasons for Documenting Sources

Generally speaking, writers document their sources for four reasons.

1. Careful documentation gives credit for words or ideas to the original writer or speaker, and relieves the writer of any indictment of plagiarism.
2. Documentation lends the writer authority as a researcher. It says to the reader, "I am honest and open to anyone wishing to retrace the steps in my research." Documentation is an important element in the ethos of the writer presenting research. Undocumented (plagiarized) sources—or sources imprecisely documented, even if only slightly—suggest that the writer is careless or even dishonest.
3. Documentation is a courtesy to later writers on the subject who may want to use some of the material. Documentation provides them with directions for finding it.
4. Documentation allows others to follow up on a writer's research in order to test its validity. Not only should writers tolerate such a procedure; they should welcome it. To have others look so carefully at one's work implies that such work is important.

On the History of Documentation

The practice of documenting sources developed out of the larger movement toward bibliography and documentation that has become a hallmark of the twentieth century. Documentation arose out of the increase of information and the growth of information systems.

In ancient times, information storage and retrieval was accomplished for the most part by individuals mnemonically and by societies through rituals. With the rise of literacy came the desire to classify information systematically in the form of writing. The first libraries were built simply to preserve but not to make available their information. That intention really did not begin to change until the late nineteenth century.

An important development in the history of documentation was the change during the late Middle Ages and Renaissance in the notion of authorship. Medieval authors did not view their work as necessarily theirs alone; there was little sense of knowledge as somehow owned or its origins as deserving acknowledgment. However, in modern times, authorship became more personalized; writers began to think in terms of "original" ideas and to believe that they had a right to be acknowledged as authors of such ideas.

The invention of the printing press and the great increase in the desire for knowledge during the Renaissance helped increase the flow of information via books and the need for some way to classify such information in order to make it more readily available. Many different and individualized systems of classification and organization of information developed until, in the late nineteenth century, American librarian Melvil Dewey invented the Dewey Decimal System which libraries quickly adopted.

The form of such acknowledgment, whether it is MLA style or APA style or any of the many other documentation styles, derives from bibliographical description. Such description is meant to record various characteristics of each book, thereby revealing the uniqueness of each.

> **Plagiarists are always suspicious of being stolen from.** —SAMUEL TAYLOR COLERIDGE

FOR TEACHING: In-Text Citations (48)

According to the MLA Web site, there is a particular way to cite electronic texts that have no page numbers. Share the following information from that site with your students:

> In the text of a paper, works on the Web are cited just like printed works. For any type of source, you must include information in your text that directs readers to the correct entry in the works-cited list (see the *MLA Handbook*, 6th ed., sec. 6.2). Web documents generally do not have fixed page numbers or any kind of section numbering. If your source lacks numbering, you cannot cite numbers when you borrow from it.
>
> If your source includes fixed page numbers or section numbering (such as numbering of paragraphs), cite the relevant numbers. For numbers other than page numbers, give the appropriate abbreviation before the numbers: "Moulthrop, pars. 19–20." (*Pars.* is the abbreviation for *paragraphs*. Common abbreviations are listed in the *MLA Handbook*, sec. 7.4.) Do not count paragraphs yourself if your source lacks numbering.
>
> For a document on the Web, the page numbers of a printout should normally not be cited, because the pagination may vary in different printouts. An exception is PDF files, which appear with the same pagination on all systems.

FOR MULTILINGUAL WRITERS: In-Text Citations (48)

You can address the concerns of multilingual writers by asking them to bring in examples of in-text citations and share them in small groups. Choose examples from student papers, write them on the board for collective review, and correct the citations as a class. It's helpful to explain the rationale for a particular citation rule as you correct it. At the end of the workshop, leave time for students to ask questions.

TEACHING WITH TECHNOLOGY: In-Text Citations (48)

Try the preceding exercise in a computer-networked classroom. See Alexandra Barron's online article "Collaborative Teaching in the Computer Classroom" (www.cwrl.utexas.edu/currents/spring02/barron.html) for ways to "teach MLA documentation to a class without putting students to sleep."

FOR COLLABORATION: Explanatory and Bibliographic Notes (49)

Ask students working in pairs to review each other's drafts by marking or highlighting places in the text that merit an explanatory note. Often, positioning students as the primary audience for a draft helps writers learn when to use explanatory or bibliographic notes.

In a variation of this exercise, ask students to evaluate each note critically and to work through the following questions:

- Is the essay's argument hidden in an explanatory note?
- Are there too many notes?
- Do the notes detract from the flow of the essay?
- Should the list of bibliographic references be alluded to in the body of the essay rather than tucked into a note?

FOR TEACHING: List of Works Cited (50)

Spend some time in class discussing the purposes for adhering to MLA style in the works-cited list. Students often view the necessity of learning technical details for MLA style as an onerous task, one without intrinsic merit. But if you remind them that they are participating in a community of scholars and that they need to cite sources as a matter of professional courtesy, they might be more enthusiastic about learning and following MLA documentation format.

FOR TEACHING: The Use of *et al.* (50)

Even though *et al.* has been the preferred MLA option for citing four or more authors, you may want to encourage students to use the second MLA option—that of naming all the authors—because *et al.* leaves all but the first author nameless. As a result, it implicitly devalues collaborative work, suggesting that the only person with any *real* authority is the first author. Yet many who have written collaboratively would agree with Mary Belenky, who argues that such work should count twice as much as that which is singly authored because it is doubly difficult. As a result of these considerations, the authors of this book routinely cite all authors of a work.

TEACHING WITH TECHNOLOGY: List of Works Cited (50)

Students might complain about the time it takes to format the MLA works-cited list properly. If so, you can inform your class about software programs that construct a works-cited list in correct MLA style. Students simply enter all the fields, and the programs do the rest. Students using such a tool may spend most of their time and attention on the writing of their essays, rather than on the finer details of documentation. Examples include RefWorks (www.refworks.com), EndNote (www.endnote.com), and the free-to-use Citation Machine (www.citationmachine.net).

FOR TEACHING: Electronic Sources (50)

Since the 2003 publication of the sixth edition of the *MLA Handbook for Writers of Research Papers*, the MLA has been working to devise a standard style for citing electronic sources. The guidelines provided in Chapter 50 of the *The Everyday Writer* adopt these latest MLA guidelines. But several other efforts have been made to adapt MLA style for electronic sources. Janice Walker and Todd Taylor developed a set of guidelines in *The Columbia Guide to Online Style* that can be used for citing electronic sources in *any* of the major styles (MLA, APA, and so on). As new stylistic conventions emerge, our best advice is to help students use *consistent* citation patterns and to alert them to the current debate.

FOR TEACHING: A Student Research Essay, MLA Style (51)

The Introduction. After students read the introductory paragraphs of David Craig's research paper (note that David takes *two* paragraphs for the introduction), direct them to the questions that open 18a in *The Everyday Writer.* Use these questions as the basis for discussing how David establishes his rhetorical stance.

The Thesis. Call students' attention to Craig's thesis, and then ask them to test it against the questions posed in "Testing your thesis" in 18a of *The Everyday Writer.*

Paraphrases. Direct students' attention to the discussion of accurate and effective paraphrasing in Chapter 17 of *The Everyday Writer.* Then ask them to evaluate how closely David Craig follows those guidelines in his paper.

Quotations. Refer students to the discussion of quotations in 17b of *The Everyday Writer,* and then ask them to examine David's use of direct quotations in his paper. What in these quotations is particularly necessary or memorable? What other functions do the quotations serve? In addition, point out the formal features of long quotations, such as rules for indentation, noting that such quotations must be clearly introduced. Finally, discuss whether David integrates quotations smoothly into his own text.

The Conclusion. Ask students to refer to 18b on drafting the conclusion. Then ask them to identify the strategies David Craig uses in his conclusion. How effective is his conclusion? What alternative conclusions can students offer?

USEFUL READINGS

Ashton-Jones, Evelyn, and Dene Thomas. "Composition, Collaboration, and Women's Ways of Knowing: A Conversation with Mary Belenky." *Journal of Advanced Composition* 10.2 (Fall 1990): 275–92. In this interview, Mary Belenky describes collaborative work as doubly difficult.

Barron, Alexandra. "Collaborative Teaching in the Computer Classroom." *Currents in Electronic Literacy* 6 (Spring 2002) <http://www.cwrl.utexas.edu/currents/spring02/barron.html>. Barron provides a list of concrete ways to use technology to encourage collaborative learning and the mastery of MLA style.

Bloom, Lynn Z. "Why I (Used to) Hate to Give Grades." *CCC* 48 (1997): 360–71. Bloom offers here an essay that is, as she says, "solidly grounded in current research without any citations." Well worth reading to see how she does it!

Connors, Robert. "The Rhetoric of Citation Systems." Parts 1 and 2. *Rhetoric Review* 17 (Fall 1998): 6–49; and 17 (Spring 1999): 219–46. This lengthy essay recounts the history of citation practices and styles in the first part and discusses "Competing Epistemic Values in Citation" in the second.

Gibaldi, Joseph. *MLA Handbook for Writers of Research Papers.* 6th ed. New York: MLA, 2003. This is the definitive sourcebook for MLA style.

Harnack, Andrew, and Gene Kleppinger. "Beyond the *MLA Handbook*: Documenting Sources on the Internet." *Kairos* 1 (1996) <http://english.ttu.edu/kairos/1.2/inbox/mla_archive.html>. This article identifies difficulties in using traditional citation styles for Internet sources and recommends alternative models. The same issue includes an interesting and helpful response from Janice Walker, author of the guidelines adopted by the Association for Computers and Writing and coauthor of *The Columbia Guide to Online Style.*

Walker, Janice, and Todd Taylor. *The Columbia Guide to Online Style.* New York: Columbia UP, 1998.

USEFUL WEB SITES

Alliance for Computers and Writing (ACW)

http://www2.nau.edu/acw/

The ACW home page introduces readers to this group's many activities.

The Bedford Research Room

http://bedfordstmartins.com/researchroom

This online research tutorial offers advice on many steps in the research process, along with links to other research and documentation resources.

Modern Language Association

http://www.mla.org

At the MLA's home page, click on MLA Style *for information and updates.*

APA, *Chicago*, and CSE Documentation

Documentation styles in different disciplines vary according to what information is valued most highly. Thus in the sciences and social sciences, where timeliness of publication is crucial, the date of publication comes up front, right after the author's name.

—ANDREA A. LUNSFORD

52 APA Style

The fifth edition of the APA Publication Manual provides expanded coverage of technological advances in publishing, as well as the most up-to-date information on APA style guidelines and more in-depth coverage of case studies, tables, and lots more.
–APA WEB SITE

The current *Publication Manual of the American Psychological Association* (APA) has evolved since 1929, when it began as a seven-page article offering general guidelines for stylistic standards, to a book of well over three hundred detail-filled pages. Now followed by writers in many fields throughout the social sciences, the APA guidelines aim to foster clear communication and easy reference.

According to the APA Web site, the *Publication Manual* is the stylebook of choice for many disciplines where effective communication in words and data is fundamental, including psychology, sociology, business, education, economics, nursing, social work, and criminology. Many of your students majoring in these fields will need to learn and use APA style on a regular basis.

FOR COLLABORATION: In-Text Citations (52a)

Send students to the APA Web site entitled "Citations in Text of Electronic Material" (www.apastyle.org/electext.html), and have students read the guidelines aloud in class:

> To cite a specific part of a source, indicate the page, chapter, figure, table, or equation at the appropriate point in text. Always give page numbers for quotations (see section 3.34). Note that the words *page* and *chapter* are abbreviated in such text citations:
>
> (Cheek & Buss, 1981, p. 332)
> (Shimamura, 1989, chap. 3)
>
> For electronic sources that do not provide page numbers, use the paragraph number, if available, preceded by the paragraph symbol or the abbreviation

para. If neither paragraph nor page numbers are visible, cite the heading and the number of the paragraph following it to direct the reader to the location of the material (see section 3.39).

(Myers, 2000, ¶ 5)
(Beutler, 2000, Conclusion section, para. 1)

Next, have students work in pairs on each other's drafts, correcting errors in APA style.

TEACHING WITH TECHNOLOGY: List of References (52c)

Ask students to bring in their working bibliographies on a CD and put them on a computer screen for collective assessment and review. Ask students working in small groups to consult the APA's "Reference Examples for Electronic Source Materials" page (www.apastyle.org/elecsource.html) and to correct their reference lists accordingly. Then have each group present to the others some common errors found in their working bibliographies. Leave time at the end of class for questions.

USEFUL READING

American Psychological Association. *Publication Manual of the American Psychological Association.* 5th ed. Washington, DC: APA, 2001.

USEFUL WEB SITES

American Psychological Association

http://www.apa.org

The APA's homepage has much useful information for students—and their instructors!

APA Style: Electronic References

http://www.apastyle.org/elecref.html

A regularly updated Web page providing guidance on citing electronic sources.

APA Style: Frequently Asked Questions

http://www.apastyle.org/faqs.html

The APA's FAQ page provides useful information about APA documentation style.

53 Chicago Style

As always, most Chicago rules are guidelines, not imperatives; where options are offered, the first is normally our preference. Users should break or bend rules that don't fit their needs, as we often do ourselves. Some advice from the first edition (1906), quoted in the twelfth and thirteenth editions and invoked in the fourteenth, bears repeating: "Rules and regulations such as these, in the nature of the case, cannot be endowed with the fixity of rock-ribbed law. They are meant for the average case, and must be applied with a certain degree of elasticity."

–*The Chicago Manual of Style*, 15th ed.

First published in 1906, *The Chicago Manual of Style* became the touchstone for use of footnote styles. Now in its fifteenth edition (2003), this classic reference work provides consistent and systematic advice about punctuation, design, and typography as well as about documentation. It is still a standard.

USEFUL READINGS

General Reference

Howell, John Bruce. *Style Manuals of the English-Speaking World.* Phoenix: Oryx, 1983.

Law

The Bluebook: A Uniform System of Citation. 17th ed. Cambridge: Harvard Law Review Assn., 2000.

Linguistics

LSA Bulletin, December issue, annually.

USEFUL WEB SITES

The Chicago Manual of Style Online

http://www.chicagomanualofstyle.org

As a supplement to the print source, this Web site provides an extensive list of questions and answers grouped by topic.

Ohio State University Libraries: *Chicago Manual of Style* Citation Guide.

http://library.osu.edu/sites/guides/chicagogd.php

An accessible guide to help students work through the Chicago *guidelines.*

54 CSE Style

A must for anyone—author, editor, publisher, student, translator, science writer—responsible for writing or publishing scientific material. The book recommends both general and scientific publication style and formats for journals, books, and other types of publications.

–*CSE Manual* Web Site

While MLA, *Chicago*, and APA styles of documentation are widely used in the humanities and social sciences, other disciplines typically use other styles. But like scholars and organizations in the humanities and social sciences, scientists also felt a growing need for a style of documentation that matched their requirements and purposes. Thus the Conference of Biological Editors (CBE)—and its newer incarnation, the Council of Science Editors (CSE)—published the first manual of scientific citation styles in 1960. CSE style continues to be widely used in the sciences today.

Major revisions and changes have produced a new seventh edition of *Scientific Style and Format* (better known by its subtitle, *The CSE Manual for Authors, Editors, and Publishers*). The CSE Style Manual Committee's Web site describes the revisions made to the seventh edition and provides links to the book's content, features, preface, and introduction (www.councilscienceeditors.org/publications/style.cfm). At the site, you can also order a copy of the *CSE Manual* for yourself and your students.

USEFUL READINGS

Biology and Natural Sciences

Council of Science Editors. *Scientific Style and Format: The CSE Manual for Authors, Editors, and Publishers.* 7th ed. Reston: CSE, 2006.

Geology

Suggestions to Authors of the Reports of the United States Geological Survey. 7th ed. Washington, DC: GPO, 1991.

Mathematics

A Manual for Authors of Mathematical Papers. 8th ed. Providence: American Mathematical Soc., 1989.

Medicine

American Medical Association Manual of Style. 9th ed. Baltimore: Williams, 1998. This comprehensive guide to publication in the medical sciences includes chapters on preparing an article for publication, ethical and legal considerations, style terminology, quantification and measurement, and technical information.

Patrias, Karen. *National Library of Medicine Recommended Formats for Bibliographic Citations.* Bethesda: National Library of Medicine, 1991. See Chapter 12, pages 101–61, on electronic formats. See also the 2001 addendum on Internet sources at <http://www.nlm.nih.gov/pubs/formats/internet.pdf>.

USEFUL WEB SITE

Scientific Style and Format: The CSE Manual for Authors, Editors, and Publishers

http://www.councilscienceeditors.org/publications/style.cfm

The Web page for the CSE Manual, *maintained by the Council of Scientific Editors Style Manual Committee, includes links to selected sections of the new seventh edition.*

For Multilingual Writers

We're all imported.

—DEREK WALCOTT

55 Writing in U.S. Academic Genres

America is woven of many strands. I would recognize them and let it so remain. Our fate is to become one, and yet many. This is not prophecy, but description. –RALPH ELLISON

Within the many strands of U.S. culture are countless multilingual students who encounter American academic conventions as confusing restrictions on the ways of reading, writing, and thinking that they have known for so long. Whether we consider these U.S. conventions in terms of "contrastive rhetorics" or "second-language issues," we need to be sensitive to the fact that U.S. academic conventions comprise a culture with a discourse and philosophy that can intimidate many multilingual students.

If the assumption "we all know good writing when we see it" governs our approach to teaching composition, how will we incorporate a concern for multilingual writers whose ways of engaging texts, assuming expectations for readers and writers, and personal or academic voices may not conform to such models? The notes provided here and the readings listed at the end of this chapter can begin to suggest alternative ways of approaching the teaching of writing to multilingual students. In particular, the work by Diane Belcher, Ilona Leki, and Vivian Zamel—to name a few—offers us suggestions on how to teach students writing in U.S. academic contexts in a way that takes Ralph Ellison's tribute to America to heart.

America's future walks through the doors of our schools each day. –MARY JEAN LETENDRE

FOR TEACHING: U.S. Academic Writing (55a)

While the "process movement" has been all the rage in composition studies, Ilona Leki tells us that ESL teaching has only recently shifted from structure-based language instruction to process-based instruction. In order to achieve the task of teaching students how to produce effective academic writing, you will need to engage your multilingual students using a process model, not a transmission model of writing pedagogy.

Share with your students Min-Zhan Lu's moving personal essay, "From Silence to Words: Writing as Struggle" (available in Sondra Perl's collection, *Landmark Essays on Writing Process*), and have them discuss Lu's writing process. What academic styles did she encounter on her journey? What academic genres have your students encountered? What counts as "standard" in their home countries? When did they make their second (or third) language acquisition? You might also share with students stories about famous novelists who chose to write in second languages, such as Joseph Conrad and Samuel Beckett. How did these writers master the particular style or genre of a given audience and make their living by it? What can your students learn from such tales? How have cultures and expectations for assimilation changed since Conrad and Beckett? How are they different in the United States versus England, Mexico, or Japan?

FOR COLLABORATION: Genre Conventions (55b)

Ilona Leki advocates immersion in language, especially reading, as vital for developing writing skills and understanding genre conventions. In her book, *Understanding ESL Writers*, Leki recommends classroom practices, analyzes student writing, and surveys findings of contrastive rhetoric for several cultures. Similarly, Vivian Zamel, in "Writing One's Way into Reading," argues that reading and writing are interactive, mutually beneficial tasks.

Building off this research, have students in your classes share their responses to the questions in the "Features of Genres" box in Chapter 55 of *The Everyday Writer*. How do native speakers approach and analyze a text's genre features in contrast to multilingual speakers? What genres seem most and least familiar to readers of certain cultures?

> America is a land of wonders, in which everything is in constant motion and every change seems an improvement. . . . No natural boundary seems to be set to the efforts of man; and in his eyes, what is not yet done is only what he has not yet attempted to do.
>
> – ALEXIS DE TOCQUEVILLE

FOR MULTILINGUAL WRITERS: Adapting Structures and Phrases (55c)

Sandra Cisneros tells her readers to "write about what makes you different." Indeed, if your students are multilingual writers, then their own experiences form a veritable treasure trove of material for academic, professional, and personal essays. Encourage your students to write from what they know but also to begin to look for models of writing in the academic texts they will encounter through their reading. Have them avoid possible plagiarism by reviewing the example of effective borrowing in 55c.

> **America's future will be determined by the home and the school. The child becomes largely what he is taught; hence we must watch what we teach, and how we live.**
>
> —JANE ADDAMS

TEACHING WITH TECHNOLOGY: Checking Usage with Search Engines (55d)

In her 1997 address to the Conference on College Composition and Communication, Cynthia Selfe discussed contemporary expectations for texts in a technological age:

> Technological literacy—meaning computer skills and the ability to use computers and other technology to improve learning, productivity and performance—has become as fundamental to a person's ability to navigate through society as traditional skills like reading, writing and arithmetic. (par. 1)

In *Literacy and Computers*, Cynthia Selfe and Susan Hilligoss expand further on the significance of technologically mediated texts for U.S. academic conventions:

> Technology, along with the issues that surround its use in reading- and writing-intensive classrooms, both physically and intellectually disrupts the ways in which we make meaning—the ways in which we communicate. Computers change the ways in which we read, construct, and interpret texts. In doing so, technology forces us to rethink what it means to be human. We need more problems like this. (1)

Share the preceding passages with your students. Do they agree that technology has transformed writing and ways of making meaning through language and genres? How does America's access to computers change the way writers communicate across the globe? How do students from other countries and cultures respond to new technological environments? What can be learned from search engines about the structure of language in U.S. contexts and the ever-changing American vernacular? How might such technologies facilitate or hinder language acquisition and usage?

FOR COLLABORATION: Checking Usage with Search Engines (55d)

Give students the following quotation to analyze. You might post it for the class through an electronic discussion board.

The last time somebody said, "I find I can write much better with a word processor," I replied, "They used to say the same thing about drugs."
—ROY BLOUNT JR.

Ask students to write a brief response— to be posted to the discussion board—about the specific words, phrases, and expressions used in the passage. Then have them comment on the textual and cultural allusions inherent in the passage, and ask them to create a thesis about the way in which the language conveys the main idea of the passage. To further the dialogue, ask each student to respond to one other student's post. Choose a few postings from the class to generate discussion on how writing in the United States reflects a dependence on technology, genres, and cultural contexts.

USEFUL READINGS

Bartholomae, David. "Inventing the University." *When a Writer Can't Write: Studies in Writer's Block and Other Composing Process Problems*. Ed. Mike Rose. New York: Guilford, 1985. 135–65. Bartholomae argues that to succeed in college, students must learn to speak the language of the university, to "try on the peculiar ways of knowing, selecting, evaluating, reporting, concluding, and arguing" that are already valued by various academic discourse communities.

Belcher, Diane, and George Braine, eds. *Academic Writing in a Second Language: Essays on Research and Pedagogy*. Norwood: Ablex, 1995.

Bizzaro, Resa Crane. "Places as Teacher-Scholars in Composition Studies: Comparing Transition Narratives." *CCC* 53.3 (Feb. 2002): 487–506. Through personal narrative, professional interviews, and a synthesis of theoretical claims, Bizzaro discusses the experiences of Native Americans and other minorities in order to offer those marginalized by ethnicity, race, class, and gender a model for entering the profession of rhetoric and composition.

Carson, Joan G., and Ilona Leki, eds. *Reading in the Composition Classroom: Second Language Perspectives*. Boston: Heinle, 1993. The authors examine how reading and writing are increasingly being taught together in ESL courses—not as technical skills but as processes imbued in cultural contexts.

Connor, Ulla. *Contrastive Rhetoric: Cross-Cultural Aspects of Second-Language Writing*. New York: Cambridge UP, 1996.

Cope, Bill, and Mary Kalantzis, eds. *Multiliteracies: Literacy Learning and the Design of Social Futures*. London: Routledge, 2000. This collection of essays from the New London Group (NLG), which includes the famous

1996 *Harvard Educational Review* manifesto, "Pedagogy of Multiliteracies: Designing Social Futures," analyzes and responds to the globalized, "fast-capitalism" economy that both fragments cultures and produces new forms of writing in terms of multimedia and information technology. With consequences for theories of public and private spheres as well as for curricula, this volume offers new perspectives on negotiating changes in literacy and writing.

Cummins, Jim. "The Sanitized Curriculum: Educational Disempowerment in a Nation at Risk." *Richness in Writing: Empowering ESL Students*. Ed. Donna M. Johnson and Duane H. Roen. White Plains: Longman, 1989. 19–38. The authors discuss how, in 1983, university curricula across the country shifted policies from "equity" to "excellence" with the consequence that increased standards and tough pedagogical strategies threatened to disempower multilingual and minority students in particular.

Ferdman, Bernardo M., Rose-Marie Weber, and Arnulfo G. Ramirez, eds. *Literacy across Languages and Cultures*. Albany: SUNY P, 1994. The essays in this collection reveal that meeting the English literacy needs of members of linguistic and cultural minorities in the United States requires rethinking many assumptions about literacy itself, especially because most research concentrates on first-language literacy.

Henry, Jim. "Writing Workplace Cultures." *CCC* 53.2 (Dec. 2001). Henry examines the dramatic changes wrought by globalization (or "fast capitalism") on both the workplace and the writing produced in it.

Huckin, Thomas, Margot Haynes, and James Coady. *Second Language Reading and Vocabulary Learning*. Norwood: Ablex, 1993. A presentation on research into the ways that ESL students learn vocabulary, including analyses of L1 vocabulary learning and the efficacy of contextual guessing, investigation of the assumption that reading improves vocabulary acquisition, and evaluation of pedagogical practices for improving vocabulary.

Kutz, Eleanor, Suzy Q. Groden, and Vivian Zamel. *The Discovery of Competence: Teaching and Learning with Diverse Student Writers*. Portsmouth: Boynton/Cook, 1993. This is a call to approach students in terms of competence, not error. The authors argue that teachers need to understand the complexities of language acquisition and help students acquire new competencies in academic discourse by building bridges between old and new languages.

Leki, Ilona. *Understanding ESL Writers: A Guide for Teachers*. Portsmouth: Boynton/Cook, 1992.

Lu, Min-Zhan. "From Silence to Words: Writing as Struggle." *CE* 49 (Apr. 1987). In this personal essay, Lu takes us on a journey between discourse communities and offers compelling points for writing teachers to ponder.

Okawa, Gail Y. "Diving for Pearls: Mentoring as Cultural and Activist Practice among Academics of Color." *CCC* 53.3 (Feb. 2002): 507–32. Okawa discusses the mentorship views of two senior scholars, Geneva Smitherman and Victor Villanueva, and offers insight into the complexities and costs of building a multiethnic/multiracial professoriate in our discipline.

Pennycook, Alastair. "Borrowing Others' Words: Text, Ownership, Memory, and Plagiarism." *TESOL Quarterly* 30 (Summer 1996): 201–30. In an interesting perspective on plagiarism, Pennycook argues that memorizing the words of others and other acts of language learning differ significantly across cultures, and that understanding the complex issues related to textual borrowing makes Western notions of plagiarism confusing and hypocritical.

Perl, Sondra. *Landmark Essays on Writing Process*. Davis: Hermagoras P, 1994.

Selfe, Cynthia. "Technology and Literacy: A Story about the Perils of Not Paying Attention." *CCC* 50.3 (Feb. 1999): 411–36.

Selfe, Cynthia L., and Susan Hilligoss. *Literacy and Computers: The Complications of Teaching and Learning with Technology*. New York: MLA, 1994. This crucial collection of essays on using computers in literacy education addresses how computer technology changes literacy instruction and how to use collaborative computer networks and hypertext; it also includes suggestions for further research on literacy and technology.

Spigelman, Candace. "Argument and Evidence in the Case of the Personal." *CE* 64.1 (Sept. 2001): 63–87. Spigelman examines the strategic versions of "the personal" as rhetorical tropes in academic essays and as sources of evidence that might replace more empirically based models in the form of "narrative probability." She builds on Aristotelian rhetorical theory to argue that "narrative too offers claims, reasons and evidence for serious analysis and critique" (83). Her works-cited list provides particularly rich material for interested readers.

Tucker, Amy. *Decoding ESL: International Students in the American College Classroom*. Portsmouth: Boynton/Cook, 1995.

Valdes, Guadalupe. "Bilingual Minorities and Language Issues in Writing." *Written Communication* 9 (Jan. 1992): 85–136. Examining the complexity of bilingualism in the United States, Valdes charges that our profession must do more research on the kinds of writing that bilingual minorities are exposed to, on how mainstream teachers respond to these students' writing, and on the linguistic and social factors that affect their writing.

Zamel, Vivian. "Strangers in Academia: The Experiences of Faculty and ESL Students across the Curriculum." *CCC* 46.4 (Dec. 1995): 506–21.

———. "Writing One's Way into Reading." *TESOL Quarterly* 26 (1992): 463–85. Zamel argues that even though reading and writing are both acts of meaning making, reading continues to be taught by a transmission or information-retrieval model. Reading is a transaction between the text and the reader's knowledge and experience, and writing can reveal and enhance this transaction by enabling students to engage the text through their responses; students thus become better readers by becoming better writers.

Zamel, Vivian, and Ruth Spack, eds. *Negotiating Academic Literacies: Teaching and Learning across Languages and Cultures.* Mahwah: Lawrence Erlbaum, 1998.

Clauses and Sentences

56

In "Dictation as a Measure of Communicative Competence," Sandra Savignon argues that a student's success in taking dictation is a strong indicator of that student's language proficiency, for that student is *hearing* the language correctly. You might use the following passage for such an exercise:

> In prerevolutionary Cambodian society, whether a family belonged to the upper class or the peasantry, and whether they were ethnic Cambodian, or of Chinese or Vietnamese origin, the mother dealt with all household matters, child rearing in particular, and the prosperity, well-being, and reputation of the household depended mostly on her. The father dealt with the outside world and provided major family support. Because social norms based on Buddhist teachings promoted male-female equality, many women engaged in business ventures. When necessary, children helped their mothers to earn extra income, and there was usually a strong empathy between mothers and children. Even after children married and set up their own nuclear households, they continued to interact closely with their parents and siblings for mutual physical, emotional, and financial needs.
>
> The legal and cultural norm of duty to family members based on Buddhist precepts covered such things as parental authority, arrangement of proper marriages for children, provision of support in the event of divorce and in old age, inheritance, adoption, guardianship, and provision of proper funeral arrangements.
>
> Children generally received a great deal of affection in the first years of life not only from parents, but also from other adults and adolescents. But as they grew, older children were expected to conform to norms of politeness and obedience.
>
> Although some competition was present in games, the stress was on playing rather than winning. . . .
>
> By age 10 or so, both sexes had been taught basic skills necessary to be useful members of society. Boys, particularly in villages, learned agricultural techniques, while girls learned household duties. In adolescent years, the two sexes were segregated in school, which was strictly a place for education, and not for entertainment or romance. Premarital sex was deplored and sexual knowledge not considered suitable for children because it was considered to

> lead to desire and trouble. Adults also did not display physical love publicly even after marriage. Ideally, marriages were arranged by parents.
>
> –USHA WELARATNA, "A Khmer Perspective"

You may also ask your students to read aloud their dictations, taking care to notice whether, as they read aloud, they correct any of the mistakes they've made in their transcriptions.

Additional exercises on clauses and sentences are available on *The Everyday Writer*'s companion Web site, **bedfordstmartins.com/everydaywriter**. Go to **Exercise Central** and click on **For Multilingual Writers**.

FOR TEACHING: Clauses and Sentences

Read aloud to the class the following passage from Amy Tan's "The Language of Discretion," and then ask students to list her allegations. After you have written their lists of allegations on the board, ask students to respond to Tan's argument, providing examples from their own language when possible.

> Having listened to both Chinese and English, I . . . tend to be suspicious of any comparisons between the two languages. Typically, one language—that of the person doing the comparing—is often used as the standard, the benchmark for a logical form of expression. And so the language being compared is always in danger of being judged deficient or superfluous, simplistic or unnecessarily complex, melodious or cacophonous. English speakers point out that Chinese is extremely difficult because it relies on variations in tone barely discernible to the human ear. By the same token, Chinese speakers tell me English is extremely difficult because it is inconsistent, a language of too many broken rules, of Mickey Mice and Donald Ducks.
>
> Even more dangerous to my mind is the temptation to compare both language and behavior *in translation.* To listen to my mother speak English, one might think she has no concept of past or future tense, that she doesn't see the difference between singular and plural, that she is gender blind because she calls my husband "she." If one were not careful, one might also generalize that, based on the way my mother talks, all Chinese people take a circumlocutory route to get to the point. It is, in fact, my mother's idiosyncratic behavior to ramble a bit.
>
> –AMY TAN, "The Language of Discretion"

USEFUL READINGS

Belcher, Diane, and George Braine, eds. *Academic Writing in a Second Language: Essays on Research and Pedagogy.* Norwood: Ablex, 1995. A "must-read" for teachers of writing.

Charles, Maggie. "Responding to Problems in Written English Using a Student Self-Monitoring Technique." *English Language Teaching Journal* 44

(1990): 286–93. Charles describes the ideal revision situation as editor-writer conferences between students and instructors. She outlines a procedure for student self-monitoring in which students engage in a written dialogue with instructors from their first draft through their final revision; such an approach gives students control, motivates them to read and incorporate comments, and encourages them to analyze their writing by placing themselves in the position of the reader.

Savignon, Sandra. "Dictation as a Measure of Communicative Competence." *Language Learning* 32 (1982): 33–51.

Spack, Ruth, and Catherine Sadow. "Student-Teacher Working Journals in ESL Freshman Composition." *TESOL Quarterly* 17 (1983): 575–93. Students and instructors exchange dialogic journals that focus on classroom issues. All students participate in the class and in the construction of their essay topics; instructors receive feedback on their techniques and topics. Journal writing has a positive impact on ESL students' writing attitudes and habits.

57 Nouns and Noun Phrases

Assessment of student writing is already a complex field of study, and the assessment of ESL student writing can be even trickier, especially when the teacher doesn't feel prepared to teach or evaluate ESL students.

But in "Assessment of ESL Students in Mainstream College Composition," Lisa Hillenbrand addresses the major concerns of writing instructors by speaking to issues of "Unraveling the Rhetoric," "Moving Away from the Error Obsession," and "Methods of Marking and Evaluating." She offers several substantive practices for classroom instructors.

Additional exercises on nouns and noun phrases are available on *The Everyday Writer*'s companion Web site, **bedfordstmartins.com/everydaywriter**. Go to **Exercise Central** and click on **For Multilingual Writers**.

FOR TEACHING: Count and Noncount Nouns (57a)

As you talk with your class about count and noncount nouns, you will have to discuss the redundancies of the English language. Ask your students to bring in an essay they're working on and to write out the first paragraph, giving themselves plenty of space to mark out the redundancies of their English prose, particularly as redundancy does or does not apply to instances involving count and noncount nouns.

FOR TEACHING: Articles (57e)

Ask students to copy out a passage from an in-progress essay and label as definite or indefinite the articles they use. Students should be able to explain their choice of article in each case. When students use nouns *without articles*, they should also be able to explain their syntactical decision.

FOR COLLABORATION: Nouns in Specific Languages

Break the class into groups, and make a list of the distinguishing characteristics among *nouns* in each group member's native language. Have students work together to prepare a lesson about these characteristics to present to the other groups. When they take the time to see and hear their native languages through the eyes and ears of a "foreigner," students will be better able to teach their own languages as well as to become more adept at learning the nuances of other languages—in this case, standard academic English.

USEFUL READINGS

Acton, William. "Some Pragmatic Dimensions of ESL Writing Tutorials." *ERIC: Educational Resources Information Center*, 1981. ED 267 581. Acton describes an "editor" model that ESL students may use with one another, especially if they ask for assistance with particular problems of mechanics, syntax, usage, idiomatic expressions, coherence, and style. If students know what their problem areas are and can ask for help with those problems, they will progress more quickly toward near-native fluency in English.

Hillenbrand, Lisa. "Assessment of ESL Students in Mainstream College Composition." *TETYC* 21 (May 1994): 125–29.

Robinson, William S. "ESL and Dialect Features in the Writing of Asian American Students." *TETYC* 22 (Dec. 1995): 303–10.

Zamel, Vivian. "Strangers in Academia: The Experiences of Faculty and ESL Students across the Curriculum." *CCC* 46.4 (Dec. 1995): 506–21.

58 Verbs and Verb Phrases

In "The Poetry of ESL Error," Melissa Allen discusses her evolution from an error-oriented, frustrated ESL instructor to a relaxed, fascinated instructor of ESL students. She writes that she began enjoying her teaching and her students when she realized that they were telling her things she didn't know; they were provoking her to think. "[T]hey were using the English language in interesting ways, with nuance and subtlety, with fascinating sounds and rhythms and silences. Even the errors sometimes had a certain something—poetry?" (120).

Allen's realization changed her attitude about the goal of ESL teaching, and she argues that to concentrate on making ESL students write like native speakers is to "deprive them, ourselves, and our language of much that is enriching about the way ESL students use English" (121). Hers is a compelling argument, which is most convincing in the list of "error-free" ESL sentences she includes. She describes these sentences as having "a nonnative flavor":

1. I went outside and smoked down my anger.
2. I cheered him on his success.
3. [I looked through the list of names] but my name didn't come out for me.
4. When I feel oppressed in the chest, I like to listen to rock music.
5. I imagined she was a ferocious person who had timid ideas.
6. Your brain wants to eat more air than you are giving it.
7. Our music filled the room with warm heart.
8. It is useless to continue this barren argument.

Additional exercises on verbs and verb phrases are available on *The Everyday Writer*'s companion Web site, **bedfordstmartins.com/everydaywriter**. Go to **Exercise Central** and click on **For Multilingual Writers**.

FOR TEACHING: Poetic Uses of Nonnative English

Ask for volunteers to share their "poetic" and other nonnative uses of English. If your students are working in groups, a native speaker of English might be able to locate such impressive examples of English usage.

USEFUL READINGS

Allen, Melissa. "The Poetry of ESL Error." *TETYC* 21 (May 1994): 21–24.

Goldstein, Lynn M., and Susan M. Conrad. "Student Input and Negotiation of Meaning in ESL Writing Conferences." *TESOL Quarterly* 24 (1990): 443–60. Conferencing in and of itself does not necessarily lead to student input or successful revision. Only when students negotiate meaning with the teacher is there a high percentage of successful revisions. The authors encourage teachers to discuss conference goals and examine their own conference behavior, especially in terms of trying to control the students' discourse.

Hafernick, Johnnie Johnson. "The How and Why of Peer Editing in the ESL Writing Class." *ERIC: Educational Resources Information Center*, 1983. ED 253 064. Hafernick discusses the advantages of peer editing and includes specific guidelines for ensuring efficient and successful editing days.

Hvitfeldt, Christina. "Guided Peer Critique in ESL at the College Level." *ERIC: Educational Resources Information Center*, 1986. ED 282 438. If writing students follow specific guidelines, they will better analyze and critique student papers. Hvitfeldt includes sample peer-critique forms.

Keh, Claudia L. "Feedback in the Writing Process: A Model and Methods for Implementation." *English Language Teaching Journal* 44 (1990): 294–304. Feedback is a fundamental element of the process approach to writing: peer feedback, often focused on sentence-level concerns, raises audience awareness and allows peer learning/teaching; instructor feedback should also stay with higher-order concerns and follow established guidelines.

59 Prepositions and Prepositional Phrases

Sandra Savignon, pioneer in communicative competence, is credited with influencing second-language teaching worldwide. Her work focuses on theoretical and research bases for language teaching, curriculum design, and testing procedures that encourage the learner to combine rule-based knowledge of several areas in order to negotiate meaning in a second language. In *Communicative Competence: Theory and Classroom Practice*, the phrase "communicative competence" includes "knowledge of sociolinguistic rules, or the appropriateness of an utterance in addition to knowledge of grammar rules." As she notes, "the development of the learners' communicative abilities is seen to depend not so much on the time they spend rehearsing grammatical patterns as on the opportunities they are given to interpret, to express, and to negotiate meaning in real life situations."

Additional exercises on prepositions and prepositional phrases are available on *The Everyday Writer*'s companion Web site, **bedford stmartins.com/everydaywriter**. Go to **Exercise Central** and click on **For Multilingual Writers**.

FOR COLLABORATION: Using Prepositions Idiomatically (59a)

Ask your students to form into groups and discuss their language backgrounds. First, consider an American attitude that all people should either know or learn English. What is their response? Second, they may want to consider the idea that everyone—including those smug Americans—should learn at least one foreign language. What are the advantages of knowing another language? another culture? Finally, ask students to focus on any prepositions and prepositional phrases they have used in this discussion, noting those that seem problematic. Use these examples for class discussion.

USEFUL READINGS

Chenoweth, N. Ann. "The Need to Teach Rewriting." *English Language Teaching Journal* 41 (1987): 25–29. Teachers who correct only sentence-level errors reinforce students' attention on the sentence only. Therefore, Chenoweth argues for assigning revisions rather than new essays.

Robb, Thomas, Steven Ross, and Ian Shortreed. "Salience of Feedback on Error and Its Effects on EFL Writing Quality." *TESOL Quarterly* 20 (1986): 83–93. Although research in ESL concludes that instructors should concentrate on higher-level concerns, most instructors continue to respond more frequently to issues of mechanics, syntax, and spelling. Instructors need to remember that the direct correction of surface errors is not a significant way to improve student writing ability.

Savignon, Sandra J. *Communicative Competence: Theory and Classroom Practice.* Reading: Addison, 1983.

———. "Communicative Language Learning." *Theory into Practice* 26 (1987): 235–42.

Writing in the Disciplines

Don't underestimate your readers' intelligence, but don't overestimate their knowledge of a particular field.

—JULIE ANN MILLER

60 Academic Work in Any Discipline

A college education should equip one to entertain three things: a friend, an idea and oneself. —THOMAS EHRLICH

The belief that writing should be the concern of the entire school community underlies this chapter. According to Art Young and Toby Fulwiler, composition researchers and theorists such as James Britton, Janet Emig, James Kinneavy, James Moffett, Mina Shaughnessy, and Lillian Bridwell-Bowles have all variously suggested that student writing will not improve until students see writing at the center of their academic experience. They will learn to value it and practice it when it is incorporated usefully into the daily process of learning in all disciplines. Writing-across-the-curriculum programs work toward these goals. Over the last two decades, dozens of these programs have emerged in U.S. colleges and universities. Individual programs may differ in scope and practice, but all of them aim to improve student writing by encouraging faculty from across the disciplines to use writing regularly and thoughtfully in their classrooms.

On Writing for Every Discipline (60a)

Writing in the disciplines—sometimes called writing across the curriculum, writing in the content areas, language for learning, or writing to learn—has two histories that Anne Herrington and Charles Moran refer to as "extraordinarily different yet intimately related" (3). In *Writing, Teaching, and Learning in the Disciplines*, they begin with two historical perspectives, the British one given by Nancy Martin and the American one discussed by David Russell. In these essays, we see how theorists and educators such as Douglas Barnes, James Britton, and Harold Rosen from the United Kingdom and Wayne Booth, James Moffett, and Albert Kitzhaber from the United States came together to provide an impetus for what came to be known as the writing-in-the-disciplines movement, which has persisted for more than twenty years. Today, many universities consider writing in the disciplines to be a central concern and use general education requirements to ensure that students are writing in their classes in several disciplines. This chapter aims to assist students in using skills and techniques from their writing courses to situate their writing in other disciplines successfully.

FOR MULTILINGUAL WRITERS: Reading for Every Discipline (60a)

Writers from diverse national backgrounds have to consider cultural expectations as well as disciplinary specifications when approaching reading required in specific disciplines. They might need additional clarification on the various standards for disciplinary work. Encourage multilingual students to visit their teachers during office hours or to make an appointment to review the assigned reading and to explain assignment expectations before commencing a task. This communication will often prevent misunderstandings and will help expedite the learning process.

> A teacher affects eternity; he can never tell where his influence stops.
>
> —Henry Brooks Adams

FOR COLLABORATION: Academic Assignments and Expectations (60b)

If your students can provide assignments from various disciplines, have them carry out an analysis using the questions in the Analyzing an Assignment checklist in 60b. Encourage them to work in groups to analyze the assignments and their expectations.

FOR COLLABORATION: Disciplinary Vocabulary (60c)

Ask students to work in groups of three. Each student should bring to class two copies of a short passage of approximately one hundred words taken from an article, an essay, or a textbook in a field with which he or she is familiar. Have students give a copy to each of their partners and ask them (1) to list terms, phrases, or concepts that seem to involve specialized or highly technical language, and (2) to define and explain these terms. Have students retrieve their articles and their partners' lists, check their efforts, and then, in discussion, clarify the terms for them. Discuss their confusion or lack of it.

This exercise gives students practice explaining basic terms in fields they are familiar with to a general audience. For example, the term *blastema* is basic knowledge to students in molecular genetics, as is *Cyrillic alphabet* to Slavic language majors. *Morpheme* is a basic concept to linguistics students, as is *hypotenuse* to geometry students. Thus, this exercise serves two purposes:

1. It helps students develop an awareness of how to adapt their language and explanations to audiences with different degrees of expertise or familiarity with a field's vocabulary.
2. It also allows students to test their own understanding of terms and concepts. One way we determine how well we understand concepts is to explain them to someone else.

For additional practice recognizing and using particular disciplinary language, divide the class into groups of no more than three students who are working in the same major field or in closely related fields. Have each group compile a glossary of twenty key terms that are essential to the field or fields. Ask students to alphabetize the terms and to define and explain each one.

TEACHING WITH TECHNOLOGY: Disciplinary Style (60d)

> There are many languages. There is the language of guns. There is the language of money. There is the language of human rights. There is the language of love.
> –JUNE JORDAN

June Jordan might well have added to this quotation, "And there is a language of science, of law, of medicine." To get students thinking about the style of disciplines, ask them to write a journal entry about their experiences with writing in different disciplines. Some will have found writing difficult or easy regardless of the discipline, but others will have noted differences in the experiences, assignments, and teacher expectations associated with different subjects. These journal entries can be shared or simply written as preparation for an initial class discussion of disciplinary writing conventions.

FOR TEACHING: Use of Evidence (60e)

In an intriguing letter to the editor, published in the *PMLA*, David Linton examines the way in which scholarly contributors to a *PMLA* roundtable entitled "The Status of Evidence" use evidence themselves to make their claims. Ask your students to write similar letters to editors of journals that they read across various disciplines. In their letters, they should analyze and comment on the use of evidence in three of the journal's articles.

> **Any place that anyone young can learn something useful from someone with experience is an educational institution.**
>
> —AL CAPP

ATTENDING TO DISABILITIES: Conventional Patterns and Formats (60f)

Students with disabilities may wish to offer alternative means of complying with disciplinary patterns and formats in order to accommodate their particular learning styles. A student with a visual impairment, for example, might provide a verbal copy of an assignment by using a voice recorder or other device availabe at the campus disability center. Take time to discuss possible variations in disciplinary formats with advisers from across the college campus. You might bring up the importance of attending to disabilities at the next faculty meeting to get the discussion started.

FOR COLLABORATION: Academic Work in Any Discipline

Have students pair up with a classmate or friend who intends to major in the same field. Then have the teams investigate the college Web site to locate two faculty members in that field and to learn about their scholarly work. One team member should contact a professor for an appointment to conduct an interview. (Make sure each group has a couple of backup professors on the list in case one is unavailable.) Before conducting their interview, remind students to review section 15e in *The Everday Writer* and to create a list of interview questions about research in the field. They might use the information in Chapter 60 of *The Everday Writer* to help them generate their questions. Finally, each team should conduct the interview and write a brief summary of what they have learned for the class.

USEFUL READINGS

Bazerman, Charles. "Codifying the Social Scientific Style: The *APA Publication Manual* as a Behaviorist Rhetoric." *The Rhetoric of the Human Sciences: Language and Argument in Scholarship and Public Affairs.* Ed. John Nelson, Allan Megill, and Donald McClosky. Madison: Wisconsin UP, 1987. 125–44. Bazerman argues that the disciplines are socially negotiated territories and conventions of disciplines are representations of actions produced through that discipline's process of inquiry—a process that is shaped and transformed by the contributions of those who work with and within the discipline.

Herrington, Anne, and Charles Moran, eds. *Writing, Teaching, and Learning in the Disciplines.* New York: MLA, 1992. This collection contains fourteen essays covering historical and theoretical perspectives on writing across the curriculum as well as several treatments of classroom practice.

Kasper, Loretta Francis. "Discipline-Oriented ESC Reading Instruction." *TETYC* (Feb. 1995): 45–53. Kasper describes three different kinds of reading courses that use discipline-specific materials.

Kirsch, Gesa. *Women Writing the Academy.* Carbondale: Southern Illinois UP, 1993. Kirsch studies women's experiences in trying to inhabit various disciplinary languages and styles.

Langer, Judith A. "Speaking of Knowing: Conceptions of Understanding in Academic Disciplines." *Writing, Teaching, and Learning in the Disciplines.* Ed. Anne Herrington and Charles Moran. New York: MLA, 1992. 69–85.

LeFevre, K. B., and M. J. Dickerson. *Until I See What I Say: Teaching Writing in All Disciplines.* Burlington: IDC Publications, 1981. This book, written by English instructors, gives several ideas for teaching writing in other disciplines. This source might prove especially useful for ideas on revision, generating content, and teaching techniques.

Linton, David. "The Framing of Evidence." *PMLA* 112 (1997): 428–29.

MacDonald, Susan Peck. *Professional Academic Writing in the Humanities and Social Sciences.* Carbondale: Southern Illinois UP, 1994. The author examines the ways disciplinary genres and forms shape knowledge-making.

Malinowitz, Harriet. "A Feminist Critique of Writing in the Disciplines." *Feminism and Composition Studies.* Ed. Susan C. Jaratt and Lynn Wosham. New York: MLA, 1998. 291–312.

Marsella, Joy, Thomas L. Hilgers, and Clemence McLaress. "How Students Handle Writing Assignments in Six Disciplines." *Writing, Teaching, and Learning in the Disciplines.* Ed. Anne Herrington and Charles Moran. New York: MLA, 1992. 174–91.

Walvoord, Barbara E., and Lucille P. McCarthy. *Thinking and Writing in College: A Naturalistic Study of Students in Four Disciplines.* Urbana: NCTE, 1990. Useful reading for teachers of first-year writing courses whose students will go on to enter a variety of disciplines.

Young, Art, and Toby Fulwiler. *Writing across the Disciplines: Research into Practice.* Upper Montclair: Boynton, 1986. This is an informative collection of research on writing-across-the-curriculum programs from four perspectives: purpose, evaluation, writing and learning connections, and the politics and effectiveness of these programs.

Writing for the Humanities

61

Books are the carriers of civilization. Without books, history is silent, literature dumb, science crippled, thought and speculation at a standstill.
–BARBARA TUCHMAN

The central focus of the humanities is to explore, interpret, and reconstruct the human experience. To that end, we teach our students the disciplines of history, literature and literary analysis, drama, film, philosophy, and language. As you facilitate your students' learning in these disciplines, you might introduce your class to texts ranging from poems and plays to novels, articles, philosophical treatises, films, and translations.

Additional examples of student writing in the humanities are available on *The Everday Writer*'s companion Web site, **bedfordstmartins.com/everydaywriter**. Go to **Writing Resources/Links** and click on **Writing in the Disciplines**.

Every man's work, whether it be literature or music or pictures or architecture or anything else, is always a portrait of himself.
–SAMUEL BUTLER

FOR TEACHING: Writing Texts in the Humanities (61b–c)

Ask students to read Bonnie Sillay's essay in 61c of *The Everyday Writer*, noting where the student writer uses material from literary texts—examples, quotations, and so on—to support her thesis. Point out the critical role that such textual evidence plays in any essay whose writer adopts a text-based stance. Have students emulate this use of evidence in their own essays.

FOR COLLABORATION: Writing Texts in the Humanities (61b)

Ask students to choose an inspiring film, literary work, or painting and to write a short essay explaining to their peers how the work affects them.

Next, have students exchange essays for peer review, reminding the reviewers to focus on how the essay's content and how learning about the writer's relationship to the work reveals the power of strong writing to move and persuade.

> Great literature should do some good to the reader: must quicken his perception though dull, and sharpen his discrimination though blunt, and mellow the rawness of his personal opinions.
>
> —A. E. HOUSMAN

ATTENDING TO DISABILITIES: Writing Texts in the Humanities (61b)

As Mark Mossman reminds us, when you ask students to write autobiographical texts, be sure to include mention of disabilities. Make a space for discussion of disabilities when teaching how to write about the humanities. Have them research figures such as Lord Byron for the myths of creativity and writing that continue to affect people with disabilities in present-day Western civilization.

TEACHING WITH TECHNOLOGY: Writing Texts in the Humanities (61b)

One difficulty students often have in writing essays for the humanities is weaving quotations smoothly into their papers. Refer students to the discussion of quotations in 17b of *The Everyday Writer*, and ask them to evaluate the use of quotations in this chapter's student essay by Bonnie Sillay (61c). Are quotations introduced clearly? Do they "fit in" to the preceding sentence? Does the student writer comment sufficiently on their significance? Next, have students work in groups of two or three on a shared computer. Each group should compose a review of one essay and use quotes from the essay in the review. Remind students to practice integrating quotations in various ways as a means to develop their writing skills.

FOR COLLABORATION: Writing for the Humanities

Ask students to work with a partner. Have half of the teams analyze Bonnie Sillay's paper (61c) and the other half analyze a paper that one of your students volunteers to use as a model, using the principles and guidelines presented throughout Chapter 61 of *The Everyday Writer*. Each team should write a two- or three-paragraph peer response to the student essay and bring it to class for discussion. Do both essays succeed in the same way, or do they have different strengths given their purposes?

USEFUL READINGS

Commeyras, Michelle. "Using Literature to Teach Critical Thinking." *Journal of Reading* 32 (1989): 703–7.

Crowley, Sharon. *Composition in the University: Historical and Polemical Essays.* Pittsburgh: U of Pittsburgh P, 1998. Tracing the history of competing composition and literature programs, Crowley views composition as a "policing mechanism" resulting from composition specialists' middle-class affiliations and claims that while English departments have colonized composition, writing in the university need not depend on first-year college English.

Elbow, Peter. "The Cultures of Literature and Composition: What Could Each Learn from the Other?" *CE* 64.5 (May 2002): 533–46.

———. "The War between Reading and Writing—and How to End It." *Critical Theory and the Teaching of Literature: Politics, Curriculum, Pedagogy.* Urbana: NCTE, 1995. Elbow examines the war between writing and literature in university English departments. His analysis covers sites of conflict, the privilege of reading over writing, the benefits of ceasing the battle, and strategies for conflict resolution.

Gere, Anne Ruggles. "Composition and Literature: The Continuing Conversation." *CE* 51 (Oct. 1989): 617–22.

Glenn, Cheryl. "The Reading-Writing Connection: What's Process Got to Do with It?" *When Writing Teachers Teach Literature.* Ed. Toby Fulwiler and Art Young. Portsmouth: Boynton, 1995. Glenn charts in detail the ways she uses writing to teach a survey-of-English-literature course.

Harmon, William. *A Handbook to Literature.* 9th ed. Upper Saddle River: Prentice, 2003. This is a useful and convenient reference guide to literary terminology.

Lindemann, Erika. "Freshman English: No Place for Literature." *CE* 55 (1993): 311–16.

Lynn, Stephen. "A Passage into Critical Theory." *CE* 52 (1990): 258–71. This is a brief guide for teachers to some schools of critical theory including new criticism, structuralism, deconstruction, psychological criticism, and feminist criticism. Lynn offers concrete examples of these critical approaches by applying each of them to the same passage.

MacDonald, Susan Peck, and Charles R. Cooper. "Contributions of Academic and Dialogue Journals to Writing about Literature." *Writing, Teaching, and Learning in the Disciplines.* Ed. Anne Herrington and Charles Moran. New York: MLA, 1992. 137–55.

Mossman, Mark. "Visible Disability in the College Classroom." *CE* 64.6 (July 2002): 645–59. Mossman argues for the importance of visible narratives of disability to transform the culture of the classroom; he contends that we need to include disability when we ask students to write autobiographical texts.

Schilb, John. *Between the Lines: Relating Composition Theory and Literary Theory.* Portsmouth: Boynton/Cook, 1996. Assessing differing definitions of rhetoric (irony to literary theory; persuasion to composition theory), Schilb traces the divergences in the fields at conferences and university departments since the 1960s. Looking alternatively to postmodernism, personal writing, and collaboration, Schilb identifies potential new trends and argues for theories tested by pedagogy.

Tate, Gary. "A Place for Literature in Freshman Composition." *CE* 55 (1993): 317–21.

USEFUL WEB SITE

The Voice of the Shuttle

http://vos.ucsb.edu

This site, created by Alan Liu, is a rich source of information on the humanities. The literature resources include cross links to world literature and minority literature and offer searches by subject and period. In addition, the site has an extensive literary theory page that is very useful for undergraduates.

62 Writing for the Social Sciences

Nothing has such power to broaden the mind as the ability to investigate systematically and truly all that comes under thy observation in life.
—MARCUS AURELIUS

In an article for *College English*, Peter Elbow compares his experiences as both a composition teacher and a teacher of literature. What characterizes composition for him is its focus on useful instruction:

> When I finally came to see myself as a composition person, I felt an enormous relief at finally feeling *useful*—as though I could make an actual difference for people. I'd never felt solidly useful trying to teach and write about literature. I'm proud that composition is the only discipline I know, outside of schools of education, where members feel their field has a built-in relationship to teaching and to students. (536)

The idea of writing instruction as inherently useful—related to purpose and student goals—is nowhere more appropriate than in composition classes, where we may need to teach students to write for the social sciences. Indeed, many students in our first-year classes go on to major in such fields as psychology, economics, anthropology, political science, and sociology. We can help prepare them for their future majors and careers through a focus on writing as a process of discovering knowledge in a particular field, for a particular audience. The same rhetorical foundations that students need to write a compelling public-policy analysis will help them craft a careful psychological study. At the same time, we can best serve our students by fostering their spirit of inquiry, showing them how to seek out the resources they need to pursue their own research interests, and leading them toward viewing writing as a critical means of communicating across all disciplines.

Additional examples of student writing in the social sciences are available on *The Everyday Writer*'s companion Web site, **bedfordstmartins.com/everydaywriter**. Go to **Student Writing** from the home page.

A sense of curiosity is nature's original school of education. —NORMAN VINCENT PEALE

TEACHING WITH TECHNOLOGY: Reading Texts in the Social Sciences (62a)

If your composition course includes social science readings, you may find it difficult to tell how comprehensively students can process the material. One solution, suggested by Joe Law in *Writing across the Curriculum*, is to design weekly quizzes for students to complete on a computer during class or through a course Web site. Law also has students log their reading, research, and field-observation notes through technological means so that he can respond quickly to each student's work.

FOR TEACHING: Writing Texts in the Social Sciences (62b)

One way for students to master material in the social sciences is through writing assignments that engage their critical and imaginative skills. In "Writing to Learn History," Donald Holsinger advocates using a variety of writing projects to engage students in the subject matter: course journals, simple writing exercises as preparation for in-class discussions, and detailed response papers that challenge students to write about specific statements and questions rather than vague topics. In addition, Holsinger suggests, giving students opportunities to write frequently and freely helps them become strong writers of texts in the social sciences. You might assign larger projects in developmental steps so that students work through the stages of writing. Have students revise and resubmit their work as if it were being submitted to a journal in the field. Finally, have students write to different audiences and from different perspectives.

Anthropology is the most humanistic of the sciences and the most scientific of the humanities. —ALFRED L. KROEBER

FOR COLLABORATION: Writing Texts in the Social Sciences (62b)

You might get students started on creative and engaging writing projects by asking them to examine various models of scholarly writing in the social sciences. Divide the class into groups of three, and send them to the library to find several journal articles from different publications in a particular field (psychology, anthropology, political science, sociology, economics, or education, for example). Ask each group to perform a rhetorical analysis of the writing in the articles, assessing it for disciplinary specific terminology, construction of knowledge (quantitative or qualitative), supporting evidence, and formal properties (organization, voice, and subsections). Then ask each group to compose a "mock" article to be published in one of the journals. Have them model their text on one of the examples and then write a brief reflection about what they have learned from this "pedagogy of models."

> **Anthropology provides a scientific basis for dealing with the crucial dilemma of the world today: how can peoples of different appearance . . . and dissimilar ways of life get along peaceably together?**
>
> —CLYDE KLUCKHOHN

FOR TEACHING: A Student's Brief Psychology Report (62c)

Your students may feel hesitant to express their own individuality in their writing for the social sciences. You might initiate a class discussion on what it means to write with an objective voice versus writing with the strategic use of ethos. Analyze Katie Paarlberg's psychology report in 62c of *The Everyday Writer* for its unique style. Ask students to write a short response to the report, commenting on the appropriateness of Katie's choices for her particular academic audience.

> **Education in our times must try to find whatever there is in students that might yearn for completion, and to reconstruct the learning that would enable them autonomously to seek that completion.**
>
> —ALLAN BLOOM

USEFUL READINGS

Abdalla, Adil E. A. "A Country Report Project for an International Economics Class." *Journal of Economic Education* 24.3 (Summer 1993): 231–36. In this semester-long, multipart writing project for an international economics class, each student wrote a report on a specific country, received instructor feedback and peer review, revised the report, and wrote a lengthy term paper, thereby using writing to comprehend economic theory, real-world phenomena, problems with data, and the research process.

Bazerman, Charles. "Codifying the Social Scientific Style: *The APA Publication Manual* as a Behaviorist Rhetoric." *The Rhetoric of the Human Sciences: Language and Argument in Scholarship and Public Affairs*. Ed.

John Nelson, Allan Megill, and Donald McClosky. Madison: Wisconsin UP, 1987. 125–44. Bazerman works within the discipline of psychology to give an interesting view of language and writing. He argues that the disciplines are socially negotiated territories and that conventions of disciplines are representations of actions produced through that discipline's process of inquiry—a process that is shaped and transformed by the contributions of those who work with and within the discipline.

Carlisle, Marcia. "Talking History." *OAH Magazine of History* 9 (Winter 1995): 57–59. Arguing that students put more effort into writing essays than into class participation, Carlisle advocates establishing a computer discussion about history in order to generate critical discussion about the readings.

CCC 36 (1985). This entire issue is devoted to the role of writing in the academic and professional disciplines. Of special interest is "Learning to Write in the Social Sciences" (140–49).

Davidson, Lawrence S., and Elisabeth C. Gumnior. "Writing to Learn in a Business Economics Class." *Journal of Economic Education* 24.3 (Summer 1993): 237–43. The authors argue that recursive writing assignments (in which students receive feedback and revise their drafts) make students more interactive, force them to spend more time on task, and give them a more accurate sense of economics as a discipline.

Elbow, Peter. "The Cultures of Literature and Composition: What Could Each Learn from the Other?" *CE* 64.5 (May 2002): 533–46. Des-cribing his career as both a literature and a composition professional, Elbow contrasts the fields, identifies his relief at teaching something "*useful*" in composition, and points out how both fields might learn from each other.

Hemmeter, Thomas, and David Connors. "Research Papers in Economics: A Collaborative Approach." *Journal of Advanced Composition* 7 (1987): 81–91. Hemmeter and Connors describe their collaboratively taught course combining writing instruction with an advanced-level economics course. The essay focuses especially on the writing of the "end-of-the-term research paper."

Herrington, Anne, and Charles Moran, eds. *Writing, Teaching, and Learning in the Disciplines.* New York: MLA, 1992. This collection contains fourteen essays covering historical and theoretical perspectives on writing across the curriculum as well as several treatments of classroom practice.

Holsinger, Donald C. "Writing to Learn History." *Social Studies Review* (Fall 1991): 59–64. Holsinger suggests several ways that professors can use writing to engage students in the subject of history, including in-class writing exercises, responses to course journals, process writing, and multiple-perspectives projects.

Johnson, William A., Jr., Richard P. Rettig, Gregory M. Scott, and Stephen M. Garrison. *The Sociology Student Writer's Manual.* 3rd ed. Upper Saddle River: Prentice, 2002.

Law, Joe. "Critical Thinking and Computer-Aided Instruction in Sociology 200." *Writing across the Curriculum* 8 (March 1998): 1+. Law suggests using computers to test student comprehension of readings in large, lecture-size class settings.

MacDonald, Susan Peck. *Professional Academic Writing in the Humanities and Social Sciences.* Carbondale: Southern Illinois UP, 1994. The author examines the ways disciplinary genres and forms shape knowledge-making.

Odell, Lee, Dixie Goswami, and Doris Quick. "Writing outside the English Composition Class: Implications for Teaching and for Learning." *Literacy for Life: The Demand for Reading and Writing.* Ed. Richard W. Bailey and Robin Melanie Fosheim. New York: MLA, 1983. 175–94. The authors assess the writing of both political science and economics majors as well as of legislative analysts; their conclusion that analysts more effectively address audience and context suggests that a pedagogy informed by such practical purposes will strengthen student writing.

Shamoon, Linda K., and Robert A. Schwegler. "Sociologists Reading Student Texts: Expectations and Perceptions." *Writing Instructor* 7 (Winter 1988). 71–81. This article examines the expectations and perceptions that instructors have of their students' writing. A group of sociology instructors are asked two questions: (1) To what extent are instructors' expectations and perceptions discipline specific? (2) What features of good expository writing do college instructors look for—thesis statements? topic sentences? paragraph coherence?

Sociology Writing Group. *A Guide to Writing Sociology Papers.* 5th ed. New York: Worth, 2001.

USEFUL WEB SITES

Exercising the Sociological Imagination

http://www.trinity.edu/mkearl

A dynamic Web site hosting links to exciting research topics, questions, and steps toward reading and writing in the social sciences.

Dartmouth Writing Program: Writing in the Social Sciences

http://www.dartmouth.edu/~writing/materials/student/soc_sciences/write.shtml

Dartmouth College's Writing Program site includes this step-by-step guide for undergraduates to writing social science papers.

63 Writing for the Natural and Applied Sciences

By looking at writing ecologically we understand better how important writing is—and just how hard it is to teach.
—MARILYN COOPER

Jacques Cousteau once wrote, "What is a scientist after all? It is a curious man looking through a keyhole, the keyhole of nature, trying to know what's going on." Many of the students in your writing classes will go on to pursue scientific majors and careers. But remember that curiosity—the spirit of inquiry that drives research—is crucial to successful writing for any purpose. Teaching students to recognize and cultivate their own spirit of inquiry will help make them more effective writers in your composition classes and in their future professions.

Additional examples of student writing in the natural and applied sciences are available on *The Everyday Writer*'s companion Web site, **bedfordstmartins.com/everydaywriter**. Go to **Student Writing**.

> The best scientist is open to experience and begins with romance—the idea that anything is possible.
> —RAY BRADBURY

TEACHING WITH TECHNOLOGY: Reading Texts in the Natural and Applied Sciences (63a)

The famous physicist Robert Millikan wrote that being a strong reader—having what he called the "habit of attention"—is crucial to academic success: "Cultivate the habit of attention and try to gain opportunities to hear wise men and women talk. Indifference and inattention are the two most dangerous monsters that you'll ever meet. Interest and attention will insure to you an education." To help familiarize students with the conventions of science writing, have them peruse online journals in several different scientific fields available through your library's database collection and conduct a detailed analysis of the differences between the way each field organizes information. How do journals for professionals in a given field present information? How does this differ from articles meant for a more general audience? You might also have students explore how different journals in one field of scientific study differ from one another. Ask students to write a brief report on their findings, using the questions on identifying arguments in 63a of *The Everyday Writer* as a guide.

FOR COLLABORATION: Writing Texts in the Natural and Applied Sciences (63b)

Have students work in peer-review groups on their literature reviews, research reports, and lab reports. You can get them started by modeling a peer review of Allyson Goldberg's lab report in *The Everyday Writer* (63c). Ask students to suggest textual revisions, alternatives in format and presentation, and an alternate introduction. As a class, make the changes collaboratively, using the board or an overhead projector. Be sure to emphasize to students the point made in this chapter—that most scientific writing is collaborative.

> **Facts are the air of scientists. Without them you can never fly.** —Linus Pauling

USEFUL READINGS

CCC 36 (1985). This entire issue is devoted to the role of writing in the academic and professional disciplines. Of special interest is "A Freshman Writing Course in Parallel with a Science Course" (160–65).

Dobrin, Sidney I., and Christian R. Weisser. "Breaking Ground in Ecocomposition: Exploring Relationships between Discourse and Environment." *CE* 64.5 (May 2002): 566–89. In a foundational article on the mutual relationship between ecology and composition, the authors argue for place and environment as critical categories in academic inquiry and for the importance of ecological approaches to composition.

Haas, Christina. "Learning to Read Biology." *Written Communication* 11 (1994): 43–84. This case study follows the development of one student's changing perceptions of literacy, focusing on her own reading and writing as well as her views about those activities, her representations of the nature of texts, and her understanding of the relationship between knowledge and written discourse within her disciplinary field.

Manual for Design Report Writing in Engineering. Sponsored by Michigan Technological University, National Science Foundation, and Whirlpool Foundation, 1991. This manual, written in collaboration with several senior engineering students and tested in engineering design courses for ten years, gives concise and useful guidelines for advanced engineering students, from conceptualizing an audience to ethics and politics in writing design reports.

McMillan, Victoria E. *Writing Papers in the Biological Sciences*. 3rd ed. Boston: Bedford, 2001.

Michaelson, Herbert B. *How to Write and Publish Engineering Papers and Reports*. 3rd ed. Phoenix: Oryx, 1990. In clear language, this book outlines several proven methods and techniques for preparing, writing, and submitting technical papers for school, business, or publication.

Powell, Alfred. "A Chemist's View of Writing, Reading, and Thinking across the Curriculum." *CCC* 36 (1985): 414–18. Powell, a chemistry professor, outlines numerous discipline-based writing and reading projects that he assigns in a two-semester course sequence in organic chemistry.

Ross, Carolyn. *Writing Nature: An Ecological Reader for Writers*. Boston: Bedford, 1995.

Weisser, Christian R. "Ecocomposition and the Greening of Identity." *Ecocomposition: Theoretical and Pedagogical Approaches*. Ed. Christian R. Weisser and Sidney I. Dobrin. Albany: SUNY P, 2001. 81–95. An examination of how social constructionist approaches to composition have changed our conception of identity by emphasizing the wide range of external influences and social conventions that shape human experience.

Weisser, Christian R., and Sidney I. Dobrin, eds. *Ecocomposition: Theoretical and Pedagogical Approaches*. Albany: SUNY P, 2001. This groundbreaking collection of essays brings together scientific approaches to ecology and composition theorists.

Winsor, Dorothy A. "Engineering Writing/Writing Engineering." *CCC* 41 (1990): 58–69. A useful general article on how engineers think and write differently about engineering, this article employs a case study to suggest similarities and differences in how engineers construct knowledge through language.

Writing for Business

64

Learning is about more than simply acquiring new knowledge and insights; it is also crucial to unlearn old knowledge that has outlived its relevance. Thus, forgetting is probably at least as important as learning. —GARY RYAN BLAIR

All professional activities require strong and persuasive writing as well as adherence to the formal conventions of a particular audience. Companies and business organizations look for solid, well-written, and carefully constructed cover letters and résumés that attend to the rhetorical situation. Grants and business proposals can be highly successful if attention is given to the writing process for each of these important genres. As writing teachers, we often find that our students need advice and instruction in writing for business situations. You can help them develop their business-writing strategies by leading them through the sections in *The Everyday Writer* on becoming strong readers and writers of texts in business.

Additional examples of business writing are available on *The Everyday Writer*'s companion Web site, **bedfordstmartins.com/everydaywriter**. Go to **Student Writing**.

FOR TEACHING: Reading Texts for Business (64a)

In a study of strong business writing, Lee Odell and Dixie Goswami examined writing done by administrators and caseworkers. By interviewing the study participants and analyzing the writing samples they collected, the authors found that while workers in different positions write differently and justify their writing choices differently, all writers are sensitive to rhetorical context. Their writing varied according to its type, audience, and subject. Nevertheless, what the study participants termed "acceptable writing" remained constant across different positions.

Conduct a version of this study with your class. Ask students to bring in articles from business magazines, memos and reports from print and online sources, and other examples of business writing. During a class discussion about the rhetorical context for each piece of writing, compile a list on the board of the shared qualities of "acceptable writing" among the different types of business writing.

FOR COLLABORATION: Writing Texts for Business (64b)

Keeping Odell and Goswami's findings in mind, as well as the class-generated list detailing the qualities of "acceptable writing," ask students to compose their own collaborative piece of writing in emulation of one of the models they selected in the preceding activity. Have each group take on a different type of writing—memos, email messages, letters, or résumés. Make sure that they consult the At a Glance guidelines for writing effective memos and effective letters in 64b of *The Everyday Writer.* Then discuss the similarities and differences among the various texts and how the qualities of each text are determined by its rhetorical situation.

FOR COLLABORATION: Writing Business Memos (64b)

Ask students to work in groups of three or four to write a memo about the course—the activities, the instructor's expectations, and the like—for students who will be enrolled in the course next term. Then, to encourage students' consideration of audience, have them write different versions of the memo to friends, teachers, and so on. This activity will provide practice in a genre that is unfamiliar to many students.

TEACHING WITH TECHNOLOGY: Writing Résumés (64b)

Because employers spend so little time reading résumés, the format, the design, and just plain good writing are especially critical. For this exercise, ask students to bring in drafts of their résumés. Have them work in groups of two or three to review each résumé and offer suggestions based on the guidelines in 64b of *The Everyday Writer.* In addition, you may want students to review the principles of document design in Chapter 4. If you are teaching in a technology-enhanced classroom, have students work with electronic versions of their résumés, revising the documents to incorporate the peer-review suggestions. Project examples on a screen, and discuss with the class the difference that small changes can make, paying particular attention to audience.

FOR MULTILINGUAL WRITERS: Special Considerations in Business Writing (64c)

Cultural norms often determine the kinds of memos, email messages, and reports that are most appropriate for a given audience. Ask your students to share a copy of an email from someone in their home country conducting a business transaction.

> **Success or failure in business is caused more by the mental attitude even than by mental capacities.**
> —Sir Walter Scott

FOR COLLABORATION: Writing for Business

Have students work in groups of two or three to analyze the Abbott and Abernathy memo, using the Guidelines for Writing Effective Memos in 64b of *The Everyday Writer* and other advice in Chapter 64. Students should note the memo's strengths and weaknesses, jot down any topics they think the memo overlooks, and mark any spots where they think information can be deleted. The groups should be prepared to explain their choices. Review the results of their analyses in a class discussion.

USEFUL READINGS

Barbour, Dennis. "Collaborative Writing in the Business Writing Classroom: An Ethical Dilemma for the Teacher." *Bulletin of the Association for Business Communication* (Sept. 1990): 33–35. Barbour examines the difficulties inherent in grading collaborative writing in business communications courses.

Caudron, Shari. "Virtual Manners." *Workforce* 79.2 (Feb. 2000): 31–34. This is a discussion of email etiquette for business situations.

Davis, Ken. "Managing Your Writing." *College Accounting*. Ed. James Heintz and Robert W. Parry Jr. Mason: South-Western, 1993. 10–11. Davis describes a twelve-step process to optimize the writer's time.

Laufer, Doug, and Rick Crosser. "The 'Writing-across-the-Curriculum' Concept in Accounting and Tax Courses." *Journal of Education for Business* (Nov./Dec. 1990): 83–87. This piece includes sample writing assignments and instruction for an accounting course.

Law, Joe. "Learning to Write with E-mail in Money and Banking." *Writing across the Curriculum* 7 (Jan. 1998): 1+. The article offers practical advice for using electronic discussion lists in courses on money and banking.

Locker, Kitty O. *Business and Administration Communication*. 6th ed. Boston: Irwin, 2003. Locker writes knowledgeably about oral and written communication, technology in the workplace, workplace ethics, organizational culture, and international and intercultural business communication.

Nelson, Sandra J., and Douglas C. Smith. "Maximizing Cohesion and Minimizing Conflict in Collaborative Writing Groups." *Bulletin of the Association for Business Communication* (June 1990): 59–62. Peer-review and collaborative writing strategies for business communication classes are included in this discussion.

Odell, Lee, and Dixie Goswami. "Writing in a Non-Academic Setting." *Research in the Teaching of English* 16.3 (Oct. 1982): 201–23. Odell and Goswami examine writing standards across diverse business conditions.

Peek, Lucia E., and George S. Peek. "Using Practitioner Articles to Develop Computer, Writing, and Critical Thinking Skills: Examples from the Accounting Curriculum." *Bulletin of the Association for Business Communication* 53.4 (Dec. 1990): 17–19. The authors call for writing assignments in accounting classes that focus on the analysis and production of computer spreadsheets.

Tebeaux, Elizabeth. "Redesigning Professional Writing Courses to Meet the Needs of Writers in Business and Industry." *CCC* 36 (Dec. 1985): 419–28. Tebeaux describes the distinctions among technical, business, and science writing; she recommends changes in business writing courses to make a better match between the writing taught and the actual writing used on the job.

USEFUL WEB SITES

Purdue University's Online Writing Lab (OWL)

http://owl.english.purdue.edu

Purdue hosts a range of model documents for writing email messages, résumés, and job application letters.

Stanford University's Program in Writing and Rhetoric (PWR)

http://www.stanford.edu/group/pwr/students/wr_resources/studrcl.html

Stanford's PWR pages provide numerous links with annotations for students in composition classes.

Answers to Exercises in *The Everyday Writer with Exercises*

Here are answers to all exercises that have specific answers. Exercises for which answers will vary are not covered here.

EXERCISE 8.9: Suggested Answers

I must make, I must confess, I have been, I have almost; first; confessions/confess; white moderate, White Citizen's Councilor, white moderate; who is more devoted, who prefers, who constantly says, who paternalistically believes, who lives, who constantly advises; to "order" than to justice, a negative peace which is the absence of tension to a positive peace which is the presence of justice; I agree with you, but I cannot agree with; timetable, mythical concept of time, "more convenient season"; Shallow understanding from people of good will, absolute misunderstanding from people of ill will; Lukewarm acceptance, outright rejection.

EXERCISE 13.1: Suggested Answers

1. Arguable
2. Arguable, depending on the acceptance of scientific data
3. Arguable
4. Not arguable
5. Arguable
6. Not arguable, unless students want to discuss boiling temperatures at different air pressures
7. Arguable
8. Arguable, depending on the acceptance of statistical reports
9. Arguable
10. Arguable, although some studies continue to show correlations between reduced speed and lower accident rates. More readily verifiable is the correlation between speed limit and mortality rate.

EXERCISE 13.3: Suggested Answers

1. The Palestinian-Israeli conflict can be managed but not solved. *Thesis*: The U.S. government should not attempt to solve the Palestinian-Israeli conflict because (1) it is essentially religious, not political; (2) neither side has a tradition of compromise; and (3) both sides will accept nothing less than possession of the same territories.
2. Prison inmates retain basic human rights, including the right not to be tested for HIV. *Thesis*: Mandatory testing of prisoners for HIV is wrong because it would infringe on their basic right to privacy.
3. Raising the minimum wage is a socially responsible way of combating poverty. *Thesis*: It's in everyone's interest to ensure that companies pay employees enough to keep employees from having to rely on taxpayer-funded welfare programs like Medicaid and Medicare.
4. The reinstatement of the U.S. military draft would force every citizen to consider whether a war would be worth his or her life, or the life of a family member. *Thesis*: Reinstating the draft would help bring the reality of war home to the United States as it would force everyone, before they agreed to let the country go to war, to consider whether they themselves would be willing to fight.

5. Music downloading is a convenient, seemingly victimless kind of petty crime. *Thesis*: Because theft should not be tolerated, even on a small scale, colleges should uniformly forbid music downloading.

EXERCISE 13.5: Suggested Answers

1. Whatever promotes the best interests of all concerned and violates no one's rights is morally acceptable.
2. Women should not be exposed to a higher risk of death.
3. Only those who can talk can feel pain.

EXERCISE 13.7: Suggested Answers

1. Concern over basic human rights if banned; concern about impacted social life; relief that pressure to drink would be lessened; concern that drinking would merely go underground and possibly become more dangerous; anger that a "right" has been restricted; resentment at being forbidden from doing something pleasurable.
2. Fear of terrorist hijackings; concern over possible invasion of privacy; anger over failure of past security measures.
3. Relief at the lessening of danger; residual anger that land mines were there to begin with; concern that some land mines might be missed; relaxation about being able to travel freely again.
4. Fear of being threatened in a place considered safe; outrage that a peaceful, civilian place would be targeted.
5. Concern for the health of student-athletes; disbelief that coaches and administrators would want to win at all costs; anger that their insistence on perfection would cause athletes to turn to drugs to stimulate performance, to relieve stress, and to relax.

EXERCISE 17.3: Answers

1. Unacceptable; misstates the writer's intent
2. Acceptable
3. Unacceptable; wording is too similar to original
4. Unacceptable; wording is too similar to original
5. Unacceptable; incomplete citation (missing page number)

EXERCISE 20.1: Suggested Answers

When you suggest something that doesn't appeal to them, they feel they must assert themselves. Their nature tells them to. They just say No in words or actions, even about things that they like to do. The psychologists call it "negativism"; many parents call it "that terrible No stage." But stop and think what would happen to children who never felt like saying No. They'd become robots. You wouldn't be able to resist the temptation to boss them all the time, and they'd stop learning and developing. When they were old enough to go out into the world, to school and later to work, everybody else would take advantage of them, too. They'd never be good for anything.

–BENJAMIN SPOCK,
Baby and Child Care (1968)

EXERCISE 22.2: Suggested Answers

1. Desdemona's attitude is that of a submissive victim; she simply lies down and dies, accepting her death as inevitable.
2. Some people feel that "The Star-Spangled Banner," which is primarily about war, should be replaced as our national anthem with "America the Beautiful."
3. The discovery of the artifacts in King Tut's tomb was one of the most important archeological events of the twentieth century.
4. The angrier she became over his actions, the more he rebelled and continued doing what he pleased.
5. My family lived in Trinidad for the first ten years of my life, and we experienced many hardships, but when we came to America, we thought our prospects were good.

EXERCISE 22.3: Answers

1. attentively
2. emphasize
3. conscientious
4. frugal

EXERCISE 22.4: Suggested Answers

1. *tragic:* distressing, alarming, disturbing; *consumes:* defeats, feeds on, erodes; *displays:* champions, thrives on, builds up, promotes; *drama:* excitement, tension, vitality
2. *girl:* young lady, miss
3. *abide:* tolerate; *turns:* changes; *vital:* alive; *hold still:* contain their energy

EXERCISE 22.5: Suggested Answers

1. The entryway of the building looked like a garbage dump: paper was littered about, all kinds of bottles lay shattered, and rotting cantaloupe and chicken parts gave off an unbearable odor.
2. The cheerful early morning sounds of birds outside my window make it easier to get up.
3. The feast at Mom's on Sunday was delicious as usual: roast chicken, garlic and sage stuffing, sweet garden peas, gravy, and half a fresh-baked apple pie each.
4. The valet stepped toward my Porsche with excitement in her eyes.
5. My alarm clock clamored insistently until I mustered up the strength to get out of bed and turn it off.

EXERCISE 22.9: Answers

1. rhetoric: from ME *rethorike* < L *rhetorica* < Gr *rhetor*, orator < *eirein*, to speak
2. student: from ME < L *studere*, to study
3. tobacco: Sp *tabaco* probably from *Taino*, roll of tobacco leaves
4. crib: ME, from OE *cribb*: akin to OHG *krippa* manger, and perh. to Gr *griphos* reed basket
5. cinema: from Fr *cinématographe* < Gr *kinema*, motion + *graphein*, to write
6. okra: a word of West African origin

EXERCISE 22.10: Answers

If *you're* looking for summer fun, *accept* the friendly *advice* of thousands of happy adventurers: spend three *weeks* kayaking *through* the inside passage *to* Alaska. For ten years, Outings, Inc., has *led* groups of novice kayakers *past* some of the most breathtaking scenery in North America. The group's goal is simple: to give participants the time of *their* lives and show them things they don't see *every day*. As one of last year's adventurers said, "*It's* a trip that is *already* one of my favorite memories. It *affected* me powerfully."

EXERCISE 24.1: Suggested Answers

The bull-riding arena was fairly crowded, but this made no impression on me. I had made a decision: it was now time to prove myself, even though I was scared. I walked to the entry window and laid my money on the counter. The clerk held up a Stetson hat filled with slips of paper. I reached in and picked one, a slip that held the number of the bull I was to ride. Ready, I headed toward the stock corral.

EXERCISE 24.2: Suggested Answers

1. The *Hindenburg*, a gigantic airship, was destroyed in an explosion.
2. Ancient Greeks relied on Athena, the goddess of wisdom, to protect the city of Athens, which was named in her honor.
3. When Stephen King stole traffic cones in 1970, he was arrested and fined one hundred dollars.
4. Flappers, who broke with 1920s social conventions by cutting their hair short and smoking in public, seemed rebellious to their parents' generation.
5. In the mid-seventies, skateboarding originated in Venice, California, where, because of a drought, the swimming pools were empty.

EXERCISE 24.3: Suggested Answers

1. The president persuaded his staff, Congress, and the American people.

2. If meteorologists are correct in their predictions, we can expect a decade of record-breaking tropical storms and hurricanes.
3. From the sightseeing boat, we saw a whale dive toward the photographer, lift itself out of the water, and crash its tail on the waves.
4. The presence of the Indian in these movies always conjures up destructive stereotypes of drunkenness, horse theft, and scalping.
5. Victorian women were warned that smoking would cause them to grow a moustache, contract tuberculosis, become sterile, or die young.

EXERCISE 25.1: Suggested Answers

1. My dream in life, to enjoy my job, has kept me in school and working hard.
   I have stayed in school and worked hard in order to achieve my life's dream of enjoying my job.
2. Many people would suffer if air pollution standards were relaxed.
   The reason air-pollution standards should not be relaxed is that many people might suffer if they were.
3. By not prosecuting white-collar crime as vigorously as we prosecute violent crime, we encourage white-collar criminals to ignore the law.
   We must prosecute white-collar crime as vigorously as violent crime unless we want to encourage white-collar criminals to ignore the law.
4. Irony occurs when you expect one thing and get something else.
   The experience of expecting one thing and getting another is irony.
5. I ate the best meal of my life, bread and cheese from a farmers' market, while sitting by a river.
   By the side of a river, I ate the best meal of my life, which consisted of bread and cheese from a farmers' market.

EXERCISE 25.2: Suggested Answers

1. Convection ovens cook more quickly and with less power than traditional ovens.
2. Argentina and Peru were colonized by Spain, while Brazil was colonized by Portugal.
3. She argued that children are even more important for men than they are for women.
4. Were the traffic jams in Texas any worse than those in other states?
5. The equipment in our new warehouse is guaranteed to last longer than the machines in our current facility.

EXERCISE 26.1: Suggested Answers

1. Before buying a used car, you should note the mileage, take it for a test drive, and get it checked by a mechanic.
2. My favorite pastimes include reading, exercising, and talking with friends.
3. Working in a restaurant taught me not only the importance of service but also the art of small talk.
4. We must either walk quickly or drive slowly.
5. Graduates find that the job market shrinks, narrows, and tightens.

EXERCISE 26.2: Suggested Answers

1. I remember watching it the first time, realizing I'd never seen anything like it, and immediately vowing never to miss an episode of *The Daily Show*.
2. A crowd stood outside the school and watched as the graduates paraded by.
3. An effective Web site is well designed, provides useful information, and gives links to other relevant sites.
4. It is impossible to watch *The Simpsons* and not to see a little of yourself in one of the characters.
5. TV networks now face the question of either coming up with new situations or acknowledging the death of the sitcom.

EXERCISE 26.3: THINKING CRITICALLY: Suggested Answers

The richness of the scene was in *its plainness, its natural condition—of horse, of ring, of girl,* even to the girl's bare feet that gripped the bare back of her proud and ridiculous mount. The enchantment grew not *out of anything that happened or was performed* but *out of something that seemed to go round and around and around with the girl,* attending her, a steady gleam in the shape of a circle—a ring *of ambition, of happiness, of youth.* (And the positive pleasures of equilibrium under difficulties.) In a week or two, *all would be changed, all (or almost all) lost; the girl would wear makeup, the horse would wear gold, the ring would be painted, the bark would be clean for the feet of the horse, the girl's feet would be clean for the slippers that she'd wear.* All, all would be lost.

EXERCISE 27.1: Suggested Answers

1. The greed of the 1980s gave way to the occupational insecurity of the 1990s, which in turn gave way to reinforced family ties in the early 2000s.
2. The building inspector suggested that we apply for a construction permit and that we check with his office again when the plans are complete.
3. She studied the package, wondered what it could be, and tore off the wrapping.
4. Suddenly, we heard an explosion of wings off to our right, and we could see a hundred or more ducks lifting off from the water.
5. In my previous job, I sold the most advertising spots and earned a sales excellence award.
6. A cloud of snow powder rose as skis and poles flew in every direction.
7. The flight attendant told us to turn off all electronic devices but mentioned that we could use them again after takeoff.
8. When workers with computer skills were in great demand, a programmer could almost name his or her salary.
9. When in Florence, be sure to see the city's famed cathedral as well as Michelangelo's statue *David*.
10. The aroma, which wafts through the house, lures the adults from their beds.

EXERCISE 27.2: THINKING CRITICALLY: Suggested Answers

third-person singular (*It has been . . .*) → first-person plural (*our time . . .*) → third-person singular (*There is no delusion . . .*) → second-person singular (*your head . . .*) → third-person singular (*The human mind . . .*) → first-person plural (*and we are obliged . . .*) → third-person singular (*It is all very well . . .*) → second-person singular (*your awareness . . .*)

(Note the shift in mood from the indicative to the imperative in the next-to-last sentence.)

EXERCISE 28.1: Suggested Answers

As humans domesticated dogs over many thousands of years, the canine species evolved into hundreds of breeds designed to perform specific tasks such as pulling sleds and guarding sheep. Over time, as human civilization grew, the need for many breeds decreased. For example, as humans evolved from hunter-gatherers into farmers, they no longer needed hunting dogs. Later, as farming societies became industrialized, people's need for shepherds diminished. But by this time humans had grown accustomed to dogs' companionship, and breeding continued. Today, most owners keep dogs simply as companions, but some dogs still do the work they were intentionally bred for, such as following a scent, guarding a home, or leading the blind.

EXERCISE 29.1: Suggested Answers

Before planting a tree, a gardener needs to choose a good location—one with the right kind of soil, sufficient drainage, and enough light for the type of tree chosen. Then he or she must be sure to dig a deep enough hole. It should be deeper than the root-ball and about twice as wide. The gardener must unwrap the root-ball since the burlap, which is biodegradable, may be treated with chemicals that will eventually damage the roots if it is not removed. The roots may have grown into a compact ball if the tree has been in a pot for some time; they should be separated or cut apart. The gardener should set the root-ball into the hole and then begin to fill the hole with loose dirt. After filling the hole completely, he or she should make sure to water the tree thoroughly, since new plantings require extra water and extra care. After about three years they become well rooted.

EXERCISE 30.1: Answers

1. My foot got tangled in the computer cord.
2. Her first afternoon as a kindergarten teacher had left her exhausted.
3. The Croatian news media is almost entirely owned by the state.
4. Our office manager, a stern taskmaster with a fondness for Chanel suits, has been terrifying interns since 1992.
5. Making bread on a dreary winter day always cheers me up.

EXERCISE 30.2: Answers

1. will ask
2. had been leaking
3. agree; does need
4. should drink
5. would be

EXERCISE 30.3: Answers

Nouns are set in italics; articles are set in boldface.

1. *Halloween*; **the**; *children*; *candy*
2. *June*; **the**; *month*; *flooding*; **the**; *spring*
3. *Manuel*; **an**; *gardener*; **a**; *garden*; *tomatoes*; *lettuce*; *sweet corn*
4. **A**; *frost*; **the**; *ground*; **a**; *field*; *ice*
5. **the**; *row*; *people*; **a**; *man*; *hair*; **a**; *woman*; *jeans*

EXERCISE 30.4: Answers

Pronouns are set in italics; antecedents are set in boldface.

1. *He*; **volunteers**; *themselves*
2. **Kiah**; *one who*; *she*
3. *Who*; **jeans**; *them*; **designer**; *himself*; *them*
4. ***They***; *themselves*
5. **Those people**; *who*; *they*; *anyone*

EXERCISE 30.5: Answers

Adjectives are set in italics; adverbs are set in boldface.

1. *An empty*; *subject*; *a* **somewhat** *familiar*; *sender's*; *the* **seemingly** *innocent*
2. **Nevertheless**; *her teenage*; **eventually**; *his*; *poor study*
3. **generally**; *quiet*; *loud*; *grunting*; *mating*
4. *The huge red*; *lovely*; **disappointingly**
5. *The youngest*; *the*; *a brilliant*

EXERCISE 30.6: Answers

1. of; from; until
2. through; across; into
3. Instead of; among
4. After; on; for
5. about; from; in

EXERCISE 30.7: Answers

1. after; and; both . . . and; so
2. not only . . . but also
3. because; and; however
4. Although; and; as if
5. because; but; still

EXERCISE 30.8: Answers

Complete subjects are set in italics; simple subjects are set in boldface.

1. *That* **container** *of fried rice*
2. *the new tour* **guide**
3. *my favorite* **car**
4. *Japanese* **animation**, *with its cutting-edge graphics and futuristic plots*

5. *Some* **women** *worried about osteoporosis*

EXERCISE 30.9: Answers

Predicates are set in italics.

1. *is proud of his heritage*: LV—is; SC—proud
2. *made me angry:* TV—made; DO—me; OC—angry
3. *seems likely in this case:* LV—seems; SC—likely
4. *will never die:* IV—will . . . die
5. *promise consumers the world:* TV—promise; IO—consumers; DO—world

EXERCISE 30.10: Answers

1. APP—the motel clerk; VERBAL (INF)—to be certified as a river guide; PREP—as a river guide
2. VERBAL (PART)—made of granite; PREP—of granite
3. ABSO—my stomach doing flips; VERBAL (PART)—doing flips
4. VERBAL (PART)—floating on my back; PREP—on my back
5. VERBAL (GER)—learning to drive a car with a manual transmission; VERBAL (INF)—to drive a car with a manual transmission; PREP—with a manual transmission

EXERCISE 30.11: Answers

1. IND—The hockey game was postponed; DEP—because one of the players collapsed on the bench
2. IND—She immediately recognized the officer; DEP—who walked into the coffee shop; REL—who
3. DEP—After completing three advanced drawing classes; SUB CONJ—after; IND—Jason was admitted into the fine arts program; IND—and he immediately rented a small studio space
4. IND—The trip was longer; DEP—than I had remembered; REL—than
5. IND—I could see that he was very tired; REL—that; IND—I had to ask him a few questions

EXERCISE 30.12: Suggested Answers

1. News of the virus, which seemed to be on every news show and in every paper, was beginning to frighten the public.
2. After hearing of an insurgent attack near her husband's base station, Simone waited nervously by the phone.
3. The new computer, which was still a mystery to its user, made a strange noise.
4. Rob, who frequently left his wallet at home, always borrowed money from his friends.
5. When the police shut down the outdoor concert, the crowd grew louder and more disorderly.

EXERCISE 30.13: Answers

1. complex, declarative
2. compound, interrogative
3. simple, declarative
4. simple, imperative
5. compound-complex, declarative

EXERCISE 31.1: Answers

1. let, came, torn
2. made, found
3. began
4. planted, gone
5. knew, ignored
6. woke, flown
7. sprang, swam
8. assumed, found
9. passed, fallen
10. decided, been

EXERCISE 31.2: Answers

1. lies
2. laid
3. set
4. sitting
5. rise

EXERCISE 31.3: Answers

1. *shows/has shown*—present action; may be seen as having started in the past and still ongoing

2. *have feared/have been fearing*—action begun in past continues
3. *emigrated*—completed action
4. *has been/was*—started in the past and still ongoing; if action is completed, then simple past tense may be used
5. *will direct/will be directing*—future (continuing) action
6. *ate/were eating*—past action, completed
7. *will have received*—future action completed by a certain time
8. *will have watched*—future action completed by a certain time
9. *expresses*—literary work
10. *last*—general truth

EXERCISE 31.4: Answers

1. When she *saw Chicago*, it *made* her want to become an actress even more.
2. *Having left* England in December, the settlers *arrived* in Virginia in May.
3. I *had hoped* to finish reading the book before today.
4. *Having worked* with great dedication as a summer intern at the magazine, Mohan called his former supervisor in the fall to ask about a permanent position.
5. When we walked home from school, we often *stopped* for ice cream.

EXERCISE 31.5: Answers

1. The lifeguard *informed* the surfers of a shark sighting.
2. A superhero with amazing crime-fighting powers *was drawn* by the comic-book artist.
3. For months, the mother kangaroo *protects* her baby, *feeds it*, and *teaches it* to survive.
4. The first snow of winter *covered* the lawns and rooftops.
5. The board members *chose* a new advertising company.

EXERCISE 31.6: Answers

1. was → were
2. was → were
3. (correct)
4. was → were
5. remains → remain

EXERCISE 32.1: Answers

1. deserve
2. races
3. appears
4. supplies
5. stops
6. was
7. comes
8. contributes
9. cause
10. leaves

EXERCISE 32.2: Answers

1. (correct; *rhythm and blues* is considered a single unit)
2. are → is; *Green Eggs and Ham* is singular, a title
3. is → are; the subject, *stations*, is plural
4. (correct; *Most* refers to *students*)
5. are → is; the subject, *Each*, is singular
6. were → was; “neither/nor”
7. make → makes; the subject, *jury*, is treated as singular
8. (correct; *who* refers to *one*)
9. was (second verb) → were; *that* refers to *countries*
10. involve → involves; the subject, *Economics*, is treated as singular

EXERCISE 32.3: THINKING CRITICALLY: Suggested Answers

none of these assumptions about marriage *add up*; plural, *none* refers to *assumptions*

Between the public statistic and the private reality *lies* a sea of contradictions; singular subject is *sea*

Marriage *seems* to me; *Marriage* is singular

the divorce rate—with or without new babies in the house—*remains* constant; *divorce rate* is singular

The fabric of men-and-women-as-they-once-were *is* so thick; *fabric* is singular

no amount of patching *can weave* that cloth together; *amount* is singular but even stronger *is* the growing perception; singular, subject is *perception*

that only people who *are* real to themselves; plural, *who* refers to *people*

that only people who are real to themselves *can connect*; *people* is plural

Two shall be as one *is* over; singular, *Two shall be as one* is an expression that forms a singular subject

no matter how lonely we get; *we* is plural

EXERCISE 33.1: Answers

1. Who (subjective)
2. Whomever (direct object of *recommends*)
3. whoever (subject of the clause)
4. whom (object of preposition *with*)
5. Who (subjective)

EXERCISE 33.2: Answers

1. she
2. them
3. me
4. their
5. we

EXERCISE 33.3 Suggested Answers

1. With tuition on the rise, students have to save money wherever they can.
2. Congress usually resists presidential attempts to encroach on what it considers congressional authority.
3. Marco and Ellen were each given a chance to voice an opinion.
4. Although firefighters spend most of their days reading and watching television, they are ready to answer an urgent call at a moment's notice.
5. Every dog and cat has its own personality.

EXERCISE 33.4: Suggested Answers

1. All scholarship applicants must fill out a financial aid form, meet with the dean, and write a letter to the committee members. The deadline is October 24, so applicants should start the process as soon as possible.
2. Patients on medication may relate better to their therapists and be more responsive to them; these patients may also be less vulnerable to what disturbs them.
3. Before Sasha flew to Brazil, she hurried to call her sister.
   Sasha hurried to call her sister before her sister flew to Brazil.
4. Texans often hear about the influence of big oil corporations.
5. Many employees resented smoking, so the company policy prohibited it.
   The company prohibited smoking, a policy that many employees resented.

EXERCISE 33.5: Suggested Answers

In the summer of 2005, the NCAA banned the use of mascots that could be considered offensive to Native Americans at any NCAA-sponsored championship games. Native Americans have been vocally criticizing the use of negative stereotypes in college sports since the 1970s. In order to understand why Native Americans feel this issue is important, consider that, for years, movies and television programs portrayed Native Americans as savage warriors who were feared and misunderstood. That stereotypical image of Native Americans is what some schools have chosen to use as their mascot, a role typically played by wild animals or fictional beasts. Derogatory terms for other ethnic groups are never used for school mascots, but Native Americans continue to suffer from this form of racism. In its new ruling, however, the NCAA asks schools to listen to the minority point of view and eliminate mascots that may be hurtful or offensive to America's Indian population.

EXERCISE 33.6: THINKING CRITICALLY: Answers

Answers are in italics.

Sexual attraction has entered the Harry Potter universe. Harry (Daniel Radcliffe) is now 14, and *Harry is* one of four contestants competing in the dangerous

Tri-Wizard Tournament. The first event requires *Harry* to capture a golden egg. *The golden egg is* guarded by a ferocious Hungarian flying dragon. Terrifying as *the first event* is, *the first event* pales in comparison with having to ask the beguiling Cho Chang (Katie Leung) to Hogwarts's Yule Ball. Now, *asking Cho Chang to the ball* takes courage . . . The uncontestable triumph of "Goblet of Fire," however, is Brendan Gleeson's Alastor (Mad-Eye) Moody, the grizzled new Defense Against the Dark Arts professor. With a face like cracked pottery and a manner both menacing and mentoring, *Alastor* becomes Harry's protector as *Harry* faces life-threatening tests. Gleeson, one of the screen's greatest character actors, steals every scene *Gleeson's* in—no small feat when *an actor is* up against Maggie Smith and Alan Rickman.

EXERCISE 34.1: Answers

1. nearly → impossible
2. violently and immaturely → behaving
3. bad → Nora
4. really _ hot and humid; frequently → below zero
5. loudly → talked
6. badly → bleeding
7. well → performed
8. terrific → Arjun
9. good → stew
10. accurately → measured

EXERCISE 34.2: Answers

1. Alicia speaks both Russian and German, but she speaks Russian better.
2. People in Rome are friendlier [or *more friendly*] to children than people in Paris are.
3. The crown is set with some of the most precious gemstones in the world.
4. Women tend to live longer than men; hence, more of the elderly are women.
5. Minneapolis is the larger of the Twin Cities.
6. She came up with a perfect plan for revenge.
7. We think you will be pleased with our unique design proposal.
8. The student cafeteria is operated by a college food service, which is part of a chain.
9. It is safer to jog in daylight than in the dark.
10. Evan argued that subtitled films are more boring to watch than films dubbed in English.

EXERCISE 34.3: THINKING CRITICALLY: Answers

Adjectives are set in italics; adverbs are set in boldface.

back, **wonderfully**, *refreshed*, *glad-hearted*, *ravenous*, **soon**, *blazing*, **up**, **again**, *clear*, *cold*, **close by**, *broad*, *oak*, *hickory*, *sweetened*, *such*, *wildwood*, *good*, **enough**

EXERCISE 35.1: Suggested Answers

1. Relating her stories in a deadpan voice, the comedian had the audience doubled over with laughter.
2. News reports that emphasize random crime or rare diseases can increase a listener's irrational fears.
3. Legal documents and court records can reveal the habits of ordinary people in the Middle Ages.
4. Civilians learn about the conflict from the firsthand accounts of journalists who risk their lives in war zones abroad.
5. With our new digital camera, we recorded a wolf pack at play near where we were camping last summer.
6. Doctors recommend a new, painless test for cancer.
7. Every afternoon I find my windshield covered with flyers for free pizza.
8. Before I decided to buy the stock, I knew the investment would pay off dramatically.
9. To the homeowners, the bank offered flood insurance underwritten by the federal government.
10. The maintenance worker shut down the turbine that was revolving out of control.

EXERCISE 35.2: Suggested Answers

1. The candidate quickly promised to reduce class size.
   The candidate promised to reduce class size quickly.
2. The soldier was apparently injured by friendly fire.
   The soldier was injured, apparently by friendly fire.
3. The collector who originally owned the painting planned to leave it to a museum.
   The collector who owned the painting originally planned to leave it to a museum.
4. Doctors can now restore limbs that have been partially severed to functioning condition.
   Doctors can now restore limbs that have been severed to partially functioning condition.
5. Ever since I was a child, I have liked only green peas with ham.
   Ever since I was a child, I have liked green peas only with ham.

EXERCISE 35.3: Suggested Answers

1. Statistics tell us that strong economic times have led to increases in the college dropout rate.
2. Due to its shock value in negotiations, sometimes a radical proposal stimulates creative thinking by labor and management.
3. The court's ruling allows cities to seize private property lawfully and sell it to the highest bidder.
4. At the pinnacle of his career, Michael Jordan earned roughly $40 million annually in endorsements.
5. Because of the sudden trading, the stock exchange became a chaotic circus.

EXERCISE 35.4: Suggested Answers

1. Determined to increase audience share, producers may make news into entertainment.
2. Late-night talk shows blend news with comedy to attract younger viewers.
3. When news programs highlight local events, important international news stories may get overlooked.
4. Chosen for their looks, newscasters may have weak journalistic credentials.
5. As a visual medium, television is not well suited for presenting complex issues.

EXERCISE 36.1: Suggested Answers

1. Listeners prefer talk shows to classical music, so the radio station is changing its programming.
2. The tallest human on record was Robert Wadlow—he reached an amazing height of eight feet, eleven inches.
3. Some students read more online than in print; some do the opposite.
4. The number of vaccine manufacturers has plummeted because the industry has been hit with a flood of lawsuits.
5. Although most crustaceans live in the ocean, some also live on land or in freshwater habitats.
6. She inherited some tribal customs from her grandmothers, including the sewing technique called Seminole patchwork.
7. Don't throw your soda cans in the trash—recycle them.
8. Even though the West Indian woman has lived in New England for years, she always feels betrayed by winter.
9. The impressive Hope diamond in the Smithsonian Institution looks even larger in person than online.
10. You adopted the puppy—now you'll have to train him.

EXERCISE 36.2: Suggested Answers

My sister Maria decided to paint her house last summer. Thus, she had to buy some paint. She wanted inexpensive paint; at the same time, it had to go on easily and cover well. That combination was unrealistic to start with. She was a complete beginner. On the other hand, she was a hard worker and willing to learn. Maria went out and bought "dark green" paint for $6.99 a gallon. It must have been mostly water; in fact, you could almost see through it. She put one coat of this paint on the house. As a result, her white house turned a streaky light green. Maria was forced to buy all new paint. The job ended up costing more than it would have if she had bought good paint at the start.

EXERCISE 37.1: Suggested Answers

1. Long stretches of white beaches and shady palm trees give tourists the impression of an island paradise.
2. Many Americans yearn to be celebrities.
3. Much of New Orleans is below sea level, which makes it susceptible to flooding.
4. Fortunately for us, Uncle Ron forgot to bring his clarinet to the party.
5. Oscar night is an occasion for celebrating the film industry and criticizing the fashion industry.
6. Diners in Creole restaurants might try shrimp gumbo or turtle soup.
7. Tupperware parties, where the hosts are salespersons, go back to the late 1940s.
8. I attempted to lose ten pounds in less than a week by eating only cottage cheese and grapefruit.
9. None of the adults realized that we were hiding under the porch.
10. Thomas Edison was famous for his inventions as well as his entrepreneurial skills.

EXERCISE 37.2: Suggested Answers

1. *Dependent-clause fragment:* As soon as the seventy-five-year-old cellist walked onstage, the audience burst into applause.
2. *Verbal-phrase fragment:* The patient has only one goal, to smoke behind the doctor's back.
3. *Noun-phrase fragment:* Alaskan king crab fishing is one of the world's most dangerous professions.
4. *Dependent-clause fragment:* After writing and rewriting for almost three years, she finally felt that her novel was complete.
5. *Prepositional-phrase fragment:* In the wake of the earthquake, relief workers tried to provide food and shelter to victims.
6. *Appositive-phrase fragment:* Forster stopped writing novels after *A Passage to India*, one of the greatest novels of the twentieth century.
7. *Subordinate-clause fragment:* Because the speaker's fee was astronomical, the student organization invited someone else.
8. *Compound-predicate fragment:* The jury found the defendant guilty and recommended the maximum sentence.
9. *Relative-clause fragment:* Production began in late September, four months ahead of schedule.
10. *Subordinate-clause fragment:* Her parents simply could not understand why she hated her childhood nickname.

EXERCISE 38.1: Answers

1. At the worst possible moment, a computer crash made me lose my document.
2. To our surprise, the charity auction raised enough money to build a new technology center.
3. Unaware that the microphone was on, the candidate made an offensive comment.
4. Whenever someone rings the doorbell, her dog goes berserk.
5. Therefore, answering the seemingly simple question is very difficult.
6. (no comma needed)
7. A tray of shrimp in one hand and a pile of napkins in the other, the waiter avoided me.
8. (no comma needed)
9. When they woke up, the exhausted campers no longer wanted to hike.
10. Covered in glitter, the children proudly displayed their art project.

EXERCISE 38.2: Suggested Answers

1. The chef did not want to serve a heavy dessert, *for* she was planning to have a rich stew for the main course.

2. My mother rarely allowed us to eat sweets, *but* Halloween was a special exception.
3. Scientists have mapped the human genome, *and* they learn more every day about how genes affect an individual's health.
4. The playwright disliked arguing with directors, *so* she avoided rehearsals.
5. Tropical fish do not bark, *nor* are they cuddly pets.

EXERCISE 38.3: Answers

1. (no commas needed)
2. (no commas needed)
3. I would feel right at home in the city dump, which bears a striking resemblance to my bedroom.
4. The rescue workers, exhausted and discouraged, stared ahead without speaking.
5. (no commas needed)
6. Viruses, unlike bacteria, can reproduce only by infecting live cells.
7. (no commas needed)
8. Hammurabi, an ancient Babylonian king, created laws that were carved on a stone for public display.
9. Birds' hearts have four chambers, whereas reptiles' have three.
10. (no commas needed)

EXERCISE 38.4: Answers

1. The students donated clothing, school supplies, and nonperishable food.
2. The tiny, brown-eyed Lafayette twins were the only children in the kindergarten class who could already read.
3. Landscape architects need to consider many aspects of a plant: how often it blooms, how much light it needs, and how tall it will grow.
4. (no commas needed)
5. The young athletes' parents insist on calling every play, judging every move, and telling everyone within earshot exactly what is wrong with the team.

EXERCISE 38.5: Answers

1. One must consider the society as a whole, not just its parts.
2. Many of the parents and students did, in fact, support the position of the teacher who resigned.
3. You don't expect me to read this speech, do you?
4. Coming in ahead of schedule and under budget, it appears, is the only way to keep this client happy.
5. Ladies and gentlemen, I bid you farewell.

EXERCISE 38.6: Answers

1. (no commas needed)
2. More than 350,000 people gathered for the protest on the Washington Mall.
3. New Delhi, India, and Islamabad, Pakistan, became the capitals of two independent nations at midnight on August 15, 1947.
4. MLA headquarters are at 26 Broadway, New York, New York 10004.
5. I was convinced that the nameplate I. M. Well, MD was one of my sister's pranks.

EXERCISE 38.7: Answers

1. (no comma needed)
2. My professor insisted, "The cutting edge gets dull very quickly."
3. (no comma needed)
4. "Learning without thought is labor lost; thought without learning is perilous," Confucius argued.
5. (no comma needed)

EXERCISE 39.1: Answers

1. Joining the chorus was a great experience for Will; it helped him express his musical talent and gave him a social life.
2. City life offers many advantages; in many ways, however, life in a small town is much more pleasant.
3. The door contains an inflatable slide to be used in an emergency; in addition,

each seat can become a flotation device.

4. Most car accidents occur within twenty-five miles of the home; therefore, you should wear your seat belt on every trip.
5. The debate over political correctness affects more than the curriculum; it also affects students' social relationships.

EXERCISE 39.2: Suggested Answers

Hosting your first dinner party can be very stressful, but careful planning and preparation can make it a success. The guest list must contain the right mix of people; everyone should feel comfortable. Good talkers and good listeners are both important, and while they don't need to agree on everything, you don't want them to have fistfights, either. Then you need to plan the menu, which should steer clear of problem areas: for vegans, no pork chops; for guests with shellfish allergies, no lobster; for teetotallers, no tequila. In addition, make sure your home is clean and neat, and check that you have enough chairs, dishes, glasses, napkins, and silverware. Leave enough time to socialize with your guests —and save a little energy to clean up when it's over!

EXERCISE 40.1: Suggested Answers

1. Social scientists face difficult questions: should they use their knowledge to shape society, merely describe human behavior, or try to do both?
2. The court denied a New Jersey woman's petition to continue raising tigers in her backyard.
3. I screamed at Jamie, "You rat! You tricked me!"
4. The reporter wondered whether anything more could have been done to save lives.
5. Trish asked the receptionist if Dr. Margolies had office hours that afternoon.
6. "Have you seen the new Spielberg film?" Mia asked casually.

EXERCISE 41.1: Answers

1. Grammar is *everybody's* favorite subject.
2. An *ibis's* wingspan is about half as long as a *flamingo's*.
3. *Charles and Camilla's* first visit to the United States as a married couple included a stop at the White House.
4. The owners couldn't fulfill all the *general manager's* wishes.
5. *Stephen King's and Nicholas Sparks's* writing styles couldn't be more different.

EXERCISE 41.2: Answers

1. There was a big revival at my Auntie *Reed's* church.
2. I heard the songs and the minister saying: "Why *don't* you come?"
3. Finally Westley said to me in a whisper: . . . "*I'm* tired *o'* sitting here. *Let's* get up and be saved."
4. So I decided that maybe to save further trouble, *I'd* better lie. . . .
5. That night . . . I cried, in bed alone, and *couldn't* stop.

EXERCISE 42.1: Answers

1. Stephen Colbert introduced Americans to the concept he calls "truthiness" on the first episode of *The Colbert Report*.
2. In his article "Race Against Time," Anthony S. Fauci warns of the critical threat posed by the avian flu virus.
3. "The little that is known about gorillas certainly makes you want to know more," writes Alan Moorehead in his essay, "A Most Forgiving Ape."
4. The "fun" of surgery begins before the operation ever takes place.
5. Should "America the Beautiful" replace "The Star-Spangled Banner" as the national anthem?
6. In the chapter called "The Last to See Them Alive," Truman Capote shows the utterly ordinary life of the Kansas family.
7. A special *Simpsons* episode called "The Treehouse of Horror" airs each Halloween.

8. A remix of Elvis Presley's "A Little Less Conversation" reached number one on the charts twenty-five years after the superstar had died.
9. My dictionary defines *isolation* as "the quality or state of being alone."
10. In his poem "The Shield of Achilles," W. H. Auden depicts the horror of modern warfare.

EXERCISE 43.1: Answers

1. The committee was presented with three options to pay for the new park: (1) increase vehicle registration fees, (2) install parking meters downtown, or (3) borrow money from the reserve fund.
2. The FISA statute authorizes government wiretapping only under certain circumstances (for instance, the government has to obtain a warrant).
3. The health care expert informed readers that "as we progress through middle age, we experience intimations of our own morality [*sic*]."
4. Some hospitals train nurses in a pseudoscientific technique, therapeutic touch (TT), that has been discredited by many rigorous studies.
5. The obnoxious actions of one marcher (who, as it turned out, was an undercover police officer) marred the otherwise peaceful protest.

EXERCISE 43.2: Answers

1. Many people would have ignored the children's taunts—but not Ace.
2. Even if marijuana is dangerous—an assertion disputed by many studies—it is certainly no more harmful to human health than alcohol and cigarettes, which remain legal.
3. If too much exposure to negative news stories makes you feel depressed or anxious—and why wouldn't it?—try going on a media fast.
4. Union Carbide's plant in Bhopal, India, sprang a leak—a leak that killed more than 2,000 people and injured an additional 200,000.
5. Hybrid vehicles—especially those that require no external electrical power—continue to grow more popular.

EXERCISE 43.3: Answers

1. The article made one point forcefully and repeatedly: the United States must end its dependence on foreign oil.
2. Another example is taken from Psalm 139:16.
3. Roberto tried to make healthier choices, such as eating organic food, walking to work, and getting plenty of rest.
4. (correct)
5. Sofi rushed to catch the 5:45 express but had to wait for the 6:19.

EXERCISE 44.1: Answers

1. The town in the South where I was raised had a statue of a Civil War soldier in the center of Main Street.
2. Reporters speculated about the secret location where Vice President Cheney had remained for several weeks.
3. The Corporation for Public Broadcasting relies on donations as well as on grants from the National Endowment for the Arts.
4. Every artist on a major label seems to want a Lexus or a Lincoln Navigator and a chauffeur to drive it.
5. Most Americans remember where they were when they heard about the *Columbia* disaster.
6. Accepting an award for his score for the John Wayne film *The High and the Mighty*, Dmitri Tiomkin thanked Beethoven, Brahms, Wagner, and Strauss.

EXERCISE 45.1: Answers

1. Every Friday, my grandmother would walk a mile to the post office and send a care package to her brother in Tennessee.

2. An MX missile, which is 71 feet long and 92 inches around, weighs 190,000 pounds.
3. Enron officials met with the vice president of the United States to discuss the administration's energy policy, but soon afterward the Texas company declared bankruptcy.
4. A large corporation like AT&T may help finance an employee's MBA.
5. Rosie always began by saying, "If you want my two cents," but she never waited to see if I wanted it or not.

EXERCISE 45.2: Answers

1. Al Gore won the popular vote with 50,996,116 votes, but he was still short by five electoral votes.
2. Twenty-five hundred people wanted tickets, but the arena held only eighteen hundred.
3. The senator who voted against the measure received 6,817 angry emails and only twelve in support of her decision.
4. (correct)
5. In that age group, the risk is estimated to be about 1 in 2,500.

EXERCISE 45.3: THINKING CRITICALLY: Answers

All semi-pro leagues, it should be understood, are self-sustaining, and have no farm affiliation or other connection with the *26* major-league clubs, or with the *17* leagues and *152* teams . . . that make up the National Association—the minors, that is. There is no central body of semi-pro teams, and semi-pro players are not included among the *650* major-leaguers, the *2,500*-odd minor-leaguers, plus all the managers, coaches, presidents, commissioners, front-office people, and scouts, who, taken together, constitute the great tent called organized ball. (A much diminished tent, at that; back in 1949, the minors included *59* leagues, about *448* teams, and perhaps *10,000* players.) Also outside the tent, but perhaps within its shade, are *five* college leagues, ranging across the country from Cape Cod to Alaska, where the most promising freshman, sophomore, and junior-college ballplayers . . . compete against each other. . . .

–ROGER ANGELL, "In the Country"

EXERCISE 46.1: Answers

1. Correct.
2. Homemade sushi can be dangerous, but so can deviled eggs kept too long in a picnic basket.
3. The Web site *Poisonous Plants and Animals* lists tobacco (*Nicotiana tobacum*) as one of the most popular poisons in the world.
4. The monster in the Old English epic *Beowulf* got to tell his own side of the story in John Gardner's novel *Grendel*.
5. In *Ray*, Jamie Foxx looks as if he is actually singing Ray Charles's songs.

EXERCISE 47.1: Answers

1. She insisted that the line workers pick up the pace.
2. Line up quietly and wait for my signal.
3. Her ability to convey her ideas clearly has made her well respected in the office.
4. After he spent four weeks in an alcohol rehabilitation program, he apologized to his wife for twenty-two years of heavy drinking.
5. Having an ignore-the-customer attitude may actually make a service-industry job less pleasant.
6. Both pro- and anti-State Department groups registered complaints.
7. At a yard sale, I found a 1964 pre-CBS Fender Stratocaster in mint condition.
8. Applicants who are over fifty years old may face age discrimination.
9. Neil Armstrong, a self-proclaimed "nerdy engineer," was the first person to set foot on the moon.
10. Carefully marketed children's safety products suggest to new parents that the more they spend, the safer their kids will be.

EXERCISE 56.1: Answers

1. The scholar who finally deciphered hieroglyphics was Jean François Champollion.
2. Champollion enjoyed studying the languages of the Middle East.
3. (correct)
4. It was of great importance that he knew Coptic, a later form of the Egyptian language.
5. In 1822 Champollion wrote a paper in which he presented his solution to the puzzle of hieroglyphics.
6. If the Rosetta Stone had not been discovered, it would have been much more difficult to decipher hieroglyphics.

EXERCISE 57.1: Answers

1. Before the middle of the nineteenth century, surgery was usually a terrifying, painful ordeal.
2. Because anesthesia did not exist yet, the only painkiller available for surgical patients was whiskey.
3. The pain of surgical procedures could be so severe that many people were willing to die rather than have surgery.
4. In 1846, one of the hospitals in Boston gave ether to a patient before he had surgery.
5. The patient, who had a large tumor on his neck, slept peacefully as doctors removed it.

EXERCISE 57.2: Answers

Hollywood is famous for hiring various experts to teach people technically what most of us learn informally. A case in point is the story about the children of one movie couple who noticed a new child in the neighborhood climbing a tree. The children immediately wanted to be given the name of his instructor in tree climbing.

EXERCISE 58.1: Answers

1. Over the past forty years, average temperatures in the Arctic have increased by several degrees.
2. A few years ago, a robin was observed in Inuit territory in northern Canada.
3. Inuit people in previous generations would never have seen a robin near their homes.
4. The Inuit language, which is called *Inuktitut*, has no word for *robin*.
5. Many Inuits are concerned that warmer temperatures may change their way of life.

EXERCISE 58.2: Answers

The notion that a chill puts you at risk of catching a cold is nearly universal. Yet science has found no evidence for it. One of the first studies on the matter was led by Sir Christopher Andrewes. He took a group of volunteers and inoculated them with a cold virus; previously, half of the group had been kept warm, and the other half had been made to take a bath and then to stand for half an hour without a towel while the wind was blowing on them. The chilled group got no more colds than the warm group.

EXERCISE 59.1: Answers

Haivan skated **on** the pond, looking **at** her new engagement ring. As she skated, she thought about the plans for her wedding. Should it be **in** September or October? Could the caterer **from** her neighborhood do a good job? Would her sister manage to be **on** time?

EXERCISE 59.2: Answers

1. *lay off:* phrasal verb
2. (correct) *count on:* prepositional verb
3. (correct) *pick up:* phrasal verb
4. *look at:* prepositional verb
   As I looked at the newspaper, I was surprised to see that I was qualified for a job that paid much better than mine.
5. (correct) *give up:* phrasal verb